LPI

Linux Essentials

Study Guide
Third Edition

Christine Bresnahan

Richard Blum

SYBEX®
A Wiley Brand

Copyright © 2020 by John Wiley & Sons, Inc., Indianapolis, Indiana

Published simultaneously in Canada

ISBN: 978-1-119-65769-9
ISBN: 978-1-119-65770-5 (ebk.)
ISBN: 978-1-119-65771-2 (ebk.)

Manufactured in the United States of America

For general information on our other products and services or to obtain technical support, please contact our Customer Care Department within the U.S. at (877) 762-2974, outside the U.S. at (317) 572-3993 or fax (317) 572-4002.

Wiley publishes in a variety of print and electronic formats and by print-on-demand. Some material included with standard print versions of this book may not be included in e-books or in print-on-demand. If this book refers to media such as a CD or DVD that is not included in the version you purchased, you may download this material at http://booksupport.wiley.com. For more information about Wiley products, visit www.wiley.com.

Library of Congress Control Number: 2019955498

V10016584_122719

Dedicated to the loving memory of Kevin E. Ryan, our longtime technical editor and friend. Kevin's gentle correction and guidance helped make our work better. His contributions will be missed.

"As iron sharpens iron, so one man sharpens another." Proverbs 27:17 (NIV)

Acknowledgments

First, all glory and praise go to God, who through His Son, Jesus Christ, makes all things possible, and gives us the gift of eternal life.

Many thanks go to the fantastic team of people at Sybex for their outstanding work on this project. Thanks to Devon Lewis, the acquisitions editor, for offering us the opportunity to work on this book. Also thanks to Stephanie Barton, the development editor, for keeping things on track and making the book more presentable. Thanks, Steph, for all your hard work and diligence. The technical editor, Jason Eckert, did a wonderful job of double-checking all the work in the book in addition to making suggestions to improve the content. We would also like to thank Carole Jelen at Waterside Productions, Inc., for arranging this opportunity for us and for helping us out in our writing careers.

Christine would particularly like to thank her husband, Timothy, for his encouragement, patience, and willingness to listen, even when he has no idea what she is talking about.

Rich would particularly like to thank his wife, Barbara, for enduring his grouchy attitude during this project and helping to keep up his spirits with baked goods.

About the Authors

Christine Bresnahan started working with computers more than 30 years ago in the IT industry as a systems administrator. Christine is an adjunct professor at Ivy Tech Community College, where she teaches Linux certification and Python programming classes. She also writes books and produces instructional resources for the classroom.

Richard Blum has also worked in the IT industry for more than 30 years as both a system and network administrator, and he has published numerous Linux and open source books. Rich is an online instructor for Linux and web programming courses that are used by colleges and universities across the United States. When he is not being a computer nerd, Rich enjoys spending time with his wife, Barbara, and his two daughters, Katie and Jessica.

Contents at a Glance

Contents

Introduction

This book you hold in your hands provides a solid introduction to the Linux operating system. As its title suggests, it will give you the essential knowledge to begin using and managing this powerful operating system (OS), which is an important one in today's computing world.

The Linux Professional Institute, or LPI (lpi.org), offers a series of Linux certifications. These certifications aim to provide proof of skill levels for employers; if you've passed a particular certification, you should be competent to perform certain tasks on Linux computers. The LPI exams include Linux Essentials, LPIC-1, LPIC-2, and the LPIC-3 series. As the name implies, the Linux Essentials exam is the lowest level of the four exams, covering the most basic tasks of using and administering a Linux computer.

The purpose of this book is to help you pass the Linux Essentials exam, updated in 2019 to version 1.6. The Linux Essentials exam is meant to certify that you:

- Understand the open source industry
- Have knowledge of the most popular open source applications
- Understand the major components of Linux
- Can work at the Linux command line
- Have basic knowledge of security and administration-related concepts
- Know where to go for help

Why Become Linux Certified?

With the growing popularity of Linux (and the increase in Linux-related jobs) comes hype. With all the hype that surrounds Linux it's become hard for employers to distinguish between employees who are competent Linux users and those who just know the buzzwords. This is where the Linux Essentials certification comes in.

With a Linux Essentials certification, you will establish yourself as a Linux user who is familiar with the Linux platform and its applications and who can use any type of Linux system. LPI has created the Linux Essentials exams as a way for employers to have confidence in knowing their employees who pass the exam will have the skills necessary to get the job done.

How to Become Certified

The certification is available to anyone who passes the LPI Linux Essentials required exam. The current version of the exam is version 1.6 and is denoted as 010-160.

The exam is administered by Pearson VUE. The exam can be taken at any Pearson VUE testing center. If you pass, you will get a certificate in the mail saying that you have passed.

To register for the exam with Pearson VUE register online at home.pearsonvue.com. You'll have to provide your name, mailing address, phone number, employer, when and where you want to take the test (which testing center), and your credit card number (arrangement for payment must be made at the time of registration).

Who Should Buy This Book

You may have been assigned this book for a class that you're taking, but if not, it can still have value for self-study or as a supplement to other resources. If you're new to Linux, this book covers the material that you will need to learn the OS from the beginning. You can pick up this book and learn from it even if you've never used Linux before. If you're already familiar with Linux, you'll have a leg up on many of the topics described in these pages.

This book is written with the assumption that you know at least a little about computers generally, such as how to use a keyboard, how to insert a disc into an optical drive, and so on. Chances are that you have used computers in a substantial way in the past—perhaps even Linux, as an ordinary user—or maybe you have used Windows or macOS. We do *not* assume that you have knowledge of how to use a Linux system.

It will also help to have a Linux system available to follow along with. Each chapter contains a simple exercise that will walk you through the basic concepts presented in the chapter. This provides the crucial hands-on experience that you'll need, both to pass the exam and to do well in the Linux world.

 Although the LPI Linux Essentials exam is Linux distribution neutral, it's impossible to write exercises that work in all Linux distributions. That said, the exercises in this book assume you have a learning environment similar to the one described in Appendix B "Setting up a Linux Environment."

How This Book Is Organized

This book consists of 15 chapters, two appendixes, plus this introduction and the assessment test after the introduction. The chapters are organized as follows:

- Chapter 1, "Selecting an Operating System," provides a birds-eye view of the world of operating systems. The chapter will help you understand exactly what Linux is and the situations in which you might want to use it.

- Chapter 2, "Understanding Software Licensing," describes copyright law and the licenses that both Linux and non-Linux OSs use to expand or restrict users' rights to use and copy software.

- Chapter 3, "Investigating Linux's Principles and Philosophy," covers Linux's history and the ways in which Linux, and other OSs, are commonly used.

- Chapter 4, "Using Common Linux Programs," looks at the major categories of Linux software, and it provides pointers to some of the most popular Linux programs.

- Chapter 5, "Getting to Know the Command Line," tackles using typed commands to control Linux. Although many new users find this topic intimidating, command-line control of Linux is important.

- Chapter 6, "Managing Hardware," provides advice on how to select and use hardware in Linux. Specific topics range from the central processing unit (CPU) to device drivers.

- Chapter 7, "Managing Files," describes how to move, rename, delete, and edit files. Directories are just a special type of file, so they are covered here as well.

- Chapter 8, "Searching, Extracting, and Archiving Data," summarizes the tools that you can use to find data on your computer, as well as how you can manipulate data archive files for data transport and backup purposes.

- Chapter 9, "Exploring Processes and Process Data," describes how to install programs in Linux and how to adjust the priority of running programs or terminate selected programs.

- Chapter 10, "Editing Files," introduces the topic of editing text files. This includes the basic features of the nano and vi text-mode text editors, as well as some common configuration file and formatted text file conventions.

- Chapter 11, "Creating Scripts," describes how to create simple scripts, which are programs that can run other programs. You can use scripts to help automate otherwise tedious manual tasks, thus improving your productivity.

- Chapter 12, "Understanding Basic Security," introduces the concepts that are critical to understanding Linux's multiuser nature. It also covers super user privileges, which Linux uses for most administrative tasks.

- Chapter 13, "Creating Users and Groups," covers the software and procedures you use to create, modify, and delete accounts and groups, which define who may use the computer.

- Chapter 14, "Setting Ownership and Permissions," describes how to control which users may access files and in what ways they may do so. In conjunction with users and groups, ownership and permissions control your computer's security.

- Chapter 15, "Managing Network Connections," covers the critical topic of telling Linux how to use a network, including testing the connection and some basic network security measures.

Each chapter begins with a list of the exam objectives that are covered in that chapter. The book doesn't cover the objectives in order. Thus, you shouldn't be alarmed at some of the odd ordering of the objectives within the book. At the end of each chapter, you'll find a couple of elements you can use to prepare for the exam:

Exam Essentials   This section summarizes important information that was covered in the chapter. You should be able to perform each of the tasks or convey the information requested.

Review Questions   Each chapter concludes with 10 review questions. You should answer these questions and check your answers against the ones provided in Appendix A. If you can't answer at least 80 percent of these questions correctly, go back and review the chapter, or at least those sections that seem to be giving you difficulty.

> The review questions, assessment test, and other testing elements included in this book are *not* derived from the actual exam questions, so don't memorize the answers to these questions and assume that doing so will enable you to pass the exam. You should learn the underlying topic, as described in the text of the book. This will let you answer the questions provided with this book *and* pass the exam. Learning the underlying topic is also the approach that will serve you best in the workplace—the ultimate goal of a certification.

To get the most out of this book, you should read each chapter from start to finish and then check your memory and understanding with the chapter-end elements. Even if you're already familiar with a topic, you should skim the chapter; Linux is complex enough that there are often multiple ways to accomplish a task, so you may learn something even if you're already competent in an area.

Additional Study Tools

Readers of this book can access a website that contains several additional study tools, including the following:

> Readers can access these tools by visiting wiley.com/go/sybextestprep.

Sample Tests   All the questions in this book are there, including the assessment test at the end of this introduction and the questions from the review sections at the end of each chapter. In addition, there are two bonus exams.

Electronic Flashcards   The additional study tools include questions in flashcard format (a question followed by a single correct answer). You can use these flashcards to review your knowledge of the exam objectives.

Glossary of Terms as a PDF File   In addition, there is a searchable glossary in PDF format, which can be read on all platforms that support PDF.

Conventions Used in This Book

This book uses certain typographic styles in order to help you quickly identify important information and to avoid confusion over the meaning of words such as onscreen prompts. In particular, look for the following styles:

- *Italicized text* indicates key terms that are described at length for the first time in a chapter. (Italics are also used for emphasis.)

- A `monospaced` font indicates the contents of configuration files, messages displayed at a text-mode Linux shell prompt, filenames, text-mode command names, and Internet URLs.

- *`Italicized monospaced text`* indicates a variable—information that differs from one system or command run to another, such as the name of a client computer or a process ID number.

- **`Bold monospaced text`** is information that you're to type into the computer, usually at a Linux shell prompt. This text can also be italicized to indicate that you should substitute an appropriate value for your system. (When isolated on their own lines, commands are preceded by non-bold monospaced $ or # command prompts, denoting regular user or system administrator use, respectively.)

In addition to these text conventions, which can apply to individual words or entire paragraphs, a few conventions highlight segments of text:

A note indicates information that's useful or interesting but that's somewhat peripheral to the main text. A note might be relevant to a small number of networks, for instance, or it may refer to an outdated feature.

A tip provides information that can save you time or frustration and that may not be entirely obvious. A tip might describe how to get around a limitation or how to use a feature to perform an unusual task.

Warnings describe potential pitfalls or dangers. If you fail to heed a warning, you may end up spending a lot of time recovering from a bug, or you may even end up restoring your entire system from scratch.

EXERCISE

An exercise is a procedure you should try on your own computer to help you learn about the material in the chapter. Don't limit yourself to the procedures described in the exercises, though! Try other commands and procedures to really learn about Linux.

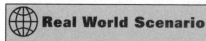

Real World Scenario

A real-world scenario is a type of sidebar that describes a task or example that's particularly grounded in the real world. This may be a situation I or somebody I know has encountered, or it may be advice on how to work around problems that are common in real, working Linux environments.

The Exam Objectives

Behind every computer industry exam you can be sure to find exam objectives—the broad topics in which exam developers want to ensure your competency. The official exam objectives are listed here. (They're also printed at the start of the chapters in which they're covered.)

NOTE Exam objectives are subject to change at any time without prior notice and at LPI's sole discretion. Please visit LPI's website (lpi.org) for the most current listing of exam objectives.

Exam 010-160 Objectives

The following are the areas in which you must be proficient in order to pass the Linux Essentials 010-160 exam. This exam is broken into five main topics, each of which has three to eight objectives. Each objective has an associated weight, which reflects its importance to the exam as a whole. Refer to the LPI website to view the weights associated with each objective. The five main topics are as follows:

Subject Area

1 The Linux Community and a Career in Open Source

2 Finding Your Way on a Linux System

3 The Power of the Command Line

4 The Linux Operating System

5 Security and File Permissions

Topic 1: The Linux Community and a Career in Open Source

1.1 Linux Evolution and Popular Operating Systems (Chapters 1 and 3)

- Knowledge of Linux development and major distributions
- Key knowledge areas:
  - Distributions:
    - Embedded Systems
    - Linux in the Cloud

1.2 Major Open Source Applications (Chapter 4)

- Awareness of major applications as well as their uses and development
- Key knowledge areas:
  - Desktop applications
  - Server applications
  - Development languages
  - Package management tools and repositories

1.3 Open Source Software and Licensing (Chapter 2)

- Open communities and licensing Open Source Software for business
- Key knowledge areas:
  - Open source philosophy
  - Open source licensing
  - Free Software Foundation (FSF), Open Source Initiative (OSI)

1.4 ICT Skills and Working in Linux (Chapters 4 and 5)

- Basic Information and Communication Technology (ICT) skills and working in Linux
- Key knowledge areas:
  - Desktop skills
  - Getting to the command line
  - Industry uses of Linux, cloud computing and virtualization

Topic 2: Finding Your Way on a Linux System

2.1 Command Line Basics (Chapters 5, 7 and 11)

- Basics of using the Linux command line
- Key knowledge areas:
    - Basic shell
    - Command line syntax
    - Variables
    - Quoting

2.2 Using the Command Line to Get Help (Chapter 5)

- Running help commands and navigation of the various help systems
- Key knowledge areas:
    - Man pages
    - Info pages

2.3 Using Directories and Listing Files (Chapter 7)

- Navigation of home and system directories and listing files in various locations
- Key knowledge areas:
    - Files, directories
    - Hidden files and directories
    - Home directories
    - Absolute and relative paths

2.4 Creating, Moving, and Deleting Files (Chapter 7)

- Create, move, and delete files and directories under the home directory.
- Key knowledge areas:
    - Files and directories
    - Case sensitivity
    - Simple globbing

Topic 3: The Power of the Command Line

3.1 Archiving Files on the Command Line (Chapter 8)

- Archiving files in the user home directory
- Key knowledge areas:
    - Files, directories
    - Archives, compression

3.2 Searching and Extracting Data from Files (Chapters 5 and 8)

- Search and extract data from files in the home directory.
- Key knowledge areas:
  - Command line pipes
  - I/O redirection
  - Basic Regular Expressions using ., [ ], *, and ?

3.3 Turning Commands into a Script (Chapters 10 and 11)

- Turning repetitive commands into simple scripts
- Key knowledge areas:
  - Basic shell scripting
  - Awareness of common text editors (vi and nano)

Topic 4: The Linux Operating System

4.1 Choosing an Operating System (Chapter 1)

- Knowledge of major operating systems and Linux distributions
- Key knowledge areas:
  - Differences between Windows, OS X, and Linux
  - Distribution life cycle management

4.2 Understanding Computer Hardware (Chapter 6)

- Familiarity with the components that go into building desktop and server computers
- Key knowledge areas:
  - Motherboards, processors, power supplies, optical drives, peripherals
  - Hard drives, solid state disks and partitions, /dev/sd*
  - Drivers

4.3 Where Data Is Stored (Chapters 7 and 9)

- Where various types of information are stored on a Linux system
- Key knowledge areas:
  - Programs and configuration
  - Processes
  - Memory addresses
  - System messaging
  - Logging

4.4 Your Computer on the Network (Chapter 15)

- Querying vital networking configuration and determining the basic requirements for a computer on a Local Area Network (LAN)
- Key knowledge areas:
  - Internet, network, routers
  - Querying DNS client configuration
  - Querying network configuration

Topic 5: Security and File Permissions

5.1 Basic Security and Identifying User Types (Chapter 12)

- Various types of users on a Linux system
- Key knowledge areas:
  - Root and standard users
  - System users

5.2 Creating Users and Groups (Chapter 13)

- Creating users and groups on a Linux system
- Key knowledge areas:
  - User and group commands
  - User IDs

5.3 Managing File Permissions and Ownership (Chapter 14)

- Understanding and manipulating file permissions and ownership settings
- Key knowledge areas:
  - File permissions and ownership
  - Directory permissions and ownership

5.4 Special Directories and Files (Chapter 7)

- Special directories and files on a Linux system including special permissions
- Key knowledge areas:
  - Using temporary files and directories
  - Symbolic links

Assessment Test

1. What elements does a Linux distribution bundle that make it unique? Choose all that apply.

   A. Kernel

   B. Applications

   C. User and group accounts

   D. GNU utilities

   E. Package management utility

2. What graphical interfaces does Linux support? (Choose all that apply.)

   A. macOS

   B. GNOME

   C. KDE Plasma

   D. Metro

   E. Cinnamon

3. True or false: The Free Software Foundation (FSF) advocates free software, which means they believe you should not have to pay money for software.

4. Which of the following are open source software licenses? (Choose all that apply.)

   A. MIT

   B. GPL

   C. BSD

   D. Creative Commons

   E. Apache

5. What are the three common categories for Linux systems?

   A. Embedded

   B. Graphical

   C. Desktop

   D. Industrial

   E. Server

6. What are some of the recent changes seen in Linux? (Choose all that apply.)

   A. Improvements in the kernel

   B. Improvements in support tools

   C. Creation of new support tools

   D. Creation of new distributions

   E. Payment is now required to install Linux.

7. Which of the following are software suites that allow you to set up a private cloud using Linux? (Choose all that apply.)

    A. Nextcloud

    B. Zoho

    C. ownCloud

    D. Castero

    E. Kdenlive

8. True or false: The dpkg and rpm package management utilities are both low-level tools.

9. True or false: When working in a terminal, the shell prompt often ends in either a dollar sign or a greater-than symbol for ordinary users.

10. Which of the following commands allow you to search the man pages for the keyword copy? (Choose all that apply.)

    A. `apropos copy`

    B. `man -k copy`

    C. `whereis copy`

    D. `whatis copy`

    E. `locate copy`

11. Which is the current version of the original ext filesystem?

    A. extfs

    B. ext2fs

    C. ext3fs

    D. ext4fs

    E. btrfs

12. What command(s) display(s) information about the CPU that your Linux system is running on? (Choose all that apply.)

    A. `uname -a`

    B. `lsusb`

    C. `lspci`

    D. `lscpu`

    E. `man cpu`

13. What type of files are typically stored in the /usr folder?

    A. User data files

    B. Configuration files

    C. Critical system files

    D. Noncritical system program and data files

    E. Program library files

14. Which wildcard character matches any character or set of characters?

   A. *

   B. ?

   C. []

   D. _

   E. -

15. Which of the following are considered characters that can be used for regular expression matching rules? (Choose all that apply.)

   A. *

   B. []

   C. >

   D. ?

   E. .

16. Which `tar` option is used to compress the archive into a tarball using `xz` compression?

   A. -X

   B. -j

   C. -z

   D. -v

   E. -J

17. What commands could you use to see if the MySQL database server is currently running on your system? (Choose all that apply.)

   A. ls

   B. ps

   C. top

   D. free

   E. yum

18. What command-line command displays the overall memory usage on your Linux system?

   A. ps

   B. top

   C. free

   D. ls

   E. yum

19. Which of the following are text editors you can use at the command line on a text-based tty terminal? (Choose all that apply.)

   A. vi

   B. nano

   C. gedit

   D. Kate

   E. emacs

20. The first line of a shell script is #!/bin/bash. What does that mean?

   A. The script won't run on most Linux systems.

   B. The script requires the Bash shell to run.

   C. The script requires the C shell to run.

   D. The script will run on Unix systems.

   E. The script can be run without specifying the full pathname to the script file.

21. What variable can you use to view the exit status of a script after it completes?

   A. $?

   B. $0

   C. $1

   D. $PATH

   E. $exit

22. Which of the following typically holds user account passwords on a modern Linux distribution?

   A. /etc/passwd

   B. /bin/bash

   C. /etc/shadow

   D. /etc/group

   E. /sbin/nologin

23. A(n) _____ account is one that most common users have as their account type.

   A. home

   B. system

   C. administrative

   D. standard

   E. root

24. When you create a new account with the useradd utility, if you did not set a password with an option the account will be locked. What command should you use with super user privileges to unlock it?

   A. usermod -u *username*

   B. password *username*

   C. passwd *username*

   D. useradd -p *password username*

   E. unlock *username*

25. True or false: When a user account is created, it is automatically assigned a primary group.

26. Which commands can you use to change the group a file is assigned to? (Choose all that apply.)

   A. chmod

   B. chgrp

   C. chage

   D. chown

   E. groupadd

27. What command would you use to make the file myfile.txt a hidden file?

   A. chmod 755 myfile.txt

   B. mv myfile.txt ~myfile.txt

   C. cp myfile.txt ./myfile.txt

   D. mv .myfile.txt myfile.txt

   E. mv myfile.txt .myfile.txt

28. If your Linux server doesn't have a graphical desktop installed, what two tools could you use to configure network settings from the command line?

   A. nmcli

   B. iwconfig

   C. ip

   D. netstat

   E. ping

29. What tool allows you to send ICMP messages to a remote host to test network connectivity?

   A. netstat

   B. ifconfig

   C. ping

   D. iwconfig

   E. ss

Answers to Assessment Test

1. **A, B, D, and E.** A Linux distribution bundles the Linux kernel, GNU utilities, applications, and a package management utility to make it unique, so options A, B, D, and E are all correct. User and group accounts are somewhat standard across Linux systems based on the software packages installed, not on the distribution, so option C is incorrect.

2. **B, C, and E.** Linux supports the GNOME, KDE Plasma, and Cinnamon graphical interfaces, so options B, C, and E are correct. Linux does not support the proprietary macOS or Metro environments, so options A and D are incorrect.

3. **False.** The FSF does advocate free software, but it defines it in terms of freedom to do things you want to do with the software, not the price of the software.

4. **A, B, C, E.** The MIT, GPL, BSD, and Apache are all open source licenses or groups of licenses. Therefore, options A, B, C, and E are correct answers. The Creative Commons is an organization that offers a suite of licenses but not for software. Instead, it targets audio recordings, video recordings, textual works, and so on, not just software programs.

5. **A, C, and E.** Linux systems are commonly used in embedded systems, as desktop workstations, and in server environments, so options A, C, and E are correct. Linux systems can use a graphical desktop in either a desktop or server environment, but graphical is not a category of Linux systems, so option B is incorrect. Linux can be used as either a desktop, embedded system, or server in an industrial environment, but industrial is not a category, making option D incorrect.

6. **A, B, C, and D.** In the Linux world, constant improvements are being made to the kernel and support tools and new support tools and distributions are being released, so options A, B, C, and D are all correct. Linux is still released under the open source license, which doesn't prohibit charging a fee for Linux, but most Linux distributions are still available free of charge for installing in any environment, making option E incorrect.

7. **A, C.** Nextcloud and ownCloud are both software suites that allow you to set up a private cloud using Linux, so options A and C are correct answers. Zoho is a cloud-based office productivity suite but does not allow you to set up a private cloud, so option B is a wrong answer. Castero is a text-based podcast client that is available on Linux, but it does not provide the ability to configure a private cloud, making option D incorrect. Kdenlive is another useful Linux application (you can use it to perform video editing), but it is not involved with the cloud. Thus, option E is also an incorrect choice.

8. **True.** The dpkg and rpm package management utilities are both low-level tools, and they are limited in what functions they can perform for maintaining software packages. It's typically better to use a higher-level utility, such as yum or apt-get, depending on your Linux distribution.

9. **True.** Typically, when working in a terminal, for regular users (users who are not logged into the root account) the default shell prompt ends in either in a dollar sign ($) or a greater-than symbol (>).

10. A, B, D. The apropos, man -k, and whatis commands can all be used to search the man pages for the keyword copy. Therefore, options A, B, and D are correct answers. The whereis program searches for files in a restricted set of locations instead of keywords within the man pages, so option C is a wrong answer. The locate command also searches for files, but it uses a database—it does not search for keywords within the man pages. Therefore, option E is also an incorrect choice.

11. D. The ext filesystem is currently at version 4, which is called ext4fs, so option D is correct. The original extfs filesystem is no longer supported, so option A is incorrect. The ext2fs and ext3fs filesystems are still supported and can be used if needed, but they are not recommended for new Linux installations, so options B and C are incorrect. The btrfs filesystem is not part of the extfs family but instead a new type of filesystem, so option E is incorrect.

12. A, D. The uname command with the -a option displays information about the host system, including the architecture the kernel was built for, which gives you a clue as to the CPU. The lscpu command provides detailed information about the CPU. Thus, both options A and D are correct. The lsusb command provides information about USB devices connected to the system, not the CPU, so option B is incorrect. Likewise, the lspci command provides information about PCI devices connected to the system, not the CPU, so option C is incorrect. The man command provides information about system and application commands, not about the CPU hardware, so option E is incorrect.

13. D. Linux installs noncritical applications, such as word processors and browsers, in the /usr directory, so option D is correct. User data files are normally stored in each user's home directory, located in the /home directory structure, so option A is incorrect. Most Linux applications store their configuration files in the /etc directory, so option B is incorrect. Linux installs critical applications in either the /bin directory for user utilities or the /sbin directory for administrator programs, so option C is incorrect. In Linux, program library files are stored within the /lib directory structure, so option E is incorrect.

14. A. The asterisk (*) wildcard character matches none, one, or a set of characters in filename globbing, so option A is correct. The question mark (?) matches only one character in filename globbing, not a set of characters, so option B is incorrect. The square brackets ([]) match only one character within a set of characters, not the entire set of characters, so option C is incorrect. The underscore (_) and dash (-) characters are not valid wildcard characters used in filename globbing, so options D and E are both incorrect.

15. A, B, D, E. The *, [], ?, and . are all characters that activate regular expression matching rules. Thus, options A, B, D, and E are correct choices. The > character is used for basic redirection, and not for regular expressions, so option C is a wrong choice.

16. E. The tar option to compress the archive into a tarball using xz compression is -J, so option E is the correct answer. The -X option has a name of a file passed to it as an argument. That file contains filenames to be excluded from the archive, so option A is a wrong answer. The -j option is for using bzip2 compression, so option B is also an incorrect answer. The -z option is for using gzip compression. Thus, option C is an incorrect choice. The -v option instructs the tar command to produce verbose output (show what files are being archived). Therefore, option D is also an incorrect choice.

17. B, C. Programs running on the Linux system are called processes. The `ps` command allows you to display a snapshot of running processes, and the `top` command produces a real-time display of running processes, so options B and C are correct. The `ls` command displays files and directories, not running processes, so option A is incorrect. The `free` command displays memory usage, so option D is incorrect. The `yum` command is a package management tool used for installing and removing software packages, so option E is incorrect.

18. C. The `free` program displays the current memory usage on the Linux system, including memory in-use, free memory, and swap space, so option C is correct. The `ps` and `top` commands display information about the processes running on the system, and they can display information about process memory usage but not the overall memory usage on the Linux system, so options A and B are incorrect. The `ls` command displays file and directory information, so option D is incorrect. The `yum` program is a package management tool that allows you to install and remove software packages, so option E is incorrect.

19. A, B, E. The `vi`, `nano`, and `emacs` editor are all text editors you can use at the command line on a text-based terminal such as tty3. Therefore, options A, B, and E are the correct answers. The `gedit` and Kate editors are GUI-only editors and cannot be used on a text-based terminal. Therefore, options C and D are incorrect choices.

20. B. The shebang command specifies the shell that the Linux system should use to process the script. The `/bin/bash` path indicates to use the Bash shell, so option B is correct. The Bash shell is the default shell on most Linux systems, so this script should run on most Linux systems, making option A incorrect. The C shell is specified using either `/bin/csh` or `/bin/tcsh`, depending on which C shell your Linux system uses, so option C is incorrect. Most Unix systems don't support the Bash shell, so option D is incorrect. The shebang specifies the path to the shell, not to the script file, so option E is incorrect.

21. A. The special `$?` variable contains the exit status of the last statement in the shell script, or the result of the `exit` statement if the shell script ends with that, so option A is correct. The `$0` variable contains the name of the shell script, not the exit status, so option B is incorrect. The `$1` variable contains the first parameter specified on the command line when the shell script is launched, not the exit status, so option C is incorrect. The `$PATH` environment variable specifies a list of directories the Linux system should search to find executable files, not the exit status of a shell script, so option D is incorrect. The `$exit` variable is a user variable that you can define either locally in a script or globally in a shell, but it has no special meaning in shell scripts, so option E is incorrect.

22. C. On modern Linux distributions, the `/etc/shadow` file typically holds user account passwords, so option C is the correct answer. Although many years ago the `/etc/passwd` file held the user account passwords, it does not (and should not) due to file permissions, so option A is incorrect. The `/bin/bash` is a shell program, not an account file, and is typically the default shell assigned to regular user accounts. Thus, option B is also incorrect. The `/etc/group` file contains group information as well as which user accounts belong to the various groups, so option D is a wrong choice. The `/sbin/nologin` is a program (not an account file) that helps to prevent system accounts from logging into the system. Therefore, option E is incorrect.

23. D. Most common users have an account type of standard, so option D is the correct answer. There is no account type of home, so option A is incorrect. A system account is one that is used by daemons, but not common users, so option B is a wrong choice. The administrative account is not for common users, nor is the root account, because they use super user privileges to perform duties such as installing software or changing other accounts' passwords, so options C and E are also incorrect.

24. C. The passwd *username* command in option C will allow you to set a password for the passwd *username* account, effectively unlocking it. Therefore, option C is the correct answer. The usermod -u command modifies an account's UID but does not unlock it, so option A is a wrong answer. The password command in option B is does not exist and is therefore incorrect. If you had used the useradd -p *password username* command in option D to create the account (not recommended for security reasons), then the account would not be locked. However, you cannot reissue the useradd command for a preexisting account, so option D is a wrong choice. There is no standard command called unlock, so option E is also incorrect.

25. True. When a user account is created, it is automatically assigned a primary group that typically has the same name as the account's username.

26. B, D. You can use either the chgrp or chown command-line command to assign a new primary group to a file or directory, making options B and D correct. The chmod command assigns permissions to a file, not the group, so option A is incorrect. The chage command changes the password options for a user account, not the group of a file, so option C is incorrect. The groupadd command adds a new group to the system and does not change the group assigned to a file, so option E is incorrect.

27. E. Linux uses a leading period in filenames to indicate hidden files. To change the name of a file, you use the mv command, thus making option E correct. The chmod and cp commands don't change the name of a file, so options A and C are incorrect. The mv command lists the original filename first and the new filename second, so option D is incorrect. Since Linux uses a period to indicate hidden files, option B is incorrect.

28. A, C. The nmcli and the ip commands both allow you to set and change network settings from the command line, so options A and C are both correct. The iwconfig command only sets wireless network information, so option B is incorrect. The netstat command displays open ports—it doesn't change any network settings—so option D is incorrect. The ping command sends ICMP packets to remote hosts for testing—it also doesn't set any network settings—so option E is also incorrect.

29. C. The ping command sends ICMP packets to a specified remote host and waits for a response, making option C the correct answer. The netstat command displays statistics about the network interface, so option A is incorrect. The ifconfig command displays or sets network information but doesn't send ICMP packets, making option B incorrect. The iwconfig command displays or sets wireless network information but doesn't handle ICMP packets, making option D incorrect. The ss command displays information about open connections and ports on the system, so option E is also incorrect.

Chapter
1

Selecting an Operating System

OBJECTIVES:

✓ **1.1** Linux Evolution and Popular Operating Systems

✓ **4.1** Choosing an Operating System

The fact that you're reading this book means you want to learn about the Linux operating system (OS). To begin this journey, you must first understand what Linux is and what an OS is. This chapter describes what an OS is, how users interact with an OS, how Linux compares to other popular OSs, and how even specific Linux implementations vary. Understanding these issues will help you as you make the switch to Linux and learn about the various Linux-based systems.

What Is an OS?

An OS provides all the fundamental features of a computer, at least from a software point of view. An OS enables you to use the computer's hardware devices, defines the user interface standards, and provides basic tools that allow applications to run on the computer. This section describes the different parts that make up an OS and how they work together to create your computing experience.

What Is a Kernel?

An OS *kernel* is a software component responsible for managing various low-level features of the computer, including:

- Interfacing with hardware devices (network adapters, hard disks, and so on)
- Allocating memory to individual programs
- Allocating CPU time to individual programs
- Enabling programs to interact with one another

When you use a program (say, a web browser), it relies on the kernel for many of its basic functions. The web browser can communicate with the outside world only by using network functions provided by the kernel. The kernel allocates memory and CPU time to the web browser, without which it couldn't run. The web browser may rely on plug-ins to display multimedia content; such programs are launched and interact with the web browser through kernel services. Any program you run on a computer relies on the kernel in a similar way, although the details vary from one OS to another and from one program to another.

The kernel is the software "glue" that holds the computer together. Without a kernel, a modern computer can do very little.

Kernels are not interchangeable; the Linux kernel is different from the macOS kernel used in Apple workstations and laptops, and from the Windows kernel used in Microsoft-compatible workstations and laptops. Each of these kernels uses a different internal design and provides different software interfaces for programs to use. Thus, each OS is built from the kernel up and uses its own set of programs that further define each OS's features.

Some programs run on multiple kernels, but most need OS-specific tweaks. Programmers create *binaries*—the program files for a particular processor and kernel—for each OS. You need to run the binary file created for the specific OS you're running the program on.

Linux uses a kernel called *Linux*—in fact, technically speaking, the word Linux refers only to the kernel. Other features that you might associate with Linux are provided by non-kernel programs, most of which are available on other platforms, as described shortly, in "What Else Identifies an OS?"

A student named Linus Torvalds created the Linux kernel in 1991. Linux has evolved considerably since that time. Today, it runs on a wide variety of CPUs and other hardware. The easiest way to learn about Linux is to use it on a desktop or laptop PC, so that's the type of configuration emphasized in this book. The Linux kernel, however, runs on everything from tiny cell phones to powerful supercomputers.

What Else Identifies an OS?

The kernel is at the core of any OS, but it's a component that most users don't directly manipulate. Instead, most users interact with a number of other software components, many of which are closely associated with particular OSs. Such programs include the following:

Command-Line Shells   Years ago, users interacted with computers exclusively by typing commands in a program (known as a *shell*) that accepted such commands. The commands would rename files, launch programs, and so on. Although many computer users today don't use text-mode shells, they're still important for intermediate and advanced Linux users, so we describe them in more detail in Chapter 5, "Getting to Know the Command Line," and subsequent chapters rely heavily on your ability to use a text-mode shell. Many different shells are available, and which shells are available and popular differ from one OS to another. In Linux, a shell known as the Bourne Again Shell (Bash) is popular.

 Graphical User Interfaces   A graphical user interface (GUI) is an improvement on a text-mode shell, at least from the perspective of a beginning user. GUIs rely on icons, menus, and a mouse pointer rather than typed commands. Windows and macOS both have their own OS-specific GUIs. Linux relies on a GUI known as the X Window System, or X for short. X is a very basic GUI, so Linux also uses *desktop environment* program suites, such as the GNU Object Model Environment (GNOME) or the K Desktop Environment (KDE), to provide a more complete user experience. It's the differences between a Linux desktop

Certification Objective

Certification Objective

environment and the GUIs in Windows or macOS that will probably strike you most when you first begin using Linux.

Utility Programs   Modern OSs invariably ship with a wide variety of simple utility programs—calculators, calendars, text editors, disk maintenance tools, and so on. These programs differ from one OS to another. Even the names and methods of launching these programs can differ between OSs. Fortunately, you can usually find the programs you want by perusing menus in the main desktop environment.

Libraries   Unless you're a programmer, you're unlikely to have to work with libraries directly; nonetheless, we include them in this list because they provide critical services to programs. Libraries are collections of programming functions that can be used by a variety of programs. For instance, in Linux most programs rely on a library called libc. Other libraries provide features associated with the GUI or that help programs parse options passed to them on the command line. Many libraries exist for Linux, which helps enrich the Linux software landscape.

Productivity Programs   Major productivity programs—web browsers, word processors, graphics editors, and so on—are the usual reason for using a computer. Although such programs are often technically separate from the OS, they are sometimes associated with certain OSs. Even when a program is available on many OSs, it may have a different "feel" on each OS because of the different GUIs and other OS-specific features.

You can search for Linux equivalents to popular macOS or Windows programs on popular open source software websites such as www.linuxalt.com.

In addition to software that runs on an OS, several other features can distinguish between OSs, such as the details of user accounts, rules for naming disk files, and technical details of how the computer starts up. These features are all controlled by software that's part of the OS, sometimes by the kernel and sometimes by non-kernel software.

Investigating User Interfaces

Earlier, we noted the distinction between text-mode and graphical user interfaces. Although most users favor GUIs because of their ease of use, Linux retains a strong text-mode tradition. Chapter 5 describes Linux's text-mode tools in more detail, and Chapter 4, "Using Common Linux Programs," covers basic principles of Linux GUI operations. It's important that you have some grounding in the basic principles of both text-mode and graphical user interfaces now, since user interface issues crop up from time to time in intervening chapters.

Using a Text-Mode User Interface

In the past, and even sometimes today, Linux computers booted in text mode. After the system had completely booted, the screen would display a simple text-mode login prompt, which might resemble this:

```
Fedora 30 (Workstation Edition)
Kernel 5.0.9-301.fc30.x86_64 on an x86_64 (tty1)

essentials login:
```

 To try a text-mode login, you must first install Linux on a computer. Neither the Linux Essentials exam nor this book covers Linux installation; consult your distribution's documentation to learn more.

The details of such a login prompt vary from one system to another. This example includes several pieces of information:

- The OS name and version: Fedora Linux version 30
- The computer's name: essentials
- The name of the hardware device being used for the login: tty1
- The login prompt itself: login:

 If you see a GUI login prompt, you can obtain a text-mode prompt by pressing Ctrl+Alt+F2 or Ctrl+Alt+F3. To return to the GUI login prompt, press Ctrl+Alt+F1 or Ctrl+Alt+F7.

To log into such a system, you must type your username at the login: prompt. The system then prompts you for a password, which you must also type. If you entered a valid username and password, the computer is likely to display a login message, followed by a shell prompt:

```
[rich@essentials:~]$
```

In this book, we omit most of the prompt from example commands when they appear on their own lines. We keep the dollar sign ($) prompt, though, for ordinary user commands. Some commands must be entered as the root user account, which is the Linux administrative user. We change the prompt to a hash mark (#) for such commands, since most Linux distributions make a similar change to their prompts for the root user.

 Chapter 13, "Creating Users and Groups," describes Linux accounts, including the root user account, in more detail.

The details of the shell prompt vary from one installation to another, but you can type text-mode commands at the shell prompt. For instance, you could type **ls** (short for list) to see a list of files in the current directory. The most basic commands are shortened by removing vowels, and sometimes consonants, to minimize the amount of typing required to execute a command. This has the unfortunate effect of making many commands rather obscure.

Some commands display no information, but most produce some type of output. For instance, the ls command produces a list of files:

```
$ ls
chapter1.doc   figure01.png
```

This example shows two files in the current directory: chapter01.doc and figure01.png. You can use additional commands to manipulate these files, such as cp to copy them or rm to remove (delete) them. Chapter 5 ("Getting to Know the Command Line") and Chapter 7 ("Managing Files") describe some common file manipulation commands.

Some text-mode programs take over the display in order to provide constant updates or to enable you to interact with data in a flexible manner. Figure 1.1, for instance, shows the nano text editor, which is described in more detail in Chapter 10, "Editing Files." When nano is working, you can use your keyboard's arrow keys to move the cursor around, add text by typing, and so on.

FIGURE 1.1   Some text-mode programs take over the entire display.

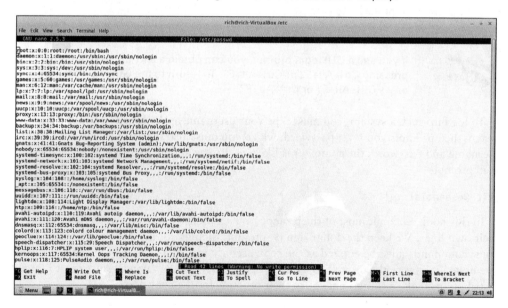

Even if you use a graphical login, you can use a text-mode shell inside a window, known as a *terminal*. With common Linux GUIs, you can launch a terminal program, which provides a shell prompt and the means to run text-mode programs.

Using a Graphical User Interface

Most users are more comfortable with GUIs than with text-mode commands. Thus, many modern Linux systems start up in GUI mode by default, presenting a login screen similar to the one shown in Figure 1.2. You can select your username from a list or type it, followed by typing your password, to log in.

Certification Objective

Some Linux GUI login screens don't prompt you for a password until after you've entered a valid username.

FIGURE 1.2 Graphical login screens on Linux are similar to those for Windows or macOS.

Unlike Windows and macOS, Linux provides a number of different desktop environments for you to choose from. Which one you use depends on the specific variety of Linux you're using, what software options you selected at installation time, and your own personal preferences. Common choices include GNOME, KDE Plasma, Cinnamon, and Xfce. Many other options are available as well. Many graphical desktops have assistive technology features built in. In Figure 1.2, the person icon at the top-right corner of the Fedora login window allows you to select an assistive technology such as a screen reader or onscreen keyboard to assist with the login entry.

Linux desktop environments can look quite different from one another, but they all provide similar functionality. Figure 1.3 shows the default Cinnamon desktop on a Mint 18.3 installation, with a couple of programs running. Chapter 4 describes common desktop environments and their features in more detail, but for now, you should know that they all provide features such as the following:

Program Launchers   You can launch programs by selecting them from menus or lists. Typically, one or more menus reside along the top, bottom, or side of the screen. In Figure 1.3, you can click the Mint leaf icon in the bottom-left corner of the screen to produce the menu that appears in that figure.

File Managers   Linux provides GUI file managers similar to those in Windows or macOS. A window for one of these is open in the center of Figure 1.3.

Window Controls   You can move windows by clicking and dragging their title bars, resize them by clicking and dragging their edges, and so on.

Multiple Desktops   Most Linux desktop environments enable you to keep multiple virtual desktops active, each with its own set of programs. This feature helps keep the screen uncluttered while you run several programs simultaneously. Typically, an icon in one of the menus enables you to switch between virtual desktops.

Logout Options   You can log out of your Linux session, which enables you to shut down the computer or let another user log in.

FIGURE 1.3   Linux desktop environments provide the types of GUI controls that most users expect.

WARNING   Logging out is very important in public computing environments. If you fail to log out, a stranger might come along and use your account for malicious purposes.

As you learn more about Linux, you'll discover that its GUI environments are quite flexible. If you find you don't like the environment that's the default for your distribution, you can change it. Although they all provide similar features, some people have strong preferences about desktop environments. Linux gives you a choice in the matter that's not available in Windows or macOS, so feel free to try multiple desktop environments.

You may need to install extra desktop environments to use them. This topic is not covered in this book.

Where Does Linux Fit in the OS World?

This chapter's title implies a comparison, and as this book is about Linux, the comparison must be to non-Linux OSs. Thus, we compare Linux to three other OSs or OS families: Unix, Apple macOS, and Microsoft Windows.

As described later in "What Is a Distribution?" Linux can be considered a family of OSs. Thus, you can compare one Linux version to another one.

Comparing Linux to Unix

If you were to attempt to draw a "family tree" of OSs, you would end up scratching your head a lot. This is because OS designers often mimic one another's features and sometimes even incorporate one another's code into their OSs' workings. The result can be a tangled mess of similarities between OSs, with causes ranging from coincidence to code "borrowing." Attempting to map these influences can be difficult. In the case of Linux and Unix, though, a broad statement is possible: Linux is modeled after Unix.

Certification
Objective

Unix was created in 1969 at AT&T's Bell Labs. Unix's history is complex and involves multiple *forks* (that is, splitting of the code into two or more independent projects) and even entirely separate code rewrites. Modern Linux systems are, by and large, the product of open source projects that clone Unix programs, or of original open source code projects for Unix generally.

Open source software is software that you can not only run, but modify and redistribute yourself. Chapter 3, "Investigating Linux's Principles and Philosophy," covers the philosophy and legal issues concerning open source software.

These projects include:

The Linux Kernel   Linus Torvalds created the Linux kernel as a hobby programming project in 1991, but it soon grew to be much more than that. The Linux kernel was designed to be compatible with other Unix kernels in the sense that it used the same software interfaces in source code. This made using open source programs for other Unix versions with the Linux kernel easy.

The GNU Project   The GNU's Not Unix (GNU) project is an effort by the Free Software Foundation (FSF) to develop open source replacements for all the core elements of a Unix OS. In 1991, the FSF had already released the most important such tools, with the notable exception of the kernel. (The GNU HURD kernel is now available but is not as popular as the Linux kernel.) Alternatives to the GNU tools include proprietary commercial tools and open source tools developed for the BSD Unix variants. The tools used on a Unix-like OS can influence its overall "flavor," but all of these tool sets are similar enough to give any Unix variety a similar feel compared to a non-Unix OS.

GNU is an example of a recursive acronym—an acronym whose expansion includes the acronym itself. This is an example of geek humor.

Xorg-X11   The X Window System is the GUI environment for most Unix OSs. Most Linux distributions today use the Xorg-X11 variety of X. As with the basic text-mode tools provided by the GNU project, choice of an X server can affect some features of a Unix-like OS, such as the types of fonts it supports. Wayland is a newer X Windows System software package used in Linux and is gaining in popularity.

Desktop Environments   GNOME, KDE Plasma, Cinnamon, Xfce, and other popular open source desktop environments have largely displaced commercial desktop environments even on commercial versions of Unix. Thus, you won't find big differences between Linux and Unix in this area.

macOS, described shortly, is technically a commercial Unix but uses a proprietary Apply GUI instead of an open source desktop environment running on the X Window System.

Server Programs   Historically, Unix and Linux have been popular as server OSs—organizations use them to run web servers, database servers, email servers, and so on. Linux runs the same popular server programs as do commercial Unix versions and the open source BSDs.

User Productivity Programs   In this realm, as in server programs, Linux runs the same software as do other Unix-like OSs. In a few cases, Linux runs more programs or runs them better. This is mostly because of Linux's popularity and the vast array of hardware drivers that Linux offers. If a program needs advanced video card support, for example, it's more likely to find that support on Linux than on a less popular Unix-like OS.

On the whole, Linux can be thought of as a member of the family of Unix-like OSs. Although Linux is technically not a Unix OS, it's similar enough that the differences are unimportant compared to the differences between this family as a whole and other OSs, such as Windows. Because of its popularity, Linux offers better hardware support, at least on commodity PC hardware. Some Unix varieties offer specific features that Linux lacks, though. For instance, Oracle's Solaris Unix uses built-in zones that handle virtual machines better than the tools currently available in Linux.

 Although computers understand only ones and zeroes, human beings prefer to write programs in a text form known as *source code*. Although source code can seem arcane to the uninitiated, it's crystal clear compared to the form a program must take for a computer to run it: *binary code*. A program known as a *compiler* translates source code to binary code. (Alternatively, some programming languages rely on an *interpreter*, which converts source code to binary code "on the fly," eliminating the need to compile source code.)

The term *open source* refers to the availability of source code, which is generally withheld from the public in the case of commercial programs and OSs. A programmer with access to a program's source code can fix bugs, add features, and otherwise alter how the program operates.

Comparing Linux to macOS

Apple macOS is a commercial Unix-based OS that borrows heavily from the BSDs and discards the usual Unix GUI (namely X) in favor of its own user interface. This makes macOS both very similar to Linux and quite different from it.

Certification Objective

You can open a macOS Terminal window and type many of the same commands described in this book to achieve similar ends. If a command described in this book isn't present, you may be able to install it in one way or another. macOS ships with some popular Unix server programs, so you can configure it to work much like Linux or another Unix-like OS as a network server computer.

macOS differs from Linux in its user interface, though. The macOS user interface is known as *Cocoa* from a programming perspective, or *Aqua* from a user's point of view. It includes elements that are roughly equivalent to both X and a desktop environment in Linux. Because Cocoa isn't compatible with X from a programming perspective, applications developed for macOS can't be run directly on Linux (or on other Unix-like OSs), and porting them (that is, modifying the source code and recompiling them) for Linux is a nontrivial undertaking. Thus, native macOS applications seldom make the transition to Linux.

macOS includes an implementation of X that runs under Aqua. This makes the transfer of GUI Linux and Unix programs to macOS relatively straightforward. The resulting programs don't entirely conform to the Aqua user interface, though. They may have buttons, menus, and other features that look out of place compared to the usual appearance of macOS equivalents.

Apple makes macOS available only for its own computers. Its license terms forbid installation on non-Apple hardware, and even aside from licensing issues, installing macOS on non-Apple hardware is a nontrivial undertaking. A variant of macOS, known as iOS, runs on Apple's iPad and iPhone devices, and is equally nonportable to other devices. Thus, macOS is largely limited to Apple hardware. Linux, by contrast, runs on a wide variety of hardware, including most PCs. You can even install Linux on Macintosh computers.

Comparing Linux to Windows

Certification
Objective

Most desktop and laptop computers today run Microsoft Windows. Thus, if you're considering running Linux, the most likely comparison is to Windows. Broadly speaking, Linux and Windows have similar capabilities; however, there are significant differences in details. These include the following:

Licensing   Linux is an open source OS whereas Windows is a proprietary commercial OS. Chapter 2, "Understanding Software Licensing," covers open source issues in greater detail, but for now you should know that open source software gives you greater control over your computer than does proprietary software—at least in theory. In practice, you may need a great deal of expertise to take advantage of open source's benefits. Proprietary software may be preferable if you work for an organization that's only comfortable with the idea of software that's sold in a more traditional way. (Some Linux variants, though, are sold in a similar way, along with service contracts.)

Costs   Many Linux varieties are available free of charge and so are appealing if you're trying to cut costs. However, the expertise needed to install and maintain a Linux installation is likely to be greater, and therefore more expensive, than the expertise needed to install and maintain a Windows installation. Different studies on the issue of total cost of ownership of Linux versus Windows have gone both ways, but most tend to favor Linux.

Hardware Compatibility   Most hardware components require OS support, usually in the form of drivers. Most hardware manufacturers provide Windows drivers for their devices or work with Microsoft to ensure that Windows includes appropriate drivers. Although some manufacturers provide Linux drivers, too, for the most part the Linux community as a whole must supply the necessary drivers. This means that Linux drivers may take a few weeks or even months to appear after a device becomes available. At the same time, Linux developers tend to maintain drivers for old hardware for much longer than manufacturers continue to support their own old hardware. Thus, a modern Linux may run better than a recent version of Windows on old hardware. Linux also tends to be less resource intensive, so you can be productive on older hardware when using Linux.

Software Availability   Some popular desktop applications, such as Microsoft Office, are available on Windows but not on Linux. Although Linux alternatives such as LibreOffice are available, they haven't caught on in the public's mind. In other realms, the situation is reversed. Popular server programs, such as the Apache web server, were developed first for Linux or Unix. Although many such servers are available for Windows, they run more efficiently on Linux. If you have a specific program you must run, you may want to research its availability and practicality on any platforms you're considering.

User Interfaces   Like macOS, Windows uses its own unique user interface. This fact contributes to poor inter-OS portability. (Tools exist to help bridge the gap, though; X Window System implementations for Windows are available, as are tools for running Windows programs in Linux.) Some users prefer the Windows user interface to any Linux desktop environment, but others prefer a Linux desktop environment.

Microsoft introduced a new user interface, called Metro, in Windows 8. The idea behind Metro is that it works the same on everything from smartphones to desktop computers. However, the Metro user interface quickly became unpopular because it made it difficult for experienced desktop Windows users to maneuver around, so it was removed as the default user interface starting with Windows 10 but is still available for those who prefer it.

Configurability   Linux is a much more configurable OS than is Windows. Although both OSs provide means to run specific programs at startup, change user interface themes, and so on, Linux's open source nature means you can tweak any detail you want. Furthermore, you can pick any Linux variant you like to get a head start on setting up the system as you see fit.

Security   Advocates of each OS claim it's more secure than the others. They can do this because they focus on different security issues. Many of the threats to Windows come from viruses, which by and large target Windows and its huge installed user base. Viruses are essentially a nonissue for Linux; in Linux, security threats come mostly from break-ins involving misconfigured servers or untrustworthy local users.

For over a decade, Windows has dominated the desktop arena. In both homes and offices, users have become familiar with Windows and are used to popular Windows applications, such as Microsoft Office. Although Linux can be used in such environments, it's a less popular choice for a variety of reasons—its unfamiliarity, the fact that Windows comes preinstalled on most PCs, and the lack of any compelling Linux-only applications for most users.

Unix generally, and Linux in particular, on the other hand, have come to dominate the server market. Linux powers the web servers, database servers, email servers, and so on that make up the Internet and that many businesses rely on to provide local network services. Thus, most people use Linux daily even if they don't realize it.

In most cases, it's possible to use either Linux or Windows on a computer and have it do an acceptable job. Sometimes, though, specific needs dictate use of one OS or another. You might need to run a particular exotic program, for instance, or your hardware might be too old for a modern Windows or too new for Linux. In other cases, your own or your users' familiarity with one OS or the other may favor its use.

What Is a Distribution?

Up until now, we've described Linux as if it were a single OS, but this isn't really the case. Many different Linux *distributions* are available, each consisting of a Linux kernel along with a set of utilities and configuration files. The result is a complete OS, and two Linux distributions can differ from each other as much as either differs from macOS or even Windows. We therefore describe in more detail what a distribution is, what distributions are popular, and the ways in which distribution maintainers keep their offerings up-to-date.

Creating a Complete Linux-Based OS

Certification Objective

We've already described some of what makes up a Linux OS, but some details need reiteration or elaboration:

A Linux Kernel   A Linux kernel is at the core of any Linux OS, of course. We've written this item as *a* Linux kernel because the Linux kernel is constantly evolving. Two distributions are likely to use slightly different kernels. Distribution maintainers also often *patch* kernels—that is, they make small changes to fix bugs or add features.

Core Unix Tools   Tools such as the GNU tool set, the X Window System, and the utilities used to manage disks are critical to the normal functioning of a Linux system. Most Linux distributions include more or less the same set of such tools, but as with the kernel, they can vary in versions and patches.

Supplemental Software   Additional software, such as major server programs, desktop environments, and productivity tools, ships with most Linux distributions. As with core Unix software, most Linux distributions provide similar options for such software. Distributions sometimes provide their own "branding," though, particularly in desktop environment graphics.

Startup Scripts   Much of a Linux distribution's "personality" comes from the way it manages its startup process. Linux uses scripts and utilities to launch the dozens of programs that link the computer to a network, present a login prompt, and so on. These scripts and utilities vary between distributions, which means they have different features and may be configured in different ways.

An Installer   Software must be installed to be used, and most Linux distributions provide unique installation software to help you manage this important task. Thus, two distributions may install in very different ways, giving you options for key features such as disk layouts and initial user account creation.

Typically, Linux distributions are available for download from their websites. You can usually download a CD-R or DVD image file that you can then burn to an optical disc. When you boot the resulting disc, the installer runs and you can install the OS. You can also use the same image to create a bootable USB flash drive if your computer lacks an optical drive. There are also cloud versions of many Linux distributions, which allow you to download a complete Linux system to run in either a private virtual machine or a commercial cloud such as Amazon Web Services (AWS) or Google Cloud Platform.

If you're curious about trying out Linux but don't have a dedicated workstation or laptop available, install a virtual machine software package such as VMWare or VirtualBox, which allows you to run a Linux OS inside an existing macOS or Windows workstation environment without having to change the system.

Some Linux installers come complete with all the software you're likely to install. Others come with only minimal software and expect you to have a working Internet connection so that the installer can download additional software. If your computer isn't connected to the Internet, be sure to get the right type of installer.

A Summary of Common Linux Distributions

Depending on how you count, there are about a dozen major Linux distributions for desktop, laptop, and small server computers, and hundreds more that serve specialized purposes. Table 1.1 summarizes the features of the most important distributions. Certification Objective

TABLE 1.1   Features of major Linux distributions

Distribution	Availability	Package format	Release cycle	Administrator skill requirements
Arch	Free	pacman	Rolling	Expert
CentOS	Free	RPM	approximately 2-year	Intermediate
Debian	Free	Debian	2-year	Intermediate to expert
Fedora	Free	RPM	approximately 6-month	Intermediate
Gentoo	Free	ebuild	Rolling	Expert
Mint	Free	Debian	6-month	Novice to intermediate
openSUSE	Free	RPM	8-month	Intermediate
Red Hat Enterprise	Commercial	RPM	approximately 2-year	Intermediate
Slackware	Free	tarballs	Irregular	Expert
SUSE Enterprise	Commercial	RPM	2–3 years	Intermediate
Ubuntu	Free	Debian	6-month	Novice to intermediate

These features require explanation:

Availability   Most Linux distributions are entirely open source or free software; however, some include proprietary components and are sold for money, typically with a support contract. Red Hat Enterprise Linux (RHEL) and SUSE Enterprise Linux are the two most prominent examples of this type of distribution. Both have completely free cousins. For RHEL, CentOS is a near-clone that omits the proprietary components, and Fedora is an open version that serves as a testbed for technologies that may eventually be included in RHEL. For SUSE Enterprise, openSUSE is a free alternative.

Package Format   Most Linux distributions distribute software in *packages*, which are collections of many files in one. Package software maintains a local database of installed files, making upgrades and uninstallations easy. The RPM Package Manager (RPM) system is the most popular one in the Linux world, but Debian packages are very common, too. Other packaging systems work fine but are distribution-specific, such as the pacman package management system used in Arch Linux. Slackware is unusual in that it uses *tarballs* for its packages. These are package files created by the standard tar utility, which is used for backing up computers and for distributing source code, among other things. The tarballs that Slackware uses for its packages contain Slackware-specific information to help with package management. Gentoo is unusual because its package system is based on compiling most software from source code. This is time-consuming but enables experienced administrators to tweak compilation options to optimize the packages for their own hardware and software environments.

Tarballs are similar to the zip files common on Windows. Chapter 8, "Searching, Extracting, and Archiving Data," describes how to create and use tarballs.

Release Cycle   We describe release cycles in more detail shortly, in "Understanding Release Cycles." As a general rule, distributions with short release cycles aim to provide the latest software possible, whereas those with longer release cycles strive to provide the most stable environments possible. Some try to have it both ways; for instance, Ubuntu releases long-term support (LTS) versions in April of even-numbered years. Its other releases aim to provide the latest software.

Administrator Skill Requirements   The final column in Table 1.1 provides our personal estimation of the skill level required to administer a distribution. As you can see, we've described most Linux distributions as requiring "intermediate" skill to administer. Some, however, provide less in the way of user-friendly GUI administrative tools and so require more skill. Ubuntu aims to be particularly easy to use and administer.

Don't be scared off by the "intermediate" classification of most distributions. This book's purpose is to help you manage the essential features of such distributions.

Most Linux distributions are available for at least two platforms—that is, CPU types: x86 (also known as IA32, i386, and several variants) and x86-64 (also known as AMD64, EM64T, and x64). Until about 2007, x86 computers were the most common variety, but now x86-64 computers have become the standard. If you have an x86-64 computer, you can run either an x86 or an x86-64 distribution on it, although the latter provides a small speed improvement. More exotic platforms, such as ARM (for tablets), PowerPC, Alpha, and SPARC, are available. Such platforms are mostly restricted to servers and to specialized devices (described shortly).

 Real World Scenario

Which Distribution to Use?

With a plethora of different Linux distributions available, one of the most often asked questions for novice Linux users is which one to try. Some Linux distributions, such as Red Hat and Oracle, focus on commercial Linux installations, providing paid customer support. These distributions can be expensive, and they are often hard for novice users to install and use.

A second type of Linux distributions are those geared toward advanced Linux users. The CentOS, Slackware, and Gentoo Linux distributions fall in this category. They expect you to know how to install and configure most of the software and hardware yourself. Advanced Linux users like to use these distributions because they can customize exactly what to install on the system.

The third type of Linux distributions are those geared toward novice Linux users. The popular Fedora, Ubuntu, and Mint Linux distributions fall in this category. The default installation takes care of most of the software and hardware configuration issues you need to worry about, and they all provide a wealth of user-friendly graphical tools for doing administrator functions, such as adding user accounts, exploring disk space, and working with network connections. These types of Linux distributions are the best way to go if you're a novice to the Linux world.

Understanding Release Cycles

Table 1.1 summarized the release cycles employed by a number of common Linux distributions. The values cited in that table are the time between releases. For instance, new versions of Ubuntu come out every six months, like clockwork. Most other distributions' release schedules provide some "wiggle room"; if a release date slides a month, that may be acceptable.

After its release, a distribution is typically supported until sometime after the next version's release—typically a few months to a year or more. During this support period, the

Certification
Objective

distribution's maintainers provide software updates to fix bugs and security problems. After the support period has passed, you can continue to use a distribution, but you're on your own—if you need updated software, you'll have to compile it from source code yourself or hope that you can find a compatible binary package from some other source. As a practical matter, therefore, it's generally a good idea to upgrade to the latest version before the support period ends. This fact makes distributions with longer release cycles appealing to businesses, since a longer time between installations minimizes disruptions and costs associated with upgrades.

Two of the distributions in Table 1.1 (Arch and Gentoo) have rolling release cycles. Such distributions have no version numbers in the usual sense; instead, upgrades occur in an ongoing manner. Using such a distribution makes it unnecessary to ever do a full upgrade, with all the hassles that creates; however, you'll occasionally have to do a disruptive upgrade of one particular subsystem, such as a major upgrade in your desktop environment.

Certification
Objective

Before the release of a new version, most distributions make pre-release versions available. *Alpha software* is extremely new and very likely to contain serious bugs, whereas *beta software* is more stable but nonetheless more likely to contain bugs than is the final release software. As a general rule, you should avoid using such software unless you want to contribute to the development effort by reporting bugs or unless you're desperate to have a new feature.

Embedded Linux Systems

In addition to the mainstream PC distributions, several other Linux distributions are available that serve more specialized purposes. The term *embedded systems* describes running a small stripped-down Linux system on a small microcomputer, such as a phone or monitoring device. Common uses of embedded Linux systems are:

Certification
Objective

Android   Many cell phones today use a Linux-based OS known as *Android*. Its user interface is similar to that of other smartphones, but underneath lies a Linux kernel and a significant amount of the same Linux infrastructure you'll find on a PC. Such phones don't use X or typical desktop applications, though; instead, they run specialized applications for cell phones.

> Android is best known as a cell phone OS, but it can be used on other devices. Some tablets and e-book readers, for instance, run Android.

Network Appliances   Many broadband routers, print servers, and other devices you plug into a local network to perform specialized tasks run Linux. You can sometimes replace the standard OS with a customized one if you want to add features to the device. Tomato (www.polarcloud.com/tomato) and OpenWrt (openwrt.org) are two examples of such customized Linux distributions. Don't install such software on a whim, though; if done improperly, or on the wrong device, they can render the device useless!

IoT Devices   In recent years the term *Internet of Things (IoT)* has exploded both in the news and in classrooms. IoT relates to creating a network of small devices that can sense physical conditions and control systems. Small microprocessors running a specialized OS monitor data from sensors, such as the temperature, humidity, light, or motion, and use that data to control motors, locks, and switches. Embedded controllers such as the Arduino and Beagle Bones devices, as well as more powerful larger controllers such as the Raspberry Pi, are becoming all the craze in schools and manufacturing environments. The larger controllers, such as the Raspberry Pi, often run a stripped-down version of Linux to provide more versatility in the applications, such as sending out email alerts for specific sensor conditions.

TiVo   This popular digital video recorder (DVR) uses a Linux kernel and a significant number of standard support programs, along with proprietary drivers and DVR software. Although many people who use them don't realize it, they are Linux-based computers under the surface.

Most embedded Linux systems typically require little or no administrative work from users, at least not in the way such tasks are described in this book. Instead, these devices have fixed basic configurations and guided setup tools to help inexperienced users set critical basic options, such as network settings and your time zone.

Linux in the Cloud

Cloud technology has greatly changed the landscape of the computer world. Moving computer resources and applications into a shared network environment changes how many companies do business and provide services to customers. Linux plays an important role in the cloud world, so it's a good idea to define just what a cloud is and what type of resources it provides. This section covers the basics of cloud computing.

What Is Cloud Computing?

The first mention of the term *cloud* came in documentation for the original ARPANET network environment in 1977, the precursor to the modern-day Internet. In that documentation, the cloud symbol was commonly used to represent the large network of interconnected servers geographically dispersed. However, in this environment each server was self-contained and self-sufficient—there was no distributed computing.

The term *cloud computing* is related to distributed computing. In distributed computing, resources are shared among two or more servers to accomplish a single task, such as run an application. This environment became the precursor to what we know today as cloud computing, popularized by companies such as Amazon Web Services (AWS), Google Cloud Platform, and Microsoft Azure.

Cloud computing provides the ability to deliver computing resources across the Internet. Now customers can purchase both hardware and software resources as needed from cloud computing vendors. This includes servers, storage space, databases, networks, operating systems, and even individual applications. Figure 1.4 demonstrates the three methods for providing cloud computing services.

FIGURE 1.4   Cloud computing methods

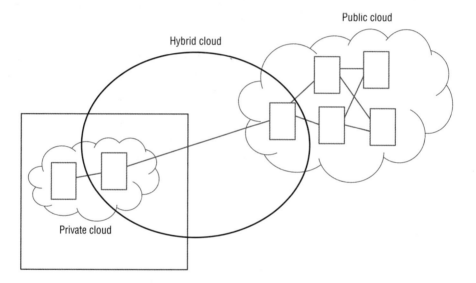

As you can see in Figure 1.4, there are three primary methods for providing cloud computing environments:

- **Public:** In the public cloud computing environments, a third party provides all of the computing resources outside of the organization. These resources are usually shared between multiple organizations.

- **Private:** In the private cloud computing environments, each individual organization builds its own cloud computing resources to provide resources internally.

- **Hybrid:** In hybrid cloud computing environments, computing resources are provided internally within the organization but also connected to an external public cloud to help supplement resources when needed.

What Are the Cloud Services?

Cloud computing environments can customize the level of resources provided to customers, depending on each customer's needs. This section describes the three most popular models for providing resource levels that you'll find from cloud computing vendors.

Infrastructure as a Service (IaaS)

In the infrastructure as a service (IaaS) model, the cloud computing vendor provides low-level server resources to host applications for organizations. These low-level resources include all of the physical components you'd need for a physical server, including CPU time, memory space, storage space, and network resources, as shown in Figure 1.5.

FIGURE 1.5   The IaaS cloud model

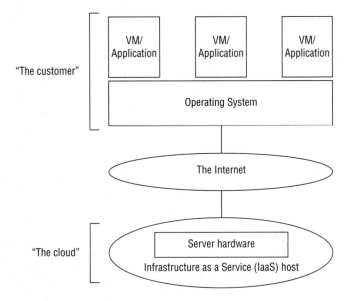

The server resources provided may be on a single server, or they may be distributed among several servers. In a distributed environment. the servers may be co-located in a single facility or they may be separated into multiple facilities located in separate cities. This helps provide for increased availability.

As shown in Figure 1.5, in an IaaS model the customer supplies the operating system and any applications that it needs to run. Most IaaS environments support a multitude of different operating systems, including Linux and Windows servers. The customer is responsible for any system administration work required for the operating system, as well as any application administration. The cloud computing vendor maintains the physical infrastructure environment.

Platform as a Service (PaaS)

In the platform as a service (PaaS) model, the cloud computing vendor provides both the physical server environment as well as the operating system environment to the customer, as shown in Figure 1.6.

FIGURE 1.6   The PaaS cloud model

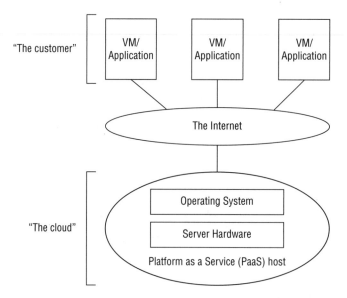

With the PaaS model. the cloud computing vendor takes responsibility for both the physical components as well as the operating system administration. It provides system administration support to ensure the operating system is properly patched and updated to keep up with current releases and security features. This allows the customer to focus mainly on developing the applications running within the PaaS environment.

Software as a Service (SaaS)

In the software as a service (SaaS) model, the cloud computing vendor provides a complete application environment, such as a mail server, database server, or web server. The vendor provides the physical server environment, the operating system, and the application software necessary to perform the function. This is shown in Figure 1.7.

FIGURE 1.7 The SaaS cloud model

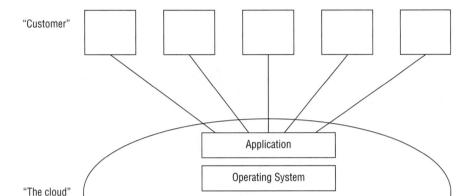

Summary

Linux is a powerful OS that you can use on everything from a cell phone to a supercomputer. At Linux's core is its kernel, which manages the computer's hardware. Built atop that are various utilities (many from the GNU project) and user applications. Linux is a clone of the Unix OS, with which it shares many programs. Apple macOS is another Unix OS, although one with a unique user interface. Although Windows shares many features with Unix, it's an entirely different OS, so software compatibility between Linux and Windows is limited. Linux comes in many varieties, known as distributions, each of which has its own unique "flavor." Because of this variety, you can pick a Linux version that best suits your needs, based on its ease of use, release cycle, and other unique features. Linux is a popular OS used for embedded systems, due to its customizable features and small size. The same customizable features also makes it ideal for large cloud computing environments that support applications distributed around the world.

Exam Essentials

Describe what makes a Linux distribution and why there are so many. A Linux distribution is a bundle of components required to run a Linux system. This includes a Linux kernel and usually utilities for managing the system, application software, and a package management system for installing and removing software. Different Linux users have different needs, such as desktop office automation, multimedia production, mathematical simulations, or server features, such as a web or database server. The different Linux distributions are each customized to support specific features and functions so that you don't have to do that yourself.

Explain how Linux is used in embedded systems.   Embedded systems often use a stripped-down Linux system that specializes in controlling specific hardware. Devices such as Android phones, IoT monitors, and TiVo recorders each use a customized Linux system that performs only the functions required for those devices.

Explain how Linux is used in cloud environments.   The cloud environment requires a distributed computing environment that can be expanded as needed. Linux servers provide an inexpensive platform that can be easily modified.

Describe the basic differences between Linux and the more popular macOS and Windows environments.   The basic difference between Linux and the macOS and Windows environments is choice. For just about every feature of the OS, Linux doesn't lock you in to a specific environment, but instead provides multiple options for you to choose from. This includes desktop features, application software, and even what you pay for software support.

Explain Linux distribution life-cycle management.   Each OS requires updating from time to time to keep up with technology, improve features, fix software bugs, and guard against security vulnerabilities. Life-cycle management relates to how often an OS is updated. Some OSs are updated on a regular basis, whereas others are updated only as needed. Different Linux distributions support different life cycles, depending on their user base. Some Linux distributions produce long-term support (LTS) versions that are maintained for three to five years, ideal for corporate environments that don't want to change OS versions for hundreds of thousands of employees.

Review Questions

You can find the answers in the Appendix A.

1. Which of the following is a function of the Linux kernel? (Choose all that apply.)
   A. Allocating memory for use by programs
   B. Allocating CPU time for use by programs
   C. Creating menus in GUI programs
   D. Controlling access to hard disks
   E. Enabling programs to use the network

2. Which of the following is an example of an embedded OS?
   A. Android
   B. CentOS
   C. Fedora
   D. Mint
   E. Red Hat

3. Which of the following is a notable difference between Linux and macOS?
   A. Linux can run common GNU programs, whereas macOS cannot.
   B. Linux's GUI is based on the X Window System, whereas macOS is not.
   C. Linux cannot run on Apple Macintosh hardware, whereas macOS can run only on Apple hardware.
   D. Linux relies heavily on BSD software, whereas macOS uses no BSD software.
   E. Linux supports text-mode commands, whereas macOS is a GUI-only OS.

4. Where did the Linux kernel come from?
   A. It was derived from Microsoft Windows.
   B. It was derived from Apple macOS.
   C. It was derived from AT&T Unix.
   D. It was derived from BSD Unix.
   E. It was created by Linus Torvalds.

5. True or false: If you log into a Linux system in graphical mode, you cannot use text-mode commands in that session.

6. True or false: CentOS is a Linux distribution with a long release cycle.

7. A Linux text-mode login prompt reads _____.

   A. login:

   B. welcome:

   C. Enter:

   D. userid:

   E. Enter your userid:

8. A common security problem with Windows that's essentially nonexistent on Linux is _____.

   A. Commercial software

   B. Network firewalls

   C. Network routers

   D. Viruses

   E. Software management packages

9. Pre-release software that's likely to contain bugs is known as _____ and _____.

   A. First and second

   B. Primary and secondary

   C. Alpha and beta

   D. Development and production

   E. Development and test

10. Linux distributions that have no version number but instead release upgrades in an ongoing manner are said to have a(n) _____ release.

   A. rolling

   B. staggered

   C. informal

   D. systematic

   E. hap-hazard

Chapter

2

Understanding Software Licensing

OBJECTIVE:

✓ 1.3 Open Source Software and Licensing

Software is a type of intellectual property that is governed by copyright laws and, in some countries, patent laws. As a general rule, this makes it illegal to copy software unless you're the software's author. Open source software, however, relies on licenses, which are documents that alter the terms under which the software is released. As described in this chapter, open source licenses grant additional rights to software users.

In general, open source software owes a great deal to three organizations: the Free Software Foundation (FSF), the Open Source Initiative (OSI), and the Creative Commons (CC). Each organization has a distinct philosophy and role to play in the open source world. There are also numerous specific open source licenses, which are summarized at the end of this chapter, along with ways that businesses can use them.

Investigating Software Licenses

Copyright law has existed for centuries, and as such, it wasn't designed with software in mind. Nonetheless, copyright law does apply to software. Licenses that authors apply to their software interact with copyright law to create the specific rights that you have—and *don't* have—to use, modify, and redistribute software. Thus you need to understand the basic principles, as well as the differences, between proprietary and open source license terms.

Exploring Copyright Protection and Software

Certification
Objective
A *copyright* is, as the name implies, a legally recognized right to create a copy of something. In most countries, if you write a book, take a photograph, or create a computer program, you (and you alone) have the right to make copies of that book, photograph, or computer program. However, you can give others the right to make such copies, or even relinquish control of the copyright to somebody else.

Copyright laws vary from one country to another, but most countries signed the Berne Convention, an international agreement that requires countries to recognize one another's copyrights. That is, if Carol writes a book (or opera, or computer program) in the United States, that work will be copyrighted not only in the United States, but also in Iceland, Kenya, the United Kingdom, and other countries that have ratified the treaty.

Because most copyright laws were written long before computers came into being, they frequently don't mesh well with the needs of computers. For instance, copyright laws forbid the copying of a work, but a computer program is useless without such copies. Examples of copies that must necessarily be made to run a program or that are advisable for safety, include the following:

- A copy of the program from an installation medium to a disk drive
- A copy of the program from the disk drive to the computer's random access memory (RAM)
- A copy of the RAM into swap space
- A copy of the RAM into various smaller caches on the motherboard or CPU used to improve performance
- One or more disk drive backups to protect against disk failures

 Swap space is disk space that serves as a supplement to RAM. For example, if RAM fills up, the operating system (OS) begins to use swap space as if it were RAM.

In the past, such copies were generally ignored on the principle of *fair use*—that is, exceptions that allow portions of copyrighted material to be copied. Other examples of fair use include quotes used in reviews or news reports and excerpts used in research or teaching. Today, copyright law explicitly recognizes the need to copy software to use it, at least in the United States.

 Real World Scenario

Patents, Trademarks, and Software   Certification Objective

Copyright is one example of intellectual property, but there are many others. One of these is *patents*. A copyright protects a single creative work, which can be considered an expression of an idea, but a patent protects the *idea* itself. Patents typically apply to inventions, such as the proverbial "better mousetrap."

In the United States, software patents are legal. Although you can't patent an entire program, you can patent the algorithms that the program uses. Such patents are both common and controversial. Some open source programs don't use certain file formats because the algorithms required to use them are patented and the patent-holders have threatened to sue unauthorized users. Critics of software patents contend that most such patents are trivial or obvious—two things that a patented invention must not be. Companies sometimes use software patents as a way to block another company from selling a product, or to demand payment from a company that sells a product.

In many other countries, software algorithms cannot be patented. Efforts are underway to change the relationships between software and patents—both to make software patentable in countries where it is not and to restrict or eliminate software patents in countries where software can currently be patented.

Trademarks are another type of intellectual property. These are names, logos, and similar identifiers of a specific company or product. Software and the companies that produce it often use trademarks, as do hardware companies. An individual with little involvement in the Linux community trademarked the name *Linux* in 1994 and attempted to charge royalties on the name. After a lawsuit, the trademark was transferred to the Linux Mark Institute, or LMI (www.linuxfoundation.org/programs/legal/trademark).

As an end user, you probably won't have to deal with software patents or trademarks. Software patent and trademark issues play out at the corporation level. This contrasts with copyright issues, which can affect individuals who violate copyright law. If you work for a company that releases software, though, patent and trademark law could affect you. This is especially true if your software potentially violates a software patent or trademark. You should consult an attorney if you believe this might be the case.

Using Licenses to Modify Copyright Terms

Certification
Objective

Although software is subject to copyright law, most software is released with a *license*, which is a legal document that claims to modify the rights granted by copyright law. In most cases, you don't sign such a license, although in some cases you must click a button to accept the license terms. In the past, licenses were sometimes printed on the boxes in which software was distributed. Such licenses are often called *end-user license agreements (EULAs)*, *click-through licenses*, *shrink-wrap licenses*, or *click-wrap licenses*. Open source software generally comes with a license in a file, often named COPYING.

Courts have often upheld the enforceability of click-through and similar licenses, although this result is not universal.

Software licenses can modify copyright terms by making the terms either more or less restrictive. For example, the *General Public License* (GPL), which is the license used by the Linux kernel, grants you the right to redistribute the software, including both the source code and binaries. This represents a loosening of the restrictions provided by copyright law.

As a general rule, licenses for proprietary software restrict your rights under copyright law, whereas open source licenses grant you additional rights. There can be exceptions to this rule, though; for instance, a *site license* is a license for a proprietary program that grants an organization the right to make a certain number of copies of the program—say, 100 copies of a word processor for all of the company's computers.

Looking at the Free Software Foundation

The Free Software Foundation (FSF) is a critical force in the open source world. Founded in 1985 by Richard Stallman, the FSF is the driving force behind the GNU's Not Unix (GNU) project described in the previous chapter. The FSF has a certain philosophy, described next, which manifests itself in the GPL, which is FSF's favored software license.

Understanding the FSF Philosophy

The FSF advocates what it calls *free software*, which it defines as freedom to do things you want to do with the software, not the price of the software. A common phrase used to make this distinction clear is "free as in speech, not free as in beer."

Certification
Objective

> Free software, as the FSF defines it, is different from *freeware*. Freeware generally refers to software that's free of charge but not necessarily free as in speech.

The FSF defines four specific software freedoms:

- Freedom to use the software for any purpose
- Freedom to examine the source code and modify it as you see fit
- Freedom to redistribute the software
- Freedom to redistribute your modified software

These freedoms are similar to the principles espoused by the OSI, described shortly. However, there are some important differences in interpretation, as you'll soon see. The FSF elaborates on the implications of each of its principles, and their interactions, at gnu.org/philosophy/free-sw.html.

In an ideal world, by the FSF's standards, all software would be free—distributed with source code and all of the freedoms just outlined. Some Linux distributions meet this ideal in isolation, whereas other distributions include proprietary software. Sometimes, this software is freeware. At other times, it's a bit of proprietary code that enables the vendor to restrict redistribution and charge money to sell the software. Since free software is not necessarily free of charge, selling it is not a problem from the FSF's point of view. However, given the other freedoms, free software's price tends toward zero as it gets passed around.

The point of all this talk of freedom is to empower users—not just developers or companies. If you can modify a program that does *almost* what you want it to do so that it does *exactly* what you want it to do, that fact is a big advantage compared to a proprietary program. If you can then redistribute your modified version of the program, you can help others (assuming they want similar functionality). Thus the FSF philosophy, when applied, can create a benefit to the wider community.

The FSF philosophy and the licenses it inspires are often referred to as *copyleft*. This term came from a play on the word copyright, reflecting the fact that copyright provisions are used to ensure freedoms that are, in some respects, the exact opposite of what copyright was created to do—that is, to guarantee the freedom of users to copy software, rather than to restrict that right. Copyleft licenses require that any modified programs derived can be distributed only under the same license terms of the original program. Thus, copyleft licensing is sometimes called *reciprocal licensing.*

Examining Free Software and the GPL

The legal expression of the FSF's principles comes in the form of the GPL (sometimes called the *GNU GPL*). Two current versions of the GPL are common: version 2 and version 3. Both versions of the GPL apply the four freedoms of the FSF philosophy to the licensed software. They also state explicitly that derivative works must be released under the GPL, thus making it a copyleft license. This clause prevents a company from wholly appropriating an open source program. For instance, many companies make Linux distributions, and some use Linux kernels that incorporate bug-fix "patches." These kernels, like the mainstream Linux kernel, are all available under the GPL. No company could legally release a distribution based on a patched Linux kernel and then refuse to make its kernel patches available.

 A Linux distribution is a collection of many programs that may use different individual licenses. No one license takes priority over the others.

The GPL version 2 (or GPLv2 for short) was released in 1991, and it held sway for many years. In 2007, GPLv3 appeared, with the intention of closing certain loopholes in the GPLv2, particularly with respect to changes in laws and practices since 1991. Specifically, the GPLv3 contains clauses to combat use of hardware restrictions that limit the FSF's four freedoms and to address issues related to software patents. Many new programs are now being released under the terms of the GPLv3, and many older programs now use the GPLv3 rather than the GPLv2. Some programs have not changed, though. Notable among these is the Linux kernel itself, which still uses the GPLv2. This is an important choice because it means that the Linux kernel can still be used at the heart of devices that are otherwise fairly closed, such as Android-based phones. Many such devices use restrictive boot processes to prevent unauthorized kernels from booting—a process that the GPLv3 would forbid.

⊕ Real World Scenario

Enforceable Legal Contract

Hancom Inc. freely obtained open source software that was covered under the GNU GPL from Artifex Software Inc. and then modified the code. Hancom allegedly violated the license by charging money for the revised software. Artifex Software sued Hancom, who in turn filed a motion to dismiss the case, claiming that the GNU GPL was not a binding contract. The Magistrate Jacqueline Scott Corley, Federal Court, denied the motion and concluded that the GNU GPL was a binding contract, case No.16-cv-06982-JSC (N.D. Cal. Sep. 12, 2017). The two companies ultimately reached a confidential settlement.

A variant of the GPL is the *Lesser GPL (LGPL)*. Developers often use the LGPL with *libraries*, which are collections of code that can be used by other programs. For instance, in Linux, libraries implement the features that create dialog boxes and menus. Many GUI programs use these features, and placing them in libraries not only helps programmers, but also reduces the size of the programs that use them. The wording of the GPL, however, would require that all programs that use a library with a GPL also be released under the terms of the GPL. This strong requirement motivated the creation of the LGPL, which enables programs that use a library with a GPL to be released under another license—even a commercial license.

Another related license is the *GNU Free Documentation License (FDL)*, for use in documentation rather than by programs. The GPL, being written for software, doesn't apply perfectly to static documents, so the FSF created the GNU FDL to fill the gap. A notable user of the FDL is Wikipedia (wikipedia.org). All of its content is available under the terms of the GNU FDL.

Looking at the Open Source Initiative

Bruce Perens and Eric S. Raymond founded the *Open Source Initiative (OSI)* in 1998 as an umbrella organization for open source software in general. Its philosophy, described in more detail shortly, is similar to that of the FSF but differs in some important details. As a general rule, more software qualifies as open source than qualifies as free (in the way the FSF means), but precisely what qualifies depends on the open source definition and, in a strict sense, on what the OSI has approved in terms of its licenses.

Understanding the Open Source Philosophy

In the 1980s and 1990s, the free software movement gathered momentum in certain circles, including academia and among hobbyists. Businesses, however, were slow to adopt free software. Many who did adopt it did so reluctantly or even unwittingly—system administrators, pressed to perform their duties with minuscule budgets, would quietly install Linux, Apache, Samba, and other free software as a way to avoid having to buy expensive commercial alternatives.

The FSF's advocacy efforts were (and are) based on a strong moral imperative—*software should be free* in the FSF's view, with "free" defined as described earlier. This approach appeals to some people, but others—particularly businesses that want to make money selling software—find this type of advocacy strange at best and threatening at worst.

For these reasons, the OSI's creators designed their organization as a way to advocate for free software. By using a new term—*open source*—and by softening some of the FSF's moral imperatives, the OSI aims to promote open source software in the business world. The difference in tone from the FSF's moral imperative can be seen in a mission statement on the OSI's website (opensource.org): "Open source enables a development method for software that harnesses the power of distributed peer review and transparency of process. The promise of open source is higher quality, better reliability, greater flexibility, lower cost, and an end to predatory vendor lock-in."

The biggest philosophical difference between the FSF and the OSI is reflected in a GPL requirement that derived works also be distributed under the GPL. The OSI has certified many licenses as being open source, including the GPL; however, many of these licenses lack similar restrictions. Software released under such licenses has, in the past, found its way into closed-source products. The OSI does not object to such a path, provided the software was licensed in a way that permits it. The FSF, on the other hand, explicitly forbade such appropriation for proprietary uses in its GPL.

Certification
Objective

Permissive

Several licenses approved by the OSI are called *permissive* licenses. These include the Apache license, BSD licenses, and the MIT license (covered later in this chapter). Like a copyleft license, a permissive license allows users to copy, share, and modify the software. However, a permissive license is not as restrictive as copyleft. Whereas copyleft licenses require that any modified programs derived from a program with the license must be distributed under the same license terms, permissive licenses have minimal requirements concerning software redistribution. Some licenses that fall under the permissive license umbrella allow additional or different license terms and conditions for the licensed software. Thus, permissive licensing is sometimes called *nonreciprocal licensing*.

Certification
Objective

Today, some tension exists between free software purists in the FSF's sense and the more pragmatic open source community. For the most part, however, the two share goals that are similar enough that their differences are minor. In fact, two terms, *free and open source software (FOSS)* and *free/libre open source software (FLOSS)*, are sometimes used as umbrella terms to refer explicitly to both types of software and development.

Defining Open Source Software

The open source definition appears at opensource.org/definition. It consists of 10 principles, which are paraphrased here:

Certification
Objective

Free Redistribution   The license must permit redistribution, including redistribution as part of a larger work.

Source Code Availability   The author must make source code available and permit redistribution of source code and (if applicable) binary code.

Permission to Derive Works   The license must permit others to modify the software and to distribute such modifications under the same license as the original.

> The open source definition permits, but does not require, that the license require redistribution under the original license.

Respect for Source Code Integrity   The license may restrict redistribution of modified source code, but only if patch files may be distributed along with the original source code. The license may require that derived works change the software's name or version number.

No Discrimination Against Persons or Groups   The license must not discriminate against any person or group of people.

No Discrimination Against Fields of Endeavor   The license must not forbid use of the program in any field, such as in business or by genetics researchers.

Automatic License Distribution   The license must apply to anybody who receives the program, without needing a separate agreement.

Lack of Product Specificity   The license must not require that the program be used or distributed as part of a larger program—that is, you may extract a single program from a larger collection and redistribute it alone.

Lack of Restrictions on Other Software   The license must not impose restrictions on other software that's distributed along with the licensed software.

Technology Neutrality   The license must not be restricted based on specific technologies or interfaces.

> The OSI's 10 principles were derived from those expressed by the Debian GNU/Linux developers.

The first three of these principles are the most important, at least in terms of understanding the point of open source technology. The collection as a whole bears a strong resemblance to the FSF's four principles and the extended description of its implications on the FSF's web page (gnu.org/philosophy/free-sw.html). As already described, however, some differences exist, particularly with respect to licensing requirements for derived works.

Looking at the Creative Commons

Certification
Objective

Whereas the FSF and the OSI are dedicated to promoting software freedoms, the objectives of the *Creative Commons* (creativecommons.org) are broader. Its licenses are aimed at audio recordings, video recordings, textual works, and so on, not just computer programs. Nonetheless, the Creative Commons as an organization helps promote the types of freedoms that also concern the FSF and the OSI.

The Creative Commons was founded by Lawrence Lessig. Its goal is to combat what its creators and supporters view as a creative culture that is increasingly tied to permissions granted (or *not* granted) by those who hold copyrights on earlier works.

Much of our current culture is derived from earlier cultural works—for instance, the *Star Wars* movie collection is inspired, in part, by common myths and legends. *Star Wars* itself is copyrighted, however, which limits the rights of current artists to distribute works that are derivative of it, at least without permission. The Creative Commons promotes its aims by providing licenses that help creators retain their works' copyrights but at the same time allow others to freely copy, distribute, and use the original artist's work in a noncommercial manner.

The Creative Commons license suite consists of six licenses that are designed for various purposes. You can select a license by answering a few questions on the Creative Commons website at creativecommons.org/choose/, such as whether you want to permit commercial use of your work.

Using Open Source Licenses

As an individual user, you might not need to delve too deeply into open source license details. The principles behind the OSI guidelines guarantee that you have the right to use open source programs as you see fit and even to redistribute those programs. If you're building a business, though, and particularly a business that creates or distributes open source software, you may need to better understand these licenses. Thus, this section describes a few of them in more detail along with some ways companies use open source licenses in their business models.

Understanding Open Source Licenses

Every open source license has its own unique characteristics. These are mostly of interest to developers who might want to contribute to a software project, but on occasion they may be important to a system administrator. The major open source licenses include the following:

GNU GPL and LGPL   As noted earlier, the Linux kernel uses the GPLv2, and many other Linux tools use the GPL (either version 2 or version 3). Many Linux libraries use the LGPL.

BSD   The Berkeley Source Definition *(BSD)* licenses are used by the open source BSD OSs and by various software components developed for them. Unlike the GPL, the BSD licenses allow modifications to be distributed under other licenses. The latest versions of this license are similar to the MIT license in brevity.

Certification
Objective

Two BSD licenses are common: the *three-clause* and the *two-clause* version. The two-clause BSD license is sometimes called the *Simplified BSD* or *FreeBSD License*. The three-clause version is sometimes called the *new* or *revised BSD license*, in reference to a still older version (the *four-clause*).

MIT   The Massachusetts Institute of Technology (MIT) was the original moving force behind the X Window System (X for short), and the MIT license continues to be used for Xorg-X11—the implementation of X that is still included with several Linux distributions. However, some Linux distributions have moved from X to Wayland, which also uses the MIT license. The MIT license is unusually short—only around 160 words.

Apache   Like the BSD and MIT licenses, the Apache license is an open source license that permits redistribution under the same or another license. If a text file called NOTICE comes with the original work, it must be included in any derived work. This enables the original developer to provide contact or other information, even to users of heavily modified versions of the program.

Certification
Objective

The original version of the Apache license (version 1.0) was created in 1995. The current version is 2.0, and thus sometimes the Apache license is referred to as *Apache 2*.

As the name implies, the Apache license originated with the Apache web browser; however, it's used by many other projects as well.

Many additional licenses meet the OSI's requirements. You can find a complete list on the Open Source Initiative website at opensource.org/licenses/.

The details of the various open source licenses are probably not important to most system administrators. You may use and redistribute any open source program as you wish. If you modify a program, though, you should be aware of redistribution requirements, particularly if you want to merge two or more programs or distribute a program under a modified license. You should also be aware that some Linux distributions may include software that doesn't qualify as open source. Some of this is commercial software, and some of it falls into a variant category.

Some combinations of open source licenses are *incompatible* with one another, meaning that you can't legally combine the code and release the modified version.

One final concern when describing software licenses is the license for Linux as a whole. When you download an image file or buy a Linux package, the software you obtain uses many licenses—the GPL, the BSD license, the MIT license, and so on. Most of these licenses are open source, but some aren't. Many distributions ship with a few shareware or not-quite-open-source packages, such as the shareware XV graphics program. Retail packages sometimes include outright commercial software. For this reason, if you've purchased a Linux package disc, you should not copy it unless you've researched the issue and found out that copying is okay. If the distribution vendor provides free-as-in-beer download links, copying is probably allowed.

Linux distributions include installation programs, configuration programs, and the like. These tools are usually all that a distribution packager can lay claim to in terms of copyright. Most distribution maintainers have made their installation and configuration routines available under the GPL or some other open source license, but this isn't always the case. Such details can turn what might seem like an open source OS into something that's not quite fully open source. Debian maintains a policy of using only open source software in its main package set, although it lets freely redistributable but non–open source programs into its "non-free" package set.

Because a complete Linux distribution is composed of components using many licenses, it's not useful to speak of a single copyright or license applying to the entire OS. Instead, you should think of a Linux distribution as a collection of products that comes with a unifying installation utility. The vast majority of all the programs use one open source license or another, though.

Understanding Open Source Business Models

Certification Objective

Some Linux distributions, such as Debian, are maintained by volunteers or by not-for-profit organizations. Others, such as Red Hat Enterprise Linux, are maintained by a company that expects to make a profit. How then can a company make a profit if its core product is available for free on the Internet? Several approaches exist to making money from open source software, including the following:

Services and Support   The product itself can be open source, and even given away for free, while the company sells services and support, such as training and a technical support phone line. For instance, a game might be open source but require a subscription to an online service to provide a full set of features.

Dual Licensing   A company can create two versions of the product: one version is completely open source, and another adds features that are not available in the open source version. The open source version is then akin to the free samples that supermarkets often provide—it's a way to draw in paying customers.

Multiple Products   The open source product may be just one offering from the company, with revenue being generated by other product lines. These other product lines could be other software or some other product, such as manuals.

Open Source Drivers   A special case of the preceding one is that of hardware vendors. They might opt to release drivers, or perhaps even hardware-specific applications, as open source as a way to promote their hardware.

 When a hardware vendor releases an open source driver, the code reveals programming information about the vendor's hardware. Thus, some vendors are reluctant to release open source drivers.

Bounties   *Bounties* are a crowdfunding method. Users can drive open source creation by offering to pay for new software or new features in existing software. Sites such as FOSS Factory (fossfactory.org) and Bountysource (bountysource.com) can help bring together users, each of whom individually might not be able to offer enough money to motivate development, to entice programmers to write the desired code. With bounties, the programmer who completes the project first is allowed to collect the project's accumulated funds.

Donations   Many open source projects accept donations to help fund development. Although this isn't a commercial funding model in the usual sense, it does help fund the operations of organizations such as the FSF.

Beyond these commercial opportunities, of course, a great deal of open source software is developed in academia, by governments, nonprofit organizations, hobbyists, and so on. Even companies can be motivated to give back changes they make for themselves, because hoarding their changes will create more internal work for the company—if an internal change is not given back to the original software author, the company will have to reapply the change with each new release of the software.

EXERCISE 2.1

- Look up the GPLv2, GPLv3, and BSD two-clause licenses. The site opensource.org/licenses is a good place to find them all. Read and compare them. Which would you use if you were to write an open source program?

- Read the OSI mission statement (on its About page at opensource.org/about) and the "Our Core Work" section of the FSF's About page (fsf.org/about/).

Summary

Many intellectual works benefit from copyright protection, but it never fully fit with software. This void gave rise to licenses, which are legal documents that modify the protection bestowed by copyrights. Where open source software licenses were concerned, various organizations such as the Free Software Foundation (FSF), the Open Source Initiative (OSI), and the Creative Commons (CC) jumped in. They produced licenses as well as guidelines for promoting this software style. For a Linux system, it's wise to view and understand the array of licenses involved for both the installed software applications and the kernel.

Exam Essentials

Summarize copyright protection and software licenses.   A copyright is a legally recognized right to create a copy of something. Software is a type of intellectual property that is governed by copyrights (and possibly patent laws). Even though these laws were not designed with software in mind, they do apply. To remedy this ill fit, most software is released with a license, which is a legal document that modifies the rights granted by copyright law. Generally licenses for proprietary software provide more restrictions to your rights under copyright law, whereas open source licenses grant you additional rights.

Detail the FSF and its freedoms.   Founded in 1985 by Richard Stallman, the Free Software Foundation (FSF) is the driving force behind the GNU's Not Unix (GNU) project. It advocates *free* software, which centers on the descriptive phrase "free as in speech, not free as in beer." The organization has four specific software freedom definitions: freedom to use the software for any purpose, freedom to examine the source code and modify it as you see fit, freedom to redistribute the software, and freedom to redistribute your modified software. The FSF philosophy and its licenses are often referred to as *copyleft*.

Describe the OSI and its guidelines.   The Open Source Initiative (OSI) was created as a way to advocate for and promote free software in the business world. Several licenses approved by the OSI are called *permissive* licenses, because they allow users to copy, share, and modify the software but are not as restrictive as copyleft licenses. The OSI's ten principles are briefly stated as free redistribution, available source code, permission to derive works, respect for source code integrity, no discrimination is tolerated against persons or groups, no discrimination is acceptable against fields of endeavor, license distribution is automatic, lack of production specificity, shortage of restrictions on other software, and technology neutrality is encouraged.

Compare the various open source licenses.   The GNU public license (GPL) version 2 was released in 1991, and in 2007 the GPL version 3 was made public. The GPLv3 is different than GPLv2 in that it contains clauses intended to combat use of hardware restrictions. The Lesser GPL (LGPL) derived from the GPL is often used by developers for software libraries. The BSD license, which allows code modifications to be distributed under other licenses, is primarily used by the open source BSD OSs. The rather short MIT license is associated with the X Window System, which also allows code modifications to be distributed under other licenses. The Apache license, first created in 1995, is similar to the BSD and MIT licenses in its handling of software modification licensing.

Review Questions

You can find the answers in the Appendix A.

1. In order for software to be certified as open source, which of the following is *not* required?

   A. The license must not discriminate against people or groups of people.

   B. The license must not require that the software be distributed as part of a specific product.

   C. The license must require that changes be distributed under the same license.

   D. The program must come with source code, or the author must make it readily available on the Internet.

   E. The license must automatically apply to anybody who acquires the software.

2. Which is true of Linux distributions as a whole?

   A. They're covered by the GPL or the BSD license, depending on the distribution.

   B. Sometimes they may not be copied because of the non–open source software they may contain.

   C. They may be copied only after software using the MIT license is removed.

   D. They all completely conform to the principles of the open source movement.

   E. They all qualify as free software as the FSF uses the term.

3. Which of the following is a key part of the FSF's philosophy?

   A. Developers should use the latest version of the FSF's GPL.

   B. Users should have the right to modify free software and distribute it under a commercial license.

   C. Developers should write software only for free operating systems such as GNU/Linux.

   D. Users should engage in civil disobedience by copying proprietary software.

   E. Users must have the right to use software as they see fit.

4. True or false: Copyright law governs the distribution of software in most countries.

5. True or false: The FSF's free software definition and the OSI's 10 principles of open source software both require that users have the ability to examine a program's workings—that is, its source code.

6. True or false: Because their hardware designs are proprietary, hardware vendors cannot release open source drivers for their products.

7. A license created by the FSF and often used for libraries is the _____.

   A. BSD

   B. Apache

   C. GPL

   D. LGPL

   E. MIT

8. An organization devoted to promoting open source–like principles in fields such as video and audio recordings is the _____.

   A. Creative Commons

   B. GNU

   C. FSF

   D. MIT

   E. OSI

9. The FSF's general principles are summarized by the term _____, which refers to using copyright laws for purposes that are in some ways contrary to copyright's original intent.

   A. patent

   B. copyright

   C. copyleft

   D. free

   E. tradmark

10. Users can motivate programmers to work on open source projects by offering a(n) _____ to whomever completes the project first.

    A. donation

    B. salary

    C. present

    D. kudos

    E. bounty

Chapter
3

Investigating Linux's Principles and Philosophy

OBJECTIVES:

✓ 1.1 Linux Evolution and Popular Operating Systems

✓ 1.3 Open Source Software and Licensing

You can frequently select a product or technology on purely pragmatic grounds—what OS works well for a given task, which software suite is the least expensive, and so on. Sometimes, though, understanding the principles and philosophy that underlie a technology can be useful, and knowing these might even guide your choice.

This is true of some Linux users; the open source model of Linux, which we introduced in Chapter 1, "Selecting an Operating System," has implications that can affect how Linux works. Furthermore, some in the Linux world can become quite passionate about these principles. Whether or not you agree with these individuals, understanding their point of view can help you appreciate the Linux culture, which you'll find in the workplace, online, at conferences, and so on.

This chapter covers these issues, beginning with information on Linux's origins and its development over time up to the present. We then describe open source principles and how they can affect the way an open source OS works in the real world. Finally, we describe some of the roles in which Linux can work—as an embedded OS, as a desktop or laptop OS, and as a server OS.

Linux Through the Ages

Although Linux's birth date of 1991 is recent by most historical standards, in the computer world 25 years is an eternity. Nonetheless, the software and culture in the early 1990s, and even before then, has conveyed quite a legacy to today's software world. After all, what we use today is built atop the foundation that was created in the past. Thus, looking at how Linux originated will help you understand Linux as it exists today.

Understanding Linux's Origins

In 1991, as is also true today, computers were classified by their sizes and capabilities. Computers could belong to any of a handful of categories, ranging from desktop personal computers (PCs) to supercomputers. x86-based computers, which are the direct ancestors of today's PCs, dominated the PC marketplace of 1991; however, other types of PCs were available, including Mac computers. Such computers generally used different CPUs and ran their own custom OSs.

Computers today can be classified in much the same way as in 1991, although some details have changed. A notable addition are embedded computers, as in smartphones.

In 1991, most PCs ran Microsoft's Disk Operating System (MS-DOS, PC-DOS, or DOS). DOS was extremely limited by today's standards; it was a single-tasking OS (it could run only one program at a time) that didn't even take full advantage of the memory or CPUs available at the time. The versions of Microsoft Windows available in 1991 ran on top of DOS. Although the initial versions of Windows helped to work around some of DOS's limitations, they didn't fundamentally fix any of them. These early versions of Windows employed *cooperative multitasking*, for instance, in which programs could voluntarily give up CPU time to other processes. The DOS kernel could not wrest control from a program that hogged CPU time.

Above the PC level, Unix was a common OS in 1991. Compared to DOS and the version of Windows of that time, Unix was a sophisticated OS. Unix supported multiple accounts and provided true *preemptive multitasking*, in which the kernel could schedule CPU time for programs, even if the programs didn't voluntarily give up control. These features were practical necessities for many servers and for multiuser computers such as minicomputers and mainframes.

Unix was not the only multiuser, multitasking OS in 1991. Others, such as Virtual Memory System (VMS), were available. Unix is most relevant to Linux's history, though.

As time progressed, the capabilities of each class of computer have grown. By most measures, today's PCs have the power of the minicomputers or even the mainframes of 1991. The OSs used on the PCs of 1991 didn't scale well to more powerful hardware, and today's PCs are now powerful enough to run the more sophisticated OSs of 1991. For this reason, DOS and its small computer contemporaries have been largely abandoned in favor of Unix and other alternatives.

Today's versions of Windows are not derived from DOS. Instead, they use a new kernel that shares many design features with VMS.

In 1991, Linus Torvalds was a student at the University of Helsinki, studying computer science. He was interested in learning about both Unix and the capabilities of the new *x*86 computer he'd just purchased. Torvalds began the program that would become the Linux kernel as a low-level terminal emulator—a program to connect to his university's larger computers. As his program grew, he began adding features that turned his terminal program into something that could be better described as an OS kernel. Eventually, he began writing with the goal of creating a Unix-compatible kernel—that is, a kernel that could run the wide range of Unix software that was available at the time.

Unix's history, in turn, stretched back two more decades, to its origin at AT&T in 1969. Because AT&T was a telephone monopoly in the United States at that time, it was legally forbidden from selling software. Therefore, when its employees created Unix, AT&T basically gave the OS away. Universities were particularly enthusiastic about adopting Unix, and some began modifying it, since AT&T made the source code available. Thus, Unix had a two-decade history of open software development to start. Most Unix programs were distributed as source code, since Unix ran on a wide variety of hardware platforms—binary programs made for one machine would seldom run on a different machine.

Early on, Linux began to tap into this reservoir of available software. As noted in Chapter 1, early Linux developers were particularly keen on the GNU's Not Unix (GNU) project's software, so Linux quickly accumulated a collection of GNU utilities. Much of this software had been written with workstations and more powerful computers in mind, but because computer hardware kept improving, it ran fine on the *x*86 PCs of the early 1990s.

The 386BSD OS was a competing Unix-like OS in the early 1990s. Today, it has forked into several related OSs: FreeBSD, NetBSD, OpenBSD, Dragon-fly BSD, and PC-BSD.Linux quickly acquired a devoted following of developers who saw its potential to bring workstation-class software to the PC. These people worked to improve the Linux kernel, to make the necessary changes in existing Unix programs so that they would work on Linux, and to write Linux-specific support programs. By the mid-1990s, several Linux distributions existed, including some that survive today. (Slackware was released in 1993 and Red Hat in 1995, for example.)

 Real World Scenario

The Microkernel Debate

Linux is an example of a *monolithic kernel*, which is a kernel that does everything a kernel is supposed to do in one big process. In 1991, a competing kernel design, known as a *microkernel*, was all the rage. Microkernels are much smaller than monolithic kernels; they move as many tasks as they can into non-kernel processes and then manage the communications between processes.

Soon after Linux's release, Linus Torvalds engaged in a public debate with Andrew Tanenbaum, the creator of the Minix OS that Torvalds used as an early development platform for Linux. Minix uses a microkernel design, and Tanenbaum considered Linux's monolithic design to be backward.

As a practical matter for an end user, either design works. Linux and the BSD-derived kernels use monolithic designs, whereas modern versions of Windows, the GNU HURD, and Minix are examples of microkernels. Some people still get worked up over this distinction, though.

Seeing Today's Linux World

By the mid-1990s, the most important features of Linux as it exists today had been established. Changes since then have included the following:

Improvements in the Kernel   The Linux kernel has seen massive changes since 1991, when it lacked many of the features we rely on today. Improvements include the addition of networking features, innumerable hardware drivers, support for power management features, and support for many non-*x*86 CPUs.

Improvements in Support Tools   Just as work has progressed on the Linux kernel, improvements have also been made to the support programs on which it relies—the compilers, shells, GUIs, and so on.

Creation of New Support Tools   New support tools have emerged over the years. These range from simple and small utilities to big desktop environments. In fact, some of these tools, such as modern desktop environments, are far more obvious to the end user than is the kernel itself.

Creation of New Distributions   As noted earlier, Slackware dates to 1993 and Red Hat (the predecessor to Red Hat Enterprise Linux, CentOS, and Fedora) originated in 1995. Other distributions have emerged in the intervening years, and some have been quite important. The Android OS used on smartphones and tablets, for instance, has become very influential over the past decade.

Linux's roots remain very much in the open source software of the 1980s and 1990s. Although a typical desktop or embedded OS user is likely to perceive the OS through the lens of the GUI, much of what happens under the surface happens because of the Linux kernel and open source tools, many of which have existed for decades.

Using Open Source Software

The philosophies that underlie much software development for Linux are different from those that drive most software development for Windows. These differing philosophies affect how you obtain the software, what you can do with it, and how it changes over time. This section describes these principles, as well as how Linux functions as a sort of "magnet," integrating software from many sources into one place.

Understanding Basic Open Source Principles

Broadly speaking, software can be described as coming in several different forms, each with different expectations about payment, redistribution, and users' rights. The number of categories varies depend on the depth of analysis and the prejudices of the person doing the categorization. As a starting point, however, four categories will do:

Commercial Software   Individuals or companies develop commercial software with the intent to sell it for a profit. Developers generally keep the source code for commercial source software secret, which means that users can't normally make changes to the software except to alter configuration settings that the software supports. In the past, commercial software was sold in stores or by mail order, but today it's often sold via downloads from the Internet. Redistributing commercial software is generally illegal. Microsoft Windows and Microsoft Office are both common examples of commercial software.

Shareware Software   From a legal perspective, *shareware* software is similar to commercial software in that it's copyrighted and the author asks for payment. The difference is that shareware is distributed on the Internet or in other ways and "sold" on an honor system—if you use the software beyond a trial period, you're expected to pay the author. Shareware was common in 1991 and is still available today, but it's much rarer.

Freeware   Freeware, like shareware, is available for free. Unlike shareware authors, though, the authors of freeware don't ask for payment. Sometimes, freeware is a stripped-down version of a more complete shareware or commercial program. At other times, the authors make it available for free to promote another product. Examples include Windows drivers for many hardware devices or the Adobe Reader program for reading Portable Document Format (PDF) files. As with commercial and shareware programs, freeware generally comes without source code.

> *Freeware* should not be confused with *free software*, which is closely related to open source software. Chapter 2, "Understanding Software Licensing," describes free software in more detail.

Certification
Objective

Open Source Software   Open source software is defined by a set of 10 principles, available at opensource.org/docs/osd. The most important of these principles are: The user has the right to redistribute the program, the source code must be made available, and the user has the right to make and distribute changed versions of the program. These principles mean that users can alter open source programs to suit their own needs, even in ways or for purposes not supported by the original author.

Variants within each of these categories exist, as well as hybrids that don't quite fit into any category. For instance, the Open Source Initiative maintains a list of licenses that it has approved as fulfilling its criteria (opensource.org/licenses); however, developers sometimes release software using obscure licenses or using licenses that impose conditions that run afoul of one of the more obscure Open Source Initiative rules. Such software is technically not open source, but it might be closer to open source than to another category.

> Chapter 2 covers specific open source licenses in greater detail.

The basic idea behind open source software is that software developed in a transparent manner is likely to be superior to software developed in a closed manner. This superiority (and arguments against it) comes in several ways:

Better Code Exposing source code to the community at large means that it can be reviewed, judged, and improved on by any interested party. Obscure bugs might be found and squashed when otherwise they might linger and cause problems in a closed-source product. However, the validity of this claim is not well supported by research, and smaller projects might not gain much in the way of interest from other programmers, so they might not benefit from outside code review.

More Flexibility By providing users with the source code, an open source project allows users to customize the software for their own needs. If users submit changes back to those individuals who maintain the software or release them as a new branch of the project, then everybody can benefit from such changes. Of course, critics would argue that this flexibility is only a benefit to those with the necessary skill and time to make such changes or to those with the money to hire somebody to do it.

Lower Cost Although the open source definition does not forbid the sale of software, the redistribution requirements mean that open source software ends up being available free of charge. If you want support, though, you may need to purchase a support contract, which can reduce or eliminate the cost benefits.

Lack of Vendor Lock-In The developers of some proprietary products, and particularly very popular ones, can make it difficult for competing products by using proprietary file formats or standards and by not supporting more open standards. Open source tools are less subject to such problems, since they can be modified to support open standards, even if they don't initially do so. As a practical matter, though, even proprietary file formats and protocols are usually reverse-engineered, so vendor lock-in usually ends up being a temporary problem rather than a permanent one.

Of course, within the Linux community the general consensus is that each of these factors is a real point in favor of Linux and of open source software in general; the downsides noted are generally regarded as minor when compared to the advantages. In the end, you'll need to make up your own mind on these matters after using different types of software.

Linux as a Software Integrator

Soon after Unix was created, the OS fragmented into a set of loosely affiliated OSs. These OSs were incompatible on the binary level but more or less compatible on the source code level. This is still true today. You can take the same program and compile it for FreeBSD, macOS, and Linux, and it will work the same on all three platforms—but the compiled binaries made for one platform won't work on the others.

There are exceptions to this rule. Some programs rely on features that are available on just some Unix-like OSs. Others have quirks that make it impossible to compile them on some OSs. If a program falls into disuse, it may become unusable on newer OSs because it relies on compiler or OS features that have changed. Such problems tend to be ironed out over time, but they do crop up periodically.

Because of Linux's popularity, most open source Unix programs compile and work fine on Linux. Commercial programs for Linux also exist, although most of these are obscure or specialized. In any event, Linux has become an OS that most open source Unix programs must support. This effect is so strong that many projects now target Linux as the primary platform.

Understanding OS Roles

Computers fill many roles in the world, and as computers have become ever more common and less expensive, those roles have multiplied. Linux can serve as the OS for most of these roles, each of which draws on its own subset of support utilities. Some of these roles also require tweaking the kernel itself. We briefly describe three of these roles: embedded computers, desktop and laptop computers, and server computers.

Looking At Embedded Computers

Certification
Objective

As noted in Chapter 1, embedded computers are specialized devices that fulfill a specific purpose. Examples include:

Mobile Phones Modern mobile phones use computers with OSs that range from simple to complex. Linux powers some of these mobile phones, usually in the form of the Android OS.

> **NOTE** Apple, Microsoft, and other vendors provide their own OSs for mobile phones.

E-book Readers These devices, like mobile phones, are specialized computers and so use an OS to power them. For many current e-book readers, that OS is Linux—either a custom Linux version or Android.

IoT Monitors The Internet of Things (IoT) consists of small embedded systems that monitor physical conditions, such as temperature, humidity, light, or motion, and use that data to control motors, switches, cameras, and other devices.

DVRs Digital video recorders (DVRs), which record TV shows for later viewing, are computers with specialized software. Some of these, including the popular TiVo models, run Linux.

> **NOTE** The MythTV package (mythtv.org) can turn an ordinary PC into a Linux-based DVR, although you'll need a TV tuner and other specific hardware to make it work.

Automotive Computers   Automobiles have included computers for years. These have mostly been tucked out of the way to monitor and control the engine and other automotive systems; however, modern cars increasingly come with computers that users more readily identify as being computers. They manage global positioning system (GPS) navigation systems, manage collision avoidance, regulate emergency braking, control the audio system, and even provide Internet access.

Appliances   Televisions, refrigerators, and other appliances are increasingly using computers to download software updates, monitor energy use, and for other purposes.

You might also think of tablet computers as falling into this category as well, although they can more closely resemble desktop or laptop computers. The distinction is mainly one of how much control the user has over the OS; embedded devices are used, not maintained, by end users. The system administration tasks described in this book are done at the factory or by using much simpler and more specialized user interfaces.

Exploring Desktop and Laptop Computers

Linux began life on a desktop computer, and although Linux doesn't come close to dominating that market, desktop computers are a good way to begin learning about Linux. Laptop computers are similar to desktop computers from a system administration perspective; both types of computers are often used by a small number of people for productivity tasks, such as word processing, web browsing, and managing digital photos. For brevity, we'll use the term *desktop* to refer to both types of computers from here on.

Certification
Objective

Desktop computers are similar to another class of computer, known as *workstations*. Workstations tend to be more powerful and specialized, and they often run Unix or Linux.

Linux software for such tasks is widely available and is quite good, although some people prefer commercial counterparts, such as Microsoft Office or Adobe Photoshop, that aren't available for Linux. This preference for a few specific commercial products is part of why Microsoft Windows continues to dominate the desktop market. Some people speculate that the open source development model doesn't lend itself to creating popular GUI applications because software developers tend to be too technically oriented to appreciate fully the needs of general users. Without an explicit way to require developers to fulfill these needs, which commercial applications create, open source software projects lag behind their commercial counterparts in usability. At worst, open source projects lag behind their commercial counterparts just a bit. Specific software that's required on most Linux-based desktop computers includes:

- The X Window System GUI (X for short)
- A popular desktop environment, such as GNOME, KDE, Xfce, or Unity
- A web browser, such as Mozilla Firefox

- An email client, such as Mozilla Thunderbird or Evolution

- A graphics editor, such as the GIMP

- An office suite, such as OpenOffice or the similar LibreOffice

Additional requirements vary depending on the user's needs. For instance, one user might need multimedia editing tools, whereas another might need scientific data analysis software.

Linux distributions such as Fedora and Ubuntu typically install these popular desktop tools by default, or as a group by selecting a single install-time option. These distributions are also designed for relatively easy maintenance so that users with only modest skill can install the OS and keep it running over time.

Investigating Server Computers

Certification
Objective

Server computers can be almost identical to desktop computers in terms of their hardware, although servers sometimes require bigger hard drives or better network connections, depending on how they're used. Many popular network server programs were written for Unix or Linux first, making these platforms the best choice for running them. Examples include:

- Web servers, such as Apache

- Email servers, such as sendmail and Postfix

- Databases, such as MySQL

- File servers, such as the Network File System (NFS) or Samba

- Print servers, such as the Common Unix Printing System (CUPS) or Samba

- Domain Name System (DNS) servers, such as the Berkeley Internet Name Domain (BIND)

- Dynamic Host Configuration Protocol (DHCP) servers, such as the Internet Software Consortium's (ISC's) dhcpd

- Time servers, such as the Network Time Protocol (NTP)

- Remote login servers, such as Secure Shell (SSH) or Virtual Network Computing (VNC)

Remote login servers enable users to run desktop-style programs on a computer remotely. Therefore, they're sometimes found even on desktop systems.

In a large organization, each of these services may have a distinct associated server computer. It's possible, though, for one computer to run many of these server programs simultaneously.

Most of these servers do not require a GUI, so server computers can do without X, desktop environments, or the typical desktop programs that you'll find on a desktop computer. One of Linux's advantages over Windows is that you can run the computer without these elements, and you can even uninstall them completely. Doing so means that the GUI won't be needlessly consuming system resources such as RAM. Furthermore, if an item such as X isn't running, any security bugs it might harbor become unimportant. Some distributions, such as Debian, Arch, and Gentoo, eschew GUI configuration utilities. This makes these distributions unfriendly to new users, but the reliance on text-mode configuration tools is not a problem to experienced administrators of server computers.

The people who maintain large server computers are generally technically quite proficient and can often contribute directly to the open source server projects that they use. This close association between users and programmers can help keep server projects on the cutting edge of applications and utilities required in the real world.

Note that the distinction between desktop and server computers is not absolute; a computer can run a mixture of both types of software. For instance, you might configure desktop computers in an office environment to run file server software. This configuration enables users to share their work more easily with others in the office. In a home or small office setting, running other servers on desktop computers can obviate the need to buy specialized hardware to fulfill those roles.

Summary

Linux's development history is tied to that of Unix and to open source development in general. Open source software is provided with source code and the right to modify and redistribute the source code. This guarantees your ability to use the software in ways that the original author did not anticipate or support, provided you have the knowledge and time to alter it or the resources to hire somebody else to do so. These open source principles have led to a great deal of popular software, particularly in the server arena; however, open source developers have been less able to capture the general public's excitement with applications designed for desktop computers.

Exam Essentials

Describe the three common uses for Linux systems.   Linux systems are commonly found in embedded systems, desktop systems, and server systems. In embedded systems a stripped-down version of Linux is used to save storage and memory space. The Linux system is usually configured to perform a single function or a limited set of functions. In desktop Linux environments the Linux system usually utilizes a graphical desktop interface to make launching programs and managing files easier. This, however, uses lots of computing power to run the graphical systems. Linux servers reserve all of their processing power for network applications, such as web servers, database servers, and email servers. They almost never incorporate a graphical desktop interface and require using command-line tools to perform all functions.

Explain the four models of providing software to customers.   The four models of software distribution are commercial, shareware, freeware, and open source. With commercial software, a company releases only the executable program files for a fee. Customers don't have the right to view the source code and only have the right to run the executable program. The shareware model allows program authors to release their executable files to the public and request payments but not demand payment. The freeware model allows program authors to release their executable files to the public without charge but also without any warranty or rights to decompile the program. In both the shareware and freeware models, the original program source code is protected by the author. The open source software model allows an author to release the executable program files and all the source code files required to build the executable program files free of charge. Customers are free to modify and recompile the source code as needed to suit their environment.

Describe the difference between a microkernel and a monolithic kernel.   A microkernel splits the kernel functions into separate small programs that interact behind the scenes to create the OS environment. A monolithic kernel includes all of the kernel functions into a single program that runs behind the scenes to create the OS environment. The monolithic kernel allows you to customize what features the kernel supports, but when you leave out a feature you can't add it back in without recompiling the kernel. The microkernel model usually allows you to add and remove kernel features from the running kernel as needed.

Review Questions

You can find the answers in the Appendix A.

1. What type of multitasking does Linux use?

   A. Preemptive

   B. Multiuser

   C. Cooperative

   D. Single-tasking

   E. Single-user

2. Which of the following is a characteristic of all open source software?

   A. The software cannot be sold for profit; it must be distributed free of charge.

   B. It must be distributed with both the source code and binaries.

   C. Users are permitted to redistribute altered versions of the original software.

   D. The software was originally written at a college or university.

   E. The software must be written in an interpreted language that requires no compilation.

3. Which of the following programs is most likely to be installed and regularly used on a desktop computer that runs Linux?

   A. Apache

   B. Postfix

   C. Android

   D. Evolution

   E. BIND

4. True or false: VMS was a common OS on x86 PCs at the time Linux was created.

5. True or false: Some DVRs run Linux.

6. True or false: A Linux computer being used as a server generally does not require X.

7. Linux uses a(n)_____ kernel design, as contrasted with a microkernel design.

   A. exo

   B. monolithic

   C. hybrid

   D. distributed

   E. unified

8.   A type of software that's distributed for free but that requires payment on the honor system if a person uses it is called _____.

   A.   open source

   B.   commercial

   C.   freeware

   D.   shareware

   E.   virus

9.   A _____ computer is likely to run a word processor and web browser.

   A.   server

   B.   desktop

   C.   distributed

   D.   client

   E.   laptop

10.   The _____ software package is an example of a web server written for the Linux server environment.

   A.   MySQL

   B.   LibreOffice

   C.   Firefox

   D.   GIMP

   E.   Apache

Chapter

4

Using Common Linux Programs

OBJECTIVES:

✓ 1.2   Major Open Source Applications

✓ 1.4   ICT Skills and Working in Linux

This chapter begins a more hands-on look at Linux, as opposed to the more abstract information presented in the previous chapters. It starts with a look at Linux desktop environments, including information on the most common desktop environments and their basic uses. If you're using a desktop environment, chances are good you're doing so in order to run productivity software; in this chapter, you'll learn about some common productivity packages for Linux. In addition, you'll likely want to install additional productivity software, so software package management is briefly covered at the chapter's end.

Another major use of a Linux system is as a network server, so this chapter covers a few common server programs that you may encounter. Although you might not need to write programs, you may have to compile programs from source code, so you should also be familiar with the common Linux programming tools described in this chapter.

Using a Linux Desktop Environment

Chances are that your first experience with a working Linux system will involve a *desktop environment*. A desktop environment is a set of programs that control the screen, and it also provides small utility programs to perform tasks such as managing files. Linux provides several desktop environment options, so if you don't like one, you can choose another. In addition to presenting information on available desktop environments, this section describes a few tools that you can use to launch programs and manage files.

Choosing a Desktop Environment

Depending on your Linux distribution and installation options, chances are good that your system has more than one desktop environment available. The most common desktop environments are as follows:

KDE Plasma   The K Desktop Environment (KDE) Plasma (kde.org) is a popular desktop environment for Linux. It's the default desktop environment for openSUSE. It includes many powerful tools that integrate well, and it's built using the Qt widget set.

A *widget set* is a library that handles GUI features such as menus and dialog boxes. Qt and GTK+ (part of the GNU project) are two popular widget sets on Linux today.

GNOME GNOME (gnome.org) is also popular in the Linux desktop environment arena. It is the default desktop environment for the Fedora and Ubuntu distributions. GNOME is built atop the GIMP Toolkit (GTK+) widget set. Like KDE Plasma, GNOME includes many powerful tools that work together. GNOME aims to provide an easy-to-use desktop environment.

Cinnamon Originally based on GNOME, the Cinnamon desktop environment was initially available only for the Linux Mint distribution but is now supported by others. Its ease of use, flexibility, clean look, and overall friendly experience makes Cinnamon a great desktop environment for those who are new to Linux. but seasoned Linux users prefer it as well.

LXDE The Lightweight X11 Desktop Environment, or LXDE (lxde.org), is, as its full name suggests, intended to consume few resources and therefore works well on old or modest computers. It is also built on the GTK+ widget set. LXDE is typically the default desktop environment on Linux distributions whose primary goal is to consume as few resources as possible while still being fully functional.

Xfce This popular lightweight desktop environment can be found at xfce.org. It was originally modeled on a commercial desktop environment known as CDE, but it is built using the GTK+ widget set. Xfce provides more configurability than GNOME. It loads and runs applications quickly but consumes fewer system resources than most other desktop environments.

Build Your Own It's possible to build a desktop environment of your own from components that you like. Because this can be a rather complex task, it's best to start with detailed guidance. Open your favorite web search engine, and type **how to create your own Linux desktop environment** to find specific information on building your custom desktop. At a minimum, you need a window manager. However, for the configuration to be a true desktop environment, you'll need other components, such as a file manager and small productivity tools. All of the components need to be accessible from some sort of menu system.

Unfortunately, it's impossible to give guidelines indicating when one desktop environment works better than another. However, the following recommendations can help. New users who are accustomed to Windows or macOS will probably be happiest with KDE Plasma. The KDE Plasma environment is similar to these traditional desktop operating systems' environments. GNOME aims for elegance and ease of use, so it's a good choice for those who want a nice-looking user interface. Xfce and LXDE are good choices on systems that are light on RAM or have low-powered CPUs. People who like to customize everything or who have less capable computers should investigate the build-your-own approach.

Before you decide to stick with a particular desktop environment, you may want to try out two or three of them. In most cases, you can install multiple environments by using a package manager, as described later in this chapter and in more detail in Chapter 9, "Exploring Processes and Process Data."

After your additional desktop environment(s) is installed, you select it when you log into the computer via a menu. The example in Figure 4.1 shows a Linux Mint system login screen.

FIGURE 4.1 A typical Linux desktop login screen where you choose the user account

To choose the desktop environment on Linux Mint, you must click the mountain peaks button that is next to the username. An example of the resulting menu is shown in Figure 4.2.

FIGURE 4.2 GUI login managers usually provide a selection of desktop environments from which you can choose.

Menu choices on your Linux system will vary, depending on which desktop environments were installed by default and which ones were added manually. How to select a desktop environment varies from one distribution to another, so you may need to peruse your login screen's options to select the environment that you want.

Launching Programs

Most desktop environments provide several ways to launch programs. Details can vary considerably from one environment to another. However, useful examples include the following:

Certification
Objective

Desktop Menus   Many desktop environments provide menus along a top, bottom, or side edge of the screen. One or more items in these menus can give you access to a preselected set of applications.

Desktop Icons   In some desktop environments you can place icons in the main area of the desktop. Clicking or double-clicking these icons then launches the applications. This approach generally requires customization. Some default configurations place a few applications in the main desktop area.

Panels   Some desktop environments provide panels where icons for common applications appear; typically panels are on the sides of the screen. GNOME Shell (a version of the GNOME desktop environment) uses such a configuration by default—although the panel appears only when you click the Activities item in the upper-left corner of the screen.

Context Menus   You can sometimes right-click in an unused part of the screen to obtain a context menu with a variety of options, which may include the option to run programs.

Searching for Programs   Some desktop environments provide a search feature that you can use to find a program by name. This search feature may be on the main screen or within a desktop menu. Typically, you type part of a program's name, and programs whose names match appear in a list. You can then select the program that you want to run from that list.

Terminals   You can launch a program called a *terminal*, which provides a text-mode user interface inside a window. You can then run either text-mode or GUI programs by typing their filenames in this window. This approach is covered in more detail in Chapter 5, "Getting to Know the Command Line."

Certification
Objective

To help clarify some of these methods, a couple of examples are in order. First, you'll launch the Firefox web browser in the Fedora 30 Workstation distribution using the GNOME Shell desktop environment.

Follow these steps after you log into the system:

1. Click the Activities item in the upper-left corner of the screen. The result is a panel (called Favorites) on the left side of the screen, as shown in Figure 4.3.

2. Move the mouse over the Firefox icon, which is the topmost icon in Figure 4.3.

3. Click the Firefox icon. After a brief delay, a Firefox window should open.

FIGURE 4.3   With panels you can launch popular programs in GNOME and some other desktop environments.

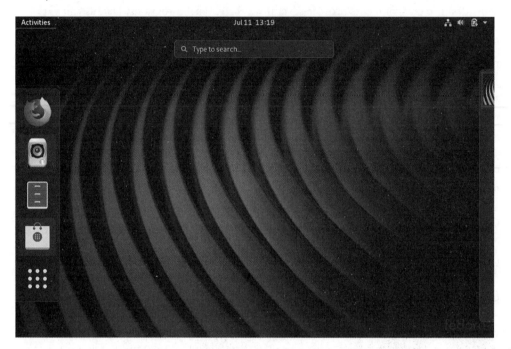

Other ways to do this also exist, such as typing the program's name in the search field (visible at the upper middle of Figure 4.3). Because only a handful of programs appear in the GNOME Shell panel, you must either add programs to it or launch programs that the Fedora developers did not include by default in some other way.

For comparison, Cinnamon under Linux Mint 18.3 provides several obvious ways to launch Firefox:

▪ By clicking its icon near the left side of the screen's bottom panel (see Figure 4.4).

▪ By finding its icon in the Favorites panel. You view this panel by clicking on the Menu icon on the far left-side of the screen's bottom panel. The Favorites panel is located on the far left-side of the menu window (see Figure 4.4).

▪ By locating it via the search feature, which is also located within the Menu system (see Figure 4.4).

▪ By finding it in the Applications list within the Menu system. You open the Firefox application by entering into the Menu system, selecting Internet, and clicking the Firefox Web Browser icon.

FIGURE 4.4   Cinnamon's desktop interface provides launch methods similar to those available in Windows.

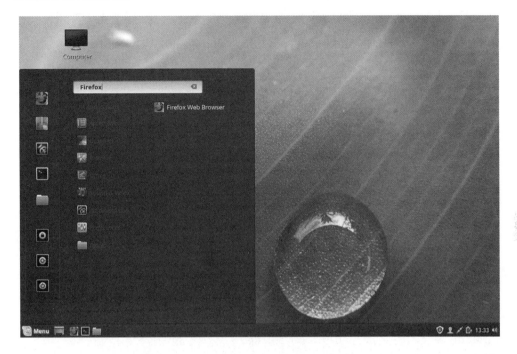

With the various desktop environments the widest range of launch options are available for a handful of popular applications, such as Firefox. For less popular programs you may need to use the more complex methods, such as locating the program in the Applications list. You can, however, reconfigure the desktop environment to add programs that you use frequently.

 Each distribution sets up its defaults in its own way. Your own GNOME or Cinnamon configuration might not resemble the ones shown here.

Using a File Manager

If you're used to Windows or macOS, you've almost certainly used a *file manager* to manipulate your files. Linux, of course, provides a file manager for this purpose too—in fact, you have a choice of several, although most of them operate in a similar way. As

Certification
Objective

an example, consider GNOME Files (formerly called Nautilus), which is GNOME's default file manager. If you were running GNOME Shell on Fedora, the GNOME Files (sometimes just called *Files*) icon resembles a filing cabinet in the Favorites panel, as shown earlier in Figure 4.3. Your desktop environment may also launch a file manager when you insert a removable disk, such as a USB flash drive or DVD disc. Figure 4.5 shows GNOME Files running on a fresh installation.

FIGURE 4.5   GNOME Files provides a view of your files similar to that in other OSs' file managers.

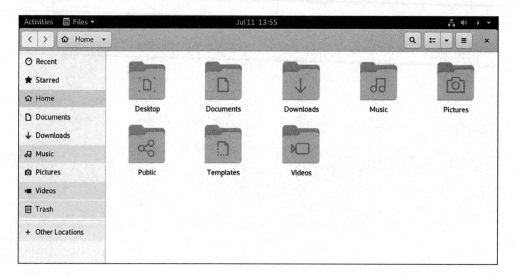

 Besides GNOME's Files, other file managers include Nemo (Cinnamon's file manager), Thunar (Xfce's file manager), and Dolphin (KDE Plasma's file manager).

Because GNOME Files is similar to the file managers in other OSs, chances are that you'll be able to use its main features quite easily. A few items do deserve mention:

Home   The Home location refers to your *home directory*—that is, the directory where you store your own user files. Ordinarily, you'll create all of your personal files in your home directory. The default view of GNOME Files, when you launch it manually, is of your home directory, as shown in Figure 4.5. The right pane shows the Home directory's files and subdirectories.

Starred   You can add bookmarks (called *Starred* in GNOME Files) for locations not shown in the main panel. Navigate to the folder above the desired location, and right-click on the folder icon to open a drop-down menu (shown in Figure 4.6). Click the Star option on the menu list. Newly added bookmarks appear in the GNOME Files' Starred panel location. You can star files as well.

FIGURE 4.6   You can star folders to enable quick access to directories that interest you.

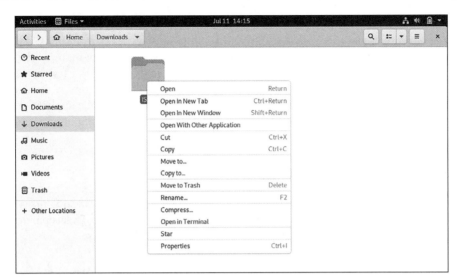

 If you double-click a location, GNOME Files will attempt to access it.

Document Properties   You can right-click a file and select Properties from the resulting drop-down menu. This produces a Properties dialog box, as shown in Figure 4.7. The Open With tab lets you associate a document type with an application.

FIGURE 4.7   GNOME Files lets you associate document types with applications.

Working with Productivity Software

The area of productivity software is extremely broad. Hundreds, if not thousands, of productivity applications exist, and entire books have been written about many of them. Therefore, in this chapter we give the names and brief descriptions of only a few productivity tools for common categories. The common tool categories include web browsers, email clients, office tools, multimedia applications, cloud computing, and mobile applications. Before describing these tools, it's best to review a few tips on how to find a program to perform a particular task in Linux.

Finding the Right Tool for the Job

Linux provides productivity applications in many broad categories, but if you're not already familiar with the field, you might have a hard time tracking them down. This is particularly true because application names don't always clearly identify their purpose.

A few techniques can help you to find suitable applications:

Using Desktop Menus   You can use the menus or other application display tools on your desktop environment to locate productivity applications. Such tools often categorize applications in helpful ways. For example, the KDE Kickoff Application Launcher (shown previously in Figure 4.4) breaks applications down into categories (Accessories, Graphics, Internet, and so on) and subcategories, Photography and Scanning in the Graphics category, for instance. This can help you track down an application, but only if it's already installed.

Using Search Features   You may be able to use a search feature, either in a desktop environment or in a web browser, to locate a suitable application. Typing in a critical word or phrase, such as **office** (in conjunction with **Linux** if you're doing a web search) may help you locate office applications (word processors, spreadsheets, and so on).

Using Tables of Equivalents   If you normally use a particular Windows application, you may be able to find a Linux substitute for it by consulting a table of equivalent applications, such as the one at wiki.linuxquestions.org/wiki/ Linux_software_equivalent_to_Windows_software.

Using Others' Expertise   You can ask other people—coworkers, friends, or people in online forums—for help in finding a suitable application. This technique is particularly helpful if you've performed a basic search but have found nothing that meets your specific criteria.

Some of these methods, such as using desktop menus, can find only software that's already installed. Other techniques, such as web searches, can find programs that you don't have installed. You can usually install software with the help of your distribution's packaging system.

Using a Web Browser

Linux supports a variety of web browsers, including the following:

Chrome   Google's Chrome browser (google.com/chrome) aims to be fast and easy to use. Since its introduction in 2008, it's gained rapidly in popularity. Although Chrome is technically a commercial project, it's available free of charge. An open source variant, known as Chromium, is also available.

Firefox   This program can be found at mozilla.org. It is the most popular browser for Linux, and it is also quite popular on Windows and macOS. It's a complete browser, and thus it can consume a lot of memory, so it may not be the best choice on an older or weaker computer.

Certification
Objective

Web   This program, originally called Epiphany, is found at wiki.gnome.org/Apps/Web. As the web browser for the GNOME desktop, it's designed to be simple and easy to use.

Konqueror   This KDE program serves a dual function: it's both a web browser and a file manager. Konqueror does a good job with most web pages. It's fairly lightweight, and so it is well worth trying, particularly if you use KDE Plasma. You can read more about it at kde.org/applications/internet/org.kde.konqueror.

Lynx   Most web browsers are GUI programs that display text in multiple fonts, show graphics inline, and so on. Lynx (lynx.browser.org) is unusual in that it's a text-based web browser. As such, it's a useful choice if you run Linux in text mode or if you don't want to be bothered with graphics. Lynx is also useful as a test browser when you develop your own web pages; if a page is readable in Lynx, chances are that visually impaired people who browse the web with speech synthesizers will be able to use your page.

Opera   An unusual commercial entrant in the Linux web browser sweepstakes, Opera (opera.com) claims to be unusually fast. Although Opera is commercial, you can download it at no charge.

Notably absent from this list is a Microsoft browser. Unfortunately, some websites won't work with anything but a Microsoft browser. Other sites are somewhat picky but can work with at least one Linux browser. Thus you should probably install at least two Linux web browsers.

Web browsers give users easy access to a world of information—literally! Unfortunately, the web has a dark side, too. Problems include the following:

Certification
Objective

- Websites can log user access data, which can be used in marketing or in other ways that you might not like.

- Much web-based content is dynamic, meaning that websites download small programs that your web browser runs. This content might be harmless, but it's increasingly being used to deliver malware.

- Malicious websites can trick users into giving up sensitive data, such as financial information, by pretending to be a trusted site. This technique is known as *phishing*.

- Some websites are not secure. Data transferred can be read on intervening computers. Most sites, especially Internet banking sites and online retailers, encrypt their sensitive data, but you should be cautious when sending such data.

- Because of security concerns, passwords used on most websites are subject to theft. This can pose a dilemma because it can be hard to remember all of your website passwords. Many browsers can do this for you, but that stores your passwords on your hard disk, which makes them vulnerable to theft or loss.

 Chapter 13, "Creating Users and Groups," describes how to create passwords that are both memorable and hard to guess.

Some of these problems aren't unique to the web, of course. For instance, most email transfers are insecure, so you shouldn't send sensitive data via email.

Using Email Clients

Email client programs enable you to read and write email messages. Such programs can either access a mailbox on your own computer or, using email network protocols described later, send and receive email with the help of network mail server computers. Common Linux email clients include the following:

Evolution   This program, located at wiki.gnome.org/Apps/Evolution, is a powerful GUI email client. It also includes address book and scheduling features.

KMail   The KDE project's KMail can be found at userbase.kde.org/KMail. It is well integrated into the KDE Plasma desktop environment, but you can use it in other desktop environments if you elect to do so.

Mutt   This is one of several text-based email readers. Despite its text-mode interface, Mutt is quite capable. You can read more about it at mutt.org.

 Certification Objective

Thunderbird   This application, located at thunderbird.net, is an email client that's closely associated with the Firefox web browser.

Email clients work in a similar way in any OS. Typically, you must configure them to know how to send and receive messages—whether to use the local computer's facilities or remote servers. Thereafter, you can read incoming messages and send outgoing messages.

Using Office Tools

Linux has several office packages available with some combination of word processors, spreadsheets, presentation programs, graphics programs, databases, and sometimes other programs. Examples include the following:

Calligra   This office suite was born out of a split from an earlier popular KDE office suite, called KOffice. Although KOffice is no longer maintained, Calligra (calligra.org) is thriving. Its office suite includes Words (word processor), Stage (presentation), Sheets (spreadsheet), Flow (flowcharting), and Kexi (database). Besides office applications, Calligra offers Graphics and Project Management software products.

Apache OpenOffice   This office suite, located at openoffice.org, was called *OpenOffice* *.org* until its corporate sponsor, Oracle, donated it in 2011 to the Apache group, who is actively maintaining it. The official name is currently *Apache OpenOffice*. It provides six applications: Writer (word processor), Calc (spreadsheet), Impress (presentation), Base (database), Draw (vector graphics), and Math (equation editor).

Certification
Objective

LibreOffice   This office suite was created as a fork of the older pre-Apache OpenOffice .org. It's becoming the most popular office suite in Linux. It provides six applications: Writer (word processor), Calc (spreadsheet), Impress (presentation), Base (database), Draw (vector graphics), and Math (equation editor). You may have noticed that these applications have the same names as the Apache OpenOffice applications. You can read more about it at libreoffice.org.

Certification
Objective

   The *fork* of a program results when a single project splits into two projects, typically because different groups of developers have diverging goals.

Most of these programs support the OpenDocument Format (ODF), which is an open set of file formats that's slowly making inroads as a standard for word processing, spreadsheet, and other office files. Although ODF is intended to enable easy transfer of files across applications, application-specific assumptions often hinder such transfers, especially on complex documents.

Many other programs exist in this space, although they are not part of an office suite. Some are unusual. For instance, LyX (lyx.org) can take the place of a word processor, but it's built in a unique way to create and edit LaTeX documents. LaTeX is a document format that's popular in computer science, mathematics, and other technical fields.

Using Multimedia Applications

Linux has an excellent reputation as a workhorse server platform, but its capacity as a multimedia OS was lacking. This was largely due to the absence of multimedia applications. In the last few decades, however, the list of multimedia applications has grown considerably. Current offerings include the following:

Audacity   This audio editor, found at sourceforge.net/projects/audacity, is similar to commercial products like Sound Forge for other platforms. You can use it to cut sections from an audio file, equalize volume, remove undesired noises, apply artificial audio effects, and more.

Blender   You can use this 3D creation suite to create complex 3D images, including both stills and animations. You can learn more about Blender at blender.org.

Castero   This text-based podcast client allows you to subscribe to your favorite podcasts (and lots of them), easily search for new podcasts, view playlists, and more. You can explore information about this program at github.com/xgi/castero.

GIMP   The GNU Image Manipulation Program (GIMP) (gimp.org) is a still-image manipulation program similar in broad strokes to Adobe Photoshop. (The GTK+ toolkit, which is the basis of GNOME and many other programs, was originally created for the GIMP.)

ImageMagick   This is a suite of graphics programs with a twist: you typically use the ImageMagick programs from the command line. You can use it to convert file formats, add frames to images, resize images, and so on. You can learn more at imagemagick.org.

Open Broadcaster Software (OBS) Studio   Live video streaming is possible with OBS Studio. In addition, this application allows you to record video and capture audio on your Linux desktop. It is a powerful program that offers lots of configurable features, so it takes some time to learn, and works best with a multiscreen setup. You obtain it from obsproject.com.

> A few motion pictures that used effects rendered via Linux include *Titanic*, the *Shrek* series, and *Avatar*. Many animated motion pictures were completely rendered using Linux, including Netflix's *Next Gen*, which was created entirely using Blender.

Kdenlive   If you need to edit the videos you are producing with OBS, Kdenlive (kdenlive .org) is the solution. It allows you to perform basic video editing all the way to professional adaptations. And almost any recorded audio or video formats can be used with Kdenlive—no need for conversion or recoding.

Given this range of multimedia applications, you can use Linux for everything from cropping photos of your two-year-old's birthday party to rendering the effects for major motion pictures. If you have very special needs, digging a bit may turn up something else—this list is just the start!

Using Linux for Cloud Computing

Public cloud computing is the storage of computer software and/or data over the Internet, rather than storing it locally on your computer. In this term, *cloud* represents the Internet and *computing* represents what you are doing over the Internet. In some cases, users access cloud-computing resources via a web browser. Thus, in theory, Linux can function as a cloud-computing client platform—just launch a web browser to access the cloud-computing provider and away you go.

In practice, complications can arise when you access public cloud-computing services. For instance, a cloud-computing provider might require that you use a particular web browser or have a specific browser plug-in installed. In some cases, it might be impossible to meet these requirements in Linux; however, if the provider supports a wide range of browsers as clients, you shouldn't have problems using cloud-computing resources.

A few notable public cloud-computing resources include the following:

- On-demand streaming media, such as Netflix (`netflix.com`)
- File storage services, such as Dropbox (`dropbox.com`)
- Office productivity suites, such as Zoho Office (`zoho.com`)
- Web-based email, such as Gmail (`mail.google.com/`)

Private cloud computing is a slightly different technology in that the *cloud* is your company's (or home's) network and its local resources, instead of the Internet. Thus, a private cloud is sometimes called an *enterprise* or *internal cloud*. Using this type of cloud provides higher security but requires more local management and resources.

Using Linux as the server, you can set up a private cloud for file hosting via one of the following software suite resources:

Certification
Objective

- ownCloud (`owncloud.org`)
- Nextcloud (`nextcloud.com`)
- FileCloud (`getfilecloud.com`)

These software suites provide services similar to Dropbox, but instead of being stored remotely in a public cloud environment, the files are typically stored locally (called *self-hosting*). However, you can get fancy with these private-cloud software suites by allowing integration of file hosting on operating systems that you install on other cloud providers, such as Amazon Web Services (AWS), Google Cloud, and Microsoft Azure. Operating systems that you install on a cloud provider are often referred to as infrastructure as a service (IAAS).

> Cloud-computing resources are often hosted on servers owned by companies called *cloud providers*. One example is the popular social media app, Twitter, which runs on Google Cloud. Cloud providers utilize powerful hardware servers to offer individual virtualized machines (simulated computer systems that appear and act as physical machines) to their clients. Typically, they use Linux as the operating system for the hardware server. But what's really interesting is that Linux is often the operating system occupying the client's virtualized computer as well.

Using Mobile Applications

Although Android is a Linux-based OS, for the most part it runs entirely different applications than do desktop or server implementations of Linux. This is understandable—chances are that you wouldn't want to try to write a long document, such as a book, with a cell phone. Many of the features in a big office program, such as LibreOffice's Write, would go to waste on a mobile computing device.

Certification
Objective

Instead, mobile computing typically focuses on small programs known as *apps*. In the case of Android, you can download apps by using an app called Google Play. (A web-based version is available at play.google.com/store.) Apps typically provide quick and specialized computation, often employing features of the phone. For instance, an app can calculate the calories that you've burned while riding a bicycle or retrieve a weather forecast for your area. Both of these examples use your phone's GPS features to identify the phone's (and your) position.

Although most Linux applications for desktop and server computers are open source and available free of charge, some Android apps are not free. Be sure to check the cost before you download an app.

Android apps are increasingly a source of malware. You can minimize your risk by downloading apps only from Google Play or other trustworthy app stores.

Using Server Programs

Linux is a powerful OS for running server programs, so it should come as no surprise that you can find a wide variety of server programs for Linux. In this section, some common server protocols and the programs that use them are described. In addition, the process of installing and launching servers is covered as well as basic information on server security issues.

Identifying Common Server Protocols and Programs

Networks, including the Internet, function by means of network *protocols*. Network protocols are clearly defined descriptions of how two computers should exchange data to achieve a particular end, such as transferring email or delivering a file to be printed. Most protocols are described in one or more standards documents, known as *request for comments (RFC)* documents, each of which has a number. Typically, one RFC document defines the protocol, and over time additional RFC documents define extensions or protocol modifications as they become necessary.

Most network protocols involve transferring data over one or more *ports*, which are numbered resources on a computer. You can think of a port as being something like a room number in a building on a college campus—the main number (an Internet Protocol, or IP, address) identifies the computer as a whole, and the port number identifies the protocol being used. A server program attaches itself to a port number and receives all incoming requests on that port.

Table 4.1 summarizes some common port numbers, the protocols with which they're associated, and the Linux programs that are often used in conjunction with these protocols. Many ports and protocols are associated with more than one program. This is because

Linux provides choices for many protocols; you can choose which of several server programs to use for a given protocol, just as you can choose which of several word processors or web browsers to use.

> The /etc/services file links common port numbers to short names that are often used in other configuration files.

TABLE 4.1   Common port numbers and their purposes

Certification
Objective

Port number	Protocol	Common server program(s)	Explanation
20–21	FTP	oftpd, ProFTPD, Pure-FTPd, vsftpd	The File Transfer Protocol (FTP) is an old protocol for transferring files over a network. It supports both anonymous and password-mediated access. FTP is unusual in that it uses two ports.
22	SSH	OpenSSH	The Secure Shell (SSH) is an encrypted remote access tool. It also supports file transfers and encrypting other protocols.
23	Telnet	telnetd	Telnet is an old unencrypted remote login protocol. It's seldom used today, although its client program, Telnet, can be a useful network diagnostic tool.
25	SMTP	Postfix, qmail, sendmail	The Simple Mail Transfer Protocol (SMTP) is the main protocol for moving email on the Internet. The sender initiates SMTP transfers.
53	DNS	dnsmasq, named	The Domain Name System (DNS) enables computers to look up an IP address by providing a hostname, or vice versa. Without it, you'd need to refer to all computers by IP address rather than by name.
67	BOOTP, DHCP	dnsmasq, dhcpd	The Bootstrap Protocol (BOOTP) and its younger cousin, the Dynamic Host Configuration Protocol (DHCP), both enable a computer on a local network to help automatically configure other computers to use a network.

TABLE 4.1   Common port numbers and their purposes *(continued)*

Port number	Protocol	Common server program(s)	Explanation
80	HTTP	Apache HTTPD, NGINX	The Hypertext Transfer Protocol (HTTP) is the basis of the World Wide Web (WWW, or simply the web).
109–110	POP2 and POP3	Courier, Cyrus IMAP, Dovecot, UW IMAP	The Post Office Protocol (POP) has gone through several revisions, each with its own port. This protocol enables a recipient to initiate an email transfer, so it's often used as the last leg in email delivery, from a server to the recipient.
118	SQL	MySQL, PostgreSQL, MariaDB	The Structured Query Language (SQL) is a network-enabled database interface language. If you run a SQL server on your network, client computers can access and modify that database.
137–139	SMB/CIFS	Samba	Microsoft uses the Server Message Block (SMB)/Common Internet File System (CIFS) protocols for file and printer sharing, and Samba implements these protocols in Linux.
143, 200	IMAP	Courier, Cyrus IMAP, Dovecot, UW IMAP	The Internet Message Access Protocol (IMAP) is another recipient-initiated email transfer protocol, similar to POP. IMAP makes it easier for recipients to store and manage email on the server computer permanently, though.
389	LDAP	OpenLDAP	The Lightweight Directory Access Protocol (LDAP) is a network protocol for accessing directories, which in this context are a type of database. LDAP is often used to store network login information, among other things.
443	HTTPS	Apache HTTPD, NGINX	This protocol is a secure (encrypted) variant of HTTP.
2049	NFS	NFS	The Network File System (NFS) is a protocol, and a server of the same name, for file sharing between Unix and Unix-like OSs.

Table 4.1 is incomplete; it summarizes only some of the more important protocols and the servers that deliver them. Numerous other protocols and servers exist, many of them for very specialized tasks.

Chapter 15, "Managing Network Connections," describes network configuration in greater detail.

Some protocols are most often used on local networks. For instance, DHCP by its nature is intended to help you manage your own local network by making it easier to configure client computers—just tell the computers to use DHCP, and that's it. SMB/CIFS is also usually employed only locally in order to enable users to access one another's files and printers more easily. Protocols like HTTPS, on the other hand, are generally used on the Internet as a whole, although they can also be used on local networks.

Real World Scenario

Server Programs and Server Computers

The term *server* can apply to an entire computer or to a single program running on that computer. When applied to a computer as a whole, the term identifies the purpose of the computer and the fact that it runs one or more server programs. Server computers typically provide services that are used by anywhere from a handful to millions of client computers—that is, the computers that use a server's services.

In the networking world, a server (computer or program) listens for a connection from a client (computer or program) and responds to data transfer requests. Server computers are often—but not always—more powerful than their clients.

When you read the word *server* (or *client*, for that matter), it may refer either to a computer or to a program. The context usually makes it clear which meaning is intended, although sometimes this isn't the case—in fact, sometimes the speaker or writer may not know! For instance, somebody might report "The Samba server isn't working." In such a case, you need to figure out whether it's the Samba server program or something else on the server computer that's causing problems.

Sometimes, the client-server lines can get blurred. For instance, in office settings, it's common for many computers to function as *file servers* by running file server software such as Samba or NFS. Such a configuration enables Sam to make her files available to Cameron and for Cameron to make his files available to Sam. In this situation, both computers function as both client and server and run both types of software. In any given exchange, though, only one is the client and one is the server.

Focusing on Web Servers

A *web server* delivers web pages to internal and/or external network users. If you have ever used the World Wide Web, you have most likely used two popular web servers that are offered on Linux:

Apache HTTPD   The Apache HTTPD server is part of the prevalent Linux, Apache, MySQL, PHP (LAMP) stack for web applications. The original web server software package was released in 1995. Within less than a year, Apache became the most popular web server on the Internet. It has continued to maintain this level of popularity due to its stability and dependability. The Apache HTTPD server is available not only for Linux, but also for Unix, BSD, Windows, and even macOS. You can learn more at httpd.apache.org.

NGINX   Released in 2002, the NGINX (pronounced *Engine X*) web server is a relative newcomer to the market. NGINX can retrieve resources on behalf of a client from one or more servers, as well as operate as a mail server. Because of these features, and the fact that it is fast and lightweight, NGINX has won over some major websites, such as Netflix. You can learn more at nginx.org.

The best feature of these two web servers is that you don't have to choose one or the other. Many server administrators choose a dual setup, using both Apache HTTPD and NGINX. Sometimes a side-by-side architecture is deployed, with each server handling what it does best—Apache managing dynamic content and NGINX managing static content (the same display for every user). Others deploy an Apache-in-Back (or NGINX-in-Front) architecture, allowing NGINX to shine with its resource-retrieval services, and the stable Apache still providing dynamic content as needed.

Installing and Launching Servers

The topic of maintaining server programs is beyond the scope of this book, but you should be aware of the basics of this task. You can install servers in the same way that you install other software, as described later in this chapter and in more detail in Chapter 9.

After the software is installed, you must launch a server. You do this differently than the way you launch a desktop application. Instead of clicking an icon or menu entry in a GUI, you typically launch a server by configuring the computer to run it automatically whenever it boots. Thereafter, the server program runs in the background, as a *daemon*—that is, as a process that runs unattended.

The word *daemon* derives from Greek mythology; daemons were helpful supernatural beings, just as Unix and Linux daemons are helpful programs.

Most servers are started automatically when Linux boots. You can also open a terminal program and type a text-mode command along with a keyword such as start or stop to start or stop the server manually. The nature of server program startup has been changing with recent distributions, and the topic is beyond the scope of this book. However, it is helpful to know that various distributions use a particular initialization daemon both to start and to manage the various server daemons. Be sure to consult your distribution's documentation to determine which initialization daemon it uses from the following list:

- System V init (SysV init)
- systemd
- Upstart

Some servers run via a *super server*, such as xinetd. These server programs run constantly, keeping the servers they manage unloaded except when they're needed. This configuration can minimize the memory impact of running many seldom-used servers. The super server can also function as a security feature, like a bouncer, and keep out the troublemakers.

Securing Servers

Whenever you run a server, you also run the risk of its being compromised and abused. Risks fall into several categories:

- Servers can contain bugs that enable outsiders to abuse the software to run programs locally.
- You can misconfigure a server, granting an outsider greater access to your system than you had intended.
- Users with accounts and remote access via a server can abuse this trust. This risk is particularly great if combined with a server bug or misconfiguration.
- A server can be used as a stepping-stone to attack others, making it appear as if an attack originated from your computer.
- Even without breaking into a computer, an attacker can swamp a server with bogus data, thus shutting it down. This technique is called a *denial-of-service (DoS) attack*.

Server security is an extremely complex topic, and details vary from one server to another. For instance, if you run a server such as a remote login server, Samba, or a POP or IMAP email server, you probably want to pay careful attention to password security, since all of these servers rely on passwords. Passwords are unimportant to a DHCP or DNS server, though. Of course, even if a DHCP or DNS server program doesn't use passwords, other server programs running on the same computer might.

Broadly speaking, securing a server requires paying attention to each of the risk factors just outlined. Specific steps that you can take to secure your servers include the following:

- You should keep your server programs up-to-date by using your package management tools to upgrade servers whenever upgrades become available. You can also research specific servers to pick ones that have good security reputations.
- You should learn enough about server configuration to be sure that you can configure your servers properly.

- You should remove unused accounts and audit necessary accounts to be sure that they use strong passwords.

- You can use firewall configurations to restrict outsiders' access to server computers that are intended for internal use only. You can also use firewalls to minimize the risk of one of your computers being used to attack others.

Managing Programming Languages

Many users never need to deal with programming languages; however, basic knowledge of what they are and how they differ from one another is important for Linux users for a variety of reasons. You might need to install languages for users on systems that you manage or for yourself to compile software from source code. You might also want to learn about programming, particularly if you want to automate computer management tasks using shell scripts.

This section presents basic information on programming languages. It begins by describing the differences between compiled and interpreted languages, which are important to understand so that you can properly handle program files or choose which you want to use. Brief descriptions of some common programming languages are also provided so that you can identify and use their source code files or choose which language you want to learn to use.

Choosing a Compiled vs. an Interpreted Language

At their core, computers understand binary codes—numbers that represent operations, such as adding two numbers or choosing which of two actions to take. People, however, are much better at handling words and symbols, such as + or if. Thus most programming involves writing a program in a symbolic programming language and then translating that symbolic code into the numeric form that computers understand. Dozens, if not hundreds, of such *programming languages* exist, each with its own unique features.

Among high-level languages, two broad categories exist:

Compiled Languages Programmers convert (or *compile*) a program written in a high-level language from its original source code form into the machine code form. The compilation process can take some time—typically a few seconds to several hours, depending on the size of the program and the speed of the computer. Compilation can also fail because of errors in the program. When the compilation succeeds, the resulting machine code executes quickly.

Interpreted Languages Programs written in interpreted languages are converted to machine code at the time they're run by a program known as an *interpreter*. The conversion happens on a line-by-line basis. That is, the program is never completely converted to machine code; the interpreter figures out what each line does and then does that one thing. This means that interpreted programs run much more slowly than compiled programs. The advantage is that interpreted programs are easier to develop, since you don't need to deal with the compilation process. Interpreted programs are also easy to modify; just open the program file in a text editor and save it back. This feature makes interpreted languages useful for helping with system startup tasks that system administrators might want to change—administrators can make and test changes quickly.

Programming in Assembly Language

In addition to compiled and interpreted languages, another option is assembly language. This is a language with a simple one-to-one correspondence between machine code numbers and the symbols that the programmer uses. Assembly language is very low-level, which means that a skilled assembly language programmer can produce compact and efficient programs. Assembly language is not very portable, though; it takes a lot of effort to convert a program written for, say, the *x*86-64 CPU to run on an ARM processor. Writing assembly language programs is also harder than writing programs in most high-level languages. For these reasons, assembly language programs have become rarer as computers have become more powerful; the speed and size advantages of assembly language just aren't very compelling for most purposes in the early 21st century.

In theory, most languages can be implemented either in compiled or interpreted form. In practice, though, most languages are most commonly used in just one form or the other.

Some languages don't fit neatly into either category. See the "Programming in Assembly Language" sidebar for one important exception. Some others fall into an in-between category, such as Java, which is compiled from source code into a platform-independent form that must be interpreted.

Identifying Common Programming Languages

Linux supports a wide range of programming languages, including the following:

Assembly   As noted earlier, this low-level language can produce efficient programs, but it is difficult to write and is not portable. In fact, referring to *assembly* as if it were one language is a bit misleading, since each CPU architecture has its own assembly language.

C   C is arguably the most important compiled language for Linux, since most of the Linux kernel, as well as a huge number of Linux applications, are written in C. C can produce fairly efficient code, but it's also easy to write buggy programs in C because it lacks some error-checking features that are common in many other languages. C source code files typically have filenames that end in .c or .h—the .c files are the main source code files, whereas the .h files are *header files*, which contain short definitions of the functions in the .c files, for reference by other files in a program. A large program can consist of dozens, if not hundreds or thousands, of individual source code files. In Linux, C programs are generally compiled with the gcc program, which is part of the GNU Compiler Collection (GCC) package.

Certification
Objective

> Although the Linux kernel is mostly written in C, parts of it are written in assembly language.

C++ C++ is an extension to C that adds *object-oriented* features, meaning that greater emphasis is given to data structures and their interactions than to the procedures used to control the flow of the program. Many complex Linux programs, such as KDE and Apache OpenOffice/LibreOffice, are written largely in C++. C++ source code files can have filenames that end in .cc, .cpp, .cxx, or .c++, with header files ending in .h, .hh, .hpp, .hxx, or .h++. In Linux, C++ is generally compiled with the g++ program, which is part of GCC.

Certification
Objective

Java Java was created by Sun Microsystems (now owned by Oracle) as a cross-platform language that's somewhere between being compiled and interpreted. It's become popular as a language for small applications delivered via websites, although some other programs are Java-based as well. Java source code usually has a name that ends in .java.

Certification
Objective

JavaScript Java and JavaScript are often confused with each other, but they are different in many ways. One difference is that JavaScript is an interpreted scripting language. Also, it is one of the most popular website programming languages—far more common than Java. It works alongside Hypertext Markup Language (HTML) and Cascading Style Sheets (CSS) to provide a majority of the Internet's web pages. Typically dynamic page information, such as animated graphics, scrolling jukeboxes, or interactive maps, is driven by JavaScript programs. Nearly all modern web browsers support JavaScript programs through built-in interpreters. A JavaScript source code file has a .js file extension.

Certification
Objective

Perl An interpreted language, Perl is designed for easy manipulation of text, but it's a general-purpose language that can be used for many other tasks as well. Perl programs typically have filenames that end in .pl, .pm, or .t.

Certification
Objective

PHP The PHP: Hypertext Preprocessor, or PHP (a recursive acronym), language was created for use on web servers in order to generate dynamic content—that is, content that varies depending on the user, the time of day, or some other criterion. PHP is an interpreted language, and it requires a PHP-aware web server, such as Apache. Given such a server and appropriate configuration, a website can support user logins, shopping carts, different content based on users' locations, and so on. PHP files most often have names that end in .php, although several variants are common.

Certification
Objective

Python The Python interpreted language makes code readability a major goal. It supports (but does not require) object orientation. It's often used for scripting purposes, but it can be used to write more complex programs, too. Python programs often use .py filename extensions, although several variants of this are common too.

> The Python programming language's name is a reference to the cult British TV show *Monty Python's Flying Circus*.

Shell Scripting   Most Linux text-mode shells—the programs that enable entirely keyboard-based use of the computer—provide their own interpreted languages. Of these, the Bourne Again Shell (Bash) is the most common, so Bash scripting is quite common. Many of the files that control the Linux startup process are in fact Bash scripts. Such scripts frequently have no unique filename extension, although some use a .sh extension.

Chapter 11, "Creating Scripts," covers the basics of creating or modifying Bash scripts.

Handling Software Packages

Installing programs on a Linux distribution has become easier through the years. However, how software is packaged, installed, and managed can vary greatly from distribution to distribution. It is important to understand these differences in order to take full advantage of the Linux programs discussed in this chapter. This section merely provides brief descriptions. More details on installing and managing software packages are provided in Chapter 9.

Understanding Software Packages

On Linux, software programs are bundled into a prebuilt package that has simplified their installation and management. Packages are managed on Linux using a package management system (PMS), which is discussed in detail in Chapter 9.

These packages are stored on *repositories*, which are official software storage servers on the Internet. The repositories can be accessed over the Internet via your Linux system's local PMS utilities. The repositories have lots of software packages stored on them, ready to be explored or installed. Each Linux distribution's developers work hard to maintain and protect their official repositories' software packages. Thus, in most cases, it's best to obtain programs from the default distribution repositories. Fortunately, your distribution's PMS typically does this by default.

Identifying Common Package Tools

Each distribution uses its own PMS and package tools, which are discussed in more detail in Chapter 9. The following are a few of the primary tools used by the major PMSs:

dpkg   A low-level package tool used as the foundation of the Debian-based family of PMS tools. It can be used directly to install, manage, and remove software packages. However, it is limited in function. For example, the dpkg tool cannot download software packages from the repositories.

rpm   The rpm tool is also a low-level package tool similar in function to the dpkg util-ity. However, it is used as the foundation of the Red Hat Linux package management system. Though you can use rpm to manage packages, it's best to use a higher-level PMS utility.

apt-get   This is a text-mode tool for the Debian PMS. With apt-get, you can install from repositories and remove software packages from your local Linux system. In addi-tion, you can perform package upgrades for individual packages, all of the packages on your system, or your entire distribution. However, you will need to use the apt-cache text-mode tool for determining various pieces of information concerning software packages.

yum   This is a text-mode tool for the Red Hat PMS. It is used on distributions, such as Red Hat Enterprise Linux (RHEL), Fedora, and CentOS. With yum, you can install from repositories, remove software packages from your local Linux system, upgrade packages, and so on. In addition, you can use yum for determining various pieces of information con-cerning packages and their management, such as displaying a list of the PMS's configured repositories.

EXERCISE 4.1

- Try at least two Linux desktop environments. Use each desktop environment for your normal computing tasks for a day or two so that you can decide which you prefer.

- Try at least two Linux web browsers. Use each to visit your favorite websites. Do you notice differences in speed or how the elements on the page are laid out? Which do you prefer?

Summary

When you're just starting out with Linux, chances are that you'll begin by using a desk-top environment—the first set of programs that you see when you log in. A desktop environment enables you to run more programs, including common productivity tools such as web browsers, email clients, office utilities, and multimedia applications. If you're configuring a computer as a server, of course, you'll want to run server programs, but you'll do this by editing configuration files rather than by launching them from a desktop environment. If you need to do programming, you should be aware of some common Linux programming languages, which enable you to write everything from trivial scripts to huge servers or productivity suites. If your distribution does not come with a needed desktop productivity program or server application preinstalled, you will have to install it via a package tool.

Exam Essentials

Summarize the major features of a Linux desktop.   A Linux desktop environment is a set of programs that control the screen, and it provides access to small utility programs to perform various productivity tasks. It consists of desktop menus (called *context menus*), which are often located around one or more of the environment window's edges. Icons used to launch programs can be located in the menus or on the main desktop window. They may also be located within panels if provided by the environment. Search features are also provided either within menus or by clicking icons on the desktop. Text-mode interfaces are offered via a terminal program as well as file managers.

Explain Linux's use in cloud computing.   Linux can function as a cloud-computing client platform by accessing cloud-based software via a web browser. It can also provide a private cloud via software such as ownCloud and Nextcloud. Due to its strong server software platform, Linux is often the hardware server operating system at cloud-computing provider companies. And it is often the OS used by the client virtual machine as well.

Specify different productivity software products.   On Linux, there are web browsers, such as Firefox, Chrome, Web, Konqueror, and Opera, available in the GUI. There's even a text-based browser, Lynx, if you need one. For reading and sending email, you have a choice of Thunderbird, Evolution, Kmail, and Mutt (which is a text-based email client). If you need to create a presentation, write a document, or maintain a spreadsheet, on Linux you can use an application from an office suite, such as Calligra, Apache OpenOffice (previously called OpenOffice.org), and LibreOffice. For creating graphics, the choices include GIMP or Blender, and there is a suite of programs that work at the command line, ImageMagik.

Describe Linux programming languages.   Because Linux is a wonderful development platform, it supports several programming languages. Assembly is a low-level language, and its name actually refers to multiple languages, because each CPU's architecture has its own version of it. Languages that require a program compiler on Linux include C and C++. JavaScript, Perl, PHP, Python, and the Bash shell are interpreted programming languages available for development on Linux. Java is also available, but it is both compiled and interpreted.

Provide an overview of the Linux PMS tools.   The tools for package management systems used on Debian-based systems include dpkg, apt-get, and apt-cache. Limited in function, the dpkg utility is used to install, manage, remove, and check the status of locally available packages. The apt-get and apt-cache tools provide the same features but can download and check on software packages residing on repositories.

Red Hat–based Linux systems use the rpm and yum PMS tools. The rpm utility provides functionality similar to dpkg, whereas yum offers services similar to a combination of what the apt-get and apt-cache tools furnish.

Review Questions

You can find the answers in the Appendix A.

1. Which of the following are Linux desktop environments? (Choose all that apply.)

    A. GTK+

    B. GNOME

    C. KDE Plasma

    D. Evolution

    E. Xfce

2. If you want to enable one Linux computer to access files stored on another Linux computer's hard disk, which of the following network protocols is the *best* choice?

    A. SMTP

    B. NFS

    C. PHP

    D. DNS

    E. DHCP

3. In which of the following languages was most of the Linux kernel written?

    A. Bash shell script

    B. Java

    C. C

    D. C++

    E. Perl

4. True or false: OpenOffice.org forked from Calligra.

5. True or false: Malicious outsiders can disrupt servers even if the computer that runs them is never broken into.

6. True or false: Python is generally implemented as an interpreted language.

7. Thunderbird is a(n) _____ program. (Specify the general category of the software.)

    A. web browser

    B. file manager

    C. email client

    D. office tool

    E. multimedia application

8. A Linux server that handles the SMB/CIFS protocol normally runs the _____ software.

    A. ProFTPD

    B. telnetd

    C. named

    D. Dovecot

    E. Samba

9. A program written in a(n)/the _____ programming language is completely converted to binary form before being run.

    A. Python

    B. compiled

    C. Javascript

    D. interpreted

    E. Perl

10. You can install and manage various Linux software applications via a(n) _____ management system.

    A. office

    B. file

    C. email

    D. package

    E. program

Chapter
5

Getting to Know the Command Line

OBJECTIVES:

✓ 1.4   ICT Skills and Working in Linux

✓ 2.1   Command Line Basics

✓ 2.2   Using the Command Line to Get Help

✓ 3.2   Searching and Extracting Data from Files

You may think of the command line as a relic from the 1970s, with not much relevance to computing today. Not so! Although Linux has numerous GUI programs, they're mostly just flashy front ends to underlying text-mode tools. By learning those command-line tools, you can unlock Linux's true power, enabling you to get your work done more quickly. You'll also be able to manage should the Linux GUI system fail entirely, or should you need to log in and administer the system remotely. Command-line tools can also be scripted, meaning that you can write a simple program that performs a task more quickly or more easily than could be achieved using the standard programs alone. For these reasons, most chapters in this book describe both the GUI and command-line methods of getting things done.

To begin command-line operations, you must know how to start one. With that task in hand, you must know how to run programs and how to get help. You should also be familiar with several labor-saving features of Linux command lines.

Starting a Command Line

A Linux command line, or *shell* as it's more properly called, is a program. Just like any other program, the shell must be launched. You can start a shell in a GUI window called a *terminal program*, or you can log into the computer locally via a text-mode console. In addition, a shell is started when you log into the computer remotely using a text-mode login protocol. However, that particular method goes beyond the scope of this book.

Certification
Objective

The default shell in most Linux distributions is the Bourne Again Shell (Bash), which is based on an older shell called the Bourne Shell. Other shells are available. Most of these are similar to Bash in broad strokes, although some details differ. Each account specifies its own default shell, so individual users can change their shells if they like. (This is done with account management tools, such as usermod, which is described in Chapter 13, "Creating Users and Groups.")

Other shells include tcsh, ksh, and zsh. Shell choice is a matter of personal preference. If you're just starting out, it's best to stick with Bash simply because it's popular.

Launching a Terminal

Most Linux distributions allow you to install various GUI terminal programs. Typically, a desktop environment comes with its own terminal, so your terminal program choices also depend on the desktop environments that you install. Many terminal programs include the word *terminal* in their names, although some don't, such as the KDE Plasma's Konsole and generic XTerm.

The details of how to launch a terminal program differ from one desktop environment to another. You can normally find an entry in your desktop environment's menus, as outlined in Chapter 4, "Using Common Linux Programs." For example, if you're using Linux Mint's Cinnamon desktop environment, you can find the available terminals on the lower panel or the menu Favorites panel, or by following this menu-driven procedure:

1. Click the Menu button, typically located at the lower-left corner of the screen.

2. Click Administration and use the scroll bar to view the various menu choices. You should see at least one terminal program in a display similar to Figure 5.1.

FIGURE 5.1   Reaching a terminal via a menu on Cinnamon

3. Click the Terminal icon, and the terminal program will launch.

Many desktop environments also provide a search method for terminal programs. For example, if you are using the GNOME desktop environment, follow this basic procedure:

1. Click Activities at the upper-left corner of the screen.

2. In the resulting search box, type **term**, as shown in Figure 5.2.

FIGURE 5.2 Reaching a terminal via a search on GNOME

3. Click the Terminal icon whose program you want to use from the resulting list, and it will launch.

The procedure to search for terminal programs can vary greatly among desktops.

 Some distributions allow you to open a terminal application quickly by pressing Ctrl+Alt+T.

When launched, the GNOME Terminal program shows a prompt; in Figure 5.3, it is [christine@localhost ~]$. This example shows the default Fedora prompt, which includes your username, your computer's hostname, your current directory (a tilde, ~, refers to your home directory), and a dollar sign ($). Some of these features are likely to change as you use the shell, as described in Chapter 7, "Managing Files." If you're using another distribution, the prompt is likely to differ in details, although most default prompts end in a dollar sign ($) or a greater-than symbol (>) for ordinary user shells.

FIGURE 5.3 GNOME's Terminal program is typical and is dominated by a textual display area.

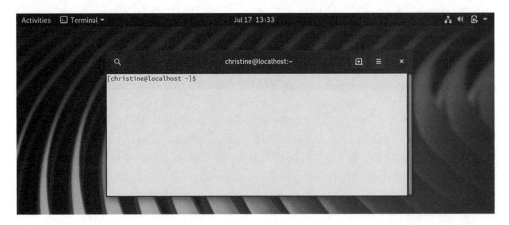

When you use the administrative account, root, the prompt normally ends in a hash mark (#). Chapter 12, "Understanding Basic Security," describes the root account in more detail.

Most terminal programs provide common features of GUI programs—you can resize them, close them, select options from menus, and so on. Details depend on the program that you're using, though. You may want to peruse the options available on your terminal program's menus so that you can set the font to one you like, change the color scheme, and so on.

Most terminal programs support *tabs*, which are similar to the tabs in a web browser. In most cases, such as in a GNOME terminal, you can open a tab by clicking on the + box at the terminal's upper right. Having multiple tabs open is handy because you can run multiple programs simultaneously, work easily in multiple directories, or run programs both as yourself and as root. Alternatively, you can run multiple terminal programs to achieve the same results.

When you're done with a terminal, you can close it like other programs by clicking on the X in the upper-right corner. Alternatively, you can type **exit** and press Enter at its shell prompt.

Logging into a Text-Mode Console

At first glance, Linux looks like Windows or macOS in that it's a GUI operating system. Scratch the surface, though, and you'll find a purely text-mode interface waiting. Linux supports *virtual terminals (VTs)*, which are virtual screens that can hold various types of information—textual or graphical. Most Linux distributions run with six or seven VTs. In CentOS and Red Hat, the first VT typically runs the GUI window system. Fedora Workstation provides a graphical login screen on VT 1—logging into this screen will start a GUI on VT 2. Many other distributions provide a graphical login screen on VT 1 and replace it with a GUI when the user logs in. Other distributions use VT 7 or VT 8 for their login screen and GUI, leaving VT 1 as a text-mode display.

You can switch between VTs by pressing Ctrl+Alt+F*n*, where F*n* is a function key. (When switching between text-mode VTs, Alt+F*n* is sufficient.)

The notation Ctrl+Alt+F*n* refers to pressing the Ctrl key and holding it; pressing the Alt key and holding it; and then pressing the desired function key and releasing all three keys at once. The function keys (F1 through F12) are located at the top of the keyboard. You pick the function key number that matches the terminal number you want to reach. For example, you'd use the Ctrl+Alt+F3 key combination to reach VT 3.

To reach and log into a text-mode console, follow these steps:

1. Press Ctrl+Alt+F3. You'll see a text-mode prompt that looks something like the first few lines in Figure 5.4.

FIGURE 5.4 Reaching and logging into a VT

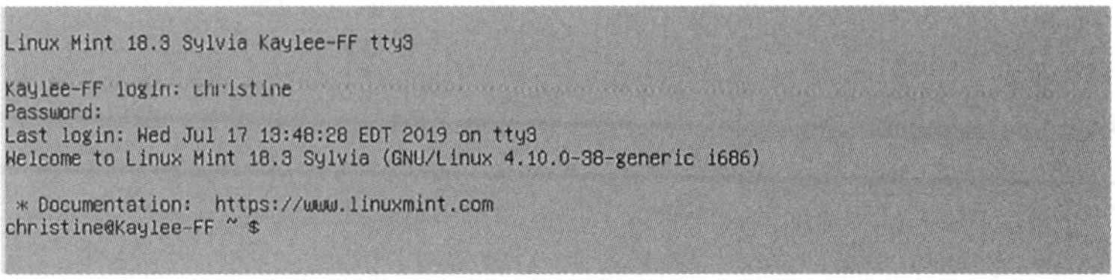

```
Linux Mint 18.3 Sylvia Kaylee-FF tty3

Kaylee-FF login: christine
Password:
Last login: Wed Jul 17 13:48:28 EDT 2019 on tty3
Welcome to Linux Mint 18.3 Sylvia (GNU/Linux 4.10.0-38-generic i686)

 * Documentation:  https://www.linuxmint.com
christine@Kaylee-FF ~ $
```

2. Type your username at this login prompt, and it will respond with a password prompt. In Figure 5.4, the username is christine.

3. At the password prompt, type in your password.

4. If your login attempt is successful, you'll see a Bash prompt like the one shown in Figure 5.4.

 When typing in your password at the password prompt for a virtual console terminal, nothing is displayed. Neither dots nor asterisks are displayed as they are when using a GUI login manager.

You can switch back and forth between your text-mode login and your GUI session by using Ctrl+Alt+F*n* keystrokes. You can also initiate multiple text-mode logins and switch between them in the same way. This feature can be handy if you're trying to debug a problem that's related to the GUI.

When you're done with your text-mode session, type **exit** to terminate it. You can also type **logout** to end your session.

Running Programs

After you've opened a terminal or logged in using a text-mode tool, you should know how to use the shell. The Bash shell includes a few built-in commands, but much of what you'll do in a shell involves running other programs. As described in the following sections, you can run text-mode and GUI programs. Sometimes you may want to run a program in the background and retain use of the shell for other purposes, which can be convenient in many situations.

Understanding Text-Mode Program Syntax

You may think that some master programmer designed and created all the various commands, but that is not true. While a few do share common programmers, many command programs were written by different individuals, so you'll find the way to use them varies as well.

Fortunately, many commands follow a basic syntax:

```
COMMAND-NAME [OPTION]... [ARGUMENT]...
```

In the command's syntax structure:

- *COMMAND-NAME* is the name of the command used to run the program.
- *[OPTION]*s are additional items added to modify the command's behavior. There are typically various *OPTION*s (also called *switches*) you can add. The brackets ([]) indicate that *OPTION*s are optional, and the three periods (...) show that you can use more than one *OPTION*.
- *[ARGUMENT]* is an item you pass to the command to let the program know you want it to operate on that item. An argument can also be a subcommand. You can see that it too is optional due to the brackets, and you can pass multiple *ARGUMENT*s to the program.

 If you want to use more than one command option, often you can squish them together. For example, to use the options -a and -b, you type **-ab**.

The who program displays which users are currently on the system:

```
$ who
rich      tty7         2020-07-16 16:40 (:0)
christine pts/1        2020-07-16 16:37 (192.168.0.102)
```

 In this book, commands you should type are in **bold monospace font**, and the program output is in standard monospace font.

However, you can modify what this command displays by adding the -b option to it. In this case, the program shows when the system was started:

```
$ who -b
         system boot  2020-07-16 16:16
```

An example of a command that accepts *arguments* is the cat command, whose name is short for *concatenate*. The cat command can quickly display a short text file on the screen. In this example, cat takes the filename MyFile.txt as an argument:

```
$ cat MyFile.txt
This is the contents of MyFile.txt.
```

Commands, arguments, and filenames are case-sensitive in the shell.

Be aware that the options (switches) are not standardized between the various programs. For example, when you use the -b switch with the cat program, it does not display information about system startup as the -b option does with the who command, but instead adds line numbers to any non-blank text file line:

```
$ cat -b MyFile.txt
     1  This is the contents of MyFile.txt.
```

You can learn about command usage details through the Linux man pages. The program to do this is called man, and you pass it the name of the command that you want to learn about as an argument, as in **man cat** to learn about the cat command.

The "Getting Help Using Man Pages" section later in this chapter describes the man page system and other documentation in more detail.

Unfortunately, several commands do not follow the basic standard command syntax. But all is not lost. The manual pages for the Linux system gives syntax structure for many programs. To find syntax structure for a particular command, view its man page and look in the Synopsis section.

The man command illustrates a feature of some text-mode programs: they can take over the entire terminal from which they're launched. In the case of man, you can scroll up or down in the documentation by using arrow keys, Page Up, Page Down, and so on. Text editors, such as vi, emacs, and nano, use similar features.

Running Text-Mode Programs

Linux stores programs in several locations, including /bin, /usr/bin, and /usr/local/bin. (Programs that are used mainly by root appear in /sbin, /usr/sbin, and /usr/local/sbin as well.) If an executable program appears in one of these directories (which make up the *path*), you can run it simply by typing its name:

```
$ free
                total      used      free    shared   buffers    cached
Mem:          3798016   3759004     39012         0     24800   1117444
-/+ buffers/cache:      2616760   1181256
Swap:         6291452         0   6291452
```

This example command displays information on the computer's use of memory. You needn't be concerned with the details of this command's output, though; just note that the free program displayed information in the same terminal in which it was launched.

Chapter 9, "Exploring Processes and Process Data," covers the free program in more detail.

You can learn what directories are included in the path—sometimes called the *defined path*—by typing the following command:

```
$ echo $PATH
```

The result will be a colon-delimited set of directory names, which the shell searches in sequence whenever you type a command that it doesn't handle directly. The *PATH* is an environment variable. Environment variables are covered in more detail in Chapter 11, "Creating Scripts."

Certification
Objective

You can run a program that is not in one of the PATH directories by typing the program's directory location along with its name, as follows:

```
$ /home/christine/myprogram
```

> **NOTE** When you run an executable program that is not located in the PATH, it is called *invoking a command outside the defined path.*

If you would like to determine how an executable program would be handled, you can use the type command as follows:

Certification
Objective

```
$ type free
free is /usr/bin/free
```

The result will show you the program's directory location (which may be a different location than what is shown in the preceding example, depending on the Linux distribution). If the PATH environment variable contains the directory location, you need to enter only the program's name to run it.

Running GUI Programs

You can run GUI programs from a terminal as well as text-based programs (however, this doesn't work if you logged in using a text-mode VT). You must know the program's filename to run it. The filename is usually related to the name you use to launch the program from a desktop's menus, but it's not always identical. For instance, the Firefox web browser's filename is firefox, so that's what you'd need to type to launch Firefox in this way.

Some GUI programs produce text-mode output that can be useful in tracking down the source of problems, so launching a program from a terminal window can be a good first step when debugging problems. You might also want to launch programs in this way because it can be quicker than tracking down programs in a desktop environment's menus, or because a program doesn't appear in the environment's menus.

Running Programs in the Background

When you launch a GUI program from a terminal window, the GUI program opens its own window or windows. The terminal window remains open but will normally become unresponsive. If you want to type more commands in this window, you can do so by selecting it and pressing Ctrl+Z. This *suspends* the running program—that is, it's sent to sleep. In its sleeping state, the GUI program won't respond to input or do any work. However, you can now use the terminal window to type in commands.

After you have suspended a program, if you want both to run the GUI program and to use the terminal from which you launched it, you can type **bg** (short for *background*) in the terminal. Both programs will now be active.

If you only want to wake the sleeping GUI program, type **fg**. This command returns the sleeping GUI program to the *foreground*, enabling it, but once again this makes your terminal unresponsive. Note that, in this context, the terms *background* and *foreground* refer to the program's relationship to the shell, not to the position of the program's windows in a "stack" of windows on the screen.

 Pressing Ctrl+Z also suspends most text-mode programs, enabling you to use the shell before returning to the program by typing **fg**.

If you know before you launch it that you want to run a program in the background, you can do so by appending an ampersand (&) to the end of the command line, as in the following:

```
$ firefox&
```

As shown in Figure 5.5, this command launches the Firefox web browser in the background, enabling you to visit web pages and to continue to use the shell.

FIGURE 5.5   Launching Firefox in the background to allow use of both the web browser and the shell

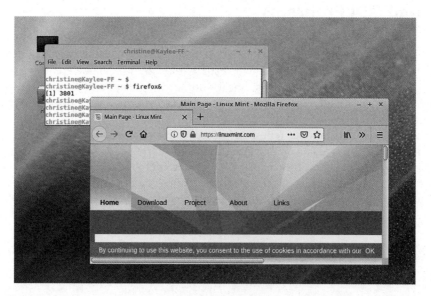

This background feature is most useful for running GUI programs, but it's sometimes used with text-mode programs too. A complex number-crunching program, for instance, might be designed to run for several minutes or hours and produce no output. You might therefore want to run it in the background and retain control of your shell. Be aware, however, that if you launch a program in the background and it produces output to the terminal, that output will continue to appear in your shell, possibly intruding on whatever else you're trying to do with the shell.

Using Shell Features

Bash includes several features that make using it much easier. Some have already been described. Many others are beyond the scope of this book. Two, however, deserve attention: command completion and command history.

Using Command Completion

Command completion is the hero of everybody who hates typing: it's a way to enter a long command or filename with a minimal number of keystrokes. To use command completion, you type part of a command or filename and then press the Tab key. If only one command on the path completes the command, Bash fills in the rest—and likewise when using command completion to refer to files.

If command completion is not working for you, the terminal program may have it configured to be turned off.

To illustrate the use of command completion, you can try it out with a few commands:

1. Launch a shell.
2. Type **wh**, then press the Tab key. The computer will probably beep or sound a tone. This indicates that your incomplete command could be completed by multiple commands, so you must type more characters. (In some configurations, the computer skips straight to the next step, as if you'd pressed Tab twice.)
3. Press the Tab key again. The shell displays a list of possible completions, such as whatis, whereis, and whoami.
4. Type **oa**, making your command so far **whoa**, and press the Tab key again. The computer will probably complete the command: **whoami**. (If it doesn't, another program that completes the command may exist on your computer, so you may need to type another character or two.)
5. Press the Enter key. The computer runs whoami, which displays the name of the account you are currently using.

Sometimes command completion can complete a command only partially. For instance, typing **gru** and then pressing Tab is likely to add a single unique character, b. However, several commands begin with grub, so you must then add more characters yourself. (These commands deal with the Grand Unified Bootloader, GRUB, which helps Linux to boot.)

Some details of how command completion works vary from one distribution to another.

Command completion also works with files. For instance, you can type **cat /etc/ser** followed by the Tab key to have Bash complete the filename, and therefore the command, as **cat /etc/services**. (This command shows you the contents of a Linux configuration file.)

Using Command History

Bash remembers the recent commands that you've typed, and you can use this fact to save yourself some effort if you need to type a command that's similar to one you've typed recently. In its most basic form, you can use the up arrow key to enter the previous command; pressing the up arrow repeatedly moves backward through earlier and earlier commands. Table 5.1 summarizes some other commonly used keystrokes that you can use in the command history—or even when editing new commands.

TABLE 5.1   Bash editing and command history features

Keystroke	Effect
Up arrow	Retrieves the previous entry from the command history
Down arrow	Retrieves an earlier entry bypassed when using the up arrow
Left arrow	Moves the cursor left one character
Right arrow	Moves the cursor right one character
Ctrl+A	Moves the cursor to the start of the line
Ctrl+E	Moves the cursor to the end of the line
Delete key	Deletes the character under the cursor
Backspace key	Deletes the character to the left of the cursor
Ctrl+T	Swaps the character under the cursor with the one to the left of the cursor
Ctrl+X and then Ctrl+E	Launches a full-fledged editor on the current command line
Ctrl+R	Searches for a command. Type a few characters, and the shell will locate the latest command to include those characters. You can search for the next-most-recent command to include those characters by pressing Ctrl+R again.

Many of the Bash command-editing features are similar to those used by the emacs text editor.

As an example of command history in use, try this:

1. Type **echo $PATH** and press the Enter key to see the directories that make up your defined path.

2. Press the up arrow key. Your echo $PATH command should reappear.

3. Press the Backspace key five times to delete $PATH.

4. Type **Hello World** to make the new command echo Hello World, and then press Enter. You should now see the words Hello World displayed on your screen.

5. Press Ctrl+R. The Bash prompt will change. It now looks like this: (reverse-i-search)`':.

6. Type **P** (without pressing Enter). Your earlier echo $PATH command will appear.

7. Press Enter. The echo $PATH command should execute again, and your Bash shell prompt should return to normal.

The Ctrl+R search feature searches on anything you enter on a command line—a command name, a filename, or other command parameters.

Certification
Objective

Another history feature is the history command. Type **history** to view all of the commands in your history, or add a number (as in **history 10**) to view the most recent specified number of commands. Along with the commands, you'll see a corresponding number. You can use this number to execute a command from your history. Just type **!**, follow it with the command number, and press Enter. The shell will display your chosen command, followed by the command's results.

You should experiment with these features. Tab completion and command history are both powerful tools that can help you avoid a great deal of repetitive typing. Command history can also be a useful memory aid. For example, if you've forgotten the exact name of a file or command that you used recently, you might be able to retrieve it by searching on part of the name that you *do* remember.

Getting Help Using Man Pages

Certification
Objective

Sometimes you need help to remember what arguments or options a command can use, or the proper syntax needed when entering a command. The *manual pages* (also called *man pages*) can help. Manual pages describe not only programs, but also configuration files and other features of a Linux installation.

Before you consult them, though, you should understand their purpose, and therefore their capabilities and limitations. With that information in mind, you can begin searching for help in the man page system, including searching for man pages by section or by searching for keywords using the whatis or apropos utility. When you're reading a man page, knowing its structure can help you quickly locate the information that you need.

Understanding the Purpose of Man Pages

Linux man pages can be an extremely helpful resource, but unlike the help systems in some OSs, Linux man pages are not supposed to be tutorial in nature. They're intended as quick references to help somebody who's already at least somewhat familiar with a command, configuration file, or other OS feature. They're most useful when you need to know the options to use with a command, the name of an option in a configuration file, or similar details. If you need to learn a new program from scratch, other documentation is often a better choice.

Manual pages also vary greatly in quality; some are very good, but others are frustratingly terse, and occasionally even inaccurate. For the most part, the programmers who wrote the program in question write them.

The upcoming section "Finding Additional Documentation" describes how to locate documentation that is more tutorial than the man pages.

In this book, many Linux commands are described in a tutorial style. However, information is often omitted on obscure options, subtle program effects, and so on. In principle, man pages should cover such finer points. This makes man pages an excellent resource for learning more about the commands described in this book, should you need to go further.

Locating Man Pages by Section Number

In the simplest case, you can read a man page by typing **man** followed by the name of a command, configuration file, system call, or other keyword. Each man page falls into one of nine categories, as summarized in Table 5.2.

TABLE 5.2   Manual sections

Section number	Description
1	Executable programs and shell commands
2	System calls provided by the kernel
3	Library calls provided by program libraries

Section number	Description
4	Device files (usually stored in /dev)
5	File formats
6	Games
7	Miscellaneous (macro packages, conventions, and so on)
8	System administration commands (programs run mostly or exclusively by root)
9	Kernel routines

If you use keywords with man, be aware that they can lead to entries in multiple sections. In such instances, the man utility returns the entry in the section based on a search order typically specified by the SECTION setting in the /etc/man_db.conf or the /etc/manpath .config configuration file (depending on your distribution).

The precise man page search order defined by SECTION varies from one distribution to another, but section 1 is usually searched first, followed by section 8 and then the others.

You can override this default search behavior by passing a section number before the keyword. For instance, typing **man passwd** returns information from manual section 1 on the passwd command, but typing **man 5 passwd** returns information from manual section 5 on the /etc/passwd file format. Some man pages have entries in sections with variant numbers that include the suffix p, as in section 1p. These refer to the Portable Operating System Interface (POSIX) standard man pages, as opposed to the Linux man pages, which are, for the most part, written by the people who wrote the open source Linux programs that the man pages describe.

If you're just starting out with Linux, chances are that you'll be most interested in section 1, executable programs and commands, which is also usually the first section in the man page search order—although section 6, games, can also be interesting if you have the time to spare! As you move on to more advanced and administrative tasks, you'll find sections 4, 5, and 8 important for device files, file formats, and programs run by root. Sections 2, 3, and 9, covering calls and kernel routines, are of most interest to programmers.

Get help on using and reading the man pages by typing **man man** at the command line.

Searching for a Man Page

One problem with man pages is that locating help on a topic can be hard unless you know the name of the command, system call, or file that you want to use. Fortunately, methods of searching the manual database exist and can help lead you to an appropriate man page:

Summary Search   The whatis command searches summary information contained in man pages for the keyword you specify. The command returns a one-line summary for every matching man page. (This summary is the Name section, described shortly, in "Reading Man Pages.") You can then use this information to locate and read the man page that you need. This command is most useful for locating all man pages on a topic. For instance, typing **whatis passwd** returns lines confirming the existence of the man page entries for passwd in various sections.

Thorough Search   The apropos command performs a more thorough search, of both the Name and Description sections of man pages. The result looks much like the results of a whatis search, except that it's likely to contain many more results. In fact, doing an apropos search on a very common keyword, such as *the*, is likely to return so many hits as to make the search useless. A search on a less common word is likely to be more useful. For instance, typing **apropos passwd** may return 16 entries on a system, including those for gpasswd, smbpasswd, and passwd—all various password utilities or tools involving password files.

The -k option to man is equivalent to apropros. Thus you can type either **apropos *keyword*** or **man -k *keyword***.

If you receive a "nothing appropriate" response from either the whatis or the apropos command, typically you need to change the keyword that you are using. However, it may indicate that the man database has not been updated. This is typically true on a fresh Linux installation or after a new program is installed. You can update the man database manually by using super user privileges and typing the command **makewhatis** (on older Linux distributions) or **mandb**. (Using super user privileges is described in Chapter 12.)

Details of what man pages are available vary from one distribution to another. This will affect the results of both whatis and apropos searches.

Reading Man Pages

The convention for man pages is a concise style that employs several sections, each of which has a particular purpose. This organization can help you locate the information that you need—you might need information that you know is in a particular section, in which case you can quickly scan down to that section. Common sections include the following:

Name   A man page begins with a statement of the command, call, or file that's described, along with a few words of explanation. For instance, the man page for man (section 1) has a Name section that reads man – an interface to the on-line reference manuals.

Synopsis   The synopsis provides a brief description of how a command is used. Optional parameters appear in square brackets, such as [-D]. An ellipsis (...) denotes an optional set of repeated elements, such as multiple filenames if a command takes one or more filenames as options. Some commands provide multiple synopsis lines, indicating that certain options are contingent on others.

Description   The description is an English-language summary of what the command, file, or other element does. The description can vary from a short summary to many pages in length.

Options   This section expands on the options outlined in the Synopsis section. Typically, each option appears in a list, with a one-paragraph explanation indented just below it.

Files   This section lists files that are associated with the man page's subject. These might be configuration files for a server or other program, related configuration files, files the page's subject modifies, and so on.

See Also   This section provides pointers to related information in the man system, typically with a section number appended. For instance, the man page for man refers to the man pages for apropos, whatis, and several other related tools.

Bugs   Many man pages provide a Bugs section in which the author describes any known bugs or limitations, or states that no known bugs exist.

History   Some man pages provide a summary of the program's history, citing project start dates and major milestones between then and the current version. This history isn't nearly as comprehensive as the changes file that comes with most programs' source code.

Author   Most man pages end with an Author section, which tells you how to contact the author of the program.

Specific manual pages may contain fewer, more, or different sections than these. For instance, the Synopsis section is typically omitted from man pages on configuration files. Manual pages with particularly verbose descriptions often split the Description section into several parts, each with its own title.

Figure 5.6 shows a typical man page in a terminal window. As you can see, section names appear in bold uppercase letters, making it easy to locate relevant sections as you page through the document.

FIGURE 5.6 The formatting of man pages helps you locate information quickly.

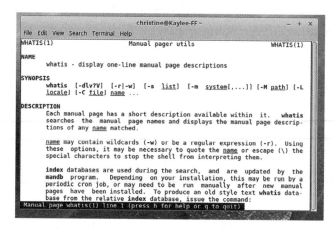

By default, man uses the less program to enable you to move back and forth in the document, and when you're done, exit the man pages. The upcoming section, "Using *less*," describes this program in detail.

Using *less*

Certification Objective

Linux's man system uses a program called less to display information. This program is a *pager*, which displays a text file one screen (that is, one page) at a time. You can move forward or backward through the file, move to a specific line, and search for information. Table 5.3 summarizes the most common ways of moving about a document using less.

An earlier pager was known as more, but less adds more features. This peculiar name is an example of geek humor.

TABLE 5.3 less file-navigation commands

Keystroke	Action
H	Displays help on using less
Page Down, spacebar, Ctrl+V, F, or Ctrl+F	Moves down one screen in the document
Page Up, Esc+V, B, or Ctrl+B	Moves up one screen in the document

Keystroke	Action
Down arrow, Enter, Ctrl+N, E, Ctrl+E, j, or Ctrl+J	Moves down one line in the document
Up arrow, Y, Ctrl+Y, Ctrl+P, K, or Ctrl+K	Moves up one line in the document
xg, x<, or x Esc+<	Goes to line x in the document—for instance, typing **100g** displays the document's 100th line. If x is omitted, the default is 1.
xG, x>, or x Esc+>	Goes to line x in the document. If x is omitted, the default is the last line of the document.
xp or x%	Goes to the point x percent through the document—for instance, typing **50p** goes to the document's halfway point
/pattern	Searches forward for *pattern* in the document, starting at the current location. For instance, typing **/BUGS** searches for the string BUGS.
?pattern	Performs a backward search, locating instances of *pattern* before the current location
N or /	Repeats the previous search
Q, :Q, or ZZ	Quits from the less pager

The notation Esc+V refers to pressing the Esc key followed by the V key.

Table 5.3 presents a small fraction of the commands available in less. To learn more about less, you can read its man page:

1. Log into the computer in text mode or open a terminal window.

2. Type **man less**. This action opens the man page for the less pager.

3. Read the first screen of text. When you finish reading the last word at the bottom of the screen, press the spacebar key. This moves the display to the next page so that you can continue reading. (You could use the PageDown key or others noted in Table 5.3 instead of the spacebar if you prefer. Similar substitutions are possible in the subsequent steps.)

4. Press the up arrow key. This moves the display up a single line, which is useful if you need to reread just a few words from the end of the last page.

5. Press the down arrow key. As you might expect, this moves the display down by one line.

6. Press the Esc key followed by the V key. This moves the display back one page.

7. Press Shift+G to move to the end of the man page.

8. Press the G key (*without* using the Shift key) to move back to the start of the man page.

9. Type **/OPTIONS** to locate the Options section. Chances are that your first hits will be to references to this section, rather than to the Options section itself.

10. Repeatedly press the N key until you find the Options section.

11. Press the Q key to quit from less, and therefore from reading the man page.

Some implementations search in a case-sensitive manner, but others are case-insensitive. In step 9, try searching on /options in lowercase) to determine which is the situation with your implementation.

Of course, when you read man pages, you aren't likely to use these exact options; you'll use whatever features you need to use to find the content that interests you. The key is to familiarize yourself with a few important features so that you can make effective use of less to read man pages and other documents.

Although less is important for reading man pages, you can also use it to read other text-mode documents, such as README files that come with many programs or other plain-text documents. To use less in this way, type its name followed by the filename of the file that you want to read, as in **less README** to read a README document. You can use all of the actions summarized in Table 5.3 (or by less's man page) on documents read in this way, just as you can on man pages.

Getting Help Using Info Pages

Certification
Objective

The man page system is typical on Unix-like OSs, including Linux, but it's also quite old and is therefore limited. A newer documentation system, known as *info pages*, is also available. The next few pages describe how info pages fill gaps in the man page system and how to use info pages.

Understanding the Purpose of Info Pages

The basic design of man pages dates back decades, so it predates some important developments in managing information. Most notably, man pages are not *hyperlinked*.

Although a See Also section is common in man pages, you can't select one of these items to read the relevant man page directly; you must quit the man system and type a new man command to read the new page. This lack of hyperlinking also makes navigating through a large man page awkward. You can use text searches to locate information that you desire, but these often find the wrong text—or if you mistype a string, your search might fail completely.

The goal of info pages is to overcome these problems by supporting hyperlinking. Each info page is known as a *node*, and the info page system as a whole is an interrelated set of nodes, similar to the World Wide Web (WWW) of the Internet. An individual program's documentation may be split up across multiple nodes, which can make each node easier to locate and search—but if you need to search for information and you're not sure in which node it resides, you may need to search multiple nodes.

Nodes are organized on *levels*, which are similar to the levels of organization in a book. This book, for instance, has chapters and two levels of headings within each chapter. Similarly, the info page for a program is likely to have one main node, similar to a chapter, along with multiple nodes at a lower level, similar to chapter headings. Some programs' info pages include further levels to help organize information.

In terms of writing style, info pages are similar to man pages—they are terse but comprehensive descriptions of their topics—intended for people who are already at least broadly familiar with the programs in question. If you're just starting out with a program, other types of documentation (described later, in "Finding Additional Documentation") may be a better choice.

The /usr/doc and /usr/share/doc directories, if available on your distribution, often contain a great deal of useful information. If you cannot find the information you are seeking in the man or info pages, look in these directories.

Broadly speaking, programs sponsored by the Free Software Foundation (FSF) use info pages in preference to man pages. Many FSF programs now ship with minimal man pages that point the user to the programs' info pages. Non-FSF programmers have been slower to embrace info pages; many such programs don't ship with info pages at all, and instead rely on traditional man pages. The info browser can read and display man pages, so using info exclusively can be an effective strategy for reading Linux's standard documentation.

Reading Info Pages

The usual tool for reading info pages is called info. To use it, you type **info** followed by the topic, as in **info info** to learn about the info system itself. When you're in the info system, you can use a number of keystrokes, summarized in Table 5.4, to move around a document.

Certification
Objective

TABLE 5.4 info file-navigation commands

Keystroke	Action
?	Displays help information
N	Moves to the next node in a linked series of nodes on a single hierarchical level. This action may be required if the author intended several nodes to be read in a particular sequence.
P	Moves back in a series of nodes on a single hierarchical level. This can be handy if you've moved forward in such a series but find that you need to review earlier material.
U	Moves up one level in the node hierarchy
Arrow keys	Moves the cursor around the screen, enabling you to select node links or scroll the screen
Page Up, Page Down	These keys scroll up and down within a single node, respectively. (The standard info browser also implements many of the more arcane commands used by less and outlined in Table 5.3.)
Enter	Moves to a new node after you've selected it. Links are indicated by asterisks (*) to the left of their names.
L	Displays the last info page that you read. This action can move you up, down, or sideways in the info tree hierarchy.
T	Displays the top page for a topic. Typically, this is the page that you used to enter the system.
Q	Exits the info page system

As an example of info pages in use, try the following:

1. Log into the computer in text mode or open a terminal window.

2. Type **info info**. You should see the top node for the info documentation appear.

3. Read the main page, using the arrow keys or the PageDown key to view the entire page.

4. Using the arrow keys, select the link to the Expert Info node near the bottom of the main page.

5. Press the Enter key to view the Expert Info node.

6. Press the U key to browse up one level—back to the main node.

7. Browse to the Advanced node.

8. Press the N key to go on to the next node on the current level, which is the Expert Info node.

9. Press the Q key to exit from the info reader.

Finding Additional Documentation

Although man pages and info pages are both useful resources, other documentation is available too, and it is sometimes preferable. Generally speaking, help on Linux can come in three forms: additional documentation on your computer, additional documentation online, and help from experts.

Documentation categories can blur together. For instance, documentation might be available online but not on your computer until you install an appropriate package.

Locating Program Documentation on Your Computer

Most Linux programs ship with their own documentation, even aside from man or info pages. In fact, some programs have so much documentation that it's installed as a separate package, typically with the word documentation or doc in the package name, such as samba-doc.

The most basic and traditional form of program documentation is a file called README, readme.txt, or something similar. Precisely what information this file contains varies greatly from one program to another. For some, the file is so terse that it's nearly useless. For others, it is extremely helpful. These files are almost always plain-text files, so you can read them with less or with your favorite text editor.

README files often contain information on building the software package that doesn't apply to program files provided with a distribution. Distribution maintainers seldom change such information in their README files, though.

If you downloaded the program as a source code file from the software package maintainer's site, the README file typically appears in the *build directory* extracted from the compressed source code file. If you installed the program from a package file, though, the README file could be in any of several locations, depending on your distribution. The most likely places are as follows:

- /usr/doc/*packagename*
- /usr/share/doc/*packagename*
- /usr/share/doc/packages/*packagename*

Certification
Objective

In the previous list, *packagename* is the software package's name. The package name sometimes includes a version number, but more often it does not.

In addition to (or instead of) the README file, many programs provide other documentation files. These may include a file that documents the history of the program in fine detail, descriptions of compilation and installation procedures, information on configuration file formats, and so on. Check the source code's build directory or the directory in which you found the README file for other files.

Some larger programs ship with extensive documentation in PostScript, Portable Document Format (PDF), Hypertext Markup Language (HTML), or other formats. Depending on the format and package, you might find a single file or a large collection of files. As with the README files, these files are well worth consulting, particularly if you want to learn how to use a package to its fullest.

Some programs rely on configuration files, typically located in the /etc/ directory, to control their behavior. Although the syntax in configuration files is often difficult to understand, many distributions provide default configuration files that include extensive comments. Details vary from one program to another, but comment lines often begin with hash marks (#). You may be able to learn enough about a program to adjust its configuration merely by reading the comments in its configuration file.

If you can't find a README or similar file, you can employ various tools to help find documentation files. Many of these searching tools, such as grep and find, are covered in more detail in Chapter 8, "Searching, Extracting, and Archiving Data," but here is a brief list:

- You can use your distribution's package management system (covered in detail in Chapter 9) to locate documentation. For instance, on an RPM-based system, you might type **rpm -ql *apackage* | grep doc** to locate documentation for *apackage*. Using grep to search for the string doc in the file list is a good trick because documentation directories almost always contain the string doc.

- The Linux find command can search your entire directory tree, or a subset of it, for files that match a specified criterion. To search for a file that includes a certain string in its name, for instance, you might type **find /usr/share/doc -name "*string*"**, where *string* is the keyword that you want to find in a filename. This command searches the /usr/share/doc directory tree, but you can search another directory tree instead. If you search a directory with lots of files and subdirectories, this command can take a long time to complete.

- The whereis program searches for files in a restricted set of locations, such as standard binary file directories, library directories, and man page directories. This tool does *not* search user directories. The whereis utility is a quick way to find program executables and related files like documentation or configuration files. To use it, type **whereis** followed by the name of the command or file, as in **whereis less** to find the less binary and related documentation.

- The Linux locate command searches a database of filenames that Linux maintains. It can therefore do its job much quicker than find can, but you can't control the part of the computer that the system searches. Type **locate** followed by the string that you want to find, as in **locate xterm** to find any files related to the XTerm terminal program.

The locate database is typically updated every 24 hours. If you are working on a freshly installed distribution, or you are searching for newly installed package files, the updatedb command will need to be run using super user privileges in order to update the locate database manually before you use the locate command.

After you've located documentation files, you must know how to read them. The details, of course, depend on the documentation's file format. You can use less to read many files. Most distributions configure less in such a way that it can interpret common file formats, such as HTML, and to automatically decompress files that are stored in compressed format to save disk space.

If you want to see a formatted text file, such as an HTML file, in a raw form, use the -L option to less, as in less -L file.html.

Table 5.5 summarizes common documentation file formats and the programs that you can use to read them. Which formats are used varies from one program to another.

TABLE 5.5   Common documentation file formats

Filename extension	Description	Programs for reading
.1 through .9	Unix man pages	man, info, less
.gz, .xz, or .bz2	File compressed with gzip, xz, or bzip2	Use gunzip, unxz, or bunzip2 to uncompress, or use less, which may be able to uncompress the file and read its underlying format.
.txt	Plain text	less or any text editor
.html or .htm	HTML	Any web browser
.odt	OpenDocument text	OpenOffice.org, LibreOffice, or many other word processors
.pdf	Portable Document Format (PDF)	Evince, Okular, Adobe Reader, xpdf
.tif, .png, .jpg	Graphics file formats	The GIMP, Eye of GNOME (eog)

Manually uncompressing a file with gunzip, unxz, or bunzip2 may require writing the uncompressed version to disk, so you may need to copy the file to your home directory. See Chapter 8 for more details.

Locating Program Documentation Online

In addition to the documentation that you find on your computer, you can locate documentation on the Internet. Most packages have associated Internet websites, which may be referred to in man pages, info pages, README files, or other documentation. Check these pages to look up documentation.

A few general Linux documentation resources are available on the Internet. The documentation offered by these sites, however, is often out-of-date. Typically, distributions have their own online sites providing up-to-date documentation. Helpful online documentation resources include the following:

- The Linux Documentation Project, or LDP (tldp.org)
- Red Hat Product Documentation (access.redhat.com/documentation)
- Official Ubuntu Documentation (help.ubuntu.com)
- openSUSE Documentation (doc.opensuse.org)
- Fedora Documentation (docs.fedoraproject.org)
- Linux Mint Documentation (linuxmint.com/documentation.php)

Be aware that items on the LDP site can be rather out-of-date. Be sure to check an item's revision date before using it!

Many Linux distributions use community volunteers to write and/or improve their documentation. These volunteers' practical experience adds to the accuracy and depth of the distribution's documentation, which makes these sites valuable resources.

Consulting Experts

Whatever issue has you looking for documentation, chances are you're not the first person to do so. In some cases, you can save a lot of time by asking another person for help. Some specific resources include the following:

Program Authors   Many open source authors are happy to answer questions or provide limited support, particularly if a bug causes your problem. Bigger projects (including most Linux distributions) have many authors, and these projects often provide web forums or mailing lists to help users and developers communicate.

Web Forums and Mailing Lists   These resources differ in format but serve similar purposes: they enable users to communicate with one another and share their expertise. Many distributions have dedicated web forums; try a web search on your distribution name and *forum* to find yours. Mailing lists are more common for individual programs. Search the program's main website for information on mailing lists.

IRC   Internet Relay Chat (IRC) is a tool for real-time text-mode communication among small groups of people. To use IRC, you need an IRC client program, such as Irssi (`irssi.org`), HexChat (`hexchat.github.io/`), or Smuxi (`smuxi.im/`). You can then join an IRC channel in which IRC users exchange messages in real time.

Paid Consultants   Paying somebody a consulting fee can often be worthwhile to fix a thorny problem, particularly if you're facing a "time is money" situation in which a delay in solving the problem will literally cost more money. A web search will turn up numerous Linux consulting firms.

Web Searches   Web search engines index many Internet resources, including man pages, program documentation sites, web forums, and even IRC channel discussions. A web search can provide you with an answer from an expert without your needing to contact the expert directly.

Some Linux distributions, such as Red Hat Enterprise Linux and SUSE Enterprise Linux, come with support. If you're using such a distribution, you may have already paid for consulting.

Careful use of these resources can help you with many Linux problems, whether those problems are simply a lack of knowledge on your part, a misconfiguration, a program bug, or some terrible disaster such as a software update that rendered your computer unbootable.

The problem today is that there's often *too much* information available; sifting through the irrelevant (or just plain bad) information to find the helpful advice can be difficult. To overcome this challenge, being specific can be helpful. You can narrow a web search by adding relevant keywords to the problem that are uncommon. Words found in error messages can be helpful in this respect. If you post a problem to a web forum or send a bug report to a program author, be as specific as possible. Include information on the distribution you're using, the version of the software, and specific details about what it's doing. If the program displays error messages, quote them exactly. Such details will help experts zero in on the cause of the problem.

EXERCISE 5.1

- Launch a GUI program, such as `firefox`, with and without a trailing ampersand (&). When you launch it without an ampersand, use Ctrl+Z to put it into the background and see how the program reacts to mouse clicks. Use `fg` to return it to the foreground, and then repeat the process but use `bg` to run the program in the background. See what happens in your terminal when you exit from the GUI program.

EXERCISE 5.1 *(continued)*

- In a shell, type a single letter, such as **m**, and press the Tab key. What happens? What happens if you type a less common letter, such as **z**, and then press Tab?

- Experiment with the command history. Use it to search on strings that are part of both command names and filenames that you've used. Use the arrow keys and editing features described in Table 5.1 to edit commands that you've used previously.

- Read the man pages for the following items: man, less, whereis, find, and locate. View their Synopsis section to understand their command syntax. What have you learned about these commands that goes beyond the descriptions in this book?

- Search /usr/share/doc for documentation on important programs that you use frequently, such as the GIMP, Firefox, or GNOME.

- Check your distribution's website, or perform a web search, to find a web forum that supports your distribution. Read some of the discussion threads to get a feel for some of the topics that come up.

Summary

Command lines are powerful tools in Linux; they're the basis on which many of the friendlier GUI tools are built. They can be accessed without the help of a GUI, and they can be scripted. To use the text-mode tools described in other chapters of this book, you should be familiar with the basics of a Linux shell. These include knowing how to start a shell, how to run programs in a shell, and how to use a shell's time-saving features.

Whether you need to learn more about a program to use it effectively, or solve a problem with a misbehaving program, getting help is often necessary. Linux provides several documentation resources for such situations. The first of these is the man page system, which documents most text-mode commands, configuration files, and system calls. The info page system is similar to the man page system, but info pages employ a more advanced hyperthreaded file format. If you need more tutorial information than the man or info pages provide, you can often obtain help in the form of extended official user manuals, web pages, and other documents, both on your computer and on the Internet. Finally, interacting with experts can help resolve a problem, so you can use numerous in-person and online resources to get the help you need.

Exam Essentials

Describe how to reach the command line.   Most Linux distributions have default GUI terminal programs that allow you to reach the command line. Some distributions let you open a terminal application with the GUI by pressing Ctrl+Alt+T, whereas others have icons on their desktop or terminal application names within their menu system. To reach a virtual terminal, which is not within the desktop environment, press Ctrl+Alt+F*n* (where F*n* is a function key typically between F2 and F6), and log in to reach the command line. The command-line prompt is provided by the shell and often ends in a dollar sign ($) for regular users or a hash mark (#) for the root user.

Explain how to run programs at the command line. If an executable program resides in a PATH directory, you can run it by typing its name, along with any needed options or required arguments. And if the program is not located in a PATH directory, you must run it by entering its directory location as well as its name and any needed options or required arguments.

Outline using basic shell features. Command completion speeds your way through the typing of commands or filenames. To use command completion, you type part of a command or filename, and then press the Tab key. As long as there is only one file or command whose name begins with what you typed, the Bash shell fills in the rest. The Bash history feature reduces your time at the command line. You can recall the most recent command with the up arrow key, view all the commands saved with the history utility, and reissue any command stored there.

Detail getting help using the man pages. The manual (man) pages are rather terse documentation aimed for those who already know the item described. They summarize commands, configuration files, and other implemented features on a Linux system. By default, the less pager is used to display information within the man pages. You can perform thorough searches for keywords stored within the man pages using the apropos utility or its equivalent—man -k. Conducting a summary search is accomplished with the whatis command.

Summarize getting help using the info pages. The info pages are as brief as the man pages but use a series of nodes (pages) that are hyperlinked and organized on levels. You can get help on how to use the info pages and its browser by typing **info info** at the command line. Interestingly, the info browser will also allow you to read man pages.

Review Questions

You can find the answers in Appendix A.

1. What keystroke moves the cursor to the start of the line when typing a command in Bash?
   - **A.** Ctrl+A
   - **B.** Left arrow
   - **C.** Ctrl+T
   - **D.** Up arrow
   - **E.** Ctrl+E

2. How can you run a program in the background when launching it from a shell? (Choose all that apply.)
   - **A.** Launch the program by typing **start** *command*, where *command* is the command that you want to run.
   - **B.** Launch the program by typing **bg** *command*, where *command* is the command that you want to run.
   - **C.** Append an ampersand (&) to the end of the command line.
   - **D.** Launch the program normally, press Ctrl+Z in the shell, and then type **bg** in the shell.
   - **E.** Launch the program normally, press Ctrl+Z in the shell, and then type **fg** in the shell.

3. Which of the following commands is an improved version of more?
   - **A.** grep
   - **B.** html
   - **C.** cat
   - **D.** less
   - **E.** man

4. True or false: Pressing Alt+F3 in the GUI brings up a text-mode display that you can use to log into Linux.

5. True or false: You can force man to display a man page in a specific section of the manual by preceding the search name with the section number, as in man 5 passwd.

6. True or false: Info pages are a web-based documentation format.

7. True or false: Linux documentation in the /usr/share/doc directory tree is almost always in OpenDocument text format.

8. Type **logout** or _____ to end a text-mode terminal session.
   - **A.** **end**
   - **B.** **bye**

   C. whoami

   D. exit

   E. man

9. Each document in an info page is known as a _____.

   A. pager

   B. site

   C. node

   D. link

   E. level

10. The _____ command searches a database of filenames, enabling you to identify files quickly whose names match a term that you specify.

   A. find

   B. whereis

   C. grep

   D. rpm

   E. locate

Chapter

6

Managing Hardware

OBJECTIVES:

✓ 4.2   Understanding Computer Hardware

Although Linux is software, it relies on hardware to operate. The capabilities and limitations of your hardware will influence the capabilities and limitations of Linux running on that hardware. Therefore, you should know these features for any computer you use extensively or that you plan to buy.

In this chapter, you'll learn about and perform basic management tasks with your hardware. We begin with low-level issues, such as the nature of your central processing unit (CPU) and motherboard. Often overlooked, the power supply can cause problems if it's undersized or misbehaves, so we cover that as well. Next, the chapter explores the various types of hard disks commonly found in both workstations and servers and discusses the special care needed in their setup. After that, the chapter focuses on monitors and display drivers, a common sticking point in Linux. Today, most external devices attach via the Universal Serial Bus (USB), so this chapter explores those types of devices. Finally, this chapter covers the common issue of drivers, which are software components that control hardware devices.

Learning About Your CPU

Certification Objective

Your CPU (sometimes called the *processor*) is the "brain" of your computer—it does most of the computer's actual computing. We've mentioned CPUs in earlier chapters in reference to distribution availability—to run on a given CPU, most software must be recompiled for that CPU. Thus, it's important that you know enough about the different CPU families to know their strengths and weaknesses and to identify what type of CPU your computer uses.

Many devices have more specialized computing circuitry. Most notably, video cards include graphics processing units (GPUs) to do specialized graphics computations.

Understanding CPU Families

CPU manufacturers tend to create product lines by making regular improvements to their products. Improvements range from minor (such as running the CPU at a faster *clock rate*, which is like running an engine at a faster speed) to moderate redesigns to improve speed (which is like shifting gears to get better speed) to radical redesigns (which are like using a bigger or more efficient engine, but one based on the original design). All these types of changes remain within a single CPU family, so they can run the same code as their predecessors. Still more radical differences exist across CPU families; two CPUs from different families can typically not run each other's binary programs, although there are exceptions to this rule, including one very important one that I describe shortly.

On desktop computers, two CPU families are common:

*x*86   This CPU type originated with Intel's 8086 CPU, but the first model capable of running Linux was the 80386 (also known as the *386*). Development continued with the 80486 (also known as the *486*), the Pentium, and related Intel CPUs, such as the Celeron. AMD, Cyrix, VIA, and others have all released CPUs that are compatible with Intel's designs.

*x*86-64   Other names for this architecture include *AMD64*, *x64*, and *EM64T*. AMD created the x86-64 architecture as a 64-bit extension to the x86 architecture. Unusually, x86-64 CPUs can run the earlier 32-bit x86 code, but when run in 64-bit mode, such CPUs have access to additional features that improve speed. Intel has created its own x86-64 CPUs. Both Intel and AMD have used the same product line names for their x86-64 CPUs as for their x86 CPUs. This fact can make it hard to tell whether you've got a 32-bit x86 CPU or a 64-bit x86-64 CPU, at least based on the CPU's marketing name.

For most desktop and laptop computers, you'll commonly run into one of the Intel Core line of processors:

- i3: The cheapest CPU, offers low-end speed and processing performance.
- i5: The mid-range CPU, offers medium speed and processing performance as well as a medium-level price.
- i7: The high-end CPU, offers advanced speeds and processing performance but at a higher price.

CPU Bit Depth

CPUs process data in binary (base 2), meaning that numbers are represented using only two digits—0 and 1. CPUs have limits to the sizes of the numbers they can process, though, and those limits are described in terms of the number of binary digits, or *bits*, the CPU can handle. A 32-bit CPU, for instance, can process numbers that contain up to 32 binary digits. Expressed as positive integers, this means that numbers can range in size from 0 to $2^{32} - 1$ (4,294,967,295 in the base 10 that people generally use). When dealing with larger numbers, the CPU must combine two or more numbers, which requires extra code.

CPUs with larger bit depths have an advantage when dealing with lots of memory, since memory addresses must fit into the CPU's basic unit size. In particular, a 32-bit CPU has a 4-gibibit (GiB) limit on memory—although some architectures, including x86, provide tricks to work around this limit. Greater bit depth does not improve speed except when dealing with very large numbers; however, the 64-bit *x*86-64 CPU architecture is faster than its 32-bit *x*86 predecessor for unrelated reasons.

In addition to x86 and x86-64 CPUs, several other model lines are available. Most of these CPUs are used in embedded applications or in very high-end servers. Here are a few that you might encounter:

ARM   The Advanced RISC Machine (ARM) processor was introduced in 1985 but has just recently taken off as the main processor in small devices, such as tablets and embedded computer systems. The RISC acronym in the name stands for Reduced Instruction Set Computing, which means it supports fewer instructions, which means less transistors are needed in the system, which in turn means less power consumption by the CPU chip. This feature is what makes ARM processors ideal for small devices that run Linux.

PowerPC   This CPU, created as a cooperative effort of Apple, IBM, and Motorola, was Apple's CPU of choice between 1994 and 2006, and so is found in Mac computers of that vintage. Today, it's used in some game consoles, embedded devices, and servers. Both 32- and 64-bit versions of this architecture are available. *PPC* is a common abbreviation for this architecture.

Itanium   Intel created the Itanium, or IA-64, architecture as a 64-bit replacement for the x86 line; however, it gained little market penetration except in the server field.

Linux can run on ARM, PowerPC, and Itanium, as well as on other CPU families, such as the Microprocessor without Interlocked Pipelined Stages (MIPS) and the Scalable Processor Architecture (SPARC); however, your choice of distribution is likely to be limited. Because software has to be recompiled and tested on new architectures, it takes effort to prepare a distribution for each architecture, and many distribution maintainers are unwilling or unable to expend this effort for more than x86 and x86-64.

The Debian Linux distribution is available on many architectures, so if you need to support Linux on a wide range of CPUs, using Debian can make sense.

Many CPUs today are *multicore* models. These CPUs package the circuitry for two or more CPUs into one unit. When plugged into a motherboard, such a CPU looks like multiple CPUs to the OS. The advantage is that Linux can run as many CPU-intensive programs as you have cores and they won't slow each other down significantly by competing for CPU resources.

Some high-end motherboards also support multiple CPUs, so you can use, say, two 4-core CPUs to get the performance of a single 8-core CPU system.

Identifying Your CPU

If you've got a working Linux system, you can learn a great deal about your CPU by using three text-mode commands at the shell command prompt:

uname -a Typing **uname -a** displays basic information on the kernel and the CPU. For instance, one of my systems returns x86_64 AMD Phenom (tm) II X3 700e Processor, among other things, indicating the manufacturer and model number of the CPU.

lscpu The lscpu command returns additional information on about 20 lines of output. Much of this information is highly technical, such as the sizes of *caches* the CPU supports. Some of it's less technical, such as the architecture and the number of CPUs or cores it supports.

cat /proc/cpuinfo The cat /proc/cpuinfo command returns still more information compared to lscpu. Chances are you won't need this information yourself, but a developer or technician might want some of this information to help debug a problem.

One thing to keep in mind is that modern x86-64 CPUs can run software compiled for the older x86 architecture. So, you might be running a 32-bit Linux distribution on a 64-bit CPU. The output of these commands can be confusing in such cases. For instance, here's part of what lscpu shows on one such system:

```
Architecture:           i686
CPU op-mode(s):         64-bit
```

The Architecture line suggests an x86 CPU (i686 being a specific variant of that architecture), but the CPU op-mode(s) line indicates that the CPU supports 64-bit operation. If you have trouble interpreting this output, you may be able to find something by looking up the CPU's model on the manufacturer's website. However, manufacturers tend to bury such information in hard-to-read specification sheets, so be prepared to read carefully.

Identifying Motherboard Capabilities

If the CPU is the computer's brain, the motherboard is the rest of the computer's central nervous system. The motherboard is a large circuit board inside the computer. It's dominated by a *chipset*, which is one or more chips that provide key functionality for the computer—they help the CPU interface with the hard disk interfaces, the USB interfaces, the network devices, and so on. Some chipsets include video circuitry for video cards, although this functionality is sometimes separate, and sometimes it's built into the CPU. Certification Objective

 Motherboards are sometimes referred to as *mainboards*.

In addition to the chipset, motherboards include plug-in interfaces for key components:

- One or more slots for the computer's CPU(s)

- Slots for random access memory (RAM)

- Slots for plug-in Peripheral Component Interconnect (PCI) or other cards

- Connectors for internal hard disks, such as the Serial Advanced Technology Attachment (SATA) interface

- Back-panel connectors that provide external interfaces for USB devices, keyboards, monitors, and so on

- Connectors for additional external devices, such as front-panel USB plugs; such devices are attached via short internal cables

Some motherboards—typically used in larger desktop and server computers—have many connectors for many purposes. Such motherboards are highly expandable, but they're physically large enough that they require bulky cases. Other motherboards are much smaller and can be used in compact computers, but such computers aren't as expandable. Laptop computers also have motherboards, which are necessarily of the small variety, with little opportunity for internal expansion.

Most of the connectors on a motherboard are managed by its primary chipset. Some high-end boards provide connectors for features beyond those of its primary chipset. Such features require a secondary chipset, such as an extra Ethernet chipset for a second network port or an extra SATA chipset for more or faster hard disk interfaces.

Whether the feature is provided by the main or by a secondary chipset, you can learn about most of the motherboard's features with the lspci command, which shows information on PCI devices. The output looks something like this shortened example:

```
$ lspci
00:00.0 Host bridge: Advanced Micro Devices [AMD] RS780 Host Bridge
00:11.0 SATA controller: ATI Technologies Inc SB700/SB800 SATAm
 Controller [IDE mode]
00:12.0 USB Controller: ATI Technologies Inc SB700/SB800 USB OHCI0m
 Controller
00:14.1 IDE interface: ATI Technologies Inc SB700/SB800 IDE Controller
00:14.2 Audio device: ATI Technologies Inc SBx00 Azalia (Intel HDA)
01:05.0 VGA compatible controller: ATI Technologies Inc Radeon HD 3200m
 Graphics
01:05.1 Audio device: ATI Technologies Inc RS780 Azalia controller
02:00.0 Ethernet controller: Realtek Semiconductor Co., Ltd.m
 RTL8111/8168B PCI Express Gigabit Ethernet controller (rev 02)
03:06.0 Ethernet controller: Intel Corporation 82559 InBusiness 10/100m
 (rev 08)
```

You may not understand everything in this output, but you should be able to glean some information from it. For instance, the computer has a number of ATI devices—a SATA controller, a USB controller, a graphics adapter, and so on. Two Ethernet devices are present—one made by Realtek and the other by Intel. Although it's not obvious from this output, the Realtek network adapter is built into the motherboard, whereas the Intel device resides on a plug-in card.

Sizing Your Power Supply

A computer's power supply takes the alternating current (AC) power from a wall outlet and converts it to the direct current (DC) that your motherboard and everything you plug into it uses. Laptop computers and some small desktop units use power adapter "bricks" that you can put on the floor. Larger desktop computers have internal power supply units. These internal units are larger, both physically and in terms of the amount of power they can deliver.

Certification
Objective

Every power supply has limits on the amount of DC power it can deliver. This is important because every device you plug into the computer consumes a certain amount of power. If your computer manufacturer cuts corners, the power supply may be barely adequate for the computer as delivered. If you add a hard disk or a power-hungry plug-in card, you could exceed the amount of power that the power supply can deliver. The result can be unreliable operation—the computer can crash or behave erratically, perhaps corrupting data or files. Such problems can be hard to distinguish from other problems, such as bad RAM or a failing hard disk.

If you need to replace your power supply, pay attention to its output in watts. You should be able to find the output of your current power supply on a sticker—but you'll need to open your computer first, at least for most desktop systems. Be sure to get a power supply that's rated for at least as many watts as the one you're replacing. Also, be sure it will fit—sizes are standardized, but a few variants are available. In the case of a laptop or a small desktop computer with an external power supply, you must ensure that a replacement provides the right type of connector to the computer. Buying a replacement from the computer's manufacturer is usually the best course of action in this case.

Understanding Disk Issues

Disks are a critical part of most Linux installations, so it's important to know how they operate and how Linux interacts with them. This section describes three basic disk issues: disk hardware interfaces, disk partitioning, and filesystems. In addition, it describes some of the issues surrounding removable disks, including optical (CD-ROM, DVD-ROM, and Blu-ray) discs.

You can install Linux in a *diskless* configuration, in which a Linux computer boots using files stored on a network server.

Disk Interfaces

 Today, three disk interfaces are common:

PATA This interface was very common in the past, but it's fading in popularity. It features wide 40- or 80-pin cables that transfer several bits of data simultaneously—hence the word parallel in the name Parallel ATA (PATA). A PATA cable can have up to three connectors—one for the motherboard or disk controller card and two more for up to two hard disks. Alternative names for PATA (or specific variants of it) include Integrated Device Electronics (IDE) or Enhanced IDE (EIDE). The ATA Packet Interface (ATAPI) standard defines a software interface that helps ATA manage devices other than hard disks. Although in some cases the differences between the technologies described by these variant terms are important, today they're often used synonymously.

SATA In 2003, a serial version of the ATA protocol was created, hence Serial ATA (SATA). SATA is more or less software compatible with PATA, but it uses thinner cables that can handle just one hard disk per cable. In 2012, SATA became the dominant disk technology on new computers. An external variant, eSATA, provides high-speed connections to external hard disks.

NVMe The Non-volatile Memory Express (NVMe) interface was designed specifically to support the solid-state drive (SSD) storage standard. SSD devices don't use physical platters and magnetic heads to read or write data; instead, data is stored electronically just like in memory, but using flash memory chips that retain the data after power is removed from the system. Because data is read and written electronically instead of magnetically, access speeds are significantly faster, and SSD drives are not susceptible to the same failures as PATA and SATA hard drives. SSD drives started out small and pricey but recently have gotten larger and cheaper, making them a realistic alternative to physical hard drives in many environments.

In addition to these technologies, others exist. The Small Computer System Interface (SCSI) is a parallel interface that was once common on servers and high-end interfaces but is less common today. The Serial Attached SCSI (SAS) is a serial variant that's quite similar to SATA. Both of these technologies are important because ATAPI is modeled after SCSI. The Universal Serial Bus (USB) interface is often used for connecting external disks.

 Most modern Linux distributions treat SATA, SAS, and USB disks as if they were SCSI disks from a software perspective and create a device file in the /dev directory that begins with sd*x*, where *x* is the drive letter, starting at a. However, for systems that utilize the new NVMe interface, Linux creates those device files as nvme*x*.

Partitioning a Disk

You can think of a hard disk as a set of *sectors*, each of which holds a small amount of data—normally 512 bytes, although some disks have larger sectors. The disk hardware itself does little to help organize data on the disk, aside from providing a means to read and write specific sectors. On-disk data management is left up to the OS. Disk partitions and filesystems are two levels of organization imposed on disks to help manage the data they store.

Partitions are a lot like the drawers in a filing cabinet. Think of a single disk as the main filing cabinet, which is then split up into multiple partitions, much like drawers. This analogy is good as far as it goes, but it has its limits. Unlike filing cabinet drawers, disk partitions can be created in whatever size and quantity are convenient, within the limits of the disk's size. A typical disk has between one and a dozen partitions, although you can create more.

Disk partitions exist to help subdivide the disk into pieces with broadly different purposes, such as partitions for different OSs or for different types of data within an OS. For instance, it's common to create separate partitions for swap space (which is used much like RAM in case you run out of RAM), for user data files, and for the OS itself.

Hard disks and their partitions are frequently represented in diagrams similar to Figure 6.1. This diagram displays partitions as subdivisions of the disk, with partition sizes in the diagram more or less proportional to their true sizes on the disk. Thus, in Figure 6.1 you can see that /root is larger compared to the memory swap space allocated. As in the figure, partitions are uninterrupted sections of a disk—that is, one partition cannot be inside another partition.

FIGURE 6.1   Disk partitions are often visualized as boxes within a hard disk.

 Some partitioning tools represent their partitions in a vertical stack rather than a horizontal chain. The principle is the same either way.

The most common partitioning scheme for x86 and x86-64 computers has gone by various names over the years, including *master boot record (MBR)*, *MS-DOS*, and *BIOS partitioning*. It supports three types of partitions:

Primary   This is the simplest type of partition. A disk can have zero to four primary partitions, one of which may be an extended partition.

Extended   This is a special type of primary partition that serves as a placeholder for logical partitions. A disk may have at most one extended partition.

Logical   These partitions are contained within an extended partition. In theory, a disk can have billions of logical partitions, thus overcoming the limit of four primary partitions, but in practice you're unlikely to see more than about a dozen of them.

MBR's use of three partition types is awkward and limiting, but inertia has kept it in place for three decades. MBR partitions have a hard limit, though: they can't support disks larger than 2 TiB (tebibytes), assuming 512-byte sectors, which are nearly universal today.

The Globally Unique Identifier (GUID) Partition Table (GPT) is the successor to MBR. GPT supports disks of up to 8 ZiB (zebibytes), which is about 4 billion times as large as MBR's limit. GPT also supports up to 128 partitions by default, with no distinction between primary, extended, and logical partitions. In these respects, GPT is a superior partitioning system to MBR; however, its support varies between OSs. Linux supports both systems quite well. Windows can boot only from MBR when the computer uses the Basic Input/Output System (BIOS), and it can boot only from GPT when the computer is based on the Unified Extensible Firmware Interface (UEFI). Thus, if you dual-boot with Windows, you may need to select your partitioning system with care.

Multibyte Units

It's common to use prefixes from the International System of Units (SI units)—*kilo* (*k*), *mega* (*M*), *giga* (G), *tera* (T), and so on—in conjunction with *byte* (B) to refer to large quantities of storage space, as in kB, MB, and so on. Technically, these units are defined as base-10 values—kilo means 1,000, mega means 1,000,000, and so on. In computers, though, base-2 values, such as 2^{10} (1024) and 2^{20} (1,048,576), are often more natural, so the SI units have often (but not always) been used to mean these base-2 values. This practice has led to confusion, since it's not always clear whether base-10 or base-2 units are being used.

To resolve this conflict, the Institute of Electrical and Electronics Engineers (IEEE) defined a new set of prefixes as IEEE-1541. Under this system, new units and prefixes describe base-2 values. The first few of these are as follows:

- A kibibyte (KiB) is 2^{10} (1024) bytes.

- A mebibyte (MiB) is 2^{20} (1,048,576) bytes.

- A gibibyte (GiB) is 2^{30} (1,073,741,824) bytes.

- A tebibyte (TiB) is 2^{40} (1,099,511,627,776) bytes.

In this book, we use IEEE-1541 units when describing features that are best expressed in this system, such as partition table size limits. Most Linux disk utilities use SI and IEEE-1541 units correctly, but which is used depends on the whim of the programs' authors. Be alert to this difference, particularly when dealing with large numbers—note that a tebibyte is almost 10 percent larger than a terabyte.

Several other partitioning systems exist, but you're unlikely to encounter most of them. One possible exception is the Apple Partition Map (APM), which Apple used on its Mac computers prior to its switch to Intel CPUs.

When it comes to partitioning a disk, Linux supports three families of tools:

fdisk Family   The fdisk, cfdisk, and sfdisk tools are simple text-based partitioning utilities for MBR disks and some more exotic partition table types. These tools work well and provide the means to recover from some disk errors, but their text-based nature can be intimidating to those who are unfamiliar with disk partitioning.

libparted-Based Tools   Tools based on the libparted library can handle MBR, GPT, and several other partition table types. Some of these tools, such as GNU Parted, are text-based, but others, such as GParted, are GUI, and so are likely to be easier for new users to use. Figure 6.2 shows GParted in action. Note how its display mirrors the structure shown in Figure 6.1. Many Linux installers include libparted-based partitioning tools that run during system installation.

FIGURE 6.2   GParted, like other GUI disk partitioning tools, provides a graphical representation of your partitions.

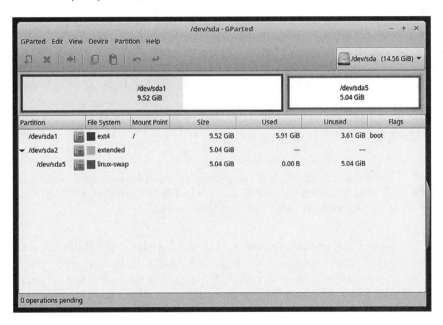

GPT fdisk Family   The gdisk, cgdisk, and sgdisk tools are modeled after the fdisk family but work with GPT disks. They provide more options for handling GPT than do libparted-based tools but at the cost of friendliness for new users.

While historically the fdisk utility focused on MBR disks and the gdisk utility focused on GPT disks, recently developers for both utilities have been experimenting with supporting both types of disks. Your Linux distribution may include a version of just one utility that supports both MBR and GPT disks.

If you're working with a preinstalled Linux system, you may not need to partition your disk; however, if you ever replace or install a new hard disk, you'll have to partition it before you can use it. You may also need to partition removable disks, although they generally come from the factory pre-partitioned with one big partition.

To partition a disk, you must know the disk's device filename. In Linux, these filenames are normally /dev/sda, /dev/sdb, and so on, with each disk taking on a new letter. Partitions are numbered starting with 1, so you might refer to /dev/sda2, /dev/sdb6, and so on. When using MBR, partitions 1 through 4 are reserved for primary or extended partitions, whereas logical partitions take numbers 5 and up.

Understanding Filesystem Issues

Most disk partitions contain filesystems, which are data structures that help the computer organize your directories and files. In Windows, each filesystem receives its own device letter. In the old days when floppy disks were commonly used, drive letters A: and B: were reserved for floppy disk drives, and that standard continues to stick around today. The C: drive letter is used for the first hard disk partition (normally the boot partition), D: for external USB disks, and so on. In Linux, by contrast, all filesystems are part of a single directory tree. The main filesystem is referred to as the root (/) filesystem. If a disk has multiple filesystem partitions, each is *mounted* at a *mount point* in the root (/) filesystem—that is, the contents of the additional filesystems are made available at specific directories, such as at /home (which holds users' data files) or /boot (which holds boot files). Several Linux filesystems exist, each with its own unique features:

The word *filesystem* is sometimes applied to the directory structure as a whole, even if it contains multiple low-level filesystems. Which meaning is intended is usually clear from the context.

Ext2fs The Second Extended Filesystem (ext2fs) was popular in the 1990s but is rarely used today because it lacks a *journal*, which is a filesystem feature that speeds filesystem checks after power outages or system crashes. A journal consumes disk space, though, so ext2fs is still useful on small disks. You might want to use it for a separate /boot partition, for instance, since such partitions are rather small. Its Linux filesystem type code is ext2.

The original Extended Filesystem (extfs) was used in the early 1990s but was quickly eclipsed by ext2fs. Extfs is no longer supported.

Ext3fs The Third Extended Filesystem (ext3fs) is essentially ext2fs with a journal. Until around 2010, it was a very popular filesystem, but ext4fs has taken its place. It supports files of up to 2 TiB and filesystems of up to 16 TiB (ext2fs imposes the same limits). Its Linux type code is ext3.

Ext4fs   The Fourth Extended Filesystem (ext4fs) is a further development of the ext filesystem line. It adds speed improvements and the ability to handle larger files and disks—files may be up to 16 TiB in size, and filesystems may be up to 1 EiB (2^{60} bytes). Linux utilities refer to it as ext4.

ReiserFS   This filesystem, referred to as reiserfs by Linux tools, is similar to ext3fs in features, with an 8 TiB file-size limit and 16 TiB filesystem-size limit. Its best feature is its capacity to make efficient use of disk space with small files—those with sizes measured in the low kibibyte range. ReiserFS development has slowed, but it remains usable.

JFS   IBM developed its Journaled File System (JFS) for its AIX OS, and its code eventually worked its way into Linux. JFS supports maximum file and filesystem sizes of 4 PiB and 32 PiB, respectively (1 PiB is 1024 TiB). JFS is not as popular as many other Linux filesystems. Linux tools use jfs as its type code.

XFS   Silicon Graphics developed the Extents File System (XFS; Linux type code xfs) for its IRIX OS and later donated its code to Linux. XFS supports files of up to 8 EiB and filesystems of up to 16 EiB, making it the choice for very big disk arrays. XFS works well with large multimedia and backup files.

Btrfs   This new filesystem (pronounced "butter-eff-ess" or "better-eff-ess") is intended as the next-generation Linux filesystem. It supports files of up to 16 EiB and filesystems of the same size. It also provides a host of advanced features, such as the ability to combine multiple physical disks into a single filesystem. As of this writing, Btrfs is still experimental, but it may provide the best overall feature mix once it's finished. Its Linux type code is btrfs.

If you're planning a new Linux installation, you should consider ext4fs, Btrfs, or XFS as your filesystems. Currently, ext4fs provides the best overall features and performance, and Btrfs and XFS are worth considering for volumes that will hold particularly small and large files, respectively. Ext4fs is a good choice for volumes that hold large files, though, so you could use ext4fs for everything and not go far wrong, particularly on a general-purpose computer.

It's possible to use several filesystems in a single Linux installation to take advantage of the benefits of each filesystem for different sets of files.

In addition to Linux's native filesystems, the OS supports several other filesystems, some of which are important in certain situations:

FAT   The File Allocation Table (FAT) filesystem was the standard with DOS and Windows through Windows Me. Just about all OSs support it. Its compatibility also makes it a good choice for exchanging data between two OSs that dual-boot on a single computer. Unlike most filesystems, FAT has two Linux type codes: msdos and vfat. Using msdos causes Linux to use the filesystem as DOS did, with short filenames with at most 8 characters plus a 3-character extension (*8.3 filenames*); when you use vfat, Linux supports long filenames on FAT.

FAT's simplicity and widespread support make it a popular filesystem on USB flash drives, cell phones, e-book readers, digital camera media, and so on.

NTFS   Microsoft developed the New Technology File System (NTFS) for Windows NT, and it is the default filesystem for recent versions of Windows. In the earlier days Linux provided only a limited read NTFS driver, but now a full read/write driver is available in the NTFS-3g software (tuxera.com). You're most likely to encounter it on a Windows boot partition in a dual-boot configuration or on larger removable or external hard disks. Under Linux, the old kernel driver is known as `ntfs`, whereas the NTFS-3g driver is called `ntfs-3g`.

 Linux's `ntfs` driver is based in the kernel, which makes it fast. The `ntfs-3g` driver, unlike most filesystem drivers, is *not* kernel-based, so it's not as fast and requires additional processing power.

HFS   Apple used its Hierarchical File System (HFS) in Mac OS through version 9.x and still supports it in macOS. You might encounter HFS on some removable media and particularly on older disks created under pre-X versions of Mac OS. Linux provides full read/write HFS support using its `hfs` driver.

HFS+   Apple's HFS+, also known as *Mac OS Extended*, is the current filesystem for macOS; you're likely to encounter it on dual-boot Mac computers and on some removable media created for use with Mac computers. Linux provides read/write HFS+ support with its `hfsplus` driver; however, write support is disabled by default on versions of the filesystem that include a journal.

 Mac users often use FAT on removable media for compatibility reasons.

ISO-9660   The ISO-9660 filesystem is used on optical media, and particularly on CD-ROMs and CD-Rs. It comes in several levels with differing capabilities. Two extensions, *Joliet* and *Rock Ridge*, provide support for long filenames using Windows and Unix standards, respectively. Linux supports all these variants. You should use the `iso9660` type code to mount an ISO-9660 disc.

UDF   The Universal Disk Format (UDF) is a filesystem that's intended to replace ISO-9660. It's most commonly found on DVD and Blu-ray media, although it's sometimes used on CD-Rs as well. Its Linux type code is, naturally, `udf`.

Most non-Linux filesystems lack support for the Unix-style ownership and permissions that Linux uses. Thus, you may need to use special mount options to set ownership and permissions as you want them. Exceptions to this rule include HFS+ and ISO-9660 when Rock Ridge extensions are in use. Rock Ridge discs are generally created with ownership and permissions that enable normal use of the disc, but if you're faced with an HFS+ disk, you may find that the user ID (UID) values don't match those of your Linux users. Thus, you may need to copy data as root, create an account with a matching UID value, or change the ownership of files on the HFS+ disk. (This last option is likely to be undesirable if you plan to use the disk again under macOS.)

To access a filesystem, you must mount it with the mount command. For instance, to mount the filesystem on /dev/sda5 at /shared, type the following command:

```
# mount /dev/sda5 /shared
```

Alternatively, you can create an entry for the filesystem in the /etc/fstab file, which stores information such as the device file, filesystem type, and mount point. When you're done using a filesystem, you can unmount it with the umount command, as in umount /shared.

The umount command's name has just one n.

Using Removable and Optical Disks

If you insert a removable disk into a computer that's running most modern Linux distributions, the computer will probably detect that fact, mount the disk in a subdirectory of /media, and launch a file manager on the disk. This behavior makes the system work in a way that's familiar to users of Windows or macOS.

Certification
Objective

When you're done using the disk, you must unmount it before you can safely remove it. Most file managers enable you to do this by right-clicking the entry for the disk in the left-hand pane and selecting an option called Unmount, Eject, or Safely Remove, as shown in Figure 6.3. If you fail to do this, the filesystem may suffer damage.

Some devices, such as optical disc drives, can lock their eject mechanisms to prevent forced removal of the media.

Most removable disks are either unpartitioned or have a single partition. They frequently use FAT, which is a good choice for cross-platform compatibility. If you need to, you can partition USB flash drives and most other removable media.

Optical discs are unusual in that they require their own special filesystems (ISO-9660 or UDF). Although you can mount and unmount these discs just like other disks, you can only read them, not write to them. If you want to create an optical disc on blank media, you must use special software, such as the text-mode mkisofs, cdrecord, or growisofs, or the GUI K3B or X-CD-Roast. These tools create an ISO-9660 filesystem from the files you specify and then burn it to the blank disc. Thereafter, you can mount the disc in the usual way.

FIGURE 6.3   Linux file managers enable you to unmount removable media.

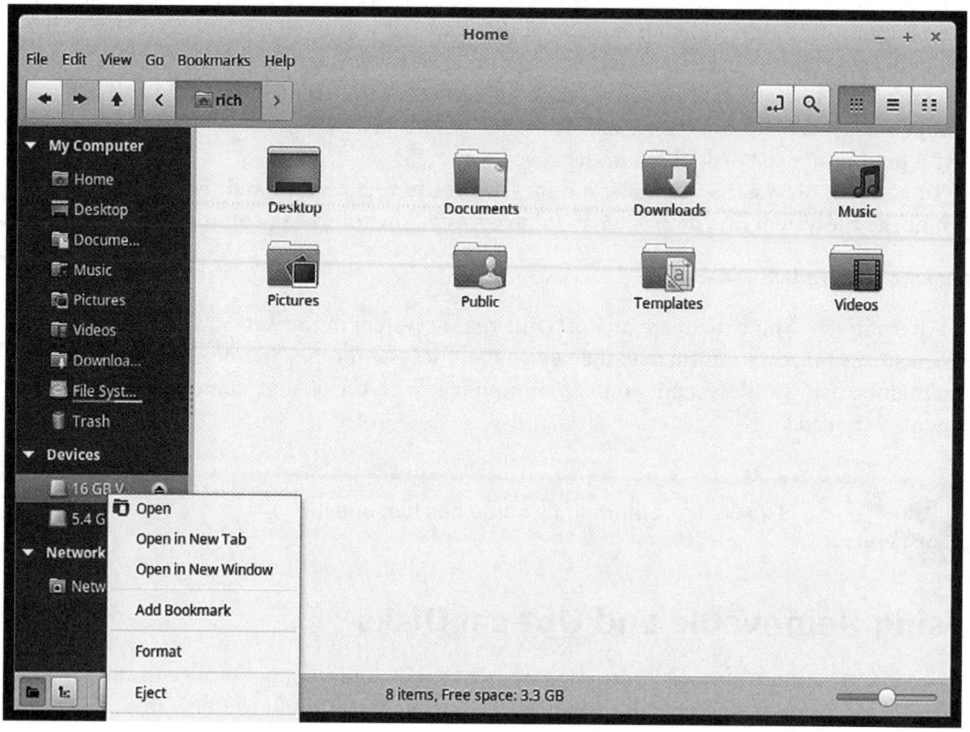

Managing Displays

Certification
Objective

Linux provides two display modes: text-mode and GUI. A text-mode display is fairly straightforward and requires little or no management. GUI displays are more complex. In Linux, the X Window System (or X for short) manages the GUI display. This section describes what X is and how it interacts with common display hardware.

Understanding the Role of X

Most people don't give much thought to the software behind their computers' displays; it all just works. Of course, behind the scenes the task of managing the display is fairly complex. Some of the tasks the software must do, on any platform, include:

▪   Initialize the video card, including set its resolution.

▪   Allocate sections of the display to hold windows that belong to applications.

- Manage windows that overlap so that only the "topmost" window's contents are displayed.
- Manage a pointer that the user controls via a mouse or similar device.
- Direct user input from a keyboard to whatever application is active.
- Display text and simple shapes within windows at the request of user programs.
- Provide user interface elements to move and resize windows.
- Manage the interiors of windows, such as displaying menus and scroll bars.

In Linux, the first six tasks are handled by X, but the seventh task is handled by a program called a *window manager* and the eighth one is handled by GUI libraries known as *widget sets*. The font display element of the sixth task can be handled by X, but in recent years many programs have begun using a library called Xft for this task. Thus, the overall job of handling the display is broken up across several programs, although X handles most of the low-level tasks.

Desktop environments include window managers, but window managers without desktop environments are also available.

Modern Linux distributions use one of two popular X software packages:

- X.org
- Wayland

Both software packages provide a version of X that can automatically detect your hardware—including the video card, monitor, keyboard, and mouse—and configure itself automatically. The result is that the software normally works properly without any explicit configuration. Sometimes, though, this autoconfiguration fails. When this happens, you must manually edit the X configuration files. For the X.org package, look in the /etc/X11/ xorg.conf file; for Wayland, the configuration settings are stored for each individual user account in the ~/.config/weston.ini file. If the X.org configuration file is missing, you can generate a sample file by typing the following command (with X not running) as root:

```
# Xorg -configure
```

Chapter 10, "Editing Files," describes the nano and Vi text-mode text editors.

The result is normally a file called /root/xorg.conf.new. You can copy this file to /etc/ X11/xorg.conf and begin editing it to suit your needs. This task is complex and beyond the scope of this book, but knowing the name of the file can help you get started—you can examine the file and locate additional documentation by searching on that name.

Using Common Display Hardware

Certification
Objective
Much of the challenge in dealing with video devices is in managing drivers for the video chipsets involved. Most modern computers use one of a handful of video drivers:

- nv, nouveau, and nvidia work with NVIDIA video hardware.

- ati and fglrx work with AMD/ATI video hardware.

- intel works with Intel video hardware.

- The fbdev and vesa drivers are generic drivers that work with a wide variety of hardware, but they produce suboptimal performance.

- Many older video cards use more obscure drivers.

The nvidia and fglrx drivers are proprietary drivers provided by their manufacturers. Check the manufacturers' websites for details or look for packages that install these drivers. These proprietary drivers provide features that aren't available in their open source counterparts, although the nouveau driver implements some of these features. In this context, video driver "features" translate into improved performance, particularly with respect to 3D graphics and real-time displays (as in playing back video files).

In the past, most video cards connected to monitors using a 15-pin Video Graphics Array (VGA) cable. Today, 19-pin High-Definition Multimedia Interface (HDMI) cables are quite common. HDMI has the advantage of being a digital interface, which can produce a cleaner display on modern light-emitting diode (LED) monitors.

Monitor resolutions are typically measured in terms of horizontal and vertical number of pixels. In the past, resolutions as low as 640×480 have been common, but today it's rare to use a monitor that has an optimum resolution of lower than 1280×1024 or 1366×768, and resolutions of 1920×1080 or higher are commonplace. Consult your monitor's manual to determine its optimum resolution. Typically, physically larger monitors have higher resolutions; however, this isn't always true.

> These days, to accommodate viewing movies, most monitors use an *aspect ratio* of 16:9, referring to the ratio of the length to the height of the display. Older monitors used a 4:3 aspect ratio, which was the old TV standard before high-definition.

In the best of all possible worlds, Linux will autodetect your monitor's optimum resolution and set itself to that value whenever you boot the computer. Unfortunately, this sometimes doesn't work. Keyboard/video/mouse (KVM) switch boxes and extension cables can sometimes interfere with this autodetection, and older monitors might not support the necessary computer–monitor communication. You may need to crack open your monitor's manual to learn what its optimum resolution is. Look for this information in the features or specifications section; it will probably be called optimum resolution, maximum resolution, or something similar. It may also include a refresh rate value, as in 1280×1024 @ 60 Hz.

In most cases, you can set the resolution using a GUI tool such as the Displays item in the GNOME System Settings panel, shown in Figure 6.4. In Figure 6.4, the Resolution drop-down enables you to set the resolution to any desired value. If you can't find the optimum resolution in the drop-down, you may need to perform more advanced adjustments involving the /etc/X11/xorg.conf file—a topic that's beyond the scope of this book. On rare occasions, you may need to upgrade your video card; some cards aren't able to handle the optimum resolutions used by some monitors.

FIGURE 6.4 Most desktop environments provide GUI tools to help you set your display's resolution.

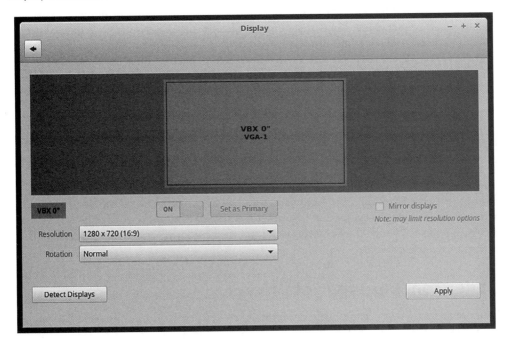

Handling USB Devices

Most modern computers use USB as the primary interface for external peripherals. Keyboards, mice, cameras, flash storage, hard disks, network adapters, scanners, printers, and more can all connect via USB. For the most part, USB devices work in a plug-and-play manner—you plug them in and they work. Some specific caveats include the following:

Human Interface Devices The X software usually manages any keyboards, mice, tablets, and similar devices when you plug them in. If you have problems, you may need to adjust your X configuration, but this is an advanced topic that's beyond the scope of this book.

Disk Storage We include USB flash drives, external hard disks, and other storage devices in this category. As described earlier, in "Using Removable and Optical Disks," it's critical that you unmount the disk before you unplug its USB cable. Failure to do so can result in data corruption.

Certification
Objective

Cell Phones, Cameras, e-Book Readers, and Music Players   You can often use these devices like disk devices to transfer photos, music, or other files. You may need to activate an option on the device to make it look like a disk device to the computer, though. When you're done, unmount the device and deactivate its interface mode.

Scanners   Linux uses the Scanner Access Now Easy (SANE; sane-project.org) software to handle most scanners. A few require obscure or proprietary software, though.

Printers   Most distributions automatically configure suitable printer queues when you plug in a USB printer. Most Linux distributions include the Common Unix Printer System (CUPS) to detect and configure printers. If you need to tweak the configuration, try entering **http://localhost:631** in a web browser on the computer in question to access the main CUPS interface. Doing so opens a web-based printer configuration utility. Some distributions provide distribution-specific printer configuration tools as well.

Managing Drivers

Most hardware devices require the presence of special software components to be useful. A piece of software that "talks" to hardware is known as a *driver*, so you should know how drivers work in Linux. This section first describes several broad classes of drivers that you may need to use in your Linux environment, and then explores how to locate and install drivers for your hardware.

Understanding Types of Drivers

Linux requires drivers because different hardware—even two devices that serve very similar purposes, such as two network adapters—can function in very different ways. That is, the methods required to initialize and use two network adapters may be entirely different. To provide generalized interfaces so that programs like the Firefox web browser can use any network adapter, the Linux kernel uses drivers as a bridge between the hardware-agnostic kernel interfaces and the hardware itself.

> In fact, several layers exist between the network hardware and a program like Firefox; the driver is just one of these layers.

Broadly speaking, drivers can exist in one of two locations:

- The kernel
- An external library or application

Most drivers are kernel-based, and in fact a large chunk of the Linux kernel consists of drivers. Kernel drivers handle most of the devices that are internal to the computer's box, such as the hard disks, network interfaces, and USB interfaces. The kernel hosts most drivers because drivers typically require privileged access to hardware, and that's the purpose of the kernel.

Some drivers reside in a library or application external to the kernel. Examples include:

- SANE, which handles scanners

- Ghostscript, which converts printed output into a form that particular printers can understand

- X, which manages the display

X is unusual in that it's a non-kernel element that communicates more or less directly with the video hardware. SANE and Ghostscript, by contrast, both communicate with external hardware devices via interfaces (such as a USB port) that are handled by the kernel. That is, you need at least two drivers to handle such devices. To print to a USB printer, for instance, you use the kernel's USB driver and a Ghostscript printer driver. Ideally, most users will be unaware of this complexity, but you may need to be familiar with it in case problems arise.

Locating and Installing Drivers

Most drivers come with the Linux kernel itself or with the library or application that handles the type of hardware. For instance, most X installations include a set of video drivers so that you can use most video cards. For this reason, it's seldom necessary to track down and install additional drivers for common hardware. There are exceptions, such as the following:

New Hardware   If your hardware is very new (meaning the model is new, not just that you purchased it recently), it might need drivers that haven't yet made their way into whatever distribution you're using.

Unusual Hardware   If you're using exotic hardware, such as a specialized scientific data-acquisition board, you may need to track down drivers for it.

Proprietary Drivers   Some manufacturers provide proprietary drivers for their hardware. For instance, the `nvidia` and `fglrx` video drivers (referred to earlier, in "Using Common Display Hardware") can improve the performance of video displays based on NVIDIA or ATI/AMD chipsets, respectively. Some hardware requires proprietary drivers. This is particularly common for some exotic hardware.

Bug Fixes   Drivers, like other software, can be buggy. If you run into such a problem, you may want to track down a more recent driver to obtain a bug fix.

One way to obtain a new kernel-based driver is to upgrade the kernel. Note that a kernel upgrade can provide both bug fixes to existing drivers and entirely new drivers. Similarly, upgrading software such as SANE, Ghostscript, or X can upgrade or add new drivers for the devices that such packages handle.

If you're using exotic hardware or need some other hard-to-find driver, your task can be more difficult. You can check with the manufacturer or perform a web search to try to find drivers.

If you obtain a driver that's not part of the kernel (or software package to handle the device), you should read the instructions that come with the driver. Installation procedures vary quite a bit from one driver to another, so it's impossible to provide a simple step-by-step installation procedure that works in all cases. Some drivers come with installation utilities, but others require you to follow a procedure that involves typing assorted commands. If you're very unlucky, the driver will come in the form of a *kernel patch*. This is a way to add or change files in the main kernel source code package. You must then recompile the kernel—a task that's well beyond the scope of this book.

Summary

Software and hardware interact in numerous ways to determine a computer's capabilities. Your CPU is one determinant of your computer's speed, and it also specifies what version of Linux you can run. CPUs are mounted on motherboards, which contain other critical circuitry for managing hard disks, displays, and other devices. Your hard disk must be partitioned and prepared with one or more filesystems before it's useful. Video hardware—both the monitor and the video circuitry inside the computer—determine how your desktop environment looks and how fast the computer can move windows and display videos. USB manages most external devices, such as keyboards, mice, and external disks. Software known as drivers manages all these hardware devices.

Exam Essentials

Describe the major hardware components Linux must interact with on a desktop or server computer. The main component of any computer system is the motherboard. The motherboard contains the CPU processor, memory, a power supply, and interfaces that connect with external devices. Desktop and server computers use the PCI connector to interface with hard drives, video cards, and network cards. The USB interface is used to connect with external devices such as the keyboard, mouse, and any external storage drives and optical drives.

Explain how Linux interacts with the various types of hardware devices. Linux uses software drivers to communicate with each specific hardware device. Linux drivers can be included as part of the kernel, or added later as a kernel module. Linux drivers exist for various printers, monitors, network cards, and other types of storage devices such as external USB drives.

Explain how Linux stores data on disks. Linux splits up storage devices into partitions for organizing the data stored on them. Linux provides several tools for partitioning storage devices, such as the fdisk and gdisk utilities. After creating the partitions, you must format each partition using a specific filesystem type. Different filesystem types have different features, such as dependability, speed of access, or file sizes, so you can choose the filesystem type that works best for your application for each partition. After creating a filesystem in the partition, you can mount it in the Linux virtual directory structure so that the Linux system can access it to read and write data.

Review Questions

You can find the answers in Appendix A.

1. Which of the following commands provides the most information about your mother-board's features?

   A. `lscpu`

   B. `Xorg -configure`

   C. `fdisk -l /dev/sda`

   D. `lspci`

   E. `http://localhost:631`

2. Why might you want to partition a hard disk? (Choose all that apply.)

   A. To install more than one OS on the disk

   B. To use ext4fs rather than ReiserFS

   C. To turn a PATA disk into an SATA disk

   D. To separate filesystem data from swap space

   E. To separate the disk's cache from its main data

3. Which of the following devices is not commonly attached via USB?

   A. Video monitors

   B. Keyboards

   C. External hard disks

   D. Printers

   E. Scanners

4. True or false: An EM64T CPU is capable of running a Linux distribution identified as being for the AMD64 CPU.

5. True or false: UDF is a good filesystem to use for a Linux installation on a hard disk.

6. True or false: The Linux kernel includes drivers for various disk controllers, network adapters, and USB interfaces, among other things.

7. The x86 CPU uses a __-bit architecture.

   A. 8

   B. 32

   C. 64

   D. 128

   E. 256

8. A computer power supply converts electricity from alternating current to _____. (two words)

    A. direct current

    B. three-phase current

    C. magnetic current

    D. static current

    E. solar electricity

9. The _____ standard is a modern digital video interface that's commonly used on computer monitors.

    A. VGA

    B. LED

    C. SVGA

    D. HDMI

    E. SDI

10. Two currently popular X software packages in Linux are _____ and _____ (Select two).

    A. xFree86

    B. X.org

    C. Wayland

    D. GNOME

    E. KDE Plasma

Chapter

7

Managing Files

OBJECTIVES:

✓ 2.3　Using Directories and Listing Files

✓ 2.4　Creating, Moving, and Deleting Files

✓ 5.4　Special Directories and Files

Much of what you do with a computer involves manipulating files. Files hold the correspondence, spreadsheets, digital photos, and other documents that you create. Files also hold the configuration settings for Linux—information on how to treat the network interfaces, how to access hard disks, and what to do as the computer starts up. Indeed, even access to most hardware devices and kernel settings is ultimately done through files. Knowing where to find the files and how to manage them is critically important for administering a Linux computer.

This chapter begins with a description of the basic layout of where Linux stores files. It then shows you how to navigate your way around the Linux filesystem to get to your files. Finally, it goes through the basic text-mode commands for manipulating files and directories.

Understanding Where Things Go

As discussed in Chapter 6, "Managing Hardware". Linux uses a unified directory tree— that is, every partition, removable disk, network file share, and other disk or disk-like storage device is accessible as a directory in a single directory tree (or filesystem). This filesystem is structured—some directories have a specific purpose, whether the directories exist as regular subdirectories on one partition or are separate devices that are mounted off the root (/) device. Understanding the purpose of the main directories will help you locate files and avoid making disastrous mistakes. Before delving into those specifics, however, you should understand the distinction between user files and system files.

The term filesystem can refer to low-level data structures or to the organization of files and directories on the computer. In this chapter, the latter meaning is the most common.

User Files vs. System Files

To understand the distinction between user files and system files, recall that Linux is a multiuser OS. In principle, a single computer can host thousands of users. Consider such a computer for a moment—perhaps it's a mainframe at a university, a large business, or a cloud-computing server. The vast majority of this computer's users will be unfamiliar with the details of Linux system administration—they want only to use their word processors, email clients, and other applications. These users don't need to deal with system configuration files, for example. Indeed, giving them access to such files—especially write access—could be disastrous. On a computer with 1,000 users, each of whom can change the system configuration, somebody will make a change that will bring down the computer, whether through ignorance or malice.

Of course, the issues involved in protecting the computer from its users are just a special case of more general user account issues—on that 1,000-user computer, you probably don't want its users to be able to read and write each others' files except in limited ways. Thus, as described in Chapter 13, "Creating Users and Groups" and Chapter 14, "Setting Ownership and Permissions," you can set permissions on files to prevent unauthorized access.

System files are files that control how the computer operates. They include the following:

Certification
Objective

- System startup scripts that launch servers and other important daemons

- Program files—both binary files and scripts

- Program support files, such as fonts and icons

- Configuration files that define how the system works (network configuration settings, disk layout information, and so on)

- Configuration files for most server services and other daemons

- Data storage for system programs, such as the database that describes what programs are installed

- System log files, which record normal system activity

Obviously, nontechnical users should not be able to alter system files, except perhaps indirectly. (Log files record activities such as login attempts, for instance.) Users must be able to read some types of system files, such as the fonts and icons they use, but some system files should be protected even from read access. (Users should not be able to read the /etc/shadow file, because it holds encrypted passwords, for instance.)

To achieve the goal of restricting ordinary users' access to system files, such files are normally owned by root or by another system account that has a more limited purpose. For instance, many server programs rely on their own specific system accounts. System files can then be protected from unwanted access by setting permissions in some appropriate way, depending on their specific needs. Ordinary users are then unable to write to most system files, protecting these files from harm. Because root can read and write any file, you must acquire root privileges to perform most system maintenance tasks.

Immediately after installing Linux, most of the files that it contains are system files, and most of the directories and subdirectories on a fresh Linux installation are system directories. As described shortly, a few directories, such as /home and /tmp, are set aside for user files, although even these are structured or configured in such a way as to prevent problems with multiuser access.

Users' home directories traditionally reside in /home, whereas /tmp is accessible to all users and holds temporary files.

   The distinction between system files and user files exists even on single-user Linux computers, such as your personal laptop computer. This may seem strange or even frustrating; after all, if you're the only user, and if you have root access, why bother with the distinction between system files and user files? The answer is that it provides a layer of protection against accidental or malicious damage. If a typo, a bug, or malware would, say, delete all the files on the computer, the damage is contained if this action is performed as a normal user rather than as root—a normal user can't delete all the files on the computer. Thus the distinction between these two account types (and, by extension, these two classes of files) is useful even on a single-user computer.

The Filesystem Hierarchy Standard

Although every Linux distribution has its own unique way of doing certain things, their developers all recognize the need for some standardization in the layout of their directories. For instance, programs should be able to locate key system configuration files consistently in the same places on all distributions. If this weren't the case, programs that rely on such features would become more complex and might not work on all distributions. To address this need, the *Filesystem Hierarchy Standard (FHS)* was created. Aside from Linux, some Unix-like OSs also follow the FHS to one degree or another.

FHS evolved from an earlier Linux-only standard, the *Filesystem Standard (FSSTND)*.

   One important distinction made by the FHS is between shareable files and unshareable files. *Shareable files*, such as user data files and program binary files, may be reasonably shared between computers. (Of course, you don't *need* to share such files, but you *may* do so.) If files are shared, they're normally shared through a Network File System (NFS) server. *Unshareable files* contain system-specific information, such as configuration files. For instance, you're not likely to want to share a server's configuration file between computers.
   A second important distinction made by the FHS is that between *static files* and *variable files*. The former don't normally change except through direct intervention by the system administrator. Most program executables are good examples of static files. Users, automated scripts, servers, or the like may change *variable files*. For instance, users' home directories and mail queues are composed of variable files.
   The FHS tries to isolate each directory into one cell of this 2 × 2 (shareable/unshareable × static/variable) matrix. Table 7.1 illustrates these relationships. Some directories contain subdirectories in multiple cells, but in these cases, the FHS tries to specify the status of particular subdirectories. For instance, /var is variable, and it contains some shareable and some unshareable subdirectories, as shown in Table 7.1.

TABLE 7.1   The FHS directory classification system

Shareable	Unshareable	
Static	/usr, /opt	/etc, /root
Variable	/home, /var/mail	/var/run, /var/lock

The FHS comes in numbered versions. Version 3.0, the latest version as we write, was released in May 2015 (see FHS's web page at linuxfoundation.org/collaborate/workgroups/lsb/fhs).

Important Directories and Their Contents

The FHS defines the names and purposes of many directories and subdirectories on a Linux system. Table 7.2 summarizes the most important of these directories. Most of these directories are system directories, the main exceptions being /home, /tmp, /mnt, and /media.

TABLE 7.2   Important Linux directories according to the FHS

Certification Objective

Directory	Purpose
/	The root directory. All files appear in this directory or subdirectories of it.
/etc	Holds system configuration files
/boot	Holds important boot files, such as the Linux kernel, the initial RAM disk, and often boot loader configuration files
/bin	Holds program files that are critical for normal operation and that ordinary users may run
/sbin	Holds program files that are critical for normal operation and that ordinary users seldom run
/lib	Holds libraries—code used by many other programs—that are critical for basic system operation
/usr	Holds programs and data used in normal system operation but that are not critical for a bare-bones boot of the system. This directory is split into subdirectories that mirror parts of the root organization—/usr/bin, /usr/sbin, /usr/lib, and so on.
/home	Holds users' home directories. Separating this directory into its own low-level filesystem effectively isolates most user data from the OS, which can be useful if you want to reinstall the OS without losing user data.

TABLE 7.2   Important Linux directories according to the FHS *(continued)*

Directory	Purpose
/root	The root user's home directory
/var	Holds miscellaneous transient files, such as log files and print spool files. One subdirectory of /var, /var/tmp, deserves special mention. Like /tmp (described next), /var/tmp holds temporary files. These files should *not* be deleted when the computer reboots.
/tmp	Holds temporary files, often including temporary files created by user programs. Such files may theoretically be deleted when the computer reboots, although in practice many distributions don't do this.
/mnt	The traditional mount point for removable media; sometimes split into subdirectories for each mounted filesystem
/media	The new mount point for removable media; typically split into subdirectories for each mounted filesystem
/dev	Holds device files, which provide low-level access to hardware
/run	Information about the running system

As an ordinary user, you will create most of your files in your home directory, which is normally a subdirectory of /home. You might also access removable media mounted at /media (or sometimes /run/media), and perhaps network resources that might be mounted elsewhere. You can use /tmp and certain subdirectories of /var, too, although most users don't need to be aware of these locations explicitly—programs are normally hard-coded to use them for temporary files or for specific types of files, such as incoming email files. As a system administrator, you might manipulate files located in any of these directories; however, for a system administrator, /etc is particularly important, since that's where most system configuration files reside. As you explore your computer with GUI or text-mode utilities, you should keep this directory structure in mind.

 Ordinary users can't write to most system directories, such as /usr. Thus, you can't damage your installation by checking out these directories—that is, *if* you're running as an ordinary user!

Of these directories, several individual directories or collections of them bear special attention:

The Configuration Directory   The /etc directory holds most system configuration files. Previous chapters have referred to several such files, such as /etc/fstab (which defines where partitions are mounted) and /etc/passwd (which is the primary account definition file). Many more exist. Indeed, you'll find subdirectories in /etc to house multiple configuration files for complex subsystems and servers, such as /etc/X11 (for the X Window System) and /etc/samba (for the Samba file server).

Executable Directories   Program files reside mainly in /sbin, /bin, /usr/sbin, and /usr/bin. (Additional directories can house program files on some systems. Most notably, /usr/local/sbin and /usr/local/bin hold locally compiled programs.)

Library Directories   *Libraries* are collections of programming functions that can be useful to many programs. They're stored in separate files to save disk space and RAM when programs run, and they enable easy updates to library files without reinstalling all of the programs that rely on them. In Linux, most libraries reside in /lib and /usr/lib, although some can reside elsewhere (such as /usr/local/lib) on some systems.

Certification
Objective

If you've administered Windows computers, you should be aware of an important difference between Windows and Linux: in Windows, it's common for a program binary, its configuration files, and all of its support files to reside in a single directory tree that belongs to the program, such as C:\Program Files\SomeProgram. In Linux, by contrast, most of a program's key files are likely to reside in standard locations that are shared with other programs and to be scattered about. For instance, the program's executable might be in /usr/bin, related libraries in /usr/lib, configuration files in /etc or in users' home directories, and so on. This works well in Linux because Linux's packaging systems, described in Chapter 9, "Exploring Processes and Process Data," keep track of where a package's many files go, enabling you to delete or upgrade a package easily. Linux has the advantage of simplifying the path, which is the list of directories in which program files reside. (Paths also exist for libraries and man pages.) If you're used to looking for files in program-specific locations, though, adjusting to the Linux system can be awkward. The key is to use your package system to identify where a package's files reside; for instance, typing **rpm -ql** *someprogram* shows where every file in the *someprogram* package resides on an RPM-based system.

The package system does not manage user configuration files, so they can linger after you delete a program. This causes no harm aside from the disk space consumed.

Exploring Files and Directories

When you're comfortable with the layout of the Linux files, you may be ready to do some exploring. In the next few pages, we describe how to learn what files are on your hard disk, how to change between directories, how to refer to files that aren't in the current directory, and how to use the most common commands for manipulating files.

Obtaining File Listings

To manipulate files, it's helpful to know what they are. The ls command, whose name is short for list, provides you with this information. The ls command displays the names of

Certification
Objective

files in a directory. If you pass it no options, it shows the files in the current directory; however, you can pass it options as well as file or directory specifications. This command supports a huge number of options; consult its man page for details. Table 7.3 summarizes the most important ls options.

Certification
Objective

TABLE 7.3 Common ls options

Option (long form)	Option (short form)	Description
--all	-a	Displays dot files. Normally, ls omits files whose names begin with a dot (.). These *dot files* (also known as *hidden files*) are often configuration files that aren't usually of interest.
--color	N/A	Produces a color-coded listing that differentiates directories and other special file types by displaying them in different colors. Some Linux distributions configure their shells to use this option by default.
--directory	-d	Changes the behavior of ls to list only the directory name. Normally, if you type a directory name as an option, ls displays the contents of that directory. The same thing happens if a directory name matches a wildcard.
N/A	-l	Produces a long listing that includes information such as the file's permission string, owner, group, size, and creation date. The ls command normally displays filenames only.
--file-type	-F	Appends an indicator code to the end of each name so that you know what type of file it is
--recursive	-R	Causes ls to display directory contents recursively. That is, if the target directory contains a subdirectory, ls displays both the files in the target directory *and* the files in its subdirectory. The result can be a huge listing if a directory has many subdirectories.

You may optionally give `ls` one or more file or directory names, in which case `ls` displays information about those files or directories, as in this example:

```
$ ls -F /usr /bin/ls
/bin/ls

/usr:
X11R6/   games/                include/   man/    src/
bin/     i386-glibc20-linux/   lib/       merge@  tmp@
doc/     i486-linux-libc5/     libexec/   sbin/
etc/     i586-mandrake-linux/  local/     share/
```

This output shows both the `/bin/ls` program file and the contents of the `/usr` directory. The latter consists mainly of subdirectories, indicated by a trailing slash (/) when `-F` is used. By default, `ls` creates a listing that's sorted by filename, as shown in this example. Note, though, that uppercase letters (as in `X11R6`) always appear before lowercase letters (as in `bin`).

> A trailing at-sign (@) denotes a *symbolic link*, which is a file that points to another file.

One of the most common `ls` options is `-l`, which creates a long directory listing like this:

```
$ ls -l t*
-rwxr-xr-x  1 rich rich        111 Aug 13 13:48  test
-rw-r--r--  1 rich rich     176322 Jul 16 09:34  thttpd-2.20b-1.i686.rpm
-rw-r--r--  1 rich rich    1838045 Jul 24 18:52  tomsrtbt-1.7.269.tar.gz
-rw-r--r--  1 rich rich    3265021 Aug 22 23:46  tripwire.rpm
```

This output includes permission strings (such as `-rwxr-xr-x`), ownership (an owner of `rich` and a group of `rich` for all of these files), file sizes, and file creation dates in addition to the filenames. This example also illustrates the use of the `*` wildcard, which matches any string; thus, `t*` matches any filename that begins with `t`.

> Chapter 14 covers file ownership and permission topics in detail.

Changing Directories

The `cd` command changes the current directory in which you're working. Although your current directory doesn't matter for many commands, it does matter when you begin to refer to files. As described in the next section, "Using Absolute and Relative File References," some types of file references depend on your current directory.

Certification
Objective

When you change your current directory, your shell's prompt may change (depending on your distribution's settings), to something like this:

```
[rich@essentials ~]$ cd /usr/bin
[rich@essentials bin]$
```

In this book, we shorten most shell prompts to a single character, such as $, when we display commands on their own lines.

The default configurations for many distributions display only the final part of the current directory—bin rather than /usr/bin in the preceding example. If you need to know the complete path of your current location, you can use pwd:

```
$ pwd
/usr/bin
```

Linux uses a slash (/) character as a directory separator. If you're familiar with Windows, you may know that Windows uses a backslash (\) for this purpose. Don't confuse the two! In Linux, a backslash serves as a "quote" or "escape" character to enter otherwise hard-to-specify characters, such as spaces, as part of a filename. Also, take note that a slash isn't a legal character in a Linux filename for this reason.

Using Absolute and Relative File References

As described in Chapter 6, "Managing Hardware," Linux uses a unified directory tree, which means that all files can be located relative to a single *root* directory, which is often referred to using the slash (/) character. If your disk contains multiple partitions, one of these devices becomes the *root filesystem*, and others are mounted at some location within the overall directory tree. The same thing happens when you mount a USB flash drive, DVD, or other removable disk device. The result might resemble Figure 7.1, which shows a subset of the directories found on a typical Linux installation, along with a couple of removable media types. Most commonly, removable media appear as subdirectories of the /media directory, but some Linux distributions prefer to use /run/media. Most subdirectories can be split off as separate partitions or even placed on separate disks. In Figure 7.1, the /home directory is on its own partition, but it's accessed in exactly the same way as it would be if it were part of the root (/) partition.

Don't confuse the root (/) directory with the /root directory, which is the root user's home directory.

FIGURE 7.1   In Linux, all files are referred to relative to a single root (/) directory.

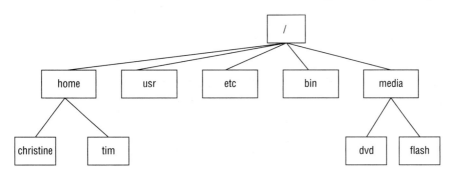

When pointing to files and directories in commands, you can refer to them in three ways:

Absolute References   Absolute file references are relative to the root (/) directory, as in /home/fred/afile.txt to refer to the afile.txt file in Fred's home directory. Such references always begin with a slash (/) character.

Home Directory References   The tilde (~) character refers to the user's home directory. If a filename begins with that character, it's as if the path to the user's home directory were substituted. Thus, for Fred, ~/afile.txt is equivalent to /home/fred/afile.txt.

Relative References   Relative file references are relative to the current directory. Thus, if Fred is working in his home directory, afile.txt refers to /home/fred/afile.txt. Relative references can include subdirectories, as in somedir/anotherfile.txt. In Linux, every directory includes a special hidden reference (..), which refers to its parent directory. Thus, if Sally is working in /home/sally, she can refer to Fred's afile.txt file as ../fred/afile.txt.

  File permissions can block your access to another user's files, an issue described in Chapter 14.

To better understand these concepts, try these operations:

1. Launch a new shell, or use an existing one.
2. Type **cd ~** to change into your home directory.
3. Type **cat /etc/fstab** to view this configuration file using an absolute file reference. Its contents should appear in your terminal.
4. Type **pwd** to view your current directory. It will probably be /home/*yourusername*, where *yourusername* is—you guessed it!—your username.
5. Type **cat ../../etc/fstab** to view this configuration file using a relative file reference. The first .. in this command refers to /home, and the second refers to the root (/) directory. (If your home directory is in an unusual location, you may need to adjust the number of ../ elements in this command, which is why we had you use pwd to find your current directory in the previous step.)
6. Type **cat ~/../../etc/fstab** to view this configuration file using a home directory reference.

Of course, steps 5 and 6 use rather awkward file references; in real life, you'd probably use an absolute file reference to access /etc/fstab from your home directory. If you were in a subdirectory of /etc, though, typing ../fstab would be slightly easier than typing /etc/fstab; and typing ~/afile.txt would be easier than typing the complete path to your home directory.

Manipulating Files

If you've used Windows or macOS, chances are that you've used a GUI file manager to manipulate files. Such tools are available in Linux, as noted in Chapter 4, "Using Common Linux Programs," and you can certainly use a file manager for many common tasks. Text-mode shells in Linux, such as Bash, provide simple but powerful tools for manipulating files, too. These tools can simplify some tasks, such as working with all the files whose names include the string invoice. Thus you should be familiar with these text-mode commands.

To begin this task, we describe some ways that you can create files. With files created, you can copy them from one location to another. You may sometimes want to move or rename files, so we explain how to do so. Linux enables you to create *links*, which are ways to refer to the same file by multiple names. If you never want to use a file again, you can delete it. *Wildcards* provide the means to refer to many files using a compact notation, so we describe them. Finally, we cover the case-sensitive nature of Linux's file manipulation commands.

Creating Files

Normally, you create files using the programs that manipulate them. For instance, you might use a graphics program to create a new graphics file. This process varies from one program to another, but GUI programs typically use a menu option called Save or Save As to save a file. Text-mode programs provide similar functionality, but the details of how it's done vary greatly from one program to another.

Chapter 10, "Editing Files," describes how to create text files with the text-mode nano and Vi editors.

Certification Objective

One program deserves special mention as a way to create files: touch. You can type this program's name followed by the name of a file that you want to create, such as **touch newfile.txt** to create an empty file called newfile.txt. Ordinarily, you don't need to do this to create a file of a particular type, since you'll use a specialized program to do the job. Sometimes, though, it's helpful to create an empty file just to have the file itself—for instance, to create a few "scratch" files to test some other command.

If you pass touch the name of a file that already exists, touch updates that file's access and modification time stamps to the current date and time. This can be handy if you're using a command that works on files based on their access times, and you want the program to treat an old file as if it were new. You might also want to do this if you plan to distribute a collection of files and you want them all to have identical time stamps.

> A programmer's tool known as make compiles source code if it's new, so programmers sometimes use touch to force make to recompile a source code file.

You can use a number of options with touch to modify its behavior. The most important of these are as follows:

Don't Create a File   The -c or --no-create option tells touch not to create a new file if one doesn't already exist. Use this option if you want to update time stamps but you do not want to create an empty file accidentally, should you mistype a filename.

Set the Time to a Specific Value   You can use -d *string* or --date=*string* to set the date of a file to that represented by the specified string, which can take any number of forms. For instance, **touch -d "July 4 2019" afile.txt** causes the date stamps on afile.txt to be set to July 4, 2019. You can achieve the same effect with -t *[[CC]YY]MMDDhhmm[.ss]*, where *[[CC]YY]MMDDhhmm[.ss]* is a date and time in a specific numeric format, such as 201907041223 for 12:23 p.m. on July 4, 2019.

Consult the man page for touch to learn about its more obscure options.

Copying Files

If you're working in a text-mode shell, the cp command copies a file. (Its name is short for *copy*.) To use it, you can pass cp a source filename and a destination filename, a destination directory name, or both. Table 7.4 outlines these three ways to use the command. Although the example filenames in Table 7.4 suggest that the original file be in your current working directory, this need not be the case; orig.txt could include a directory specification, such as /etc/fstab or ../afile.txt.

Certification Objective

TABLE 7.4   Examples of the use of cp

Example command	Effect
cp orig.txt new.txt	Copies orig.txt to new.txt in the current directory
cp orig.txt /otherdir	Copies orig.txt to the /otherdir directory. The copy will be called orig.txt.
cp orig.txt /otherdir/new.txt	Copies orig.txt to the /otherdir directory. The copy will be called new.txt.

The critical point to understand is how the destination filename is specified. This can be less than obvious in some cases, since file and directory specifications can look alike. For instance, consider the following command:

```
$ cp outline.pdf ~/publication
```

This command can produce any of three results:

- If ~/publication is a directory, the result is a file called ~/publication/outline.pdf.

If you follow a directory name with a slash (/), as in ~/publication/, cp returns an error message if ~/publication doesn't exist or is a regular file.

- If ~/publication is a file, the result is that this file will be replaced by the contents of outline.pdf.
- If ~/publication doesn't yet exist, the result is a new file, called ~/publication, which is identical to the original outline.pdf.

Keeping these results straight can be confusing if you're new to command-line file copying. We encourage you to experiment by creating a test directory using mkdir (described later, in "Creating Directories"), creating subdirectories in this directory, and copying files into this test directory tree using all of these methods of referring to files. (This is the type of situation where touch can be handy for creating test files.)

The cp command provides many options for modifying its behavior. Some of the more useful options enable you to modify the command's operation in helpful ways:

Force Overwrite The -f or --force option forces the system to overwrite any existing files without prompting.

Use Interactive Mode The -i or --interactive option causes cp to ask you before overwriting any existing files.

Preserve Ownership and Permissions Normally, the user who issues the cp command owns a copied file and uses that account's default permissions. The -p or --preserve option preserves ownership and permissions, if possible.

Chapter 13, "Creating Users and Groups," describes Linux accounts. Chapter 14, "Setting Ownership and Permissions," describes file permissions.

Perform a Recursive Copy If you use the -R or --recursive option and specify a directory as the source, the entire directory, including its subdirectories, is copied. Although -r also performs a recursive copy, its behavior with files other than ordinary files and directories is unspecified. Most cp implementations use -r as a synonym for -R, but this behavior isn't guaranteed.

Perform an Archive Copy   The -a or --archive option is similar to -R, but it also preserves ownership and copies links as is. The -R option copies the files to which symbolic links point rather than the symbolic links themselves. (Links are described in more detail later in this chapter, in "Using Links.")

Perform an Update Copy   The -u or --update option tells cp to copy the file only if the original is newer than the target or if the target doesn't exist.

This list of cp options is incomplete but covers the most useful options. Consult cp's man page for information about additional cp options.

Moving and Renaming Files

In a text-mode shell you use the same command, mv, both to move and rename files and directories. Its use is similar to that of cp; for instance, if you wanted to move outline.pdf to ~/publication, you would type:

```
$ mv outline.pdf ~/publication
```

If you specify a filename with the destination, the file will be renamed as it's moved. If you specify a filename and the destination directory is the same as the source directory, the file will be renamed but not moved. In other words, mv's effects are much like cp's, except that the new file replaces, rather than supplements, the original.

Behind the scenes, mv does the following:

- When the source and target are on the same filesystem, mv rewrites directory entries without actually moving the file's data.

Linux uses mv for renaming files because the two operations are identical when the source and destination directories are the same.

- When you move a file from one filesystem to another, mv copies the file and then deletes the original file.

The mv command takes many of the same options as cp does. From the earlier list, --preserve, --recursive, and --archive don't apply to mv, but the others do.

Using Links

Sometimes it's handy to refer to a single file by multiple names. Rather than create several copies of the file, you can create multiple *links* to one file. Linux supports two types of links, both of which are created with the ln command:

Hard Link   A *hard link* is a duplicate directory entry. Both entries point to the same file. Because they work by tying together low-level filesystem data structures, hard links can exist only on a single filesystem. In a hard link scenario, neither filename holds any sort of priority over the other; both tie directly to the file's data structures and data. Type **ln** ***origname linkname***, where origname is the original name and linkname is the new link's name, to create a hard link.

Symbolic Link A *symbolic link* (aka *soft link*) is a file that refers to another file by name. That is, the symbolic link is a file that holds another file's name, and when you tell a program to read to or write from a symbolic link file, Linux redirects the access to the original file. Because symbolic links work by filename references, they can cross filesystem boundaries. Type **ln -s** ***origname linkname*** to create a symbolic link.

 Symbolic links are similar to *shortcuts* on the Windows desktop.

You can identify links in long directory listings (using the -l option to ls) in a couple of ways. The following example illustrates this:

```
$ ln report.odt hardlink.odt
$ ln -s report.odt softlink.odt
$ ls -l
total 192
-rw-r--r-- 2 rich users 94720 Sep 10 11:53 hardlink.odt
-rw-r--r-- 2 rich users 94720 Sep 10 11:53 report.odt
lrwxrwxrwx 1 rich users    10 Sep 10 11:54 softlink.odt -> report.odt
```

This example began with a single file, report.odt. The first two commands created two links, a hard link (hardlink.odt) and a symbolic link (softlink.odt). Typing **ls -l** shows all three files. The original file and the hard link can be identified as links by the presence of the value 2 in the second column of the ls -l output; this column identifies the number of filename entries that point to the file, so a value higher than 1 indicates that a hard link exists. The symbolic link is denoted by an l (a lowercase *L*, not a digit *1*) in the first character of the softlink.odt file's permissions string (lrwxrwxrwx). Furthermore, the symbolic link's filename specification includes an explicit pointer to the linked-to file.

Both types of links are useful for referring to files by multiple names or in multiple directories. For instance, if you write a letter that you send to multiple recipients, you might want to store copies in directories devoted to each recipient. In such a situation, either type of link will probably work fine, but each type has implications. Most importantly, if you use symbolic links, deleting the original file makes the file completely inaccessible; the symbolic links remain but point to a nonexistent file. If you use hard links, by contrast, you must delete *all* copies of the file to delete the file itself. This is because hard links are duplicate directory entries that point to the same file, whereas symbolic links are separate files that refer to the original file by name.

If you modify a file by accessing its soft link, or by any hard-linked name, you should be sure that the program you use will modify the original file. Some programs create a backup of the original file that you can use to recover the original in case you find that your changes were in error. Most editors do this in such a way that the backup is a new file, and they write changes to the original file, thus affecting it as well as the link. Some programs, though, rename the original file and then write a new file with the changes. If a program does this and you've accessed the file via a link, the linked-to file will be unaffected by your changes. If in doubt, test your program to be sure that it does what you expect.

If you want to create a link to a directory, be aware that you can normally do this only via symbolic links. Hard links between directories are potentially dangerous in terms of low-level filesystem data structures, so the ln utility permits only the superuser to create such links. Even then, most filesystems disallow hard links between directories, so in practice even root usually can't create them. Any user can create symbolic links to a directory, though.

Linux installations make use of links (mostly symbolic links) in various places. For instance, system startup scripts are often referred to via symbolic links located in directories dedicated to specific startup conditions, known as *runlevels*. Runlevel management is beyond the scope of this book.

Deleting Files

The rm command deletes files in a text-mode shell. As you might expect, you pass the names of one or more files to this command:

 The rm command's name is short for *remove*.

```
$ rm outline.pdf outline.txt
```

This example deletes two files, outline.pdf and outline.txt. If you want to delete an entire directory tree, you can pass rm the -r, -R, or --recursive option along with a directory name:

```
$ rm -r oldstuff/
```

The -i option causes rm to prompt before deleting each file. This is a useful safety measure. You can use the -f (--force) option to override this setting, if -i is configured as the default. Several other options to rm exist; consult its man page to learn about them.

 Distributions sometimes set the -i option by default for root, but not for ordinary users.

It's important to realize that rm does *not* implement any functionality like a file manager's "trash can." After you delete a file with rm, it's gone, and you can't recover it except by using low-level filesystem tools—a topic that's well beyond the scope of this book. Thus, you should be careful when using rm—and even more careful when using it with its -r option or as root!

Using Wildcards

A *wildcard* is a symbol or set of symbols that stands in for other characters. You can use wildcards to refer to files. (Using wildcards is also sometimes called *globbing*.) Three classes of wildcards are common in Linux:

?   A question mark (?) stands in for a single character. For instance, b??k matches book, balk, buck, or any other four-character filename that begins with b and ends with k.

*   An asterisk (*) matches any character or set of characters, including no character. For instance, b*k matches book, balk, and buck just as does b??k. b*k also matches bk, bbk, and backtrack.

Bracketed Values   Characters enclosed in square brackets ([]) normally match any character within the set. For instance, b[ao][lo]k matches balk and book but not buck. You can also specify a range of values; for instance, b[a-z]ck matches back, buck, and other four-letter filenames of this form whose second character is a lowercase letter. This differs from b?ck—because Linux treats filenames in a case-sensitive way and because ? matches any character (not just any letter), b[a-z]ck doesn't match bAck or b3ck, although b?ck matches both of these filenames.

Wildcards are implemented in the shell and passed to the command that you call. For instance, if you type **ls b??k** and that wildcard matches the three files balk, book, and buck, the result is precisely as if you'd typed **ls balk book buck**.

WARNING   The way Bash expands wildcards can lead to unexpected, and sometimes undesirable, consequences. For instance, suppose that you want to copy two files, specified via a wildcard, to another directory, but you forget to give the destination directory. The cp command will interpret the command as a request to copy the first of the files over the second.

Understanding Case Sensitivity

Linux's native filesystems are case-sensitive, which means that filenames that differ only in case are distinct files. For instance, a single directory can hold files called afile.txt, Afile.txt, and AFILE.TXT, and each is a distinct file. This case sensitivity also means that, if you type a filename, you must enter it with the correct case—if a file is called afile.txt but you type its name as Afile.txt, the program you're using will tell you that the file doesn't exist. This is different from what happens in Windows or (usually) in macOS, in which filenames that differ only in case are treated identically. In these OSs, you can't have two files that differ only in case in the same directory, and you can specify a filename using any case variant that you like. Windows also creates a short filename (eight characters with an optional three-character extension) for every file with a longer name in order to help out older software that works only with such filenames. Linux doesn't create such alternate filenames.

Apple's Hierarchical File System Plus (HFS+) supports both case-sensitive and case-insensitive variants. Apple uses the case-insensitive mode by default.

Case sensitivity is primarily a function of the filesystem, not of the operating system. Thus if you access a non-Linux filesystem (on a removable disk, a non-Linux partition on a dual-boot computer, or using a network filesystem), you may find that case-insensitive rules will apply. This is particularly likely when accessing File Allocation Table (FAT) and New Technology File System (NTFS) volumes, which are common on Windows computers, external hard disks, and USB flash drives. A further twist on this rule is that many Linux programs, such as Bash, assume case sensitivity even on case-insensitive filesystems. Features such as command completion, described in Chapter 5, "Getting to Know the Command Line" may work only if you use the case in which filenames are recorded, even on case-insensitive filesystems.

Ordinarily, case sensitivity creates few real problems, particularly if you use GUI programs that enable you to point-and-click to select files. You should be aware of these issues, however, when copying files or directories to FAT, NTFS, HFS+, or other case-insensitive filesystems. If a directory that you want to copy contains files with names that differ only in case, you'll end up with a disk that contains just one of the offending files.

Manipulating Directories

You are probably familiar with the concept of directories, although you may think of them as "folders," since most GUI file managers represent directories using file folder icons. Naturally, Linux provides text-mode commands to manipulate directories. These include directory-specific commands to create and delete directories, as well as use of some of the file manipulation commands described earlier to manage directories.

Creating Directories

You can use the mkdir command to create a directory. Ordinarily, you'll use this command by typing the name of one or more directories following the command:

Certification Objective

```
$ mkdir newdir
$ mkdir dirone newdir/dirtwo
```

The first example creates just one new directory, newdir, which will then reside in the current directory. The second example creates two new directories: dirone and newdir/dirtwo. In this example, mkdir creates dirtwo inside the newdir directory, which was created with the preceding command.

> Chapter 5 includes information on how to specify locations other than the current directory, as well as how to change your current directory with the cd command.

In most cases, you'll use mkdir without options, other than the name of a directory, but you can modify its behavior in a few ways:

Set Mode The -m *mode* or --mode=*mode* option causes the new directory to have the specified permission mode, expressed as an octal number. (Chapter 14 describes these topics in more detail.)

Create Parent Directories Normally, if you specify the creation of a directory within a directory that doesn't exist, mkdir responds with a No such file or directory error and doesn't create the directory. If you include the -p or --parents option, though, mkdir creates the necessary parent directory. For instance, typing **mkdir first/second** returns an error message if first doesn't exist, but typing **mkdir -p first/second** succeeds, creating both first and its subdirectory, second.

Deleting Directories

The rmdir command is the opposite of mkdir; it destroys a directory. To use it, you normally type the command followed by the names of one or more directories that you want to delete:

```
$ rmdir dirone
$ rmdir newdir/dirtwo newdir
```

These examples delete the three directories created by the mkdir commands shown earlier.

Like mkdir, rmdir supports few options, the most important of which handle these tasks:

Ignore Failures on Non-Empty Directories Normally, if a directory contains files or other directories, rmdir doesn't delete it and returns an error message. With the --ignore-fail-on-non-empty option, rmdir still doesn't delete the directory, but it doesn't return an error message.

Delete Tree The -p or --parents option causes rmdir to delete an entire directory tree. For instance, typing **rmdir -p newdir/dirtwo** causes rmdir to delete newdir/dirtwo, then newdir. You could use this command rather than the second one shown earlier to delete both of these directories.

You should understand that rmdir can delete only *empty* directories; if a directory contains any files at all, it won't work. (You can use the -p option, however, to delete a set of nested directories, as long as none of them holds any nondirectory files.) Of course, in real life you're likely to want to delete directory trees that hold files. In such cases, you can use the rm command, described earlier in "Deleting Files," along with its -r (or -R or --recursive) option:

```
$ rm -r newdir
```

This command deletes newdir and any files or subdirectories that it might contain. This fact makes rm and its -r option potentially dangerous, so you should be particularly cautious when using it.

 Real World Scenario

Linux Security Features

When you log in as an ordinary user, you can accidentally delete your own files if you err in your use of rm or various other commands. You cannot, however, do serious damage to the Linux installation itself. This is because Unix was designed as a multiuser OS with multiuser security features in mind, and because Linux is a clone of Unix, Linux has inherited these security features. Among these features are the concepts of file ownership and file permissions. You can delete only your own files—or more precisely, you can delete files only if you have write access to the directories in which they reside. You have such access to your own home directory but not to the directories in which Linux system files reside. Therefore, you can't damage these Linux system files.

Chapter 13 covers these concepts in more detail. Chapter 13 also describes how you can acquire the power to administer the computer. With this power comes the ability to damage the system, though, so you should be careful to do so only when necessary.

Managing Directories

Directories are just special files—they're files that hold other files. This means you can use most of the file manipulation tools described elsewhere in this chapter to manipulate directories. There are some caveats, though:

- You can use touch to update a directory's time stamps, but you can't use touch to create a directory; mkdir handles that task.

- You can use cp to copy a directory; however, you must use the -r, -R, --recursive, -a, or --archive option to copy the directory and all its contents.

- You can use mv to move or rename a directory.

- You can use ln with its -s option to create a symbolic link to a directory. No common Linux filesystem supports hard links to directories, though.

As an example, suppose that you have a directory in your home directory called Music/Satchmo, which contains Louis Armstrong music files. You want to reorganize this directory so that the files appear under the performer's last name, but you want to retain access to the files under the name Satchmo, since your music players refer to them this way. You could type the following commands to achieve this goal:

```
$ cd ~/Music
$ mv Satchmo Armstrong
$ ln -s Armstrong Satchmo
```

Alternatively, you could omit the first command and specify the complete path to each of the directories or links in the mv and ln commands. As written, the first two of these commands rename the ~/Music/Satchmo directory to ~/Music/Armstrong. The final command creates a symbolic link, ~/Music/Satchmo, that points to ~/Music/Armstrong.

Summary

Much of what you do with a computer qualifies as file management, so you must understand the basic tools for managing files in Linux. These include commands to create, delete, copy, move, and rename files, as well as to create links to files. Directories in Linux are just files that contain other files, so most of the same commands that you can use on files also work on directories. Special commands to create and delete directories exist, too.

Exam Essentials

Describe where you would find most application files on the Linux system.   Applications that are critical and that most normal users would run are normally stored in the /bin directory. Applications that are critical but mostly used by the administrator are stored in the /sbin directory. Noncritical applications are normally stored in the /usr directory.

Explain the basic commands to create, copy, move, or delete a file.   You can create an empty file using the touch command. In Linux you copy files using the cp command, or move a file to a new filename by using the mv command. To delete a file, you use the rm command.

Describe the /tmp directory and what Linux uses it for.   The /tmp directory is intended for temporary files that do not need to be saved. Theoretically the Linux system can clear out any files in the /tmp directory when it reboots, although many Linux distributions don't do that. However, never expect a file that you store in the /tmp directory to be there after the next system reboot.

Review Questions

You can find the answers in Appendix A.

1. Which of the following commands would you type to rename `newfile.txt` to `afile.txt`?

   A. `mv newfile.txt afile.txt`

   B. `cp newfile.txt afile.txt`

   C. `ln newfile.txt afile.txt`

   D. `rn newfile.txt afile.txt`

   E. `touch newfile.txt afile.txt`

2. You want to copy a directory, `MyFiles`, to a USB flash drive that uses the FAT filesystem. The contents of `MyFiles` are as follows:

   ```
   $ ls MyFiles/
   contract.odt
   outline.pdf
   Outline.PDF
   ```

   The USB flash drive is mounted at /media/usb, and so you type **cp -a MyFiles/ /media/usb**. What problem will occur when you attempt to copy these files?

   A. The command will fail because it tries to create links.

   B. The `MyFiles` directory will be copied, but none of its files will be copied.

   C. One file will be missing on the USB flash drive.

   D. One file's name will be changed during the copy.

   E. Everything will be fine; the command will work correctly.

3. You type **mkdir one/two/three** and receive an error message that reads, in part, `No such file or directory`. What can you do to overcome this problem? (Choose all that apply.)

   A. Add the --parents parameter to the `mkdir` command.

   B. Issue three separate `mkdir` commands: **mkdir one**, then **mkdir one/two**, and then **mkdir one/two/three**.

   C. Type **touch /bin/mkdir** to be sure the `mkdir` program file exists.

   D. Type **rmdir one** to clear away the interfering base of the desired new directory tree.

   E. Type **rm -r one** to clear away the entire interfering directory tree.

4. True or false: You can create a symbolic link from one low-level filesystem to another.

5. True or false: You can easily damage your Linux installation by mistyping an `rm` command when you log into your regular account.

6. True or false: You can set a directory's time stamps with the `touch` command.

7. You want to copy a file (origfile.txt) to the backups directory, but if a file called origfile.txt exists in the backups directory, you want to go ahead with the copy only if the file in the source location is newer than the one in backups. The command to do this is cp _____ origfile.txt backups/.

   A. -f

   B. -r

   C. -s

   D. -u

   E. -v

8. You've typed **rmdir junk** to delete the junk directory, but this command has failed because junk contains word processing files. A command that will work is _____.

   A. rmdir -r junk

   B. rmdir -P junk

   C. rmdir -v junk

   D. rm -r junk

   E. rm -f junk

9. The __ wildcard character matches any one symbol in a filename.

   A. ?

   B. _ (underscore)

   C. *

   D. . (period)

   E. - (dash)

10. What directory primarily contains system configuration files?

   A. /bin

   B. /etc

   C. /usr

   D. /var

   E. /sbin

Chapter

8

Searching, Extracting, and Archiving Data

OBJECTIVES:

✓ 3.1   Archiving Files on the Command Line

✓ 3.2   Searching and Extracting Data from Files

An important part of any OS's job, including Linux, is the storage, management, and analysis of data. Data is valuable because of the knowledge that can be gleaned from it, so you need to be able to search and extract it properly, as well as protect it. This chapter covers some of the tools that you can use to search, extract, and archive data.

The chapter begins with a look at *regular expressions*, which are a way to describe patterns that you might want to look for in data files. You can use regular expressions with many commands, two of which (find and grep) are described in more detail. This chapter also covers tools that you can use to redirect programs' input and output, which is a useful trick in many situations. Finally, tools for creating archive files are described, which can be useful in transferring many files over a network or in creating backups.

Using Regular Expressions

Certification
Objective

Many Linux programs employ regular expressions, which are tools for expressing patterns in text. Regular expressions are similar in principle to the wildcards that can be used to specify multiple filenames, as described in Chapter 7, "Managing Files." At their simplest, regular expressions can be plain text without adornment, although certain characters are used to denote patterns.

Documentation sometimes uses the abbreviation *regexp* to refer to a regular expression.

Two forms of regular expression are common: basic and extended. The form that you must use depends on the program. Some accept just one expression form, whereas others can use either type (depending on the options passed to the program). The differences between basic and *extended regular expression* forms can be complex and subtle, but the fundamental principles of both are similar.

The simplest type of regular expression is an alphabetic or alphanumeric string, such as HWaddr or Linux3. These regular expressions match any string of the same size or longer that contains the regular expression. For instance, the HWaddr regular expression matches HWaddr, This is the HWaddr, and The HWaddr is unknown. The real strength of regular expressions comes in the use of nonalphanumeric characters, which activate advanced matching rules.

The most powerful basic regular expression features include the following:

Bracket Expressions   Characters enclosed in square brackets ([]) constitute bracket expressions, which match any *one* character within the brackets. For instance, the regular expression b[aeiou]g matches the words bag, beg, big, bog, and bug. The brackets represent a *single* character in the word. Thus, the regular expression p[ai]n matches pan and pin but not pain. Including a caret (^) after the opening square bracket matches against any character *except* the ones specified. For instance, b[^aeiou]g matches bbg or bAg but not bag or beg.

Range Expressions   A range expression is a variant on a bracket expression. Instead of listing every character that matches, range expressions list the start and end points separated by a dash (-), as in a[2-4]z. This regular expression matches a2z, a3z, and a4z.

Any Single Character   The dot (.) represents any *single* character except a newline. For instance, a.z matches a2z, abz, aQz, or any other three-character string that begins with a and ends with z.

> A newline is a hidden special character used in text files. When a text file is displayed, a newline character on the end of each line is often what is causing each line to display below the previous line.

Start and End of Line   A text line (sometimes called a *record*) consists of all the characters before the line is terminated with a newline. When not used inside brackets, the caret (^) represents the start of a line. The dollar sign ($) denotes the end of a line. For instance, ^bag matches bag only if it is *first* in a line of characters, whereas bag$ matches bag only if it is *last* in a line of characters.

Repetition   A full or partial regular expression may be followed by a special symbol to denote repetition of the matched item. Specifically, an asterisk (*) denotes zero or more matches. The asterisk is often combined with the dot (as in .*) to specify a match with any substring. For instance, A.*Lincoln matches any string that contains A and Lincoln, in that order—Abe Lincoln and Abraham Lincoln are just two possible matches.

Escaping   If you want to match one of the special characters, such as a dot, you must *escape* it—that is, precede it with a backslash (\). For instance, to match a computer hostname (say, www.sybex.com), you must escape the dots, as in www\.sybex\.com.

Extended regular expressions add more features that you can use to match in additional ways:

Additional Repetition Operators   Other repetition operators work like an asterisk, but they match only certain numbers of matches. Specifically, a plus sign (+) matches one or more occurrences, and a question mark (?) specifies zero or one match.

Multiple Possible Strings   The vertical bar (|) separates two possible matches; for instance, car|truck matches either car or truck.

Parentheses   Ordinary parentheses (()) surround subexpressions. Parentheses are often used to specify how to apply operators; for example, you can put parentheses around a group of words that are concatenated with the vertical bar to ensure that the words are treated as a group, any one of which may match, without involving surrounding parts of the regular expression.

If you use an extended regular expression with the grep command, you must include its -E option.

Whether you use basic or extended regular expressions depends on which form the program supports. For programs such as grep that support both, you can use either; which you choose is mostly a matter of personal preference. Note that a regular expression that includes characters associated with extended regular expressions will be interpreted differently depending on which type you're using. Thus, it's important to know which type of regular expression a program supports or how to select which type to use if the program supports both types.

Regular expression rules can be confusing, particularly when you're first introduced to them. Some examples of their use, in the context of the programs that use them, will help. The next section provides such examples, with reference to the grep program.

Searching For and Extracting Data

The grep command uses regular expressions and is helpful in locating data. The grep utility locates files by scanning their contents. The grep program also returns some of the data included in files, which can be useful if you want to extract just a little data from a file or from a program's output.

As its name suggests, find locates files. It uses surface features, such as the filename and the file's date stamps. Another command, wc, provides basic word statistics on text files. To extract individual data items from a file's lines, the cut command is useful. Two additional commands, sort and cat, allow the display of resulting data to be manipulated, which can be helpful in your search.

Unlike grep, find does not use regular expressions, by default. However, it does support pattern matching by using a similar mechanism.

Using *grep*

Certification
Objective

The grep command searches for files that contain a specified string and returns the name of the file and (if it's a text file) the line containing that string. You can also use grep to search a specified file for a specified string. To use grep, you type the command's name, an optional set of switches (options), a regular expression, and an optional filename specifica-tion. The grep command supports a large number of options, the most common of which appear in Table 8.1.

TABLE 8.1   Common grep options

Option (long form)	Option (short form)	Description
--count	-c	Displays the number of lines that match, rather than the lines that contain matches to the regular expression
--file=*file*	-f *file*	Takes pattern input from the specified file rather than from the command line. The fgrep command is a shortcut for this option.
--ignore-case	-i	Performs a case-insensitive search, rather than the default case-sensitive search
--recursive	-R or -r	Searches in the specified directory and all subdirectories rather than simply the specified directory. The rgrep command is a shortcut for this option.
--extended-regexp	-E	Pass this option to use an extended regular expression. Alternatively, you can call egrep rather than grep; this variant command uses extended regular expressions by default.

If you don't specify a filename, grep uses standard input. This can be use-ful with pipelines, as described shortly in "Redirecting Input and Output."

A simple example of grep uses a regular expression with no special components:

```
$ grep -r bash /etc/
```

This example finds all files in /etc that contain the string bash (the Bash shell). Because the example includes the -r option, it searches recursively, so grep searches files in subdi-rectories of /etc as well as those in /etc itself. For each matching text file, the line that contains the string is printed.

Ordinary users can't read some files in /etc. If you type this command as a non-super user, you'll see error messages relating to grep's inability to open some files.

Suppose that you want to locate all files in /etc that contain the string bash or dash. You can enter the following command, which uses a bracket regular expression to specify both variant devices:

```
$ grep -r [bd]ash /etc/
```

A more complex example searches just the /etc/passwd file for lines that contain the word games or mail and, later on the same line, the word nologin. This task requires extended regular expression notation; the command looks like this:

```
$ grep -E "(games|mail).*nologin" /etc/passwd
```

If you type this command on your computer, it may find no matches because of your distribution's configuration. Try other words within the parentheses instead of games and mail, such as nobody or lp.

Certification
Objective

The preceding command illustrates another feature that you may need to use: *shell quoting*. Because the shell uses certain characters, such as the vertical bar (|) and the asterisk (*), for its own purposes, you must enclose certain regular expressions in quotes. Otherwise, the shell will incorrectly treat the regular expression as shell commands. Shell quoting is useful for other programs that may use characters with special meaning to the shell, such as the echo command (covered in Chapter 11, "Creating Scripts").

You can use grep in conjunction with commands that produce a lot of output in order to sift through that output for the material that's important to you. (Several examples throughout this book use this technique.) To accomplish this, you need to use input and output redirection. This topic is covered (along with additional grep examples) in the upcoming section, "Redirecting Input and Output."

Using *find*

The find utility implements a brute-force approach to finding files. This program finds files by searching through the specified directory tree, checking filenames, file creation dates, and so on to locate the files that match the specified criteria. Because of this operation method, find tends to be slow. It's flexible, however, and likely to succeed, assuming the file you seek exists. To use find, type its name, optionally followed by a directory tree pathname (sometimes called a *starting point directory*) and a series of options, some of which use specifications that are similar to regular expressions.

In practice, you must use a directory tree pathname or a search criterion with find, and often both.

You can specify one or more paths in which find should operate; the program will restrict its operations to these paths. The man page for find includes information about its search criteria, but Table 8.2 summarizes common criteria.

TABLE 8.2   Common find search criteria

Option	Description
-name *pattern*	Search for files using their names. Doing so finds files that match the specified *pattern*. This *pattern* is a shell wildcard pattern, as described in Chapter 7, and not a regular expression.
-perm *mode*	To find files that have certain permissions, use the -perm *mode* expression. The *mode* may be expressed either symbolically or in octal form. If you precede *mode* with a +, find locates files where any specified permission bits are set. If you precede *mode* with a -, find locates files where *all* specified permission bits are set. (Chapter 14, "Setting Ownership and Permissions," covers file permissions.)
-size *n*	Search for files based on size. Normally, *n* is specified in 512-byte blocks, but you can modify this by trailing the value with a letter code, such as c for characters (bytes) or k for kilobytes.
-group *name*	Search for files that belong to the specified group.
-gid *GID*	Search for files whose group ID (GID) is set to *GID*.
-user *name*	Search for files that are owned by the specified user.
-uid *UID*	Search for files by user ID (UID) number.
-maxdepth *levels*	Limit the search of a directory and, perhaps, some limited number of subdirectories.

Many variant and additional options exist; find is a powerful command. As an example of its use, consider the task of finding all Python script files, which normally have names that end in .py, in all users' home directories. If these home directories reside in the /home directory tree, you might issue the following command:

```
# find /home -name "*.py"
```

The result will be a listing of all files that have names ending in .py and reside within the /home directory tree. Notice that shell quoting is used, "*.py", because the asterisks (*) have special meaning to the shell.

 If you lack permission to list a directory's contents, find will return that directory name and the error message Permission denied.

Using *wc*

Certification Objective

A file's size in bytes, as revealed by ls or searched for using find, can be a useful metric. This size value isn't always the most useful one for text files, though. You might need to know how many words or lines are in a text file—say, because you want to know how many pages a text document will consume when printed at 52 lines per page. The wc utility provides this information. For instance, to discover the information for a newly created file named newfile.txt in your present working directory:

```
$ wc newfile.txt
  37   59   1990  newfile.txt
```

This output reveals that the file newfile.txt contains 37 lines, 59 words, and 1,990 bytes. By default, wc displays a count of lines, words, and bytes for each file you pass to it.

You can pass options to limit or expand wc's output, as summarized in Table 8.3. Of the options in Table 8.3, -l, -w, and -c are the defaults, so typing **wc file.txt** is equivalent to typing **wc -lwc file.txt**. The program's man page describes a few more options, but you're most likely to use the ones in Table 8.3.

TABLE 8.3 Common wc options

Option (long form)	Option (short form)	Description
--bytes	-c	Displays the file's byte count
--chars	-m	Displays the file's character count
--lines	-l	Displays the file's newline count
--words	-w	Displays the file's word count
--max-line-length	-L	Displays the length of the longest line in the file

Some text files use multibyte encodings, meaning that one character can consume more than one byte. Thus, the -c and -m options may not produce identical results, although they often do.

Be aware that wc works correctly on plain-text files, but it may produce incorrect or even nonsensical results on formatted text files, such as HTML files or word processor files. You're better off using a word processor or other specialized editor to find the number of words and other statistics for such files.

Using *cut*

When extracting data, grep is helpful in pulling out entire file lines (records). Sometimes, though, you need only parts of a file record. The cut command can help in this case. It extracts text from fields in a file record. It's frequently used to extract variable information from a file whose contents are highly patterned.

Certification
Objective

Table 8.4 shows the options that you're most likely to need with the cut command. Consult its man page for additional options and a complete description of the cut command.

TABLE 8.4 Common cut options

Option (long form)	Option (short form)	Description
--characters	-c	Selects only designated character position(s)
--delimiter	-d	Uses the designated delimiter as the field delimiter instead of the default delimiter (Tab)
--fields	-f	Selects only designated fields
--only-delimited	-s	Lines without a delimiter are not printed (default is to print them when the -f option is used).

To use cut, you pass to it one or more options that specify what information you want, followed by one or more filenames. For instance, users' home directories appear in the sixth colon-delimited field of the /etc/passwd file. Therefore, to extract only the directory names issue this command:

```
$ cut -f 6 -d ":" /etc/passwd
```

You can capture the cut command's results into a file by using output redirection. Redirection is covered later in this chapter, in the "Redirecting Input and Output" section.

When using the cut command, the extracted information is displayed to the screen. Be aware, however, that the specified file(s) remains unchanged.

Using *sort*

When dealing with a large amount of data, being able to sort it is often useful. The sort command does just that. However, you need to be aware of its features in order to achieve the desired results.

For a simple data list with only words, you can use sort without any options to sort it alphabetically, as shown here:

```
$ cat pets.txt
fish
cat
dog
bird
$ sort pets.txt
bird
cat
dog
fish
```

 As with the cut command, when using sort, no changes are made to the file's data. Only the output is sorted.

You may need to use options when sorting numeric data to achieve the desired results. The example in Figure 8.1 shows what happens when the sort command is used to sort a numeric data list. The numbers are not properly sorted in numerical order until the -n option is used.

FIGURE 8.1   Sorting a numeric data list

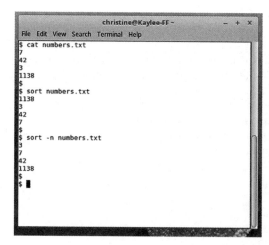

Figure 8.1 shows the importance of using the appropriate sort command option to achieve the results you desire. A few of the more popular sort options are listed in Table 8.5.

TABLE 8.5 Common sort options

Option (long form)	Option (short form)	Description
--dictionary-order	-d	Considers only blanks and alphanumeric characters; doesn't consider special characters
--ignore-case	-f	Ignores case (default is to consider case and order capitalized letters first)
--numeric-sort	-n	Sorts by string numeric value
--output=*file*	-o	Writes results to file specified
--reverse	-r	Sorts in descending order (default is to sort ascending)

Many other useful sort options are available besides those listed in Table 8.5. To explore the other options, review the man pages for sort.

Using *cat*

Certification Objective

Chapter 5, "Getting to Know the Command Line," introduced the cat command. Though cat is often used for displaying short text files on the screen, it can also concatenate files together. The example in Figure 8.2 shows both of these uses in action.

Notice in Figure 8.2 that when the cat command is issued with a single filename as an argument, it displays the file's contents on the screen, as you would expect. However, when two files are used as an argument, the files' contents are chained together. The files themselves are not modified; only the output is concatenated. This can be quite handy. The "Redirecting Input and Output" section in this chapter details how to preserve this output for future use.

To display only the *first* 10 lines of a file, use the head command instead of cat. To view only the *last* 10 lines of a file, the tail command can be helpful. Find out how to display fewer or additional file lines with these commands by viewing their man pages.

FIGURE 8.2   Using cat to display and concatenate files

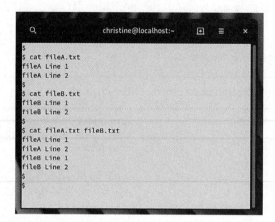

Redirecting Input and Output

If you want to save a program's output for future reference, you can *redirect* it to a file. You can also redirect the input to a program from a file. Although input redirection may sound strange, some programs rely on this feature to enable them to process data, such as raw text files fed through a program that searches the text for patterns. In addition to redirecting output to files or input from files, you can pass one program's output to another one as its input. A related technique involves the xargs command, which enables you to generate command-line options from files or other programs' output.

Using Basic Redirection Operators

Certification
Objective

Redirection is achieved with the help of *redirection operators*, which are short strings that appear after the command and its arguments. Table 8.6 shows the most common redirection operators. Be aware that output comes in two types:

Standard Output   This is for normal program messages.

Standard Error   This contains error messages.

Having two types of output enables them to be separated so that error messages don't confuse programs that might be expecting certain types of input from another program.

TABLE 8.6   Common redirection operators

Redirection operator	Effect
>	Creates a new file containing standard output. If the specified file exists, it's overwritten.
>>	Appends standard output to the existing file. If the specified file doesn't exist, it's created.
2>	Creates a new file containing error messages (standard error). If the specified file exists, it's overwritten.
2>>	Appends standard error to the existing file. If the specified file doesn't exist, it's created.
&>	Creates a new file containing both standard output and standard error. If the specified file exists, it's overwritten.
<	Sends the contents of the specified file to be used as standard input.
<<	Accepts text on the following lines as standard input.
<>	Causes the specified file to be used for both standard input and standard output.

As an example of redirecting output, consider a grep command to search for information on a particular user in all the configuration files in the /etc/ directory tree. Without redirection, such a command might look like this:

```
# grep -r christine /etc/
```

Assuming that super user privileges are used, this command will return a series of output lines like the following:

```
[...]
/etc/group:adm:x:4:syslog,christine
/etc/group:cdrom:x:24:christine
/etc/group:sudo:x:27:christine
/etc/group:dip:x:30:christine
/etc/group:plugdev:x:46:christine
[...]
```

Such output can be quite lengthy, and you might want to peruse it later. To do so, you could redirect the output to a file, like this:

```
# grep -r christine /etc/ > christine-in-etc.txt
```

 WARNING Be careful when using the > redirection operator. If the file already exists, this operator will overwrite the file's current contents.

Using the > redirection operator takes the output from the grep command and puts it into a file called christine-in-etc.txt. If you then want to see the output, use less:

```
# less christine-in-etc.txt
[...]
/etc/group:adm:x:4:syslog,christine
/etc/group:cdrom:x:24:christine
/etc/group:sudo:x:27:christine
/etc/group:dip:x:30:christine
/etc/group:plugdev:x:46:christine
[...]
```

In this example, you haven't gained much compared to simply typing **grep -r christine /etc/,** but you might in other cases. For instance, suppose a command is producing several error messages. You might then redirect standard error to a file and search for strings that might be relevant, even as you attempt to run the command, or a modified version of it, once more.

This next example illustrates how error messages (standard error) and normal program messages (standard output) are separate. If you type **grep -r christine /etc/** as a normal user (substituting your own username for *christine*), you're likely to see output such as that shown earlier, specifying the files in which your username appears; however, you're also likely to see error messages, since you lack permission to read some of the files in /etc:

```
grep: /etc/cups/subscriptions.conf.0: Permission denied
grep: /etc/security/opasswd: Permission denied
```

The information on the files in which *christine* appears is shown via standard output, but the errors are shown via standard error.

 NOTE The only difference between redirecting standard output by using the > redirection operator and redirecting standard error by using the 2> operator is the number 2. This is because the number 2 represents *standard error* at the command line.

If you're not interested in the errors, you can redirect them to /dev/null—a device file that serves as a trash can for data that you want to discard:

```
$ grep -r christine /etc/ 2> /dev/null
```

Likewise, if you redirect standard output to a file but do *not* redirect standard error, you'll see the error messages on your screen. However, the file you create (such as christine-in-etc.txt from the earlier command) will not contain the error messages. You may want to try all of the different types of output redirection by using **grep -r christine /etc/** (substituting your own username for *christine*) to get a feel for how they work.

Using Pipes

Another type of redirected output is a command-line *pipe* or *pipeline*. In a pipe, the standard output from one program is redirected as the standard input to a second program. You create a pipe by using a vertical bar (|) between the two commands; this key is usually above the Enter key on the keyboard and accessed with Shift. Pipelines can be useful when applied in various ways. For instance, you might pipe the lengthy output of a program through the less pager, which enables you to page up and down through the output. In this example, the cut command pulls the users' home directories from the /etc/passwd file and then pipes it as input into the less command (originally described in Chapter 5) for an easier viewing of the results:

Certification Objective

```
$ cut -f 6 -d ":" /etc/passwd | less
```

> **NOTE**   The /etc/passwd file and user accounts are covered in detail in Chapter 12, "Understanding Basic Security."

Often grep is used in pipelines to search for keywords in the output. In this example, the cut command pulls the users' default shells from the /etc/passwd file and then pipes it as input to the grep command to search for the bash keyword:

```
$ cut -f 7 -d ":" /etc/passwd | grep bash
```

You are not limited to one pipe in your command line. For example, you can make the previous example more useful by putting in a second pipe. To determine the number of users who have the bash shell in their /etc/passwd record, use another pipe and tack the wc command onto the pipeline's end:

```
$ cut -f 7 -d ":" /etc/passwd | grep bash | wc -l
237
```

The previous example included three commands in the pipeline. There are 237 user accounts that have the bash shell in their /etc/passwd record on this system.

Real World Scenario

Creating Custom Tools

When you use filter commands such as grep, cut, and wc with pipes and redirection, you can create powerful tailor-made utilities. With these utilities, you can conduct security audits, create usage reports, analyze text-based log files, and so on. You're limited only by your command-line knowledge and imagination.

In Chapter 11, "Creating Scripts," you'll learn how to create programs to automate many of the necessary and routine system administration tasks. When you understand how to use these utilities at the shell prompt, you can quickly engage them within shell scripts later.

Generating Command Lines

Pipelines can be useful for tricky tasks. For instance, suppose you want to remove every file in a directory tree with a name that ends in a tilde (~). (This filename convention denotes backup files created by certain text editors.) With a large directory tree, this task can be daunting. The usual file-deletion command (rm, described in detail in Chapter 7) doesn't provide an option to search for and delete every file in a directory tree that matches such a specific criterion. The find command could do the search part of the job (described in depth earlier), but not the deletion.

The solution is to combine the output of find to create a series of command lines using rm. This can be accomplished in three primary ways:

xargs   The xargs command's purpose in a pipeline is to build a command from its standard input. The basic syntax for this command is as follows:

```
xargs [OPTIONS] [COMMAND [INITIAL-ARGUMENTS]]
```

The COMMAND is the command that you want to execute, and INITIAL-ARGUMENTS is a list of arguments that you want to pass to the command. The [OPTIONS] are xargs options; they aren't passed to COMMAND. When you run xargs, it runs COMMAND once for every word passed to it on standard input, adding that word to the argument list for COMMAND. If you want to pass multiple options to the command, you can protect them by enclosing the group in quotation marks.

For instance, consider the task of deleting all those backup files, denoted by tilde characters. You can do this by piping the output of find to xargs, which then calls rm:

```
$ find ./ -name "*~" | xargs rm
```

The first part of this pipeline (**find ./ -name "*~"**) finds all the files in the current directory (./) or its subdirectories with a name that ends in a tilde (*~). This list is then piped to xargs, which adds each found file to its own rm command. The tricky task of finding and deleting all of those backup files is accomplished.

Backticks   A tool that's similar to xargs in many ways is the backtick (`` ` ``), which is a character to the left of the number 1 key on most keyboards. The backtick is *not* the same as the single quote character ('), which is located to the right of the semicolon (;) on most keyboards.

Text placed within two backticks is treated as a separate command whose results are substituted on the command line. For instance, to delete those backup files, you type the following command:

```
$ rm `find ./ -name "*~"`
```

Using backticks in this way is called *command substitution*, because you are providing a substitution for one of the command's arguments. In the previous example, the results of the find command took the place of the file's name as the rm command argument.

$() Format   Because it is so easy to confuse a backtick (`` ` ``) with a single quotation mark ('), using backticks for command substitution is generally falling out of favor. If it is available on your distribution, it's better to use another form of command substitution, the $() format:

```
$ rm $(find ./ -name "*~")
```

The results are the same using this form of command substitution, and they are generally easier to read due to the parentheses containing the first command to execute and not the small backticks (which look like quotation marks).

Archiving Data

A file-archiving tool collects a group of files into a single "package" file that you can easily move around on a single system; back up to a USB flash drive, or other removable media; or transfer across a network. Linux supports several archiving commands, the most prominent being tar and zip. In addition to understanding these commands, you should be familiar with the consequences of using compression with them.

Another archive program, cpio, is sometimes used in Linux. It's similar in principle to tar but different in operational details.

Using *tar*

The tar program's name stands for *tape archiver*. Regardless of its name, you can use tar to back up (also called *archive*) data to your hard disk or other media, not just to tapes. The tar program is a popular tool used to archive various data files into a single file, called an *archive file* (the original files remain on your disk). Because the resulting archive file can be quite large, it is often compressed on the fly via the tar program into a *tarball*. In fact, tarballs are often used for transferring multiple files between computers in one step, such as when distributing source code.

The tar program is a complex package with many options, but most of what you'll do with the utility can be covered with a few common options. Table 8.7 lists the primary tar options, and Table 8.8 lists the qualifiers that further modify what the options do. Whenever you run tar, you use exactly one option, and you usually use at least one qualifier.

TABLE 8.7 tar commands

Option (long form)	Option (short form)	Description
--create	-c	Creates an archive
--concatenate	-A	Appends tar files to an archive
--append	-r	Appends non-tar files to an archive
--update	-u	Appends files that are newer than those in an archive
--diff or --compare	-d	Compares an archive to files on disk
--list	-t	Lists an archive's contents
--extract or --get	-x	Extracts files from an archive

TABLE 8.8 tar qualifiers

Qualifier (long form)	Qualifier (short form)	Description
--directory *dir*	-C	Changes to directory *dir* before performing operations

Qualifier (long form)	Qualifier (short form)	Description
`--file [host:]file`	`-f`	Uses the file called `file` on the computer called `host` as the archive file
`--listed-incremental file`	`-g`	Performs an incremental backup or restore, using `file` as a list of previously archived files
`--one-file-system`	(none)	Backs up or restores only one filesystem (partition)
`--multi-volume`	`-M`	Creates or extracts a multitape archive
`--tape-length N`	`-L`	Changes tapes after N kilobytes
`--same-permissions`	`-p`	Preserves all protection information
`--absolute-names`	`-P`	Retains the leading / on filenames
`--verbose`	`-v`	Lists all files read or extracted; when used with `--list`, displays file sizes, ownership, and time stamps
`--verify`	`-W`	Verifies the archive after writing it
`--exclude file`	(none)	Excludes `file` from the archive
`--exclude-from file`	`-X`	Excludes files listed in `file` from the archive
`--gzip or --ungzip`	`-z`	Processes an archive through `gzip`
`--bzip2`	`-j` (some older versions used -I or -y)	Processes an archive through `bzip2`
`--xz`	`-J`	Processes an archive through `xz`

An example of archiving and compressing files to create a tarball is shown in Figure 8.3. The files, which are located in the /home/christine/Project42/ directory, are archived to a USB flash drive. The flash drive is mounted at /media/christine/USB20FD, as shown in Figure 8.3. The -czvf options are used with the tar command to create (c), compress using gzip (z), display the files being archived (v), and create an archive file (f).

FIGURE 8.3   Creating an archive tarball

```
                              christine@Kaylee-FF ~          – + ×
  File  Edit  View  Search  Terminal  Help
  $
  $ ls -l /home/christine/Project42/
  total 24
  -rw-rw-r-- 1 christine christine   12 Jul 23 18:43 DevOps-WeeklyMeeting.odt
  -rw-rw-r-- 1 christine christine 9948 Jul 23 18:42 P42-Data.txt
  -rw-rw-r-- 1 christine christine 2487 Jul 23 18:44 TeemMemberContactInfo.odt
  -rw-rw-r-- 1 christine christine 2487 Jul 23 18:42 timeline.odt
  $
  $ tar -czvf /media/christine/USB20FD/P42.tgz /home/christine/Project42
  tar: Removing leading `/' from member names
  /home/christine/Project42/
  /home/christine/Project42/timeline.odt
  /home/christine/Project42/DevOps-WeeklyMeeting.odt
  /home/christine/Project42/TeemMemberContactInfo.odt
  /home/christine/Project42/P42-Data.txt
  $
  $ ls -l /media/christine/USB20FD/P42.tgz
  -rwxrwxrwx 1 christine christine 1345 Jul 23 18:52 /media/christine/USB20FD/P42.
  tgz
  $
  $
```

Notice in Figure 8.3 that the leading / is automatically removed from the archived filenames (called *member names* in the figure). This allows you to extract the files easily to a
new location. For example, if you transfer the flash drive from Figure 8.3 to another system, mount it, copy the P42.tgz tarball file to a directory, and want to extract the archive,
you can do so with another command:

```
$ tar -xzvf P42.tgz
```

This command creates a subdirectory in the current working directory called
home/christine/Project42 and populates it with the files from the tarball. Notice that
only one tar command option change is needed from the tar options used in Figure 8.3:
the c (create) was switched to an x for extracting the files.

> The tar utility preserves Linux's ownership and permission information,
> even when the archive is stored on a filesystem that doesn't support such
> metadata.

If you don't know what's in an archive, it's a good practice to examine it with the --list
command before extracting its contents. Although common practice creates tarballs that
store files within a single subdirectory, sometimes tarballs drop many files in the current
working directory, which can make them difficult to track down if you run the command
in a directory that already has many files.

Using Compression

In Linux, the gzip, bzip2, and xz programs all compress individual files. For instance, you might compress a large graphics file like this:

$ **xz biggraphics.tiff**

The result is a file with a name like the original but with a new filename extension to identify it as a compressed format. In this specific case, the result would be biggraphics .tiff.xz.

Most graphics programs won't read files compressed in this way. Thus, to use a file that's been compressed, you must uncompress it with a matching program. To uncompress the biggraphics.tiff.xz file compressed in the previous example, use this command:

$ **unxz biggraphics.tiff.xz**

Table 8.9 summarizes the compression programs, their matching uncompression programs, and the filename extensions that they create.

TABLE 8.9   Compression and uncompression programs and filename extensions

Compression program	Uncompression program	Filename extension
gzip	gunzip	.gz
bzip2	bunzip2	.bz2
xz	unxz	.xz

 As a general rule, gzip provides the least compression and xz the most compression. This is why the Linux kernel is now compressed with xz.

The tar program provides explicit support for all three of these compression standards, and tarballs often have their own unique filename extensions that indicate the compression used:

 Sometimes two extensions are used on a tarball file, resulting in a filename such as my-work.tar.bz2.

- .tgz for tarballs compressed with gzip
- .tbz or .tbz2 or .tb2 for tarballs compressed with bzip2
- .txz for tarballs compressed with xz

When you use compression to create a tarball (using the z, j, or J option to tar), the compression program works on the entire tarball with all of its files rather than individually compressing each file within the tarball. This can improve the compression ratio compared to compressing individual files and then bundling them together. However, it makes it harder to extract data from a file if it becomes damaged.

> Typically, plain-text files compress extremely well, binary program files compress moderately well, and precompressed data (such as most video file formats) compress poorly or may even expand in size when compressed again.

The gzip, bzip2, and xz compression programs all apply *lossless* compression, meaning that the data recovered by uncompressing the file is identical to what went into it. Some graphics, audio, and audiovisual file formats apply *lossy* compression, in which some data is discarded. Lossy compression tools should never be used on program files, system configuration files, or most user data files; any loss in such files could be disastrous. That's why tar supports only lossless compression tools.

Using *zip*

Certification
Objective

Outside of the Unix and Linux world, the zip file format is a common one that fills a role similar to a compressed tarball. Linux provides the zip command to create zip files and the unzip utility to extract files from a zip archive. Zip files typically have filename extensions of .zip.

In most cases, you can create a zip archive by passing the utility the name of a target zip file followed by a filename list:

```
$ zip newzip.zip afile.txt figure.tif
```

This command creates the newzip.zip file, which holds the afile.txt and figure.tif files. (The original files remain on your disk.) In some cases, you'll need to use options to zip to achieve the desired results. Table 8.10 summarizes the most important zip options; however, the program supports many more. Consult its man page for details.

TABLE 8.10 Common zip options

Option (long form)	Option (short form)	Description
N/A	-0 through -9	Sets the amount of compression; -0 applies no compression, -1 applies minimal (but fast) compression, and so on through -9, which applies maximum (but slow) compression.

Option (long form)	Option (short form)	Description
--delete	-d	Deletes the specified files from the archive file
--encrypt	-e	Encrypts the archive with a password (zip prompts you for this password.)
--freshen	-f	Updates files in an archive if they've changed since the original archive's creation
--fix or --fixfix	-F or -FF	Performs repairs on a damaged archive file. The --fix/-F option performs minimal repairs, whereas --fixfix/-FF is more thorough.
--filesync	-FS	Updates files in an archive if they've changed since the original archive's creation, and deletes files from the archive if they've been deleted on the filesystem
--grow	-g	Appends files to an existing archive file
--help	-h or -?	Displays basic help information
--move	-m	Moves files into the zip archive—that is, the original files are deleted
--recurse-paths	-r	Includes files and subdirectories inside the directories that you specify
--split-size *size*	-s *size*	Creates a potentially multifile archive, with each file no larger than *size* bytes (A k, m, g, or t can be appended to the size to specify larger units.)
--exclude *files*	-x *files*	Excludes the specified *files*
--symlinks	-y	Includes symbolic links (Ordinarily, zip includes the linked-to files.)

Of the options in Table 8.10, the -r option is probably the most important, at least if you want to compress an entire directory tree. If you fail to use this option, your archive will contain no subdirectories. Given the speed of modern CPUs, using -9 on a regular basis also makes sense to achieve maximum compression.

To uncompress and extract files in a zip archive file, you can use the unzip program:

```
$ unzip anarchive.zip
```

This example uncompresses the files in the anarchive.zip file into the current directory. Like zip, unzip supports a large number of options, the most important of which appear in Table 8.11.

TABLE 8.11 Common unzip options

Option	Description
-f	Freshens files from the archive—that is, extracts only those files that exist on the main filesystem and that are newer in the archive than on the main filesystem
-l	Lists files in the archive but does not extract them
-p	Extracts files to a pipeline
-t	Tests the integrity of files in the archive
-u	Updates files; similar to -f but also extracts files that don't exist on the filesystem
-v	Lists files in the archive in a more verbose format than -l does
-L	Converts filenames to lowercase if they originated on an uppercase-only OS, such as DOS
-n	Never overwrites existing files
-o	Overwrites existing files without prompting

 Zip files typically contain "loose" files in the main directory, so you should generally extract zip archives in an empty subdirectory that you create for this purpose.

As a general rule, using unzip without any options except for the input filename works well. However, you might want to use one or more of its options on occasion. The -l option is particularly useful for examining the archive's contents without extracting it.

EXERCISE 8.1

- Use find and grep to locate files in your own directory and on the Linux computer at large. For instance, try locating references to your own username in configuration files in /etc.

- Use gzip, bzip2, and xz to compress a couple of instances of various types of files, such as text files and digital photos. What file types compress well? Which compression tool works best for each file type?

Summary

Managing your files often requires locating them, and tools such as grep and find help you with this task. The grep utility in particular makes use of regular expressions, which provide a way to describe patterns that you might want to find in files or in the output of another program. The wc, cut, and sort utilities assist in extracting information and reorganizing it for desired analysis. The cat command also allows you to reorganize data by combining multiple files into one, and it lets you view simple text files. If you need to view only a portion of a file, the head and tail programs are better to use. You can redirect such output into grep (or other programs or files) by using redirection operators, and many Linux command-line tools and techniques rely on such redirection. The tar and zip programs both enable you to create archive files that hold many other files. In fact, the tarballs that tar creates are a common means of distributing source code and even binary programs between Linux computers. The tar command uses xz, gzip, and bzip2 compression for creating tarballs. However, these utilities are available to use for general lossless file compression as well.

Exam Essentials

Describe using basic regular expressions. Regular expressions are used with programs, such as grep, to match text data with patterns. Bracket regular expressions are characters enclosed in square brackets ([]). The brackets represent a single character and that character may match any *one* character within the brackets. A variation of bracket expressions is the range expression, where you designate a range of potential character matches by using the first and last possible character with a dash between them, such as [a-z]. When you need to match a single character but that character can be anything, use a question mark (?) instead of a bracket expression. If the pattern you are searching for is at the beginning of a text line, put a caret (^) symbol before the pattern. If it is at the end of the line, tack a dollar sign ($) onto the pattern's end. To specify a pattern that can match with any substring, use the dot asterisk (.*).

Summarize the commands used to search for and extract data.   Use the grep command to search for a specified string or regular expression pattern within a file or a directory of files. To locate files in a specified directory tree by their name, size, owner, creation date, or other data, use the find utility. If you want to display a file, the cat command can help, and it will also display multiple files one after the other (concatenated) to your screen. To see only the first 10 lines of a file, use head, and for the last 10 lines, use the tail command. If you want to display a text file sorted, use the sort utility. To extract out only portions of text file records, use the cut command. If you'd like some statistical information about a text file, such as the number of lines, words, and bytes contained within it, then the wc tool is the one to use.

Explain how to redirect standard input and output.   Standard output is where normal program messages are sent, whereas error messages are sent to standard error (and it is represented by the number 2). To send a command's standard output to a file and over-write the file's current contents, use the > operator. Use >> to append the output to the file's existing data instead. For standard error, use the 2> operator to send a command's standard error to a file and overwrite the file's current contents and the 2>> operator to append the error messages instead. To send a program's output as input to another program, use the pipe, which is a vertical bar (|), between the commands.

Detail archiving data with tar and zip.   The tar utility archives various files into a single file, called an archive file, which is sometimes compressed at the same time resulting in a tarball. Multiple options exist for use with tar, including long options, short options, and even the single-letter old-style options. The utility preserves Linux's ownership and permission information, and it uses special options to unpack (and, if needed, to reverse the compression) archive files. Also available to create tarball-like archives is the zip utility. Unlike with the tar program, you do *not* need to add special options to automatically compress the resulting archive file. However, you will need to use the unzip program to reverse the compression and unpack it.

Outline the compression utilities on Linux.   The gzip, bzip2, and xz utilities can be used with tar or by themselves to compress files, The oldest is gzip, and the one that provides the most compression is xz. To reverse their compression, use their corresponding "un" tools—gunzip, bunzip2, and unxz.

Review Questions

You can find the answers in Appendix A.

1. Which of the following commands will print lines from the file world.txt that contain matches to changes and changed?

   A. grep change[ds] world.txt

   B. tar change[d-s] world.txt

   C. find "change'd|s'" world.txt

   D. cat world.txt changes changed

   E. find change[^ds] world.txt

2. Which of the following redirection operators appends a program's standard output to an existing file without overwriting that file's original contents?

   A. |

   B. 2>

   C. &>.

   D. >

   E. >>

3. You've received a tar archive called data79.tar from a colleague, but you want to check the names of the files it contains before extracting them. Which of the following commands would you use to do this?

   A. tar uvf data79.tar

   B. tar cvf data79.tar

   C. tar xvf data79.tar

   D. tar tvf data79.tar

   E. tar Avf data79.tar

4. True or false: The regular expression Linu[^x].*lds matches the string Linus Torvalds.

5. True or false: The find command enables you to locate files based on their sizes.

6. True or false: To compress files archived with zip, you must use an external compression program such as gzip or bzip2 in a pipeline with zip.

7. The character that represents the start of a line in a regular expression is _____.

   A. ^

   B. $

   C. |

   D. (

   E. "

8. The _____ command can extract specified data fields from a file's records.

    A. grep

    B. cut

    C. sort

    D. find

    E. cat

9. Complete the following command to redirect both standard output and standard error from the `bigprog` program to the file `out.txt`.

    $ **bigprog** ____ **out.txt**

    A. |

    B. 2>

    C. &>

    D. >

    E. >>

10. The gzip, bzip2, and xz programs all perform _____ compression, in which the compressed data will exactly match the original data, when uncompressed.

    A. zip

    B. tar

    C. high

    D. lossy

    E. lossless

Chapter

9

Exploring Processes and Process Data

OBJECTIVES:

✓ 1.2 Major Open Source Applications

✓ 4.3 Where Data Is Stored

Computers are dynamic and multipurpose machines; they do a variety of jobs using many tools. This chapter describes the ways you can manage these tools. One aspect of software management is installing, uninstalling, and upgrading software packages. Another aspect of this task is in managing programs after they're running. Finally, this chapter covers log files, which record details of what running programs do—particularly programs that run automatically and in the background.

Understanding Package Management

Package management is an area of Linux that varies a lot from one distribution to another. Nonetheless, certain principles are common across most Linux distributions. This section describes these principles, followed by some of the basics of the two major Linux package management systems. It then describes how to manage packages using both the RPM Package Manager (RPM; a recursive acronym) and Debian package systems.

Linux Package Management Principles

Certification
Objective

If you've installed software in Windows, you're likely familiar with the procedure of double-clicking on an installer program, which places all the files associated with a program where they should go. A Windows software installer is similar to a Linux package file, but there are a few differences. Linux packages have the following characteristics:

- Each package is a single file that can be stored on a disk or transmitted over the Internet.

- Linux package files, unlike Windows installers, are not programs; packages rely on other programs to do the work of installing the software.

- Packages contain *dependency* information—that is, they can tell the packaging software what other packages or individual files must be installed in order for the package to work correctly.

Many program packages depend on *library* packages; libraries provide code that can be used by many programs.

- Packages contain version information so that the packaging software can tell which of two packages is more recent.

- Packages contain architecture information to identify the CPU type (x86, x86-64, ARM, and so on) for which they're intended. A separate code identifies packages that are architecture-independent, such as fonts and desktop themes.

- *Binary* packages (that is, those that contain executable programs that are CPU-specific) are typically built from *source* packages (which contain source code that a programmer can understand). It's possible to build a new binary package, given the source package, which can be useful in some unusual circumstances.

 You can compile and install software from source code manually, without using a packaging tool. This advanced topic is beyond the scope of this book.

Certification
Objective

The package software maintains a database of information about installed packages (the *package database*). This information includes the names and version numbers of all the installed packages, as well as the locations of all the files installed from each package. This information enables the package software to quickly uninstall software, establish whether a new package's dependencies have been met, and determine whether a package you're trying to install has already been installed and, if so, whether the installed version is older than the one you're trying to install.

 Packages can, and frequently do, contain files that will be installed to many directories on the computer. This fact makes tracking package contents critical.

Understanding Package Systems

As noted earlier, two package systems, RPM and Debian, are common, although others exist as well. These systems differ in various technical details, as well as in the commands used to manage packages and in the format of the package files they use. You cannot install a Debian package on an RPM-based system, or vice versa. Indeed, installing a package intended for one distribution on another is a bit risky even when they use the same package type. This is because a non-native package may have dependencies that conflict with the needs of native packages.

 Table 1.1 in Chapter 1, "Selecting an Operating System," summarizes some features of several popular Linux distributions, including the package system each uses.

Originally, package systems worked locally—that is, to install a package on your computer you would first have to download a package file from the Internet or in some other way. Only then could you use a local command to install the package. This approach, however, can be tedious when a package has many dependencies—you might attempt an installation, find unmet dependencies, download several more packages, find that one or more of them has unmet dependencies, and so on. By the time you've tracked down all these depended-upon packages, you might need to install a dozen or more packages. Thus, modern distributions provide network-enabled tools to help automate the process. These tools rely on network software *repositories*, from which the tools can download packages automatically. The network-enabled tools vary from one distribution to another, particularly among RPM-based distributions.

In practice, then, the process of managing software in Linux involves using text-mode or GUI tools to interface with a software repository. A typical software installation task works something like this:

1. You issue a command to install a program.
2. The software locates dependencies of the specified program and notifies you of any additional software that must be installed.
3. You issue a final approval for software installation (or decide against it, in which case the process stops).
4. The software downloads all the necessary packages.

> You can configure most distributions to use local media instead of or in addition to Internet repositories.

5. The software installs all the packages.

Upgrading software works in a similar way, although upgrades are less likely to require downloading depended-upon packages. Removing software can be done entirely locally, of course. Many distributions automatically check with their repositories from time to time and notify you when updates are available. Thus, you can keep your system up-to-date by clicking a few buttons when you're prompted to do so. As an example, Figure 9.1 shows the Software Update utility in Linux Mint 18.3, which shows a list of available updates.

> Immediately after installing a distribution, you may find that a large number of updates are available.

Package management necessarily involves root access, which is described in more detail in Chapter 13, "Creating Users and Groups." If you follow the automatic prompts to update your software, you can keep the system up-to-date by entering the root password, or on some distributions your regular password, when the update software prompts for it.

FIGURE 9.1   Most Linux distributions tell you when updates are available for your software.

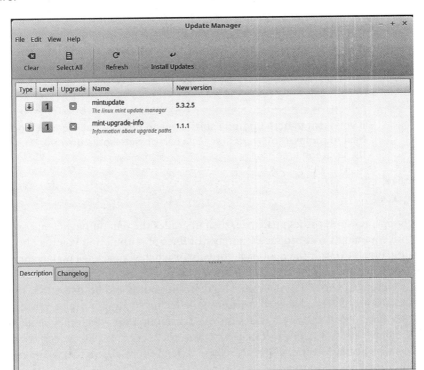

Managing Red Hat Systems

RPM-based distributions include Red Hat, Fedora, CentOS, SUSE Enterprise, openSUSE, and Mandriva. The basic tool for installing software on these distributions is the text-mode rpm command. This program works on local files, though; to use a network repository, you must use another tool, which varies by distribution:

- Red Hat, Fedora, and CentOS use the text-mode yum or dnf, or various GUI front ends to them, such as PackageKit and Yumex.

- SUSE Enterprise and openSUSE use zypper or a GUI front end such as YaST 2.

Because of the variability between these distributions, particularly for network-enabled updates, providing a complete description of all these tools is impractical here. Fortunately, the GUI tools are easy to use and accessible. Even the text-mode tools are fairly straightforward, although you may need to consult their man pages to learn the details. Typically, they use logical subcommands, such as install to install a package, as in:

```
# dnf install yumex
```

You might use this command to install the GUI Yumex tool on a Red Hat, Fedora, or CentOS system. Similarly, you can remove a specific package by using the remove subcommand or upgrade all of a computer's packages by using upgrade:

> If you want to both upgrade software and remove packages, it's generally best to remove software first. This can obviate some downloads, reducing the upgrade time.

```
# dnf remove zsh
# dnf upgrade
```

This example removes the zsh package, then upgrades the remaining packages on the system. Both commands will produce a number of lines of output, and you may be asked to verify their actions. Consult the man page for yum (or whatever package management software your distribution uses) to learn more about this tool.

If you need to deal with RPM package files directly, you should be aware that they have filename extensions of .rpm. These files also usually include codes for architecture type (such as i386 or x86_64), and often codes for the distribution for which they're intended (such as fc30 for Fedora 30). For instance, samba-4.10.2-0.fc30.x86_64.rpm is a package file for the samba package, version 4.10.2, release 0, for Fedora 30, on the x86-64 platform. To install it using the rpm command, you'd type.

```
# rpm -Uvh samba-4.10.2-0.fc30.x86_64.rpm
```

That takes a bit more work than using the yum command, as you need to know the complete filename of the installation package.

Managing Debian Systems

The Debian GNU/Linux distribution created its own package system, and distributions based on Debian, such as Ubuntu and Mint, use the same system. Atop the basic Debian package system lies the Advanced Package Tool (APT), which provides access to network repositories.

> Third-party implementations of APT for many RPM-based distributions also exist. See apt4rpm.sourceforge.net for details. At least one RPM-based distribution, PCLinuxOS, uses APT natively.

The dpkg command is the lowest-level interface to the Debian package system; it's roughly equivalent to the rpm utility on RPM-based systems. Just as with the rpm utility, to use the dpkg command you need to know the exact name of the package to install:

```
# dpkg -i samba_4.9.5+dfsg-5+deb10u1_amd64.deb
```

Several tools provide text-mode and graphical interfaces atop dpkg, the most important of these being the text-mode apt-get or the newer apt tool and the GUI Synaptic. As their names imply, apt-get and Synaptic provide access to network repositories via APT. Figure 9.2 shows Synaptic in use.

FIGURE 9.2   Synaptic enables you to search for, select, install, and uninstall software on Debian-based systems.

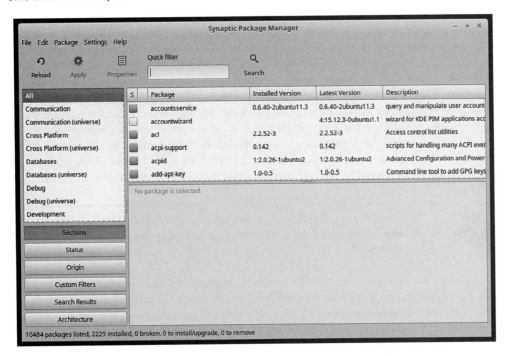

Debian package files have names that end in .deb. Like RPM packages, these names typically include codes for the software version and architecture (such as i386 or amd64). For instance, samba_3.6.1-3_amd64.deb is a Debian package file for the samba package, version 3.6.1, revision 3, for AMD64 (x86-64) CPUs. You can install such files using dpkg or apt-get, or you can use apt-get to download a package and its dependencies from the Internet, using its install command, as in:

```
# apt install samba
```

As with RPM packages, you can remove packages or upgrade your computer's software, too:

```
# apt remove zsh
# apt upgrade
```

APT is a powerful tool, as is the underlying dpkg. You should consult these programs' man pages to learn more about how to use these programs.

Understanding the Process Hierarchy

The Linux *kernel* is the core of a Linux installation. The kernel manages memory, provides software with a way to access the hard disk, doles out CPU time, and performs other critical low-level tasks. The kernel is loaded early in the boot process, and it's the kernel that's responsible for managing every other piece of software on a running Linux computer.

One way the kernel imposes order on the potentially chaotic set of running software is to create a sort of hierarchy. When it boots, the kernel runs just one program—usually either /lib/systemd or /sbin/init. These processes are then responsible for starting all the other basic programs that Linux must run, such as the programs that manage logins and always-up servers. Such programs, if launched directly by systemd or init, are called its *children*. The children processes can in turn launch their own children. This happens when you log into Linux. The process that launched a given process is called its *parent*.

You can change which program runs as the first process by adding the init= option to your boot loader's kernel option line, as in init=/bin/bash to run bash.

Certification
Objective

The result of this system is a treelike hierarchy of processes, as illustrated in Figure 9.3. ("Trees" in computer science are often depicted upside down.) Figure 9.3 shows a small subset of the many processes that run on a typical Linux installation: just a few processes associated with a text-mode login, including the login tool that manages logins, a couple of bash shells, and a few user programs. A working Linux system will likely have dozens or hundreds of running processes. The one on which I'm typing these words has 213 processes going at once!

Occasionally, a process will terminate but leave behind children. When this happens, init "adopts" those child processes.

Every process has a process ID (PID) number associated with it. These numbers begin with 1, so init's PID is normally 1. Each process also has a parent process ID (PPID) number, which points to its parent. Many of the tools for managing processes rely on these numbers, and particularly on the PID number.

FIGURE 9.3   Linux processes are arranged in a hierarchical tree.

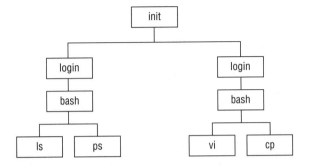

Internally, the kernel maintains process information in the *process table*. Tools such as ps and top (described shortly) enable you to view and manipulate this table.

Identifying Running Processes

Before you can manage processes, you must be able to identify them. The ps and top utilities can help you identify processes. In either case, you can search for processes in various ways, such as by name or by resource use. You may also want to identify how much memory your processes are consuming, which you can do with the free command.

Using *ps* to Identify Processes

The simplest tool for identifying processes is ps, which produces a process listing. Listing 9.1 shows an example of ps in action. In this example, the -u option restricts output to processes owned by the specified user (rich), whereas --forest creates a display that shows parent/child relationships.

Certification
Objective

Listing 9.1: Output of ps -u rich --forest

```
$ ps -u rich --forest
  PID TTY          TIME CMD
 2451 pts/3     00:00:00 bash
 2551 pts/3     00:00:00 ps
```

LISTING 9.1: Output of ps -u rich --forest *(continued)*

```
2496 ?          00:00:00 kvt
2498 pts/1      00:00:00 bash
2505 pts/1      00:00:00  \_ nedit
2506 ?          00:00:00        \_ csh
2544 ?          00:00:00              \_ xeyes
19221 ?         00:00:01 dfm
```

Listing 9.2 shows a second example of ps. In this example, the u option adds informational columns, whereas U rich restricts output to processes owned by rich. The ps command supports a huge number of options (consult its man page for details).

 The version of ps used in most Linux distributions combines features from several earlier ps implementations. The result is a huge selection of sometimes redundant options.

Listing 9.2: Output of ps u U rich

```
$ ps u U rich
USER      PID %CPU %MEM   VSZ  RSS TTY    STAT START  TIME COMMAND
rich 19221  0.0  1.5  4484 1984 ?      S    Sep07  0:01 dfm
rich  2451  0.0  0.8  1856 1048 pts/3  S    16:13  0:00 -bash
rich  2496  0.2  3.2  6232 4124 ?      S    16:17  0:00 /opt/kd
rich  2498  0.0  0.8  1860 1044 pts/1  S    16:17  0:00 bash
rich  2505  0.1  2.6  4784 3332 pts/1  S    16:17  0:00 nedit
rich  2506  0.0  0.7  2124 1012 ?      S    16:17  0:00 /bin/cs
rich  2544  0.0  1.0  2576 1360 ?      S    16:17  0:00 xeyes
rich  2556  0.0  0.7  2588  916 pts/3  R    16:18  0:00 ps u U
```

Given the large number of ps options, different users can have favorite ways to use the program. One popular combination of options is ax, which produces the information most system administrators want, including PID values and command names (including command-line options) for all the processes on the computer. Adding u (as in ps aux) adds usernames, CPU loads, and a few other tidbits. The sheer scope of the information produced, however, can be overwhelming. One way to narrow this scope is to pipe the results through grep, which eliminates lines that don't include the search criterion you specify. For instance, if you want to know the PID number for the gedit process, you can do so like this:

```
$ ps ax | grep gedit
27946 pts/8    Sl      0:00 gedit
27950 pts/8    S+      0:00 grep --colour=auto gedit
```

> **TIP** Because ps ax produces commands with their options, using grep to search for a string in the output returns the searched-for command, as well as the grep command itself.

This command reveals that gedit has a PID value of 27946. This is usually the most important information when you use ps, since you'll use the PID value to change a process's priority or terminate it.

Using *top* to Identify Processes

Certification
Objective

Although ps can return process priority and CPU use information, the program's output is usually sorted by PID number and provides information at only a single moment in time. If you want to quickly locate CPU- or memory-hogging processes, or if you want to study how resource use varies over time, another tool is more appropriate: top. This program is essentially an interactive version of ps. Figure 9.4 shows top running in a GNOME Terminal window.

FIGURE 9.4   The top command shows system summary information and information about the most CPU-intensive processes on a computer.

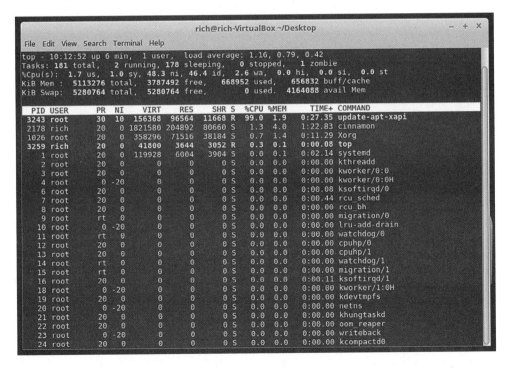

By default, top sorts its entries by CPU use, and it updates its display every few seconds. You'll need to be familiar with the purposes and normal habits of programs running on *your* system to determine if a CPU-hungry application is misbehaving. In the example shown in Figure 9.4, an APT update process is taking up almost all of the CPU time. To determine that, note the %CPU column entry, then scan to the far-right COMMAND column to note the process that's using the CPU time. Although this is a useful tool, be careful not to jump to conclusions too quickly. In this example, yes, the APT update process is taking up lots of CPU time at that moment, but that's a short burst of activity and drops when the update completes. The legitimate needs of different programs vary so much that it's impossible to give a simple rule for judging when a process is consuming too much CPU time.

You can do more with top than watch it update its display. When it's running, you can enter any of several single-letter commands, some of which prompt you for additional information, as summarized in Table 9.1. Additional commands are described in top's man page.

TABLE 9.1 Common top commands

Command	Description
h or ?	Display help information.
k	Kill a process. The top program will ask for a PID number, and if it's able to kill the process, it will do so.
q	Quit from top.
r	Change a process's priority.
s	Changes the display's update rate, which you then enter in seconds.
P	Set the display to sort by CPU usage, which is the default.
M	Change the display to sort by memory usage.

One piece of information provided by top is the *load average,* which is a measure of the demand for CPU time by applications. In Figure 9.4, you can see three load-average estimates on the top line; these correspond to the current load average and two previous measures. Load averages can be interpreted as follows:

- A system on which no programs are demanding CPU time has a load average of 0.
- A system with one program running a CPU-intensive task has a load average of 1.
- Higher load averages on a single-CPU system reflect programs competing for available CPU time.

- On a computer with multiple CPUs or CPU cores, load averages can reach the number of CPUs or cores before competition for CPU time begins. For instance, a load average of 4.0 on a system with a four-core CPU reflects processes demanding exactly as much CPU time as the computer has available.

> Most computers sold today are multicore models, but if you're running Linux on an older system, single-core models dominated the marketplace prior to about 2006. Use the `lscpu` command to see how many CPUs your system contains.

The load average can be useful in detecting runaway processes. For instance, if a system normally has a load average of 0.5 but it suddenly gets stuck at a load average of 2.5, a few CPU-hogging processes may have *hung*—that is, become unresponsive. Hung processes sometimes needlessly consume a lot of CPU time. You can use top to locate these processes and, if necessary, stop them.

> The w command, described in Chapter 13, can tell you how much CPU time entire terminal sessions are consuming.

Measuring Memory Use

Processes consume a number of system resources, the most important of these being CPU time and memory. As already noted, top sorts your processes by CPU time by default, so you can identify processes that are consuming the most CPU time. You can press the M key within top to have it sort by memory use, thus identifying the processes that are consuming the most memory. As with CPU time, you can't say that a process is consuming too much memory simply because it's at the top of the list, though; some programs legitimately consume a great deal of memory. Nonetheless, sometimes a program consumes too much memory, either because of inefficient coding or because of a *memory leak*—a type of program bug in which the program requests memory from the kernel and then fails to return it when it's done with the memory. A program with a memory leak consumes increasing amounts of memory, sometimes to the point where it interferes with other programs. As a short-term solution, you can usually terminate the program and launch it again, which resets the program's memory consumption, something like draining a sink that's filled with water from a leaky faucet. The problem will recur, but if the memory leak is small enough, you'll at least be able to get useful work done in the meantime.

Certification
Objective

> The kernel grants programs access to sets of memory addresses, which the programs can then use. When a program is done, it should release its memory back to the kernel.

If you want to study the computer's overall memory use, the free command is useful. This program generates a report on the computer's total memory status:

```
$ free
                total      used      free    shared   buffers    cached
Mem:          7914888   7734456    180432         0    190656   3244720
-/+ buffers/cache:      4299080   3615808
Swap:         6291452   1030736   5260716
```

The Mem: line reveals total random access memory (RAM) statistics, including the total memory in the computer (minus whatever is used by the motherboard and kernel), the amount of memory used, and the amount of free memory. This example shows that most of the computer's memory is in use. Such a state is normal, since Linux puts otherwise unused memory to use as buffers and caches, which help speed up disk access. Thus, the Mem: line isn't the most useful; instead, you should examine the -/+ buffers/cache: line, which shows the total memory used by the computer's programs. In this example, 4,299,080 KiB of 7,914,888 KiB are in use, leaving 3,615,808 KiB free. In other words, a bit over half the computer's memory is in use by programs, so there should be no memory-related performance problems.

The Swap: line reveals how much *swap space* Linux is using. Swap space is disk space that's set aside as an adjunct to memory. Linux uses swap space when it runs out of RAM, or when it determines that RAM is better used for buffers or caches than to hold currently inactive programs. In this example, 1,030,736 KiB of swap space is in use, with 6,291,452 KiB total, for 5,260,716 free. Swap space use is generally quite low, and if it rises very much, you can suffer performance problems. In the long run, increasing the computer's RAM is generally the best solution to such problems. If you're suffering from performance problems because of excessive swap use and you need immediate relief, terminating some memory-hogging programs can help. Memory leaks, described earlier, can lead to such problems, and terminating the leaking program can restore system performance to normal.

The free command supports a number of options, most of which modify its display format. The most useful of these is -m, which causes the display to use units of mebibytes (MiB) rather than the default of kibibytes (KiB).

Using Log Files

Many programs that run in the background (that is, daemons) write information about their normal operations to *log files*, which are files that record such notes. Consulting log files can therefore be an important part of diagnosing problems with daemons. The first step in doing this is to locate your log files. In some cases, you may need to tell the program to produce more verbose output to help track down the problem, so this section provides some pointers on how to do that. This section also describes the kernel ring buffer, which isn't technically a log file but can fill a similar role for kernel information.

Locating Log Files

Linux stores most log files in the /var/log directory tree. Some log files reside in that directory, but some servers create entire subdirectories in which to store their own log files. Table 9.2 summarizes some common log files on many Linux systems. In addition, many server programs not described in this book add their own log files or subdirectories of /var/log. If you experience problems with such a server, checking its log files can be a good place to start troubleshooting.

Certification
Objective

Log file details vary between distributions, so some of the files in Table 9.2 may not be present on your system, or the files you find may have different names.

TABLE 9.2   Important log files

Log file	Contents
boot.log	Services that are started late in the boot process via SysV startup scripts
cron	Processes run at regular intervals via the cron daemon. Although this book doesn't cover cron, a problem with it can cause glitches that recur at regular intervals, so you should be aware of it.
cups/	Directory holding log files related to the Linux printing system
gdm/	Directory holding log files related to the GNOME Display Manager (GDM), which handles GUI logins on many systems
messages or syslog	A general-purpose log file that contains messages from many daemons that lack their own dedicated log files
secure	Security-related messages, including notices of when users employ su, sudo, and similar tools to acquire root privileges
Xorg.0.log	Information on the most recent startup of the X Window System (X)

Log files are frequently *rotated*, meaning that the oldest log file is deleted, the latest log file is renamed with a date or number, and a new log file is created. For instance, if it's rotated on December 1, 2019, /var/log/messages will become /var/log/messages-20191201, /var/log/messages-1.gz, or something similar, and a new /var/log/messages will be created. This practice keeps log files from growing out of control.

Log file rotation occurs late at night, so it won't happen if you shut off your computer. Leave it running overnight periodically to ensure log files are rotated.

Most log files are plain-text files, so you can check them using any tool that can examine text files, such as less or a text editor. One particularly handy command is tail, which displays the last 10 lines of a file (or as many lines as you specify with the -n option). For instance, typing **tail /var/log/messages** shows you the last 10 lines of that file.

Note that not all programs log messages. Typically, only daemons do so; ordinary user programs display error messages in other ways—in GUI dialog boxes or in a text-mode terminal. If you think a program should be logging data but you can't find it, consult its documentation. Alternatively, you can use grep to try to find the log file to which the program is sending its messages. For instance, typing **grep sshd /var/log/*** finds the files in which the string sshd (the SSH daemon's name) appears.

Certification Objective

🌐 Real World Scenario

Creating Log Files

Some programs create their own log files; however, most rely on a utility known generically as the *system log daemon* to do this job. This program's process name is generally journald, syslog, or syslogd. Like other daemons, it's started during the boot process by the system startup scripts. Several system log daemon packages are available. Some of them provide a separate tool, klog or klogd, to handle logging messages from the kernel separately from ordinary programs.

You can modify the behavior of the log daemon, including adjusting the files to which it logs particular types of messages, by adjusting its configuration file. The name of this file depends on the specific daemon in use, but it's typically /etc/rsyslog.conf or something similar. The details of log file configuration are beyond the scope of this book, but you should be aware that such details can be altered. This fact accounts for much of the distribution-to-distribution variability in log file features.

After it's running, a log daemon accepts messages from other processes using a technique known as *system messaging*. It then sorts through the messages and directs them to a suitable log file depending on the message's source and a priority code.

Producing More Verbose Log File Entries

Sometimes log files don't provide enough information to pin down the source of a problem. Fortunately, many programs that produce log file output can be configured to produce more such output. Unfortunately, doing so can sometimes make it harder to sift through all the entries for the relevant information.

The procedure for increasing the verbosity of log file output varies from one program to another. Typically, you must set an option in the program's configuration file. You should consult the program's documentation to learn how to do this.

Examining the Kernel Ring Buffer

The kernel ring buffer is something like a log file for the kernel; however, unlike other log files, it's stored in memory rather than in a disk file. Like regular log files, its contents continue to change as the computer runs. To examine the kernel ring buffer, you can type **dmesg**. Doing so creates copious output, though, so you'll typically pipe the output through less:

Certification Objective

 Because the kernel ring buffer has a limited size, its earliest entries can be lost if the computer runs for a long time or if something produces many entries.

```
$ dmesg | less
```

Alternatively, if you know that the information you want will be associated with a particular string, you can use grep to search for it. For instance, to find kernel ring buffer messages about the first hard disk, /dev/sda, you might type the following:

```
$ dmesg | grep sda
```

Kernel ring buffer messages can be particularly arcane; however, they can also be invaluable in diagnosing hardware and driver problems, since it's the kernel's job to interface with hardware. You might try searching the kernel ring buffer if a hardware device is behaving strangely. Even if you don't understand a message you find, you could try feeding that message into a web search engine or passing it on to a more knowledgeable colleague for advice.

Some distributions place a copy of the kernel ring buffer when the system first boots in /var/log/dmesg or a similar file. You can consult this file if the computer has been running for long enough for its earliest entries to be lost. If you want to create such a file on a distribution that doesn't do so by default, you can edit the /etc/rc.d/rc.local file and add the following line to its end:

```
dmesg > /var/log/dmesg
```

Summary

An operating Linux computer can be thought of as consisting of running programs—that is, processes. Managing processes begins with managing the programs installed on the computer, which is a task you can perform with package management tools such as rpm or dpkg. You can learn what processes are running by using tools such as ps and top. Log files can help you learn about the actions of daemons, which may not be able to communicate error messages through the type of text-mode or GUI output that other programs can generate.

Exam Essentials

Explain how package management makes installing software easy.   Package management bundles all the files required for an application into a single installation process. When you install an application using a package management system, it places the files in the correct location automatically and tracks the version of each file required for the application. If a newer version of the application is available, the package management software can inform you and make updating the application files a simple one-step process.

Describe how you can view the programs running on your Linux system.   Programs running on the Linux system are called processes. You can view currently running processes using either the ps or top commands. The ps command provides a snapshot view of what processes are running when you run the command. It has lots of options that allow you to customize what information it displays. The top command produces a real-time chart of running processes, allowing you to sort the chart data based on different criteria, such as CPU usage, memory usage, or program name.

Describe how you can see error messages generated by the kernel.   Linux stores messages generated by the kernel in the kernel ring buffer, a circular buffer area reserved in memory. As new messages enter the buffer area, old messages are deleted to make room. You use the dmesg command to view the messages currently stored in the kernel ring buffer, but any old messages are lost and can't be retrieved.

Review Questions

You can find the answers in Appendix A.

1. Which of the following tools is best suited to installing a software package and all its dependencies on a Debian computer?

   A. yum

   B. zypper

   C. dmesg

   D. rpm

   E. apt-get

2. What are the two most popular utilities used as the first process that the Linux kernel runs, aside from itself? (Choose two.)

   A. init

   B. bash

   C. systemd

   D. login

   E. grub

3. Where do most log files reside on a Linux computer?

   A. /var/log

   B. /etc/logging

   C. /usr/log

   D. /home/logging

   E. /log/usr

4. True or false: When using suitable commands, you can normally install a program and be sure that all the software on which it depends will also be installed, provided you have an Internet connection.

5. True or false: By default, the first process listed in top is currently consuming the most CPU time.

6. True or false: The dmesg command may produce different output after a computer has been running for weeks than when it first started.

7. Most Linux distributions maintain information on what packages are installed in the _____.

   A. kernel

   B. package database

   C. graphical desktop

   D. /usr/lib directory

   E. Software updater

8. You're using Bash, and you type **emacs** to launch the emacs editor. In this case, emacs is Bash's _____ process.

A. child

B. parent

C. server

D. client

E. parallel

9. General system messages are likely to be found in /var/log/messages or /var/log/_____, depending on your distribution.

A. secure

B. dmesg

C. syslog

D. mail

E. wtmp

10. The command you use to read messages generated during the boot process and stored in the kernel ring buffer is the _____ command.

A. ls

B. pwd

C. chmod

D. cat

E. dmesg

Chapter

10

Editing Files

OBJECTIVES:

✓ 3.3   **Turning Commands into a Script**

Computer documents come in many forms, but one of the most basic and flexible is a text file. Typically, configuration files and shell scripts are text files. Because you will often be modifying configuration files and creating shell scripts, you must be able to edit text files. This chapter covers this task with an emphasis on the simple text-mode nano and vi editors. A few roles played by text files are described first; then how to select a text editor is explained. To edit text files, of course, you must be able to start the editor, either on an existing document or to create a new one. The nano editor is fairly simple, so its operation is described first, followed by vi, which is a more unusual editor, by modern standards.

Understanding the Role of Text Files

A text editor lets you edit documents that are stored in plain-text format. The American Standard Code for Information Interchange (ASCII) used to be the common form, but now files typically use Unicode formats to support additional characters.

Text files encode the ends of lines by using one or two special ASCII characters. End-of-line encoding differs between Unix (or Linux) and Windows, but most programs can handle either method.

These formats store text documents that, by themselves, include no special formatting or embedded features. Text files cannot include graphics, use multiple fonts, emphasize words by italicizing them, or use other features that you probably associate with word processors (although markup tools provide a partial exception to this rule).

 Real World Scenario

ASCII and Unicode

ASCII dates to the 1960s. It's a 7-bit code, meaning that it supports a maximum of 2^7, or 128, characters. (In practice, ASCII uses 8 bits, so an extra 128 characters are available. These bits encode various control characters or are used in ASCII extensions.) ASCII was created to encode the letters used in English, digits, and symbols. This original intent, combined with ASCII's limited character count, makes it rather unhelpful for many non-English languages. ASCII just doesn't have enough characters to handle all the requirements of non-English languages.

Over the years, extensions to, and variants of, ASCII have been used to support additional characters and alphabets that ASCII doesn't support. One way to do this is to use a code page to specify an alphabet. Each code page specifies a variant of ASCII that's suitable for a particular alphabet. For instance, code page 866 encodes Cyrillic (the alphabet used by Russian and most other Slavic languages). The problem with code pages is that you can generally use only one at a time.

Unicode is a more modern approach. It provides a much larger character set, allowing the encoding of any alphabet in common use on Earth, including the huge logographic writing systems used in languages such as Chinese and Japanese. The problem is that Unicode requires many more bits, and several ways to encode it efficiently exist. Fortunately, these Unicode Transformation Format (UTF) schemes are limited in number compared to code pages. Some, such as UTF-8, map the first characters in the same way as ASCII, so an ASCII file is also a valid UTF-8 file. Many text editors today handle UTF-8 (or other Unicode formats) automatically, so you can use a text editor to write text files in any language that you like. You may still need to set localization options to tell Linux what sort of keyboard you use and what code page to use by default for programs that still rely on code pages.

If your text file is encoded in ASCII, it's encoded in Unicode too. ASCII encoding is considered a subset of Unicode.

Text files consist of lines that can vary in length from 0 characters to the file's entire size and that can hold any number of data types. You might want to create or edit some of these as an ordinary user; others are important for administering a Linux system. The main file types include the following:

- Human language files
- Programming language files
- Formatted text files
- Program and system configuration files
- Program log files

Formatted text files encode special formatting using unique character sequences. Although you can edit such files with a text editor, specialized editors also exist for many of these file types.

Some files contain elements of multiple categories. Email, for instance, can be stored in text files. An email file consists largely of human language, but email messages include headers, which describe the origin and destination computers, along with information on how the message traveled from one site to the other, which is similar to formatted text or log file data.

Choosing an Editor

All Linux distributions ship with many text editors. Broadly speaking, text editors fall into one of two categories: text-mode and GUI. Beginners are generally more comfortable with GUI editors, which can be more convenient to use even for experts. But when a GUI is not available, you may have to use a text-mode editor. You should therefore familiarize yourself with at least one text-mode editor.

Some popular text-mode editors include the following:

Certification Objective

vi The vi editor is a Unix staple. It's small and usually installed by default, so you can be fairly certain that it's present on any Linux computer. It is, however, strange by modern standards—it uses multiple *editing modes*, and you must switch between them to accomplish various tasks. Many longtime Unix and Linux administrators like vi for its flexibility, power, and small size.

Most Linux distributions use a version of vi called "vi improved," or vim; you can typically still launch it by typing **vi**.

emacs The emacs editor is another Unix staple. It's a big editor with lots of features, so it's less likely to be installed by default, particularly on small, lightweight distributions. Its operating model is more like those of the text editors familiar to novices, but its commands can seem rather odd.

Bash's text-editing commands are modeled on those of emacs, so learning emacs can improve your ability to work in the Bash shell.

nano Several small editors are modeled after emacs, but they omit many of its advanced features in an effort to simplify the editor. One of these editors is nano, which is small, lightweight, and easy to use.

The nano editor is probably the best place to start, because of its ease of use. If nano is not already installed, it's typically available in most distribution's software repositories. (If you don't find nano installed on your distribution, see Chapter 9, "Exploring Processes and Process Data," for help installing the nano package.) Figure 10.1 shows nano in operation within a text-mode login session, editing a file called pets.txt.

FIGURE 10.1   The nano editor enables you to edit a text file in text mode.

As with text-mode editors, several GUI editors are available, including the following:

emacs   The emacs editor is both a text-mode editor and a GUI editor. The GUI features of emacs, however, are sometimes a bit odd; for instance, the scroll bar to move through the file appears on the left side of the window rather than on the more common right side.

gedit   The GNOME desktop environment has an associated text editor known as gedit. It's a fairly typical text editor, and it's often installed by default.

KWrite and Kate   Just as gedit is associated with GNOME, KWrite and Kate are editors that are associated with the K Desktop Environment (KDE). KWrite is slightly more sophisticated than gedit, and Kate adds some more features, but neither is nearly as powerful as emacs.

Geany   The Geany editor is not tied to any particular desktop environment, and it's small, lightweight, and rather powerful. It also runs under other OSs besides Linux, such as Windows, which is handy if you want to use one editor for multiple platforms.

For a new Linux user, any of these is a good starting GUI editor; all offer the basic features that you need for light text-file editing. Your choice may depend on which is installed by default on your system. In the long term, you should probably try a variety of editors to find the one that you like best.

Editing Files with *nano*

If you're familiar with text-mode text editors, you should have few problems learning nano. If you've used only GUI editors to edit text, you'll have to learn a few keyboard conventions. You must move about the document by using the keyboard rather than the mouse, for instance. You can insert, replace, and delete text much as you do in a GUI text editor or word processor.

If nano is not installed on your system, you can use the information from Chapter 9 to install the nano package.

You can launch the nano text editor from the command line. You can do this as a normal user, using your default privileges to edit text files you own. To edit system files, you'll need to use super user privileges. Chapter 12, "Understanding Basic Security," describes how to obtain super user privileges needed to edit system text files. This example launches nano:

$ **nano**

When it opens, you'll see a display similar to the one shown in Figure 10.1, but the bulk of the window or text-mode console will be empty, since you didn't specify a filename. Instead, as shown in Figure 10.2, the center of the top line will read New Buffer. You can begin typing in the desired text. When you save the file, as described later in "Saving Your Changes from nano," nano will ask for a filename.

FIGURE 10.2 The nano editor launched with no filename provided.

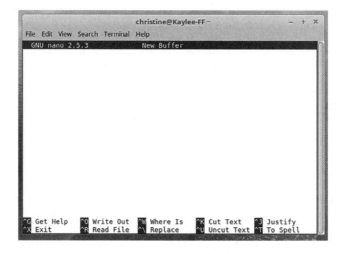

Alternatively, you can provide a filename when you launch the text editor as follows:

$ **nano great_american_novel.txt**

This example opens the great_american_novel.txt file and displays it. If the file doesn't exist, nano displays New File near the bottom of the display, where Read 4 lines appears in Figure 10.1. If you see Warning: no write permission in the third line from the bottom, you've loaded a file that you have no permission to change. You'll need to run nano using super user privileges or modify file permissions, as described in Chapter 14, "Setting Ownership and Permissions," if you want to save the file's modified contents.

If you mistype the filename of a preexisting file, nano will show an empty file. Thus, if you see an empty file instead of the file that you were expecting to see, you may have mistyped the filename.

Using Text Editor Conventions

Every text editor has its own conventions for displaying information on the screen, manipulating text, and so on. Most text-mode text editors are similar up to a point—for instance, one or more lines at the top or bottom of the display typically show summary information or brief command prompts. Figure 10.1 and Figure 10.2 show this information for nano, which includes the following:

Title Bar   The first line of the display is the title bar. This line includes nano's version number, the name of the file being edited, and the modification status.

Status Bar   The third line from the bottom of the display is reserved for status information and interactions with the user. This line will prompt you for information such as a filename to write when you save your document or terms that you want to find in the document when you perform a search operation.

Shortcut List   The bottom two lines of the editor show a summary of some of the most common operations, along with the keystrokes that trigger them.

In nano documentation, a caret (^) preceding a letter refers to a control character. In this book, such key combinations are indicated with Ctrl+ rather than a caret.

In addition to control characters, nano uses *metacharacters* to activate some functions. These key combinations use either the Esc, Alt, or Meta key (depending on your keyboard's configuration) followed by another key. In nano's documentation, meta sequences are denoted by M-*k*, where *k* is a key. For instance, M-? is the key sequence to move to the last line of the document. Note that these are distinct keystrokes, unlike Ctrl key sequences; that is, you would press Esc (or Alt or Meta), release it, and *then* press the question mark (?) key, including its Shift modifier, to move to the last line of the document.

Typically, modern keyboards do not have a Meta key (consult your keyboard manufacturer's documentation). As a substitute, first try using the Esc key in place of the Meta key for meta key sequences in nano. If that does not work, try the Alt key as the Meta key.

Exploring Basic *nano* Text-Editing Procedures

To learn nano, consider the tasks of creating and editing pets.txt, as shown in Figure 10.1. You can easily follow along on your system using this example. First populate the file with the pet types, as shown in Listing 10.1. After you save the file's data to disk, add a new pet type using the text editor.

Listing 10.1: Sample pets.txt file

```
dog
cat
bird
fish
```

For this example, the first step to using nano is to launch it and have it create a blank empty file called pets.txt as follows:

1. Open a terminal program, and in your home directory, type **nano pets.txt** and press the Enter key. You should see the words File: pets.txt displayed at the center of the title bar as well as the words New File listed in the status bar's center. This indicates that you have created an empty new file called pets.txt.

2. Type **dog** and press Enter to add the first pet type to the file. Continue with the pet types from Listing 10.1 until you have added all four pet types.

At this point, your result should resemble Figure 10.1 (shown earlier), which illustrates nano editing the pets.txt file. You can add a new entry to pets.txt in a couple of ways. The first way is to create a new empty line and type an entry manually. You can do this as follows:

1. Press the arrow keys as needed to move the cursor over the f in fish.

2. Press the Enter key. This action opens a new line between the bird line and the fish line.

3. Press the up arrow key once to reposition the cursor on the empty new line.

4. Type **reptile**, and do *not* press the Enter key.

A second way of creating a new entry demonstrates how to copy, cut, and paste text in the editor:

1. Move the cursor to the beginning of the reptile line that you've just created by using the arrow keys; you should see the cursor resting on the r in reptile.

2. Press M-6. (The second keystroke is the digit 6, not the letter g, and the Meta key may be the Esc or the Alt key, depending on your keyboard's configuration.) It may not look like anything happened, but this keystroke copies the line on which the cursor resides into a buffer. Your cursor should now be resting on the f on the fish line.

3. Press Ctrl+U. This keystroke pastes the contents of the buffer into the file in the current location. You should see that the reptile pet type is shown on two lines.

4. Use the arrow keys to move the cursor to the beginning of the second reptile line that you've just created; you should see the cursor resting on the r in reptile.

5. Press Ctrl+K to cut the entire second reptile line. The cursor should be at the start of the fish line.

6. Press Ctrl+N to go to the next line in the file. Your cursor should be below the fish line.

7. Type **rodent** to add another pet type.

> To save the new pets.txt file that you created with nano, read the upcoming section, "Saving Your Changes from *nano*."

You can make additional changes in a similar way. Although nano lacks a GUI version, most of its principles are the same as the ones in GUI text editors and word processors; you just need to know the keystroke to activate the feature that you want.

Pressing Ctrl+G displays the nano help documentation, which summarizes the program's features. This can be handy as you get to know the editor. Some additional features that you might want to use include the following:

Move to the Start or End of the File You can use the arrow keys, PageUp, PageDown, Home, and End to move the cursor around in ways that are common to other editors. To move to the start of the file, press M-\, and to move to the end of the file, press M-/. (Remember that M stands for the Meta key covered in the "Using Text Editor Conventions" section of this chapter.)

Copy or Move Multiple Lines If you need to copy or move multiple consecutive lines, you can repeat the M-6 or Ctrl+K operation; nano retains all of the lines that you copy or cut so that when you press Ctrl+U, all of them will be pasted back.

Insert a File Pressing Ctrl+R or F5 enables you to insert another file into the current one at the cursor's current position.

Search for a String Pressing Ctrl+W or F6 activates a search feature. When activated, nano prompts you for a search term. Type it, followed by the Enter key, and nano finds the next instance of that search term in the file. When you press Ctrl+W or F6 again, the default search term is the last one used, so you can search repeatedly for the same term by pressing Ctrl+W or F6 followed by Enter for each search operation. Alternatively, M-W repeats the last search.

Replace a String You can replace one string with another by pressing Ctrl+\ or M-R. The program prompts you to enter a search term and the term to take its place. The search then commences, and nano asks you to verify each replacement. If you want to replace *all* of the occurrences without prompting, you can press the A key at the first prompt.

Saving Your Changes from *nano*

After you've made changes to a text file, of course, you probably want to save them. One way to do this is with the Ctrl+O option. (That's the letter O, not the number 0.) When you press this key, nano asks the following:

```
Write Selection to File:
```

Ordinarily, the prompt will include the file's original name, so you can press the Enter key to save the file using that name. If you want to use a different name, you can delete the old one and type a new name. If you launched nano without specifying a filename, you can type one at this prompt.

Another way to save the file is to press Ctrl+X. This command exits from nano, but if you've modified the file, it produces the following prompt:

```
Save modified buffer (ANSWERING "No" WILL DESTROY CHANGES) ?
```

Type **y** at this prompt to save the file. The program then shows you the filename prompt that you'd have seen if you'd pressed Ctrl+O, so you can change the filename if you like. After nano saves the file, it terminates.

If you were following along on your system, creating and editing the pets.txt file from earlier in this chapter, here are the steps to follow to save your changes and exit the nano text editor:

1. In the nano text editor with the pets.txt file displayed, press Ctrl+O to start the process of saving the file.

   The status bar should show the words File Name to Write: pets.txt.

2. Press Enter to save the file. You should see something similar to Wrote 6 lines on the status bar.

3. Press Ctrl+X to exit the nano text editor and return to the command-line prompt.

To gain more experience, try editing the pets.txt file again with nano, making various changes and trying out the different editing commands. Be sure to peruse the help feature as well, using Ctrl+G to access it and Ctrl+X to exit from the help documentation.

Editing Files with *vi*

Certification
Objective

vi was the first full-screen text editor written for Unix. It was designed to be small enough to fit on the old-fashioned, tiny, floppy-based emergency boot systems. Later, a new version with several improvements was created and called "vi improved," or vim. Even though most Linux distributions ship with vim, it is still often referred to as the vi editor. vim is upward compatible with the vi editor, and the command to launch vim is typically vi—though some distributions have a vim command instead. The information presented in this chapter applies to both vi and vim.

Although the vi editor is useful for editing configuration files, it shines in editing program files, such as shell scripts. Thus, you will benefit from learning the vi editor, though it is considered by many to be the most complicated text editor to use.

Understanding *vi* Modes

To use vi, you should first understand the modes in which it operates. Then you can begin to learn about the text-editing procedures that vi implements. At any given moment, vi is running in one of three modes:

Command Mode   The command mode accepts commands, which are usually entered as single letters. For instance, i and a both enter insert mode, though in somewhat different ways as described shortly, and o opens a line below the current one.

Ex Mode   To manipulate files (including saving your current file and running outside programs), you use ex mode. You enter ex mode from command mode by typing a colon (:), typically directly followed by the name of the ex mode command that you want to use. After you run the ex mode command, vi returns automatically to command mode.

Insert Mode   You enter text in insert mode. Most keystrokes result in text appearing on the screen. One important exception is the Esc key, which exits insert mode and returns to command mode.

Unfortunately, terminology surrounding vi modes is inconsistent at best. For instance, command mode is sometimes referred to as *normal mode*, and insert mode is sometimes called *edit mode* or *entry mode*. Ex mode often isn't described as a mode at all but is referred to as *colon commands*.

Checking your vi/vim Editor Package

Your Linux system may not have the full vi/vim editor package installed by default. For example, your distribution may come only with the vim.tiny or vim.minimal package installed. With these packages, you can still access a form of the vi editor, though you may not have full access to the editor's various features, including some of those described in this chapter. If you wish to learn and properly use the vi editor, you should have the full vim package installed.

To check your system, enter **type vi** at the command line. You should receive the program name (vi or vim), including its directory location, similar to what is shown here:

```
$ type vi
vi is hashed (/usr/bin/vi)
```

When you have the program name and its location, type **readlink -f /location/program** to determine whether the program is linked to another program. (Linked files are covered in Chapter 7, "Managing Files.") You may receive something similar to the following:

```
$ readlink -f /usr/bin/vi
/usr/bin/vim.tiny
```

Next, you still need to check the software package that provided the program. (In some cases, the program name does *not* indicate which software package provided it.) Use the appropriate software package tool to determine this required information. The example here is on a Linux Mint distribution, so the dpkg -S command is used along with super user privileges (obtaining super user privileges is covered in more detail in Chapter 12).

```
$ sudo dkpg -S /usr/bin/vim.tiny

[sudo] password for christine:
vim-tiny: /usr/bin/vim.tiny
```

You can see that in this case the vim-tiny package is installed. If you find that the vim, vim-enhanced, vim-runtime, or vim-basic package is installed, you should have no problems using the vi editor commands in this chapter. However, if you do not find any of these packages, you'll want to install the vim package in order to follow along with the rest of this chapter. For the preceding example on the Linux Mint distribution, you would enter **sudo apt-get install vim** to install the full vim package. On the Fedora Workstation distribution, type **sudo yum install vim**. (Installing packages is covered in Chapter 9.)

You can now begin to learn about the text-editing procedures that vi implements. You'll also examine how to save files and exit vi.

Exploring Basic *vi* Text-Editing Procedures

As a method for learning vi, consider the task of creating and editing the pets.txt file—the same task described earlier in "Exploring Basic nano Text-Editing Procedures." Listing 10.1 (in that earlier section) shows the pets.txt file to create for the next example.

If you created the pets.txt file earlier and want to follow along in this section, delete the file first by typing **rm pets.txt** and pressing Enter.

For this example, the first step to using vi is to launch it and have it create a blank file called pets.txt as follows:

1. Open a terminal program and, in your home directory, type **vi pets.txt** and press Enter. You should see the words "pets.txt" [New File] displayed on the message line at the bottom of the window. This indicates that you have created a new empty file called pets.txt.

2. You are in command mode. Press the I key to enter insert mode. This mode should be indicated on the message line by the word --INSERT-- at the bottom of the window.

3. Type **dog** and press Enter to add the first pet type to the file. Continue with the pet types from Listing 10.1 until you have added all four pet types.

4. Press Esc to exit insert mode. Notice that the message --INSERT-- is no longer displayed in the message line. The vi editor is now in command mode.

5. Type **:** to enter ex mode, and finish the command by typing **wq** and pressing Enter. This writes (w) the vi buffer contents to the pets.txt file, quits (q) the vi editor, and returns you to the command line.

6. Reopen the pets.txt file in the vi editor by typing **vi pets.txt** and pressing Enter.

Your result should resemble Figure 10.3, which shows vi displaying the pets.txt file in command mode. As shown in Figure 10.3, some systems display a line of tildes (~) down the left side of the screen to indicate the end of the file. The file in Figure 10.3 was newly loaded, and therefore the bottom line shows the status of the last command—an implicit file-load command that loaded 4 lines and 18 characters from the pets.txt file.

FIGURE 10.3   The last line of a vi display is a status line that shows messages from the program.

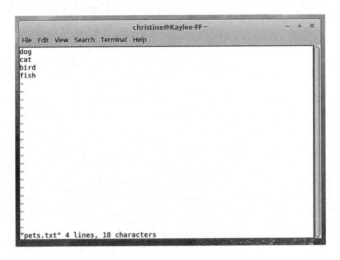

 It may be tempting to try word processor shortcut keys in a text editor, such as Ctrl+S to save the file. This is not a wise practice, as this keystroke combination may cause your terminal to freeze. If you have done this, you can unfreeze your terminal by pressing Ctrl+Q.

As with nano, you can add a new entry to pets.txt by using vi, either by typing a new line in its entirety or by duplicating an existing line and modifying it. To type a new line, follow these steps:

1. Move the cursor to the beginning of the bird line by using the arrow keys.

2. Press the O key (letter O, not number 0). This opens a new line immediately below the current line, moves the cursor to that line, and enters insert mode.

3. Type in a new entry: **reptile**.

4. Press the Esc key to return from insert mode to command mode.

To practice making changes by modifying an existing entry, follow these steps:

1. Move the cursor to the beginning of the reptile line that you just created by using the arrow keys if necessary. You should see the cursor resting on the r of reptile.

2. You will now copy (yank) one line of text. The term *yank* is used much as *copy* is used in most text editors—you copy the text to a buffer from which you can later paste it back into the file. To yank text, you use the yy command preceded by the number of

lines you want to yank. Therefore, type **1yy** (*do not* press the Enter key, though). It doesn't look like anything happened, but this keystroke copies the line on which the cursor resides into a buffer.

3. Move the cursor to the bird line, which is the line *before* the one where you want the new line to appear.

4. Type **p** (again, without pressing the Enter key). vi pastes the contents of the buffer (reptile) starting on the line after the cursor. The file should now have two identical reptile lines. The cursor should be resting at the start of the first one.

5. Move the cursor to the r in the word reptile on the line that you've just pasted, if it's not there already. You're about to delete this line.

6. The dd command works much like yy, but it deletes the lines as well as copying them to a buffer. Type **dd** to delete the reptile line. The file should now have only one reptile line.

7. Save the file and quit by typing **ZZ**. This command is equivalent to :wq.

If you need to change a text file's end-of-line encoding from the Windows method to the Unix/Linux method, open the file in the vi editor and type the command **:set ff=unix**.

Many additional commands are available that you may want to use in some situations. Here are some highlights:

Change Case Suppose that you need to change the case of a word in a file. Instead of entering insert mode and retyping the word, you can use the tilde (~) key in command mode to change the case. Position the cursor on the first character that you want to change, and press ~ repeatedly until the task is done.

Undo To undo any change, type **u** in command mode.

Open Text In command mode, typing **o** (a lowercase letter O) opens text—that is, it inserts a new line immediately below the current one and enters insert mode on that line.

Search To search forward for text in a file, type **/** in command mode, followed immediately by the text that you want to locate. Typing **?** searches backward rather than forward.

Change Text The c command changes text from within command mode. You invoke it much like the d or y command, as in cw to change the next word or cc to change an entire line.

Go to a Line The G key brings you to a line number that you specify. The H key *homes* the cursor—that is, it moves the cursor to the top line of the screen. The L key brings the cursor to the bottom line of the screen.

Replace Globally To replace all occurrences of one string with another, type **:%s/original/replacement/g**, where *original* is the original string and *replacement* is its replacement. Change % to a starting line number, comma, and ending line number to perform this change on a small range of lines.

 The /g at the command's end is not needed if *original* is listed only one time in each file's line.

vi offers a great deal more depth than is presented here; the editor is quite capable, and some Linux users are very attached to it. Entire books have been written about *vi*. Consult one of these, or a *vi* web page such as www.vim.org, for more information.

Saving Your Changes from *vi*

To save changes to a file without exiting the editor, type **:w** in command mode. This enters ex mode and runs the w ex-mode command, which writes the file using whatever filename you specified when you launched *vi*. Related commands enable other functions:

Edit a New File   The :e command edits a new file. For instance, **:e /etc/inittab** loads /etc/inittab for editing. *vi* won't load a new file unless the existing one has been saved since its last change or unless you follow :e with an exclamation mark (!). Keep in mind if you use the explanation point, you'll lose any modifications made to the original file.

Include an Existing File   The :r command includes the contents of an old file in an existing one, appending it to the existing file.

Execute an External Command   The ex mode command :! executes the external command that you specify. For instance, typing **:!ls** runs ls, enabling you to see what files are present in the current directory.

Quit   Use the :q command to quit the program. As with :e, this command won't work unless changes have been saved or you append an exclamation mark to the command (as in :q!). Keep in mind if you use the exclamation point, you'll lose any modifications made to the original file.

You can combine ex commands such as these to perform multiple actions in sequence. For instance, as shown previously, typing **:wq** writes changes and then quits from *vi*.

EXERCISE 10.1

- Launch nano to create a new file, and type in a complete paragraph from this chapter. Proofread the text and correct any typos that you find. (If you do not find any, congratulations! Now create a few "errors" and correct them.)

- Launch vi to create a new file. Type in this chapter's review questions and include the answers. Try out the various editing features, such as changing case and searching for text.

Summary

Plain-text files, which encode text using ASCII or Unicode, are important on most computer platforms, but they're particularly important on Linux. This is because many of Linux's configuration files use plain-text formats, so understanding how to use an editor such as nano or vi to edit these files enables you to edit a wide variety of configuration files. In addition, to be able to create shell scripts on Linux, you must be able to handle at least one text editor. Basic text-editing skills are required, but the more you know about moving around, searching, and modifying a text file, the quicker you can complete needed tasks.

Exam Essentials

Describe editing files with nano. Launch the nano text editor along with the name of the current file you wish to edit or the new file you want to create. You can reach the line you want to change by using arrow or control keys, some of which are displayed in the shortcut list. For editing, basic keyboard keys or control and/or meta keys are also available. For example, Ctrl+K allows you to cut a line of text, whereas Ctrl+U pastes any cut text.

Explain how to save modified text files with nano. You can save any changes made to the text file within the nano editor by pressing the Ctrl+O key combination. The editor will prompt for the filename, and if it is the name displayed, you can simply press Enter. You can also initiate this process by pressing Ctrl+X.

Describe editing files with vi. Start the vi text editor along with the name of the current file you want to edit or the new file you want to create. The initial editor mode is command mode. It is easiest for those new to vi to start editing by entering insert mode by pressing I on the keyboard. After you have completed your edits, leave insert mode by pressing the Esc key.

Detail the various methods to save changes with vi. To save your edits when using the vi editor, you can use ex mode, but you first must be out of insert mode (press the Esc key to leave insert mode if needed). Type **:w** to write out the editor's buffer to the file on the disk. You can save the changes and quit the vi editor at the same time by typing **:wq**. If you need to quit without saving changes, type **:q!**. You can also use command mode to save your modifications by typing **ZZ**.

Summarize needed super user privileges for editing. To successfully edit system files, which include some configuration files, you must obtain super user privileges prior to editing them. This also includes other files that only allow users with such privileges to write to the file. When using nano, you will see near the bottom of the editor screen the message `Warning: no write permission` if you have loaded a file that you have no permission to change.

Review Questions

You can find the answers in Appendix A.

1. For which type of file is nano *least* likely to be useful for examining or editing?

    A. A text file encoded in Unicode

    B. A shell script file

    C. A text file encoded in ASCII

    D. A LibreOffice word processing document

    E. A Linux configuration file

2. Which keystrokes invoke the nano search function? (Choose all that apply.)

    A. F3

    B. F6

    C. Esc-S

    D. Ctrl+F

    E. Ctrl+W

3. How would you remove two lines of text from a file when using vi?

    A. In command mode, position the cursor on the first line and type **2dd**.

    B. In command mode, position the cursor on the last line and type **2yy**.

    C. In insert mode, position the cursor at the start of the first line, hold down the Shift key while pressing the down arrow key twice, and press the Delete key on the keyboard.

    D. In insert mode, position the cursor at the start of the first line and press Ctrl+K twice.

    E. Select the text with the mouse, and then select File ➤ Delete from the menu.

4. True or false: Unicode is useful for encoding most European languages but not languages in Asia.

5. True or false: GUI text editors for ASCII are superior to text-mode ASCII text editors because the GUI editors support underlining, italics, and multiple fonts.

6. True or false: If you have never used a text editor before, the nano text editor is usually the best one to learn first.

7. ASCII supports _____ unique characters (not including control characters).

    A. 64

    B. 128

    C. 512

    D. 1024

    E. 2048

8. Three keystrokes that can initiate a search-and-replace operation in nano are _____, _____, and _____.

   A. Esc+R

   B. F6

   C. F14

   D. Ctrl+F

   E. Ctrl+\

9. While in vi's command mode, you can type _____ to undo a change.

   A. ~

   B. :wq

   C. ZZ

   D. u

   E. /

10. To save a file and exit the vi text editor in command mode, type _____.

    A. ~

    B. ?

    C. ZZ

    D. cw

    E. /

Chapter

11

Creating Scripts

OBJECTIVE:

✓ 3.3 Turning Commands into a Script

A *script* is a program written in an interpreted language, typically associated with a shell or other program whose primary purpose is something other than as an interpreted language. In Linux, many scripts are *shell scripts*, which are associated with Bash or another shell. (If you're familiar with *batch files* in DOS or Windows, scripts serve a similar purpose.) You can write shell scripts to help automate tedious repetitive tasks or to perform new and complex tasks. Many of Linux's startup functions are performed by scripts, so mastering scripting will help you manage the startup process.

This chapter covers Bash shell scripts, beginning with the task of creating a new script file. It then describes several important scripting features that help you to perform progressively more complex scripting tasks.

Like any programming task, shell scripting can be quite complex. Consequently, this chapter barely scratches the surface of what you can accomplish through shell scripting. Consult a book on the topic, such as our *Linux Command Line and Shell Scripting Bible, Third Edition* (Wiley, 2015), for more information.

Beginning a Shell Script

Certification Objective

Shell scripts are plain-text files, so you create them in text editors such as vi, nano, or pico, as described in Chapter 10, "Editing Files." You shouldn't use standard word processing programs, such as LibreOffice Writer, to create shell scripts as by default they embed binary code into the final document to indicate fonts, font sizes, and special characters. These binary codes confuse the Linux shell.

A shell script begins with a line that identifies the shell that's used to run it, such as the following:

```
#!/bin/bash
```

Certification Objective

The first two characters are a special code that tells the Linux kernel that this is a script and to use the rest of the line as a pathname to the program that interprets the script. (This line is sometimes called the *shebang*, *hashbang*, *hashpling*, or *pound bang* line.) Shell scripting languages use a hash mark (#) as a comment character, so the script utility ignores this line, although the kernel doesn't. On most systems, /bin/sh is a symbolic link that points to /bin/bash, but it can point to some other shell. Specifying the script as using /bin/sh guarantees that any Linux system will have a shell program to run the script, but if the script uses any features specific to a particular shell, you should specify that shell instead—for instance, use /bin/bash or /bin/tcsh instead of /bin/sh.

This chapter describes Bash shell scripts. Simple Bash scripts can run in other shells, but more complex scripts are more likely to be shell-specific.

When you're done writing the shell script, you should modify it so that it's executable. You do this with the chmod command, which is described in more detail in Chapter 14, "Setting Ownership and Permissions." For now, know that you use the a+x option to add execute permissions for all users. For instance, to make a file called my-script executable, you issue the following command:

```
$ chmod a+x my-script
```

You'll then be able to execute the script by typing its name, possibly preceded by ./ to tell Linux to run the script in the current directory rather than searching the current path. If you fail to make the script executable, you can still run the script by running the shell program followed by the script name (as in **bash my-script**), but it's generally better to make the script executable. If the script is one you run regularly, you may want to move it to a location on your path, such as /usr/local/bin. When you do that, you won't have to type the complete path or move to the script's directory to execute it; you can just type **my-script**.

Using Commands

One of the most basic features of shell scripts is the ability to run commands. You can use both commands that are built into the shell and external commands—that is, you can run other programs as commands. Most of the commands you type in a shell prompt are external commands; they're programs located in /bin, /usr/bin, and other directories on your path. You can run such programs, as well as internal commands, by including their names in the script. You can also specify parameters to such programs in a script. For instance, suppose you want a script that launches two xterm windows and the KMail mail reader program. Listing 11.1 presents a shell script that accomplishes this goal.

Listing 11.1: A simple script that launches three programs

```
#!/bin/bash
/usr/bin/xterm &
/usr/bin/xterm &
/usr/bin/kmail &
```

Aside from the first line that identifies it as a script, the script looks just like the commands you might type to accomplish the task manually, except for one fact: the script lists the complete paths to each program. This is usually not strictly necessary, but listing the complete path ensures that the script will find the programs even if the PATH environment variable changes. On the other hand, if the program files move (say, because you upgrade the package from which they're installed and the packager decides to move them), scripts that use complete paths will break. If a script produces a No such file or directory error for a command, typing **which** *command*, where *command* is the offending command, should help you locate it.

The Linux File Hierarchy Standard (FHS) defines specific directories for different types of files, such as /usr/bin for local application executable files. Many Linux distributions are incorporating the FHS structure in their directory hierarchy.

Each program-launch line in Listing 11.1 ends in an ampersand (&). This character tells the shell to go on to the next line without waiting for the first to finish. If you omit the ampersands in Listing 11.1, the effect will be that the first xterm will open but the second won't open until the first is closed. Likewise, KMail won't start until the second xterm terminates.

Although launching several programs from one script can save time in startup scripts and some other situations, scripts are also frequently used to run a series of programs that manipulate data in some way. Such scripts typically do not include the ampersands at the ends of the commands because one command must run after another or may even rely on output from the first. A comprehensive list of such commands is impossible because you can run any program you can install in Linux as a command in a script—even another script. A few commands that are commonly used in scripts include the following:

Normal File Manipulation Commands   The file manipulation commands, such as ls, mv, cp, and rm, are often used in scripts. You can use these commands to help automate repetitive file maintenance tasks.

grep   The grep command locates files that contain the string you specify, or it displays the lines that contain those strings in a single file. grep is described in detail in Chapter 8, "Searching, Extracting, and Archiving Data."

find   The find command searches for patterns based on filenames, ownership, and similar characteristics. Chapter 8 covers this command.

cut   The cut command extracts text from fields in a file. It's frequently used to extract variable information from a file whose contents are highly patterned. To use it, you pass it one or more options that specify what information you want, followed by one or more filenames. For instance, users' home directories appear in the sixth colon-delimited field of the /etc/passwd file. You can therefore type **cut -f 6 -d ":" /etc/passwd** to extract this information. The same command in a script will extract this information, which you'll probably save to a variable or pass to a subsequent command.

sed   The sed program provides many of the capabilities of a conventional text editor (such as search-and-replace operations) but via commands that can be typed at a command prompt or entered in a script.

echo   The echo command is the tool to use when a script must provide a message to the user. You can pass various options to echo or just a string to be shown to the user. For instance, echo "Press the Enter key" causes a script to display the specified string. You can also use echo to display the value of variables (described later, in "Using Variables").

mail   The mail command can be used to send email from within a script. Pass it the -s *subject* parameter to specify a subject line, and give it an email address as the last argument. If it's used at the command line, you then type a message and terminate it with a Ctrl+D keystroke. If it's used from a script, you may omit the subject entirely or pass it an external file as the message using input redirection. You may want to use this command to send mail to the superuser about the actions of a startup script or a script that runs on an automated basis.

 Chapter 8 describes input redirection.

Many of these commands are extremely complex, and completely describing them is beyond the scope of this chapter. You can consult these commands' man pages for more information. A few of them are described elsewhere in this book, as noted in their descriptions.

Even if you have a full grasp of how to use some key external commands, simply executing commands as you would when typing them at a command prompt is of limited utility. Many administrative tasks require you to modify what you type at a command, or even what commands you enter, depending on information from other commands. For this reason, scripting languages include additional features to help you make your scripts useful.

Using Arguments

Variables can help you expand the utility of scripts. A variable is a placeholder in a script for a value that will be determined when the script runs. Variables' values can be passed as parameters to a script, generated internally to a script, or extracted from a script's environment. (An *environment* is a set of variables that any program can access. The environment includes things like the current directory and the search path for running programs.)

Variables that are passed to the script are frequently called *parameters* or *arguments*. They're represented in the script by a dollar sign ($) followed by a number from 0 up—$0 stands for the name of the script, $1 is the first parameter to the script, $2 is the second parameter, and so on. To understand how this might be useful, consider the task of adding a user. As described in Chapter 13, "Creating Users and Groups," creating an account for a new user typically involves running at least two commands—useradd and passwd.

You may also need to run additional site-specific commands, such as commands that create unusual user-owned directories aside from the user's home directory.

As an example of how a script with an argument variable can help in such situations, consider Listing 11.2. When you run the script, you must provide the user account as a parameter on the command line. The script retrieves that value using the $1 variable and creates an account based on the value with the useradd command. It then changes the account's password using the passwd command (the script prompts you to enter the password when you run the script). It creates a directory in the /shared directory tree corresponding to the account, and it sets a symbolic link to that directory from the new user's home directory. It also adjusts ownership and permissions in a way that may be useful, depending on your system's ownership and permissions policies.

Listing 11.2: A script that reduces account-creation tedium

```
#!/bin/bash
useradd -m $1
passwd $1
mkdir -p /shared/$1
chown $1.users /shared/$1
chmod 775 /shared/$1
ln -s /shared/$1 /home/$1/shared
chown $1.users /home/$1/shared
```

If you use Listing 11.2, you need to type only three things: the script name with the desired username and the password (twice). For instance, if the script is called mkuser, you can use it like this:

```
# mkuser rblum
Changing password for user rblum
New password:
Retype new password:
passwd: all authentication tokens updated successfully
```

Most of the script's programs operate silently unless they encounter problems, so the interaction (including typing the passwords, which don't echo to the screen) is a result of just the passwd command. In effect, Listing 11.2's script replaces seven lines of commands with one. Every one of those lines uses the username, so by running this script, you also reduce the chance of a typo causing problems.

Using Variables

Certification
Objective

Another type of variable that can be set from the output of a command is also identified by leading dollar signs, but typically is given a name that at least begins with a letter, such as $Addr or $Name. (When values are assigned to variables, the dollar sign is omitted, as illustrated shortly.) You can then use these variables with normal commands as if they were command parameters, but the value of the variable is passed to the command.

Consider Listing 11.3, which checks to see if the computer's router is up with the help of the ping utility. This script uses two variables. The first is $ip, which is extracted from the output of route using the grep, tr, and cut commands. When you assign a value to a variable from the output of a command, that command should be enclosed in backtick characters (`), which appear on the same key as the tilde (~) on most keyboards. These are *not* ordinary single quotes, which appear on the same key as the regular quote character (") on most keyboards. The second variable, $ping, simply points to the ping program. It can just as easily be omitted, with subsequent uses of $ping replaced by the full path to the program or simply by ping (relying on the $PATH environment variable to find the program). Variables like this are sometimes used to make it easier to modify the script in the future. For instance, if you move the ping program, you need to modify only one line of the script. Variables can also be used with conditionals to ensure that the script works on more systems—for instance, if ping were called something else on some systems.

Listing 11.3: Script demonstrating assignment and use of variables

```
#!/bin/bash
ip=`route -n | grep UG | tr -s " " | cut -f 2 -d " "`
ping="/bin/ping"
echo "Checking to see if $ip is up..."
$ping -c 5 $ip
```

In addition to several commands, the ip= line uses backticks (`) to assign the output of that command chain to ip. Chapter 8 describes this technique.

In practice, you use Listing 11.3 by typing the script's name. The result should be the message Checking to see if *192.168.1.1* is up (with *192.168.1.1* replaced by the computer's default gateway system) and the output from the ping command, which should attempt to send five packets to the router. If the router is up and is configured to respond to pings, you'll see five return packets and summary information, similar to the following:

```
$ routercheck
Checking to see if 192.168.1.1 is up...
PING 192.168.1.1 (192.168.1.1) 56(84) bytes of data.
64 bytes from 192.168.1.1: icmp_seq=1 ttl=63 time=23.0 ms
64 bytes from 192.168.1.1: icmp_seq=2 ttl=63 time=0.176 ms
64 bytes from 192.168.1.1: icmp_seq=3 ttl=63 time=0.214 ms
64 bytes from 192.168.1.1: icmp_seq=4 ttl=63 time=0.204 ms
64 bytes from 192.168.1.1: icmp_seq=5 ttl=63 time=0.191 ms

--- 192.168.1.1 ping statistics ---
5 packets transmitted, 5 received, 0% packet loss, time 4001ms
rtt min/avg/max/mdev = 0.176/4.758/23.005/9.123 ms
```

If the router is down, you'll see error messages to the effect that the host was unreachable.

Listing 11.3 is of limited practical use and contains bugs. For instance, the script identifies the computer's gateway merely by the presence of the string UG in the router's output line from route. If a computer has two routers defined, this won't work correctly, and the result is likely to be a script that misbehaves. The purpose of Listing 11.3 is to illustrate how variables can be assigned and used, not to be a flawless working script.

Scripts like Listing 11.3, which obtain information from running one or more commands, are useful in configuring features that rely on system-specific information or information that varies with time. You can use a similar approach to obtain the current hostname (using the hostname command), the current time (using date), the total time the computer's been running (using uptime), free disk space (using df), and so on. When combined with conditional expressions (described shortly), variables become even more powerful because then your script can perform one action when one condition is met and another in some other case. For instance, a script that installs software can check free disk space and abort the installation if insufficient disk space is available.

In addition to assigning variables with the assignment operator (=), you can read variables from standard input using read, as in read response to read input for subsequent access as $response. This method of variable assignment is useful for scripts that must interact with users. For instance, instead of reading the username from the command line, Listing 11.2 may be modified to prompt the user for the username. Listing 11.4 shows the result. To use this script, you type its name *without* typing a username on the command line. The script will then prompt for a username, and after you enter one, the script will attempt to create an account with that name.

Listing 11.4: Modified version of Listing 11.2 that employs user interaction

```
#!/bin/bash
echo -n "Enter a username: "
read name
useradd -m $name
passwd $name
mkdir -p /shared/$name
chown $name.users /shared/$name
chmod 775 /shared/$name
ln -s /shared/$name /home/$name/shared
chown $name.users /home/$name/shared
```

One special type of variable is an *environment variable*, which is assigned and accessed just like a shell script variable. The difference is that the script or command that sets an environment variable uses Bash's export command to make the value of the variable accessible to programs launched from the shell or shell script that made the assignment. In other words, you can set an environment variable in one script and use it in another script that the first script launches. Environment variables are most often set in shell startup scripts, but the scripts you use can access them. For instance, if your script calls X programs, it might check for the presence of a valid $DISPLAY environment variable and abort if it finds that this variable isn't set. By convention, environment variable names are all uppercase, whereas non-environment shell script variables are all lowercase or mixed case.

One special variable deserves mention: $?. This variable holds the *exit status* (or *return value*) of the most recently executed command. The exit status is an integer value that you can check to determine whether or not the command completed correctly. Most programs return a value of 0 when they terminate normally and return another value to specify errors. You can display this value with echo or use it in a conditional expression (described next) to have your script perform special error handling.

Consult a program's man page to learn the meanings of its return values.

Using Conditional Expressions

Scripting languages support several types of *conditional expressions*. These enable a script to perform one of several actions contingent on some condition—typically the value of a variable. One common command that uses conditional expressions is if, which allows the system to take one of two actions depending on whether some condition is true. The conditional expression for the if keyword appears in brackets after the if keyword and can take many forms. Conditional expressions use options and operators to define just what condition to check. For instance, the condition:

Certification Objective

```
[ -f file ]
```

uses the -f option and is true if *file* exists and is a regular file; whereas the condition:

```
[ -s file ]
```

uses the -s option and is true if *file* exists and has a size greater than 0. You can also use some string operators in conditions. For example:

```
[string1 == string2 ]
```

uses the == operator and is true if the two strings have the same values.

To better understand the use of conditionals, consider the following code fragment:

Certification Objective

```
if [ -s /tmp/tempstuff ]
    then
        echo "/tmp/tempstuff found; aborting!"
        exit
fi
```

This fragment causes the script to exit if the file /tmp/tempstuff is present. The then keyword marks the beginning of a series of lines that execute only if the conditional is true, and fi (if backward) marks the end of the if block. Such code may be useful if the script creates and then later deletes this file, because its presence indicates that a previous run of the script didn't succeed or is still underway.

Certification Objective

An alternative form for a conditional expression uses the test keyword rather than square brackets around the conditional:

```
if test -s /tmp/tempstuff
```

You can also test a command's return value by using the command as the condition:

```
if [ command ]
    then
        additional-commands
fi
```

In this example, the *additional-commands* will be run only if *command* completes successfully. If *command* returns an error code, *additional-commands* won't be run.

Conditional expressions may be expanded by use of the else clause:

```
if [ conditional-expression ]
    then
        commands
    else
        other-commands
fi
```

Code of this form causes either *commands* or *other-commands* to execute, depending on the evaluation of *conditional-expression*. This is useful if *something* should happen in a part of the program, but precisely what should happen depends on some condition. For instance, you may want to launch one of two different file archiving programs depending on a user's input.

Certification Objective

What do you do if more than two outcomes are possible—for instance, if a user may provide any one of four possible inputs? You can nest several if/then/else clauses, but this gets awkward quickly. A cleaner approach is to use case:

```
case word in
    pattern1) command(s) ;;
    pattern2) command(s) ;;
    ...
esac
```

Certification Objective

For a case statement, a *word* is likely to be a variable, and each *pattern* is a possible value of that variable. The patterns can be expanded much like filenames, using the same wildcards and expansion rules (* to stand for any string, for instance). You can match an arbitrary number of patterns in this way. Each set of commands must end with a double semicolon (;;), and the case statement as a whole ends in the string esac (case backward).

Filename expansion using asterisks (*), question marks (?), and so on is sometimes called *globbing*.

Upon execution, bash executes the commands associated with the first pattern to match the *word*. Execution then jumps to the line following the esac statement; any intervening commands don't execute. If no patterns match the word, no code within the case statement executes. If you want to have a default condition, use * as the final *pattern*; this pattern matches any *word*, so its commands will execute if no other *pattern* matches.

Using Loops

Conditional expressions are sometimes used in *loops*. Loops are structures that tell the script to perform the same task repeatedly until some condition is met (or until some condition is no longer met). For instance, Listing 11.5 shows a loop that plays all the WAV audio files in a directory.

 The aplay command is a basic audio file player. On some systems, you may need to use play or some other command instead of aplay.

Listing 11.5: A script that executes a command on every matching file in a directory

```
#!/bin/bash
for d in `ls *.wav` ; do
    aplay $d
done
```

The for loop as used here executes once for every item in the list generated by ls *.wav. Each of those items (filenames) is assigned in turn to the $d variable and so is passed to the aplay command.

The seq command can be useful in creating for loops (and in other ways, too). This command generates a list of numbers starting from its first argument and continuing to its last one. For instance, typing **seq 1 10** generates 10 lines, each with a number between 1 and 10. You can use the seq command in a for loop to iterate through a series of numbers:

```
for x in `seq 1 10` ; do
    echo $x
done
```

The loop executes 10 times, with the value of x incrementing with each iteration. If you pass just one parameter to seq, it interprets that number as an ending point, with the starting point being 1. If you pass three values to seq, it interprets them as a starting value, an increment amount, and an ending value.

Another type of loop is the `while` loop, which executes for as long as its condition is true. The basic form of this loop type is:

```
while [ condition ]
do
    commands
done
```

The `until` loop is similar in form, but it continues execution for as long as its condition is *false*—that is, until the condition becomes true.

Using Functions

A *function* is a part of a script that performs a specific subtask and that can be called by name from other parts of the script. Functions are defined by placing parentheses after the function name and enclosing the lines that make up the function within curly braces:

```
myfn() {
    commands
}
```

The keyword `function` may optionally precede the function name. In either event, the function is called by name as if it were an ordinary internal or external command.

Functions are very useful in helping to create modular scripts. For instance, if your script needs to perform half a dozen distinct computations, you can place each computation in a function and then call them all in sequence. Listing 11.6 demonstrates the use of functions in a simple program that copies a file but aborts with an error message if the target file already exists. This script accepts a target and a destination filename and must pass those filenames to the functions.

Listing 11.6: A script demonstrating the use of functions

```
#/bin/bash

doit() {
    cp $1 $2
}

function check() {
  if [ -s $2 ]
    then
        echo "Target file exists! Exiting!"
        exit
    fi
```

```
}

check $1 $2
doit $1 $2
```

If you enter Listing 11.6 and name it **safercp**, you can use it like this, assuming the file original.txt exists and dest.txt doesn't:

```
$ ./safercp original.txt dest.txt
$ ./safercp original.txt dest.txt
Target file exists! Exiting!
```

The first run of the script succeeded because dest.txt didn't exist. On the second run, though, the destination file did exist, so the script terminated with the error message.

Note that the functions aren't run directly and in the order in which they appear in the script. They're run only when called in the main body of the script—which in Listing 11.6 consists of just two lines, each corresponding to one function call, at the very end of the script.

 Real World Scenario

Administrator Shell Scripts

The job of a Linux administrator can be somewhat tedious at times. There are lots of different log files the administrator must check daily to ensure things are running properly and that no security breaches have occurred on the system. That task can take quite a long time to accomplish. However, many Linux administrators use shell scripts to help take some of the tediousness out of examining pages of log files.

Instead of manually looking through logs, administrators write scripts that use Linux text processing tools, such as grep and cut, to search the log files for errors and warnings, copy those errors and warnings to a separate text file, and then email the resulting file to themselves. They then schedule the scripts to run each evening so that they have a summary of any system issues first thing in the morning when they arrive at work. Then they can focus their energy on resolving system issues rather than just looking for them!

Setting the Script's Exit Value

Ordinarily, a script's exit status is the same as the last command the script called—that is, the script returns $?. You can control the exit value, however, or exit from the script at any point, by using the exit command. Used without any options, exit causes immediate termination of the script, with the usual exit value of $?. This can be useful in error handling or in aborting an ongoing operation for any reason—if the script detects an error or if the user selects an option to terminate, you can call exit to quit.

 Certification
Objective

If you pass a numeric value between 0 and 255 to `exit`, the script terminates and returns the specified value as the script's own exit value. You can use this feature to signal errors to other scripts that might call your own script. You may have to include extra code to keep track of the causes of abnormal termination, though. For instance, you can set aside a variable (say, $termcause) to hold the cause of the script's termination. Set it to 0 at the start of the script and then, if the script detects a problem that will cause termination, reset $termcause to some non-0 value. (You can use any numeric codes you like; there's no set meaning for such codes.) On exit, be sure to pass $termcause to `exit`:

```
exit $termcause
```

Summary

Serious Linux users and administrators must have at least a basic understanding of shell scripts. Many configuration and startup files are in fact shell scripts, and being able to read them, and perhaps modify them, will help you administer your system. Being able to create new shell scripts is also important, because doing so will help you simplify tedious tasks and create site-specific tools by gluing together multiple programs to accomplish your goals. Linux shell scripts allow you to combine standard shell commands with a few specialized programming commands, such as conditional expressions, loops, and functions, to implement logic features often found in larger-scale programs.

Exam Essentials

Describe the format of a basic shell script file.   Shell script files must be plain-text files; they cannot be generated using a word processing application. The first line in the shell script should be the shebang combination (`#!/bin/sh`). This indicates the shell that should be used to run the script. The remainder of the shell script is a list of commands or shell statements arranged in the order in which they are to be run by the shell. Though not required, it's common to use the `exit` statement at the end of a shell script to control the exit status generated by the shell, especially if the shell exists with any type of error condition.

Explain how using variables helps when writing a shell script.   Shell scripts use variables to store data or other information for use later in the shell script. You assign data to a variable using the equal sign (=). The data can be any type of text or numerical data, or if you redirect the output of a command to store in a variable by placing backtick characters around the command. To reference the value of a variable inside the shell script, precede the variable with a dollar sign ($). You can reference variables in shell commands as well as in shell statements.

Explain how to pass data to a shell script.   Shell scripts can use parameters, or arguments, to pass data from the command line to the shell script. Just include the data parameters on the command-line command when starting the shell script. Inside the shell script you can retrieve any command-line parameters by using positional variables. The $0 positional variable is special; it references the shell command used to launch the shell script. Positional variable $1 references the first parameter entered on the command line, variable $2 the second parameter, and so on.

Describe the different types of programming features you can use in shell scripts.   Shell scripts can use conditional statements to evaluate data and make programming decisions based on the outcome of the evaluation. The if and case statements are two conditional statements that you can use for that. The if statement can be paired with the else statement to create a true/false scenario for executing one set of statements if a condition is true, and another set of statements if a condition is false. The case statement allows you to specify a range of possible values that a condition can evaluate to and execute separate sets of statements for each possible value. Besides conditional statements, shell scripts can use loops to iterate through a set of statements multiple times, based on either a series of values or a condition. Finally, shell scripts also support defining functions, which are a set of statements bundled together to be called from anywhere in the shell script as needed.

Review Questions

You can find the answers in Appendix A.

1. After using a text editor to create a shell script, what step should you take before trying to use the script by typing its name?

   A. Set one or more executable bits using chmod.

   B. Copy the script to the /usr/bin/scripts directory.

   C. Compile the script by typing **bash *scriptname***, where *scriptname* is the script's name.

   D. Run a virus checker on the script to be sure it contains no viruses.

   E. Run a spell checker on the script to ensure it contains no bugs.

2. Describe the effect of the following short script, cp1, if it's called as **cp1 big.c big.cc**:

   ```
   #!/bin/bash
   cp $2 $1
   ```

   A. It has the same effect as the cp command—copying the contents of big.c to big.cc.

   B. It compiles the C program big.c and calls the result big.cc.

   C. It copies the contents of big.cc to big.c, eliminating the old big.c.

   D. It converts the C program big.c into a C++ program called big.cc.

   E. The script's first line is invalid, so it won't work.

3. What is the purpose of conditional expressions in shell scripts?

   A. They prevent scripts from executing if license conditions aren't met.

   B. They display information about the script's computer environment.

   C. They enable the script to take different actions in response to variable data.

   D. They enable scripts to learn in a manner reminiscent of Pavlovian conditioning.

   E. They cause scripts to run only at specified times of day.

4. True or false: A user types **myscript laser.txt** to run a script called myscript. Within myscript, the $0 variable holds the value laser.txt.

5. True or false: Valid looping statements in Bash include for, while, and until.

6. True or false: The following script launches three simultaneous instances of the terminal program.

   ```
   #!/bin/bash
   terminal
   terminal
   terminal
   ```

7. You've written a simple shell script that does nothing but launch programs. To ensure that the script works with most user shells, the first line should be _____.

   A. `#!/bin/sh`

   B. `/bin/sh`

   C. `# /bin/sh`

   D. `bash`

   E. `#!bash`

8. The _____ Bash scripting command is used to display prompts for a user in a shell script.

   A. `case`

   B. `while`

   C. `if`

   D. `echo`

   E. `exit`

9. The _____ Bash scripting command is used to control the program flow based on a variable that can take many values (such as all the letters of the alphabet).

   A. `case`

   B. `while`

   C. `if`

   D. `echo`

   E. `exit`

10. The _____ Bash scripting command controls the return value generated by a script, independent of the other commands used in the script.

   A. `case`

   B. `while`

   C. `if`

   D. `echo`

   E. `exit`

Chapter

12

Understanding Basic Security

OBJECTIVES:

✓ **5.1 Basic Security and Identifying User Types**

Linux is a multiuser OS, meaning that it provides features to help multiple individuals use the computer. Collectively, these features constitute *accounts*. Previous chapters of this book have referred to accounts in passing but haven't covered them in detail.

This chapter changes that; it describes important account principles and a few commands that you can use to begin investigating accounts. Related to accounts are *groups*, which are collections of accounts that can be given special permissions on the computer, so this chapter also describes groups. One account, known as root, has special privileges on the computer. Some administrators use this account to perform system administration tasks, but that is now considered a bad practice. So you should understand this account and what to use in its place before tackling the administrative tasks described in the last few chapters of this book. These important topics are at the foundation of system security.

Understanding Accounts

Accounts enable multiple users to share a single computer without causing one another too much trouble. They also enable system administrators to track who is using system resources and, sometimes, who is doing things they shouldn't be doing. Account features help users use a computer and administrators administer it. Understanding these features is the basis for enabling you to manage accounts.

Even a single-user workstation uses multiple accounts. Such a computer may have just one *user account*, but several *system accounts* to help keep the computer running.

Some account features help you identify accounts and the files and resources associated with them. Knowing how to use these features will help you track down account-related problems and manage the computer's users.

There are various account types—common user accounts, system accounts, and the root account. Common accounts are built for users who do not need special privileges to complete their daily tasks, such as creating a word processing document. System accounts are set up for special services or programs, such as one that serves up web pages. The root account was historically (and sometimes still today) used for performing system administration tasks. These topics are covered in more detail in the "Understanding User Types" section later in this chapter.

Understanding Account Features

Most account features are defined in the /etc/passwd file, which consists of colon-delimited lines, with each line (or record) defining a single account. An entry might resemble the following:

 Certification Objective

```
rich:x:1001:1001:Richard Blum:/home/rich:/bin/bash
```

The information contained in the fields of this record includes the following:

Username An account's username is its most relevant feature. Most Linux account usernames consist of lowercase letters, and occasionally numbers, as in rich or thx1138. Underscores (_) and dashes (-) are also valid characters in some Linux distributions' usernames.

Password User accounts are typically protected by a password, which is required to log into the computer. Direct login to most system accounts is disabled, so they lack passwords. (The root account is an important exception on some distributions; it may have a password.) The password field in the /etc/passwd file usually contains an x, which is a code meaning that the password is stored in /etc/shadow, as described shortly.

UID In reality, the username is just a label that the computer displays to us numerically challenged humans. The computer employs a user identification (UID) number to track accounts. UID numbers begin with 0 (which refers to the root account). In most distributions, user accounts have UID numbers at 1,000 and above, with lower numbers reserved for system accounts.

 Some distributions number user accounts starting at 500 rather than 1,000.

GID Accounts are tied to one or more groups, which are similar to accounts in many ways; however, a group is a collection of accounts. One of the primary purposes of groups is to enable users to give certain other users access to their files, while preventing users not in a designated group from accessing them. Each account is tied directly to a primary group via a group ID (GID) number (100 in the preceding example). By including an account in a group's definition, accounts can be tied to several groups as described in Chapter 13, "Creating Users and Groups."

 File ownership and permissions are described in Chapter 14, "Setting Ownership and Permissions."

Comment Field The *comment field* normally holds the user's full name (Richard Blum in this example), although this field can hold other information instead of or in addition to the user's name.

Home Directory User accounts, and some system accounts, have *home directories* (/home/rich in this example). A home directory is an account's "home base." Normally, ownership of an account's home directory belongs to the account. Certain tools and procedures make it easy for users to access their home directories; for instance, the tilde (~) refers to a user's home directory when used at the start of a filename.

Default Shell   A *default shell* is associated with every account. In Linux, this shell is normally Bash (/bin/bash), but individual users can change this if they like. Most non-root system accounts set the default shell to /usr/sbin/nologin (or /sbin/nologin) as an added security measure—this program displays a message stating that the account is not available. Using /bin/false works in a similar way, although without the explanatory message.

Certification
Objective

You might guess by its name that /etc/passwd holds password information. This isn't normally the case today, although it was many years ago. For historical reasons, /etc/passwd must be readable by all users, so storing passwords there, even as a salted and hashed password, is risky.

> Passwords are stored using a *salted hash*, a one-way mathematical process with additional random input (salt), that produces what looks like nonsense to humans. When a user types a password, it's salted and hashed, and if the salted hashes match, access is granted.

Passwords today are stored in another file, /etc/shadow, that ordinary users can't read. This file associates a salted and hashed password, as well as other information, with an account. This information can disable an account after a period of time or if the user doesn't change the password within a given period of time. A typical /etc/shadow entry looks like this:

```
rich:$6$E/moFkeT5UnTQ3KqZUoA4Fl2tPUoIc[...]:18114:5:30:14:-1:-1:
```

The meaning of each colon-delimited field on this line is as follows:

Username   Each line begins with the username. Note that the UID is *not* used in /etc/shadow; the username links entries in this file to those in /etc/passwd.

Password   The password is stored as a salted hash, so it bears no obvious resemblance to the actual password. An asterisk (*) or exclamation mark (!) denotes an account with no password (that is, the account doesn't accept logins—it's locked). This is common for accounts used by the system itself.

Last Password Change   The next field (18114 in this example) is the date of the last password change. This date is stored as the number of days since January 1, 1970.

> Unix Epoch time, which is also called POSIX time, is the number of seconds since January 1, 1970, although the /etc/shadow file expresses it in days. It has a long history with Unix and Linux systems. You don't have to drag out your calculator to determine what a field's date is using the Epoch. Instead, the chage utility does that for you by displaying the /etc/shadow file record for a designated user account in a human-friendly format. POSIX time may cause problems in the year 2038 on any small systems still using 32-bit processors, because the computer will run out of storage to track time properly in this way.

Days Until a Change Is Allowed   The next field (5 in this example) is the number of days before a password change is allowed. This is used to prevent users from changing their passwords (as required) and then changing them right back to the original password.

Days Before a Change Is Required   This field (30 in this example) is the number of days before another password change is required (since the last password change).

Days of Warning Before Password Expiration   If your system is configured to expire passwords, you may set it to warn the user when an expiration date is approaching. A value of 7 is typical. However, 14 days, as shown in the preceding example, may be appropriate if your company's employees take two-week vacations.

Days Between Expiration and Deactivation   Linux allows a gap between when the account expires and when it is completely deactivated. An expired account either can't be used or requires that the user change the password immediately after logging in. In either case, its password remains intact. A deactivated account's password is erased, and the account can't be used until the system administrator reactivates it. A -1 in this field, as shown in the preceding example, indicates that this feature is disabled.

Expiration Date   This field shows the date on which the account will expire. As with the last password change date, the date is expressed as the number of days since January 1, 1970. A -1 in this field, as shown in the preceding example, indicates that this feature is disabled.

Special Flag   This field is reserved for future use and normally isn't used or contains a meaningless value. This field is empty in the preceding example.

For fields relating to day counts, typically a value of -1 or 99999 or no value (blank) indicates that the relevant feature has been disabled. The /etc/shadow values are generally best left to modification through commands such as usermod (described in Chapter 13) and chage. Understanding the format of the file enables you to review its contents and note any discrepancies, which could indicate that your system has been compromised.

The terms *encrypted* and *hashed* are often confused when used with computer objects. You can decrypt an encrypted object, but you cannot "dehash" a hashed object. Passwords on Linux are salted and hashed, though often you'll see the term *encrypted* mistakenly used instead in Linux documentation.

The /etc/shadow file is usually stored with restrictive permissions, with ownership by root. This fact is critical to the shadow password system's utility because it keeps non-super users from reading the file and obtaining the password list, even in a salted and hashed form. By contrast, /etc/passwd must be readable by ordinary users and usually has less restrictive permissions.

It's important to realize that an account isn't a single entity like a program binary file. Account information is scattered across several configuration files, such as /etc/passwd, /etc/shadow, /etc/group, and possibly in other configuration files that refer to accounts. User files reside in the user's home directory and perhaps elsewhere. Thus, managing accounts can require doing more than just maintaining a file or two. For this reason, various utilities exist to help create, manage, and delete accounts, as described in the rest of this chapter and in Chapter 13.

Examples of user files stored outside the user's home directory may include email in /var/spool/mail and temporary files in /tmp.

Identifying Accounts

One way to identify user accounts is to use a GUI tool for account management. Such tools vary from one distribution to another. One example is the Users and Groups account tool on a Linux Mint system. You can reach this tool by clicking Menu in the main window and then typing **user** in the search box, as shown in Figure 12.1.

FIGURE 12.1   Locating the Users and Groups account tool on Linux Mint

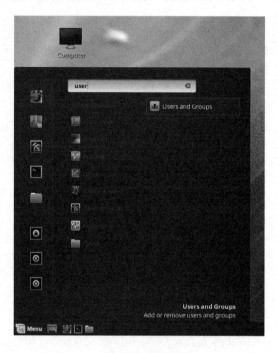

Accessing this option produces a window similar to the one shown in Figure 12.2 but only if you have super user privileges and provide the appropriate password. This tool shows only user accounts, not system accounts. It enables changing a few features, such as a user's password, by clicking them, but its usefulness as an account management tool is limited.

Passwords are typically displayed as dots or asterisks in a GUI environment as a security feature.

FIGURE 12.2   The Users and Groups account tool provides minimal account information.

You can identify *all* of a computer's accounts by viewing the /etc/passwd file's contents with cat or less. Doing so will reveal all accounts, including both system and user accounts.

Alternatively, if you're searching for information on a specific account, you can use grep to find it in /etc/passwd, as in **grep rich /etc/passwd** to find information on any account that's tied to a user with the username rich. (This specific example assumes that the string rich appears in the passwd file, of course.)

 You can pull out individual records by using the getent command too. Just add the username to the command's end—for instance, getent passwd rich.

An alternative that's similar to perusing /etc/passwd is to type **getent passwd**. The getent command retrieves entries from certain administrative databases, including the /etc/passwd file. In most cases, typing **getent passwd** produces results that are identical to typing **cat /etc/passwd**; however, sometimes the two aren't identical. The /etc/passwd file defines only *local* user accounts. It's possible to configure Linux to use a network account database to define some or all of its accounts. If you use such a configuration, typing **getent passwd** returns *both* local accounts and accounts defined on the network server.

 Real World Scenario

Network Account Databases

Many networks employ network account databases. Such systems may include the Lightweight Directory Access Protocol (LDAP), Kerberos realms, and Active Directory (AD) domains. All of these systems move account database management onto a single centralized computer (often with one or more backup systems) or distributed across a designated system set. The advantage is that users and administrators need not deal with maintaining accounts independently on multiple computers. A single-account database can handle accounts on dozens (or even hundreds or thousands) of different computers, greatly simplifying day-to-day administrative tasks and also simplifying users' lives. Using such a system, though, means that most user accounts won't appear in /etc/passwd and /etc/shadow, and groups may not appear in /etc/group (described shortly, in "Understanding Groups"). These files will still hold information on local system accounts and groups, though.

Linux can participate in these systems. In fact, some distributions provide options to enable such support at OS installation time. Typically, you must know the name or IP address of the server that hosts the network account database, and you must know what protocol that system uses. You may also need a password or some other protocol-specific information, and the server may need to be configured to accept accesses from the Linux system that you're configuring.

Activating use of such network account databases after installing Linux is a complex topic that is not covered in this book. Such systems often alter the behavior of tools such as passwd and usermod (described in Chapter 13) in subtle or not-so-subtle ways. If you need to use such a system, you'll have to consult documentation specific to the service that you intend to use.

Understanding Groups

Certification
Objective

As noted earlier, groups are collections of accounts that are defined in the /etc/group file. Like /etc/passwd, the /etc/group file contains colon-delimited lines (records), each defining a single group. An example looks like this:

```
users:x:100:games,christine
```

The fields in /etc/group are as follows:

Group Name   The first field, users in the preceding example, is the name of the group. You use it with most commands that access or manipulate group data.

Password   Groups, like users, can have passwords. A value of x means that the password is defined elsewhere (but may be disabled), and an empty password field means that the group has no password.

 The use and management of group passwords is a topic that's beyond the scope of this book. However, group passwords are typically frowned on by security professionals.

GID   Linux uses GID values, like UID values, internally. Translation to and from group names is done by the system for the benefit of users and administrators.

User List   You can specify users who belong to the group in a comma-delimited list at the end of the /etc/group record.

It's important to recognize that users can be identified as members of a group in either of two ways:

By Specifying the Group's GID in Users' Individual /etc/passwd Entries   Because /etc/passwd has room for only one GID value, only one group can be defined in this way. This is the user's primary (or default) group.

By Specifying Usernames in the User List in the /etc/group File   A single user can appear multiple times in /etc/group, and a single group can have multiple users associated with it in this way. If a user is associated with a group in this way but not via the user's /etc/passwd entry, this group association is secondary.

When you create new files, those files will be associated with your current group. When you log in, your current group is set to your primary group. If you want to create files that are associated with another group to which you belong, you can use the newgrp command, as follows:

```
$ newgrp project1
```

This command makes project1 your current group, so that the files you create will be associated with that group. Group ownership of files is important in file security, which is described in more detail in Chapter 14.

Using Account Tools

A few commands can help you learn about the users and groups on your computer. Most notably, the whoami and id utilities can tell you about your own identity, and the who and w utilities can give you information about who is currently using the computer.

Discovering Your Own Identity

If you maintain multiple accounts for yourself and you don't recall which one you used to log in, you might become confused about your current status. In such a case, the whoami command can come in handy. It displays your current user ID:

```
$ whoami
christine
```

This example reveals that the current account is christine. If you need more information, you can use the id utility:

```
$ id
uid=1002(christine) gid=100(users) groups=100(users)[...]
```

This example shows information on both users and groups:

- **Your User ID and Username:** uid=1002(christine) in this example
- **Your Current Group:** gid=100(users) in this example
- **All Your Group Memberships:** the entries following groups= in this example

The id command displays both the numeric UID and GID values and potentially the associated names. The current group is the one that's active, either by default or because you used the newgrp command.

 On some distributions, the id command provides more information than shown in our examples.

You can limit id's output by specifying various options, as summarized in Table 12.1. In addition, you can specify a username, as in **id rich**, to obtain information on that user rather than on yourself.

TABLE 12.1 Options for id

Long option	Short option	Effect
--group	-g	Displays only the effective group ID
--groups	-G	Displays all the groups to which you belong
--user	-u	Displays only the user data
--name	-n	Used in conjunction with -g, -G, or -u; displays only the name, not the UID or GID
--real	-r	Used in conjunction with -g, -G, or -u; displays only the UID or GID, not the name

Learning Who's Online

Linux permits multiple users to access the computer simultaneously. Most often, this is done by means of remote access servers such as the Secure Shell (SSH); however, you can use Linux's virtual terminal (VT) feature to log in multiple times with a single keyboard and monitor. Sometimes, you might want to know who is using the computer. You might do this before shutting down the computer, for instance, to ensure that you don't inconvenience another user.

To learn who is online, you can use a command known as who:

Certification
Objective

```
$ who
christine tty7         2019-08-06 10:14 (:0)
steph     tty2       2019-08-06 10:57
rich      pts/0      2019-08-06 10:56 (192.168.0.102)
devon     tty3       2019-08-06 10:57
ken       tty4       2019-08-06 10:57
$
```

This example shows five logins—christine, steph, rich, devon, and ken. Information provided in the default output includes the following:

Username   The first column of who's output shows the username.

Terminal Identifier   The second column of who's output shows a code associated with the terminal. In this example, christine's first login shows tty7 and it is a local GUI login, but some distributions use the 0 as a GUI identifier. The remaining logins all have terminal identifiers of the form pts/# or tty#, indicating text sessions. A text session can be a terminal launched in a GUI, a text-mode console login, or a remote login via SSH or some other protocol.

Login Date and Time   who displays the date and time of each login. You can see that christine's session began several minutes before steph logged in.

Remote Host   The final column of who's output, if present, shows the login source. Console logins (including both text-mode and GUI-based logins) don't include a source. A source of the form# or#.# or :# often indicates a terminal opened in a GUI, such as in christine's source: (:0). A hostname or IP address, as in rich's session, indicates remote access from the specified computer.

By default, the who command pulls its data from the /var/run/utmp file.

You can obtain additional information, most of which is obscure or specialized, by passing options to who. One that's more likely than others to be useful is --count (or -q), which produces a more compact summary of the data:

```
$ who -q
christine steph rich devon ken
# users=5
$
```

This output includes just the usernames and a line specifying the total number of sessions. Notice that the users number counts one user with multiple logins multiple times.

NOTE   Different distributions have varying minor details for the who command. However, the major elements are the same.

Similar to the whoami command but showing more information, passing the am i arguments to the who command displays data only for your current user ID:

```
$ who am i
rich       pts/0        2019-08-06 10:56 (192.168.0.102)
$
```

NOTE   The who command, on some distributions, ignores the am i arguments and returns nothing. If your system does accept them, for a little humor, use the arguments mom likes in place of the am i arguments.

In this example, the current user account is rich, who is logged into the pts/0 terminal session. For information on additional who options and arguments, consult its man page.

Certification
Objective

An alternative to who is w, which is similar to who but produces somewhat more verbose output:

```
$ w
 11:17:26 up  1:10,  5 users,  load average: 0.00, 0.03, 0.04
USER      TTY      FROM           LOGIN@   IDLE   JCPU   PCPU WHAT
christin tty7     :0             10:14    1:09m 17.12s  0.64s cinnamon[...]
steph    tty2                    10:57    4:30   0.21s  0.16s -bash
rich     pts/0    192.168.0.102  10:56    1.00s  0.20s  0.00s w
devon    tty3                    10:57    20:05  0.21s  0.15s -bash
ken      tty4                    10:57    19:58  0.23s  0.16s -bash
$
```

As you can see, w displays much of the same information as who, including the terminal identifier (TTY) and login time (in a different format). In addition, w displays further information:

▪   The session's idle time tells you how long it's been since the user has interacted with this session. This information can help you identify sessions that the user may have abandoned.

▪   The JCPU column identifies the total amount of CPU time associated with the session. This can be useful debugging information if the computer has become sluggish because of out-of-control processes.

- The PCPU column identifies the total amount of CPU time associated with the current process running in the session. Again, this information can help you track down out-of-control processes.
- The WHAT column tells you what program the session is running.

Some configurations also display a FROM column, which shows a remote hostname. Using the -f option toggles this option on or off. A few other options can eliminate or modify w's output. Consult the program's man page for details.

Working as *root*

Linux is modeled after Unix, which was designed as a multiuser OS. In principle, you can have thousands of accounts on a single Unix (or Linux) computer. At least one user, though, needs extraordinary power in order to manage the features of the computer as a whole. Historically, this is the root user account, also known as the *super user* or the *administrator*. Knowing why root exists, how to do things as root (if you must), and how to use root privileges safely is important for managing a Linux system.

Understanding User Types

Most people use computers to do ordinary day-to-day computer tasks—browse the web, write letters, manage a music collection, and so on. These activities are known collectively as *user tasks*, and they don't require special privileges. As just noted, a Linux computer can have many user accounts, and the users can use the computer from these user accounts (also known as *unprivileged accounts*, *unprivileged users*, or *standard users*) to perform such user tasks.

Certification
Objective

The root account exists to enable you to perform *administrative tasks*. These tasks include installing new software, preparing a new disk for use in the computer, and managing ordinary user accounts. Such tasks require access to system files that ordinary users do not need to modify or even read.

Certification
Objective

Another user type is a *system user*. These are nonlogin accounts for daemons, services, or applications. System user accounts typically have a low UID number; no password (so the account is locked); and /usr/sbin/ nologin, /sbin/nologin, or /bin/false as their default shell.

To facilitate performing these tasks, root can read and write every file on the computer. Since Linux relies on files to store system settings, this effectively gives root the power to change any detail of the OS's operation, which is the point of having a super user account. If the computer is a workstation that's used by just one individual, you may wonder why the distinction between root and the user account is necessary. The explanation is that the power of the root account can lead to accidental damage. For instance, take the rm command. If you mistype an rm command as an ordinary user, you can accidentally delete your own files but not system files. Make the same mistake as root, however, and you can delete system files, perhaps making the computer unbootable. Therefore, you should be cautious when using the root account (or not use it at all), a topic covered more thoroughly in the upcoming "Using root Privileges Safely" section.

Acquiring *root* Privileges

When you need to perform a command-line task that requires root privileges, you can do so in any of three ways:

Log In as root   You can log in directly as root at a text-mode shell or by using a remote login tool such as SSH. You can even log into GUI mode as root on some Linux distributions. Some distributions don't allow root to log in directly by default because it's dangerous.

Certification
Objective

Use su   The su command enables you to change your identity within a shell. Type **su *username*** to change your identity to that of the specified *username*. If you omit *username*, root is assumed, so typing **su** enables you effectively to become root.

You must, however, know the password for the target account (root or otherwise) for this command to work. After you acquire root privileges in this way, you can type as many commands as root as you like. When you're done, type **exit** to relinquish your super user status.

You can also use su to run a single command as root. Use the -c option, as in **su -c *command*** to run *command* as root.

If you use a dash (-) within the command, as in **su -** or **su - luke**, the program opens a login session that runs the target user's login scripts. This can be important because these scripts often set environment variables such as $PATH that can be important for that user.

su stands for *switch user* or *substitute user*.

Certification
Objective

Use sudo   The sudo command is similar to su, but it works for just one command at a time, which you type after sudo, similar to using su -c. For instance, typing **sudo cat /etc/shadow** enables you to see the contents of the /etc/shadow file, which is not readable by ordinary users. You must type either your own password or the root password, depending on the sudo configuration, when you use this program. (When using su -c, you must always type the root password.) The next command you type will be executed using your ordinary account privileges. Some distributions, such as Ubuntu and Fedora, rely heavily on sudo and don't permit direct root logins by default.

Many modern distributions do not let you log into the root account. However, if you can acquire root privileges by logging in directly as root or by using su -, your shell prompt will change:

```
[rey@jakku ~]$ su -
Password:
[root@jakku ~]#
```

 It's a good idea to always use su -, instead of just the su command. The dash (-) sets up the user account environment correctly. If you don't use the dash, you may experience command problems.

In this example, the username has changed from rey to root and the last character of the prompt has changed from a dollar sign ($) to a hash mark (#). Because just the last prompt character was used for most examples printed on their own lines in this book, such examples implicitly specify whether a command requires root privileges by the prompt used. For instance, consider accessing the /etc/shadow file mentioned earlier:

```
# cat /etc/shadow
```

The use of the hash mark prompt indicates that you *must* type this command using root privileges.

 To use root commands in Linux Mint and Fedora Workstation, you must either precede them with sudo (as in **sudo cat /etc/shadow**) or type **sudo su** to acquire a longer-lasting root shell.

Some of this book's chapters describe both GUI and text-mode methods of system administration. How, then, can you administer Linux in GUI mode if you must use the text-mode sudo command to acquire root privileges? Most distributions allow you to launch administrative tools from the computer's desktop menus, and the GUI tools will then prompt you for the super user password when administrative privileges are needed, as shown in Figure 12.3. If you type the password correctly, the program will continue. The result is similar to that of launching the program from a shell using sudo.

FIGURE 12.3   Administrative tools in the GUI ask for a password when administrator privileges are needed.

Using *root* Privileges Safely

As already described, root power is dangerous. You could accidentally wipe out critical application files and cause hours of downtime. Imagine what would happen if you mistakenly corrupted an important configuration file or destroyed a set of important backups. Everyone makes mistakes—unfortunately, some mistakes can be absolutely disastrous for a company.

Imagine intruders gaining root access to your computer: unintended changes to configuration files, damage to some (even if not all) of the computer's system files, and changes to ownership or permissions on ordinary user files, rendering them inaccessible to their true owners. You should take the following precautions whenever you need root access:

- Ask yourself if you really need root access. Sometimes there's a way to achieve a goal without super user privileges or by using those privileges in a more limited way than you'd originally planned. For instance, you might find that only root can write to a removable disk. Such a problem can usually be overcome by adjusting permissions on the disk in one way or another, thus limiting the use of root.

- Before pressing the Enter key after typing any command as root (or clicking any confirmation button in a GUI program running as root), take your hands *off* the keyboard and mouse, look over the command, and verify that it's correct in every respect. A simple typo can cause a world of pain.

Working as *root* 267

- Never run a suspicious program as root. On multiuser systems, unscrupulous users can try to trick administrators into running programs that will do nasty things or give the attacker root privileges. Programs downloaded from random Internet sites could in principle be designed to compromise your security, and such programs are much more dangerous when run as root.

If a program asks you for your password, or the root password, and it's not an administrative program that you trust, be suspicious! Research the program before giving it the password!

- Use root privileges for as brief a period as possible. If you need to type just one or two commands as root, do so and then type **exit** in the root shell to log out or return to your normal privileges. Better yet, use sudo to run the commands. It's easy to overlook the fact that you're using a root shell and therefore type commands as root that don't need that privilege. Every command typed as root is a risk.

- Never leave a root shell accessible to others. If you're performing root maintenance tasks and are called away, type **exit** in your root shell before leaving the computer.

- Be careful with the root password. Don't share the password with others, and be cautious about typing it in a public area or when others might be looking over your shoulder. If you're using Linux professionally, your employer may have guidelines concerning who may have root access to a computer. Learn those rules and obey them! Be sure to select a strong root password, too.

Chapter 13 describes how to select a strong password.

Following these rules of thumb can help keep you from damaging your computer or giving somebody else root access to the computer.

EXERCISE 12.1

- Type **whoami** followed by **id** to review your ordinary user account status. Chances are that the id command will reveal that you're a member of various groups. Perform a web search to learn what each one does.

- Read the /etc/passwd file or type **getent passwd** to review what accounts are defined on the computer. Are there ordinary user accounts (those with UIDs above 500 or 1,000, depending on your distribution) other than your own? Try performing a web search to learn the purpose of a few of the system accounts (those with UIDs below 500 or 1,000, depending on your distribution).

Summary

Accounts are critical to Linux's normal functioning. Ordinarily, most of the tasks that you perform on a Linux computer require the privileges of a standard user, so you'll use your own user account to handle these tasks. You can use tools such as whoami, id, who, and w to identify your account and to determine who else might be using the computer. Occasionally, you'll need to perform administrative tasks that require the root account's privileges, which can read and write any ordinary file, access hardware in a low-level way, reconfigure the network, and perform other tasks that ordinary users aren't allowed to do. Because root is so powerful, you should use that power sparingly and be extremely careful when you do use it, lest a typo or other accident cause serious problems.

Exam Essentials

Explain the difference between various Linux accounts.   User accounts generally fall into three categories: the root user, standard users, and system accounts. The root account has a UID of 0 and is often disabled on many modern Linux distributions so that no one can directly log into it. This is due to the fact that root can read and write every file on the computer, making it a rather dangerous user. In addition, if multiple individuals use the root account, it sets up an insecure repudiation environment.

Users are each given an account on the system to perform productive work. They typically have regular privileges, but those who perform special administrative system duties may have access to super user privileges through commands such as sudo. These accounts have UIDs that start at 500 or 1,000 depending on the distribution configuration.

System accounts help keep the computer running. You cannot log into these accounts, because they lack passwords, and their default shell is often set to /sbin/nologin. The UIDs for system accounts are numbers that are lower than the configured base for user account UIDs.

Describe the files involved in Linux account configuration.   The /etc/passwd file has a record for each account on the system. These records consist of the following fields: username, password, UID, GID, comment, home directory, and default shell.

The /etc/shadow file has password information and data for each account on the system. Each records contains the following fields: username, salted and hashed password (if a password is set for the account), the last password change in Epoch format, days until a password modification is allowed, days before a password change is required, number of days warning before the password expires, days between account expiration and deactivation, account expiration date, and a special flag.

The /etc/group file has a record for every defined group on the system. These records consist of the following fields: group name, group password, GID, and the group's user list.

Compare the utilities to show who is on the system.   The whoami command will display the current account name in use. For additional information, you can use the id command. To learn who is currently online besides yourself, the who utility works, but the w command provides more information.

Summarize methods to gain super user access.   You can directly log into the root account on distributions that allow such access to gain super user access, but it is generally frowned on due to security issues. The su command will allow you to switch to another account as long as you have its password; this includes the root account if it is enabled for such use. The sudo command is the preferred method for gaining super user privileges. Type **sudo** in front of the command that needs the privileges and press Enter. It will demand your password if not recently used.

Review Questions

You can find the answers in Appendix A.

1. What is the purpose of the system account with a UID of 0?

   A. It's the system administration account.

   B. It's the account for the first ordinary user.

   C. Nothing; UID 0 is left intentionally undefined.

   D. It varies from one distribution to another.

   E. It's a low-privilege account that's used as a default by some servers.

2. What type of information will you find in /etc/passwd for ordinary user accounts? (Choose all that apply.)

   A. A user ID (UID) number

   B. A complete listing of every group to which the user belongs

   C. The path to the account's home directory

   D. The path to the account's default GUI desktop environment

   E. The path to the account's default text-mode shell

3. You want to run the command cat /etc/shadow as root, but you're logged in as an ordinary user. Which of the following commands will do the job, assuming that the system is configured to give you super user access via the appropriate command?

   A. sudo cat /etc/shadow

   B. root cat /etc/shadow

   C. passwd cat /etc/shadow

   D. su cat /etc/shadow

   E. admin cat /etc/shadow

4. True or false: whoami provides more information than id.

5. True or false: Linux stores information on its groups in the /etc/groups file.

6. True or false: As a general rule, you should employ extra care when running programs as root.

7. The file that associates usernames with UID numbers in Linux is _____.

   A. /etc/shadow

   B. /etc/group

   C. /etc/UID

   D. /etc/passwd

   E. /etc/usernames

8. To learn who is currently logged into the computer and what programs they're currently running, you can type _____.

    A. who

    B. w

    C. whoami

    D. who -q

    E. id

9. UIDs above 0 and below 500 or 1,000 (depending on the distribution) are reserved for use by _____ account(s).

    A. administrator

    B. standard user

    C. unprivileged

    D. root

    E. system

10. A _____ environment means that a person cannot deny actions, and the sudo command helps establish this environment.

    A. secure

    B. standard

    C. nonrepudiation

    D. repudiation

    E. locked-down

Chapter

13

Creating Users and Groups

OBJECTIVES:

✓ 5.2   Creating Users and Groups

Linux is a multiuser OS, meaning that a single Linux computer can support many users, each with a unique account. With this capability comes the need to manage users' accounts, and this chapter covers the procedures you'll use to do so.

The chapter begins with information on how to create accounts. With the accounts created, you then need to know how to modify those accounts and, when necessary, delete them. Finally, groups are similar to accounts in many ways, so you'll learn how to create and manage groups.

Creating New Accounts

In many environments, the task of adding accounts is quite common. Large businesses hire new employees, universities recruit new students, charitable organizations obtain fresh volunteers, and so on. Therefore, you must know how to create new accounts. But first, this section looks at the important issues of deciding how to use groups and selecting a good password. You'll then learn how to create accounts using both GUI and text-mode tools.

Deciding on a Group Strategy

As described in Chapter 12, "Understanding Basic Security," Linux *groups* are collections of users. You can use groups to control who can access particular files. As will be described in Chapter 14, "Setting Ownership and Permissions," individuals can change the group affiliations and group permissions of their own files. Thus, the way you use groups can influence your computer's overall security strategy. Two approaches are common:

User Groups   Each user can have an associated group; for instance, the user luke can have a group called luke. This user can then set group ownership on his files to luke or set group permissions to whatever is desired, and the system administrator can add users to the luke group. Thereafter, members of the luke group may access files in this group by using the permissions determined by the user luke. This approach emphasizes controlling access to individual users' files.

Project Groups   In this method, you create groups based on work projects, departmental affiliations, or other real-world groupings of users. For instance, you might have a group called sales for users in the sales department. Members of this group who want to share files with other members of this group would assign group ownership and permissions appropriately and store files in an agreed-upon location. This approach works best when the computer is used by a large number of people who collaborate in easily defined groups.

These two approaches are not mutually exclusive; you can mix and match or create your own approach. You should also realize that users can be members of multiple groups. In fact, this is required for the user groups approach to work at all—otherwise, groups are redundant with accounts.

By default, some distributions employ a user groups strategy and others use a project groups strategy. In the latter case, most users are in a group called users or something similar by default.

If you use the project group approach, you should think about which group should be a new user's primary group. This is the group that will be assigned group ownership of the user's files by default.

Selecting a Good Password

When you create an account, you typically should create a password for it. Sometimes, the user can select the password when the account is created. At other times, you'll need to select a password that the user will use initially. In such cases, instruct the user to change the password as soon as possible. In either case, it's important to educate users about selecting a good password.

Be sure to follow the advice in this section yourself, especially for the root password if you use the root account!

Poor but common passwords include those based on the following:

- The names of family members, friends, and pets
- Favorite books, movies, television shows, or the characters in any of these
- Telephone numbers, street addresses, or Social Security numbers
- Any other meaningful personal information
- Any single word that's found in a dictionary (in *any* language)
- Any simple keyboard or alphanumeric combination, such as qwerty or 123456

The best possible passwords are random collections of letters, digits, and punctuation. Unfortunately, such passwords are difficult to remember. A reasonable compromise is to build a password in two steps:

1. Choose a base that's easy to remember but difficult to guess.

2. Modify that base in ways that increase the difficulty of guessing the password.

One approach to building a base is to use two or more *unrelated* words, such as *bun* and *pen*. You can then merge these two words (bunpen). Another approach, and one that's arguably better than the first, is to use the first letters of a phrase that's meaningful to the user. For instance, the first letters of "yesterday I went to the dentist" become yiwttd.

In both cases, the base should not be a word in any language. As a general rule, the longer the password, the better.

Many distributions place lower limits on password length, such as six or eight characters.

With the base in hand, it's time to modify it to create a password. The user should apply at least a couple of several possible modifications:

Adding Numbers or Punctuation   One important change is to insert random numbers or punctuation in the base. This step might yield, for instance, bu3npe?n or y+i9wttd. As a general rule, add at least two symbols or numbers.

Mixing Case   Linux uses case-sensitive passwords, so jumbling the case of letters can improve security. Applying this rule might produce Bu3nPE?n and y+i9WttD, for instance.

Reversing Order   A change that's very weak by itself but that can add to security when used in conjunction with the others is to reverse the order of some or all letters. You might apply this to just one word of a two-word base. This could yield Bu3nn?EP and DttW9i+y, for instance.

Growing the Haystack   A would-be intruder's task of discovering a password has been likened to finding a needle in a haystack. One way to make this task harder is to increase the size of the haystack. In password terms, this means making a password larger. You can do this by using larger words or phrases, of course, but this can make a password harder to remember and type. Even a size increase that simply repeats a single character can be helpful. Thus you might turn the passwords into Bu3nn?EPiiiiiiiiii or Dtt!!!!!!!!!!!W9i+y.

The National Institute of Standards and Technology (NIST) is a nonregulatory U.S. agency. They publish many commerce recommendations, including business computer security. NIST proposals are typically turned into procedures for companies and government organizations. In 2017, NIST issued new guidelines regarding secure passwords, and surprisingly long complicated passwords are no longer recommended. However, it may take a while before the new NIST password guidelines filter down into your day-to-day world, if ever.

Your best tool for getting users to pick good passwords is to educate them. Here are some insights to share with users:

- Passwords can be guessed by malicious individuals who know them or even who target them and look up personal information on social media, web-based telephone directories, business profiles, and so on.

- Although Linux salts and hashes its passwords internally, programs exist that feed entire dictionaries through Linux's password salting/hashing algorithms for comparison to a Linux system's passwords. If a match occurs, the password has been found.

- User accounts might be used as a first step toward compromising the entire computer or as a launching point for attacks on other computers.

- Users should *never* reveal their passwords to others, even people claiming to be system administrators. This is a common scam, because real system administrators don't need users' passwords.

- The same password should not be used on multiple systems, because doing so quickly turns a compromised account on one computer into a compromised account on all of them.

- Writing passwords down or emailing them are both risky practices. Writing a password on a sticky note stuck to the computer's monitor is particularly foolish.

Telling your users these things will help them understand the reasons for your concern, and it's likely to help motivate at least some of them to pick good passwords.

Don't Use These Passwords!

If you do a web search on **common passwords** or a similar phrase, you'll quickly discover websites that provide surveys showing the most typical and easily guessed passwords that security researchers have uncovered. Details vary from one survey to another, but typically common passwords include the following:

- 123456

- password

- 12345678

- qwerty

- 111111

- sunshine

- iloveyou

- princess

- football

- password1

Such passwords are easily discovered by brute-force password-guessing programs and are included in collections of passwords distributed on the Internet. Using such a password is barely better than using no password at all. Do yourself a favor and create a better one!

Creating Accounts Using GUI Tools

Now that you have some idea of what type of group policy you want to use and how to create a good password, you can begin creating accounts. Some distributions allow you to accomplish this task, at least partially, via a GUI tool. Such tools vary from one Linux distribution to another. Important variations include how you access these tools and the tool names. On several distributions, using the desktop's search utility, you can type **user** to find the appropriate account creation utility. On other distributions, you will need to navigate through the desktop menus to locate the correct tool. The utility's name may be something similar to Users, User Accounts, or User and Groups Administration.

When you launch the Users and Groups Administration utility on Linux Mint, a dialog appears, prompting you to type your account's password before you can proceed. If you have super user privileges, you'll then see the utility screen in Figure 13.1.

   As an example of a GUI user account management tool, Figure 13.1 shows Linux Mint's User and Groups Administration utility. You can do a great deal more than add accounts with this particular utility. However, the focus here is on creating accounts.

FIGURE 13.1   The Linux Mint User and Groups Administration utility provides many options for creating and managing accounts.

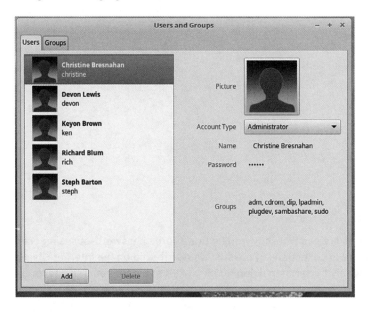

To add a user with User and Group Administration, follow these steps:

1. Click the Add button. The result is the dialog shown in Figure 13.2.

FIGURE 13.2 You can enter all the basic account information using this dialog.

2. Type the user's full name in the User's Full Name field. This entry is stored in the comment field of /etc/passwd and may be displayed in various tools; for instance, it appears in some desktop environments when a user logs into the desktop.

3. Type the username in the Username field. This is what the user will type at Linux login prompts.

4. Click the Add button to finish creating the account.

5. Click the username, and then click the words "no password set" in the account's description to open the Change Password dialog shown in Figure 13.3.

6. Type the password twice, once in the Password field and again in the Confirm Password field.

7. When the utility considers the password strong enough, the Change button is available (not grayed out) for you to click in order to modify the password.

The new account appear in the Users tab list. You can subsequently modify or delete it, as described later in this chapter.

FIGURE 13.3   Set the user account's password using the Change Password dialog.

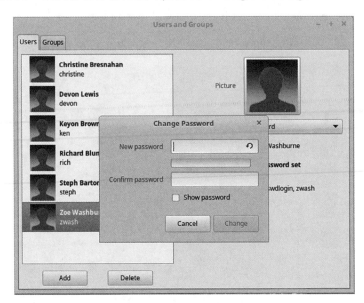

Creating Accounts from the Shell

With any distribution, you use the useradd utility to create an account from the command line. To use this utility, you type its name and the username that you want to associate with a new account. You may also include options between useradd and the username, as summarized in Table 13.1. The useradd command supports options in addition to those shown in Table 13.1; consult its man page for details.

TABLE 13.1   Options for useradd

Option name	Option abbreviation	Effect
--comment *comment*	-c	Specifies the comment field for the user. (GUI tools generally describe this as the "full name.")
--home *home-dir*	-d	Specifies the account's home directory. It defaults to /home/*username*.
--expiredate *expire-date*	-e	Sets the date on which the account will be disabled, expressed in the form *YYYY-MM-DD*. The default is for an account that does not expire.

Option name	Option abbreviation	Effect
`--inactive` *inactive-days*	`-f`	Sets the number of days after a password expires, after which the account becomes completely disabled. A value of -1 disables this feature and is the default.
`--gid` *default-group*	`-g`	Sets the name or GID of the user's default group. The default for this value is a new group named after the user.
`--groups` *group[,...]*	`-G`	Sets the names or GIDs of groups to which the user belongs—more than one may be specified by separating them with commas.
`--create-home`	`-m`	When included with `useradd`, creates a home directory for the user. This option is typically enabled by default.
`--skel` *skeleton-dir*	`-k`	Normally, default user configuration files are copied from `/etc/skel`, but you may specify another template directory with this option, which is valid only in conjunction with `-m`.
None	`-M`	Forces the system *not* to automatically create a home directory.
`--shell` *shell*	`-s`	Sets the name of the user's default login shell with this option. The default is `/bin/bash`.
`--uid` *UID*	`-u`	Creates an account with the specified user ID value (*UID*).
`--non-unique`	`-o`	Enables a single UID number to be reused; this option is passed when creating the second or subsequent account that reuses a UID.
`--system`	`-r`	Specifies the creation of a system account. `useradd` doesn't create a home directory for system accounts, and it gives them UID values below 100.
`--no-user-group`	`-N`	Disables creation of a group for the user.

On Debian-based distributions, such as Ubuntu and Linux Mint, you can use a friendlier front end to the useradd utility by typing **adduser**. Be aware that on some distributions, such as Fedora, the adduser command, if available, is not a front end to the useradd utility but rather a link to it.

Some of these options aren't readily accessible when you're creating accounts using GUI tools, but the details differ from one GUI utility to another. In some cases, options can be set in a GUI utility *after* the account has been created but not when creating it.

A complete useradd command, including setting a few options, looks like this:

```
$ sudo useradd -m -c "Hoburn Washburne" -u 1006 hwash
[sudo] password for christine:
```

This example creates an account with a username hwash, a home directory, a comment field containing the user's full name, and a UID of 1006. Notice in the preceding example that the sudo command was used to obtain super user privileges, a requirement to complete this command successfully.

You may want to specify a UID to keep these values synchronized across computers that share files with the Network File System (NFS), which identifies file ownership via UIDs.

When you create an account with useradd, it will be in a *locked* state—the user will not be able to log in. To unlock it, you must use the passwd command, as described next, in "Modifying Accounts."

You can add a password with the useradd command's -p option. However, for security reasons, this is not recommended. It is better to use the passwd command, as described later in this chapter.

Certification
Objective

Behind the scenes, useradd (or by extension its GUI front end) modifies the contents of the following files (described in detail in Chapter 12):

/etc/passwd

/etc/shadow

/etc/group

If you use --create-home or -m (or if this option is the default for your distribution), the program creates a home directory and copies files from /etc/skel to that location. Creating an account will also usually create a mail spool file in which the user's incoming email will be stored. (This file may go unused on many desktop systems, but it can be important if you run mail server software on the computer.) You can see that useradd makes quite a few modifications to your computer's files and directories in creating the account.

Modifying Accounts

As you've just learned, when creating an account you can specify many options that affect accounts, such as giving an account a specific UID number. Sometimes, though, it's necessary to change account options after an account has been created. Fortunately, Linux provides both GUI and text-mode tools to help you do this. Before delving into operational details of these tools, though, you should understand when you might want to make changes to accounts and know how to check whether a user is currently logged in.

Deciding When to Modify Accounts

In an ideal world, you'll create your accounts perfectly every time; however, sometimes this isn't possible. You might lack information that's necessary to create a flawlessly tuned account (such as the length of time an employee will be with a company), or your needs might change after the account has been created. Some common specific causes of account changes include (but are by no means limited to) the following:

- Account expiration data may need to be updated. A contract employee might have their contract extended, for instance. Sometimes an expired account must be reenabled.

- UID numbers may need to be synchronized with other computers in order to facilitate file sharing across computers or for other reasons.

- Users' home directories might change because you've added disk space and have to move some users' home directories to a new location.

- A user might forget a password. The system administrator can change the password for any account without knowing the original password, so system administrators frequently have to help users with faulty memories.

When working in a GUI, many of the preceding changes can be handled from the distribution's GUI account management tool. When working in a text-mode shell, though, you'll need to master a few different programs to handle this range of account modifications.

Checking for Logged-in Users

Be aware that some account changes could be disruptive if the user is logged in at the moment that you perform them. Changing the account's username and home directory, in particular, are likely to cause problems. Therefore, you should make such account changes only when the user is logged out. Several tools can help you check who's using the computer and thus avoid problems:

who This utility, described in Chapter 12, produces a list of users who are currently logged into the computer, along with some details of their login sessions, such as their terminal identifiers and login dates.

w   This command, also described in Chapter 12, is similar to who in broad strokes, but it provides different details. Most notably, it identifies the program that's currently running in each session.

 For a quick and simple list of who's using the computer, most distributions offer the users command as well.

last   This program produces a list of recent login sessions, including their starting and ending times, or a notice that the user is still logged in:

```
$ last
christin pts/2        192.168.0.102    Tue Aug 20 11:46    still logged in
[...]
reboot   system boot  4.10.0-38-generi Tue Aug 13 10:09 - 11:22  (01:12)
ken      tty4                          Tue Aug  6 10:57 - 11:40  (00:43)
devon    tty3                          Tue Aug  6 10:57 - 11:40  (00:43)
steph    tty2                          Tue Aug  6 10:57 - 11:40  (00:43)
rich     pts/0        192.168.0.102    Tue Aug  6 10:56 - 11:40  (00:43)
christin tty2                          Tue Aug  6 10:34 - 10:57  (00:22)
```

One notable limitation of last is that it includes only text-mode logins. This makes its utility for identifying users who are currently using the computer rather limited, since such users are likely to be logged in using a GUI session.

 The lastb command displays information similar to last, but it displays only failed login attempts and pulls its data from /var/log/btmp.

The last command displays data that is stored in the /var/log/wtmp file. You should be aware that some distributions do not create this file by default. See the last command's man pages for more information.

Modifying Accounts Using GUI Tools

As with adding accounts, the procedure for modifying accounts using GUI tools varies from one tool to another. Most GUI tools provide similar options, although some are more complete than others. In this section, you'll learn how to modify accounts using Linux Mint's User and Group Administration utility.

To make such changes, after you have the User and Groups Administration utility open, click the account name and then click Item To Modify. An example is shown in Figure 13.4.

FIGURE 13.4   The User and Groups Administration utility enables you to edit a few account properties.

This dialog presents a few account properties. Each of the four items provides access to particular types of data:

Account Type   The account type for the user Richard Blum is shown as Standard in Figure 13.4. A standard account, also called an *unprivileged user account,* was first described in Chapter 12. If you want this user to be able to acquire super user privileges when needed via the sudo command, select Administrator from the drop-down menu.

 To use the sudo command, the administrator account will also need to be part of the sudo or wheel group, depending on your distribution. Adding accounts to groups is covered in the upcoming section "Managing Groups."

Name   As shown in Figure 13.4, you can adjust the account's comment field (identified as Name). Name changes and, if your company wants job titles in this field, position advancements can be handled as well.

Password   You can modify an account's password by clicking the account's Password field. A dialog appears, as shown earlier in Figure 13.3. The utility will not allow you to change the account's password until it considers the password strong enough. If needed, you can have the utility set a strong password for you by clicking the circular arrow. In this case, you'll need to check the Show Password box so that you can view the new setting.

Groups   To add this account to a new group, click the Groups setting. A dialog pops open, allowing to you to choose additional group memberships.

> If you want to add the user to an entirely new group, you must first create the new group, as described in "Managing Groups."

Users can change their own passwords by using GUI options in their desktop environments. For instance, on Fedora within the Users utility, a user's account information automatically displays when the program is open. Click the password (displayed as a series of dots) to launch the Change Password screen, shown in Figure 13.5. Administrators can also use this tool to add and modify accounts.

FIGURE 13.5   The Users utility enables users to change their own passwords.

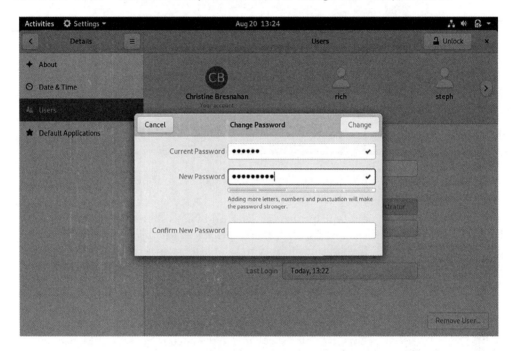

Modifying Accounts from the Shell

One of the most frequent account modifications is to change a user's password, either as part of account creation or because a user has forgotten their password. You can make this change with the passwd program. Ordinary users can type **passwd** to change their own passwords, but not other user accounts' passwords. Those with super user privileges, however, can pass a username to the command to change any account's password:

```
$ sudo passwd hwash
Enter new UNIX password:
Retype new UNIX password:
passwd: password updated successfully
$
```

As a security measure, the password you type does not echo to the screen as you type it. If the passwords you type don't match, the program refuses to accept your change and prompts you again for a fresh pair of passwords. The program also checks the password's strength and may refuse to accept the new password or display a warning message if it deems the password to be too weak. Notice in the preceding example that the sudo command is used, indicating that the person changing the hwash account's password has access to super user privileges, which are required to complete this command successfully.

In addition to setting passwords, the passwd utility enables you to adjust password expiration and aging options. Consult its man page for details.

You can handle most other account modifications by using the usermod program. This command works much like useradd, but instead of creating a new account, it modifies an existing one. Many usermod options are identical to useradd options. Table 13.2 summarizes the most important usermod options.

Certification
Objective

TABLE 13.2   Options for usermod

Option name	Option abbreviation	Effect
--append	-a	Used with --groups (-G), causes the specified groups to be added to (rather than replaced) the existing set of groups for the user.
--comment *comment*	-c	Specifies the comment field for the user. (GUI tools generally describe this as the "full name.")
--home *home-dir*	-d	Specifies the account's home directory. It defaults to /home/*username*.
--expiredate *expire-date*	-e	Sets the date on which the account will be disabled, expressed in the form *YYYY-MM-DD*. The default is for an account that does not expire.
--inactive *inactive-days*	-f	Sets the number of days after a password expires, after which the account becomes completely disabled. A value of -1 disables this feature and is the default.
--gid *default-group*	-g	Sets the name or GID of the user's default group. The default for this value is a new group named after the user.

TABLE 13.2   Options for usermod *(continued)*

Option name	Option abbreviation	Effect
--groups *group*[,...]	-G	Sets the names or GIDs of groups to which the user belongs—more than one may be specified by separating them with commas.
--login *username*	-l	Changes the account's username to the specified value.
--lock	-L	Locks the account's password, preventing logins.
--move-home	-m	When this option is included with --home (-d), usermod moves the user's existing home directory to the new location.
--shell *shell*	-s	Sets the name of the user's default shell with this option.
--uid *UID*	-u	Changes the account's UID number to the specified value.
--unlock	-U	Unlocks a locked account password.

For example, consider the following use of usermod:

```
$ sudo usermod -u 1072 -m -d /home2/hwash hwash
```

This command makes three changes to the hwash account:

- It changes the UID value to 1072.
- It changes the account's home directory to /home2/hwash.
- It moves the contents of the account's original home directory to its new location.

You might issue a command like this one if you were migrating user accounts to an NFS server mounted at /home2. Such a change might require a new home directory location and a change in the UID value to match the one used on the NFS server.

> Be careful when making changes to the UID value, because although usermod changes the UID values of files in common locations such as the user's home directory and email files, it can miss user files in unusual locations.

If you need to make group changes that require adding new groups, consult the upcoming section, "Managing Groups," for information on that topic.

Deleting Accounts

Deleting accounts can sometimes be as important as adding or modifying them. Unused accounts can be abused, either by their former owners or by others who might be able to break into an account if it has a weak password. Therefore, you should routinely delete unused accounts. Before you do so, though, you should understand what happens when you delete an account and decide precisely how to do it, lest you create problems by deleting an account in an inappropriate way. With that knowledge in hand, you can delete accounts by using either GUI or text-mode tools.

Avoiding Account Deletion Pitfalls

Deleting an account may sound simple enough, but a mistake can cause problems, either immediately or in the future. In addition to obvious issues such as accidentally deleting the wrong account, consider these two factors:

User File Preservation   Users' files might be extremely valuable, either to the users themselves or to the organization that owns the computer. You should check your company's file retention policies when considering whether to delete the user's home directory or do something else with it, such as move it into another user's home directory and change permissions on the files it contains. The same is true of the user's mail queue (normally stored in /var/spool/mail/*username*, where *username* is the account's username).

Consider archiving a deleted account's home directory to a long-term backup medium. This strategy will enable you to recover the files should they become valuable in the future.

UID and GID Reuse   When an account is deleted, the account's UID and GID become available for reuse. In many cases, these numbers will not be reused, since most Linux distributions assign these values based on the highest current value. If you delete any but the highest-numbered current user, the user's old UID and GID numbers won't be reused unless intervening accounts are also deleted. Nonetheless, if a UID is *reused*, any files previously owned by the old user will suddenly appear to be owned by the new user. This may not cause any problems, but it may cause confusion about who created the files. In some cases, it can even cause suspicion of wrongdoing by the new user (if the old files contain information the new user shouldn't have, or if the files reside in directories to which the new user shouldn't have access).

To avoid any chance of confusion or misbehavior claims falling on new users due to UID or GID reuse, you can use the find command (covered in detail in Chapter 8, "Searching, Extracting, and Archiving Data") to locate all files with particular UID or GID values. You must use the -uid and -gid options, as shown here:

```
$ sudo find / -uid 1004
```

While you can issue this command without using super user privileges, it will return errors and may miss some files. Therefore, it's best to use find in this manner with super user privileges.

Our previous example finds all files on the computer with a UID of 1004. (Searching on a GID works the same way but using the -gid option.) You can then reassign ownership of these files by using the chown command (covered in Chapter 14) or delete them. Ordinarily, you'd issue this command only after deleting or reassigning ownership of the user's home directory, since that directory will probably contain far too many matching files.

Deleting Accounts Using GUI Tools

As with other account management tasks, using a GUI is fairly intuitive, but details vary from one distribution to another. As an example, to delete an account from Linux Mint's User and Groups Administration utility, after you have the utility open, click the account and then click the Delete button. The result is a confirmation dialog similar to the one shown in Figure 13.6. If you're certain of the action, click the Yes button. The account will be immediately deleted.

FIGURE 13.6 When you delete an account with a GUI utility, you are typically asked to confirm the action.

If the user is currently logged in, the utility will often complain about this fact. You'll most likely still be able to delete the account, but the user won't be logged out immediately.

Deleting Accounts from the Shell

The userdel command deletes accounts from a text-mode shell. In its simplest form, using super user privileges you pass it a username and nothing more:

```
$ sudo userdel hwash
[sudo] password for christine:
```

The program doesn't prompt you for confirmation; it just deletes the account. It does not, however, delete the user's home directory by default. To have it do so, pass it the --remove (-r) option.

If the user is currently logged in, userdel notifies you of that fact and does nothing. You can pass it the --force (-f) option to delete the account even though it's in use. To both force account deletion and remove the user's files, you can pass both options:

```
$ sudo userdel -rf zwash
[sudo] password for christine:
userdel: user zwash is currently used by process 4800
$
```

The program still complains about the user being "used by a process" (logged into the system), but it deletes the account and files just the same.

Managing Groups

In many respects, groups are comparable to accounts. They're defined in similar files and managed with similar utilities. Groups are also tied to accounts in that accounts include group definitions. Until now, it has been assumed that you'll be using standard groups or the groups that are defined as part of account creation. Sometimes, though, you need to create, delete, or modify groups for specific purposes, such as if you use a project group strategy. Just like account management, you can use either GUI or text-mode tools.

Managing Groups Using GUI Tools

Many GUI account maintenance tools, such as Linux Mint's User and Groups Administration utility, provide group management tools that are similar to the user management tools described throughout this chapter. Referring back to Figure 13.1, you'll see that the User and Groups Administration window includes both Users and Groups tabs. To manage groups, click the Groups tab. This produces a display resembling Figure 13.7.

FIGURE 13.7   The User and Groups Administration utility enables you to manage groups as well as users.

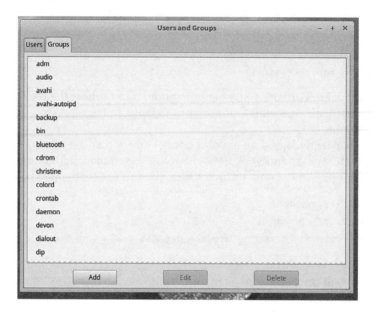

You can add, modify, and delete groups in a manner that's comparable to adding, modifying, and deleting accounts, though the number of options available may be much smaller. Groups don't have home directories, comment fields, login shells, and so on. You might, of course, want specific users to be members of your new group from the start. To do so, follow these steps:

1. Create a group by clicking the Add button on the Groups tab.

2. Specify the group name in the resulting dialog box.

3. Add the group by clicking OK.

4. Add group members by selecting the Users tab, selecting the account's username, and clicking the current groups in the Groups field to open a dialog.

5. Select the new group name check box in the dialog to make that account a member, as shown in Figure 13.8, and click OK.

> You don't have to add the account to only one group at a time. You can click multiple groups in the dialog to add the account to several groups at once.

Alternatively, you can manage group membership by altering each user's group membership individually, as described next in "Managing Groups from the Shell."

FIGURE 13.8 You can add users to a group after creating the group.

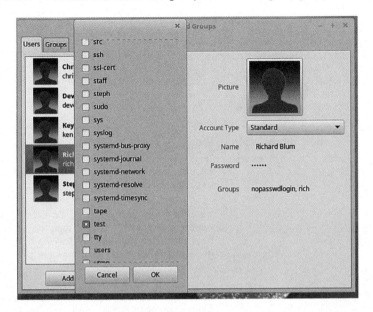

The *wheel* Group

Linux distributions invariably provide several groups by default. One of these, wheel (on some distributions), is particularly important for system administration. Members of the wheel group are granted certain special administrative privileges, such as the right to use the sudo command. The group name comes from the slang term *big wheel*, which refers to an important person.

Not all distributions provide this particular group—for example, Linux Mint uses the sudo group to allow access to the sudo command. You can type **grep wheel /etc/group** to determine whether the wheel group exists on your distribution. If it does, see if membership in this group provides access to the sudo command by typing **grep wheel /etc/sudoers** and look for a result similar to %wheel   ALL=(ALL) ALL.

Some distributions enable you to add your primary user account to the wheel group when you install the OS. Be aware that this phrasing is not used often; instead, the installer asks if you want to add the account to the "administrators group" or some similar term.

Managing Groups from the Shell

Certification
Objective
You can create groups from the shell by using the groupadd command, which works much like useradd for users but takes a smaller set of options, the most important of which appear in Table 13.3. Consult the program's man pages for information on more obscure options.

TABLE 13.3   Options for groupadd

Option name	Option abbreviation	Effect
--gid *GID*	-g	Provide a specific GID. If you omit it, groupadd uses the next available GID.
--system	-r	Instruct groupadd to create a system group, which is one with a GID of less than 500 or 1,000, depending on the distribution. Nonsystem groups are normally used as user private groups.
--force	-f	Normally, if you try to create a group that already exists, groupadd returns an error message. This parameter suppresses that error message.

Using the groupadd command, including setting an option, looks like this:

```
# groupadd -g 1001 consultants
```

This example creates a group with a GID of 1001 and a group name of consultants. Notice in the preceding example that the # prompt is shown, indicating that the root account was used to obtain the super user privileges required to complete this command successfully.

After the group is added, new members can be added to the group. This requires the use of the usermod command and super user privileges, as follows:

```
# usermod -aG consultants rich
#
# groups rich
rich: users consultants
```

The -aG options were used together to add the account, rich, to the new consultants group. If the -a option was not used, the rich account on some distributions would be *removed* from its current group memberships and belong only to the consultants group. Thus, it is wise to use -aG by default.

You can check an account's primary group. Using super user privileges type **id -gn *username*** at the command line. The *username*'s primary group will display.

Another good habit is to check if the modification was successful by using the groups command. The groups command shows all the group memberships for the specified user account.

 To modify the group itself, you can use the groupmod command. The --gid (-g) and --non-unique (-o) options from Table 13.3 can be used with this command, as well as --new-name *name* (-n *name*), which changes the group's name.

Deleting groups from the shell involves use of the groupdel command, which takes a group name as a single option, as in **groupdel consultants** to delete the consultant group.

EXERCISE 13.1

- Create a test account by using the GUI tool provided by your distribution, and then log into the account that you've created to verify that it's working as you expected.

- Create another test account by using useradd, but do *not* use passwd to set its password. Were you able to log in? Use passwd to create a password for the new test account and try logging in again.

Summary

In a GUI environment, you can perform most common account maintenance tasks with GUI tools, which enable you to add, modify, and delete accounts by selecting options from menus and lists. Some operations, however, require you to use command-line tools, such as useradd, usermod, userdel, and passwd. (The groupadd, groupmod, and groupdel commands provide similar functionality for groups.) Even if you don't need to use the more obscure features provided by the text-mode tools, they can be quicker to use than the GUI tools once you're familiar with them.

Exam Essentials

List the various files involved in account creation and management.   When an account is created on a Linux system, the /etc/passwd and /etc/shadow files get new records in them for the account. The /etc/group file also receives a new record for a newly created account, because by default a group is created with the same name as the account. These three files lose records when an account is deleted. By the same token, records in the files are changed when certain modifications are made to accounts.

When an account is created, a home directory is also produced, and files from the /etc/skel/ directory are copied into it. This home directory is typically named /home/*username*, but the name can be different based on the distribution's account creation configuration.

Summarize the tools used for account creation and management.   The tools used to create, modify, and delete accounts are useradd, usermod, and userdel, respectively. The passwd command also modifies or sets an account's password.

Outline the utilities used for group creation and management.   The utilities used to create, modify, and delete groups are groupadd, groupmod, and groupdel, respectively. The groups command allows you to view all the various group memberships for a particular account. The id -gn command shows a user's current primary group.

Describe the commands used to determine logged-in users.   Before modifying an account, it is a good idea to ensure the account user is not currently logged into the system. To learn who is currently online besides yourself, the who utility works, but the w command provides more information. The last program will display any users who are still logged on the system, as well as recent login sessions, including their starting and ending times.

Review Questions

You can find the answers in Appendix A.

1. What would a Linux system administrator type to remove the nemo account *and* its home directory?

   A. userdel nemo

   B. userdel -f nemo

   C. userdel -r nemo

   D. rm /home/nemo

   E. rm -r /home/nemo

2. Of the following, which is the *best* password?

   A. LinusTorvalds

   B. uB2op%4q++7K9_z5A++

   C. 123456

   D. password

   E. peanutbuttersandwich

3. Describe the effect of the following command, assuming that it completes successfully:

   ` # groupadd henry`

   A. It creates a new group called henry.

   B. It adds the user henry to the current default group.

   C. It imports group information from the file called henry.

   D. It changes the user's default group to henry.

   E. It adds the group henry to the user's list of groups.

4. True or false: User accounts have higher UID numbers than do system accounts.

5. True or false: Command-line users should normally use usermod to change their passwords.

6. True or false: After deleting an account, files formerly owned by the deleted account may remain on the computer.

7. You want to create an account for a new user, using the username thor and giving the user a UID of 2019. The command to do this is useradd _____.

   A. -uid 2019 thor

   B. -g 2019 thor

   C. +uid 2019 thor

   D. -u 2019 thor

   E. 2019 -u thor

8. You want to change the username of a user from carol to marvel without altering anything else about the account. To do so, you would type _____.

   A. useradd -l marvel carol

   B. usermod -l marvel carol

   C. useradd -l carol marvel

   D. usermod -l carol marvel

   E. useradd --login carol marvel

9. To create a system group, you must pass the _____ option to groupadd.

   A. -system

   B. -s

   C. --sys

   D. --r

   E. -r

10. Information on various groups, such as group name, GID, and group members, is stored in the _____ file.

   A. /etc/passwd

   B. /etc/shadow

   C. /etc/group

   D. /etc/groups

   E. /etc/GID

Chapter

14

Setting Ownership and Permissions

OBJECTIVES:

✓ 2.3 Using Directories and Listing Files

✓ 5.3 Managing File Permissions and Ownership

✓ 5.4 Special Directories and Files

As a multiuser OS, Linux provides tools to help you secure your files against unwanted access—after all, you wouldn't want another user to accidentally (or intentionally) read personal files or even delete your files! Linux handles these tasks through two features of files and directories: their *ownership* and their *permissions*. Every file has an associated owner (that is, an account with which it's linked) as well as an associated group. Three sets of permissions define what the file's owner, members of the file's group, and all other users can do with the file. Thus, ownership and permissions are intertwined, although you use different text-mode commands to manipulate them. (GUI tools often combine the two, as described in this chapter.)

Setting Ownership

The security model for Linux is based on that of Unix, which was designed as a multiuser OS. This security model therefore assumes the presence of multiple users on the computer and provides the means to associate individual files with the users who create them—that is, files have *owners*. You should thoroughly understand this concept, and with that knowledge, you can help protect your files, using either a GUI file manager or a text-mode shell command.

Ownership also applies to running programs (that is, *processes*). Most programs you run are tied to the account you used to launch them. This identity, in conjunction with the file's ownership and permissions, determines whether a program may modify a file.

Understanding Ownership

Chapter 12, "Understanding Basic Security," and Chapter 13, "Creating Users and Groups," described Linux's system of accounts. These accounts are the basis of file ownership. Specifically, every file has an owner—an account with which it's associated. The *user ID (UID)* number associates the file with an owner, whereas the *group ID (GID)* number associates the file with a *group*.

As described later, in the section "Setting Permissions," you control access to the file through permissions you set independently for the file's owner, the file's group, and all other users of the computer. As root, you can change the owner and group of any file. The file's owner can also change the file's group, but only to a group to which the user belongs.

The same principles of ownership apply to directories as apply to files: directories have owners and groups. They can be changed by root or, to a more limited extent, by the directory's owner.

Setting Ownership in a File Manager

As described in Chapter 4, "Using Common Linux Programs," you can manipulate files with a *file manager.* You're probably familiar with file managers in Windows or macOS. Linux's ownership and permissions are different from those of Windows, though, so you may want to know how to check on, and perhaps change, ownership features using a Linux file manager. As noted in Chapter 4, you have a choice of several file managers in Linux. Most are similar in broad strokes but differ in some details. In this section we'll use GNOME Files file manager as an example.

If you want to change the file's owner, you must run Files as root, but you can change the file's group to any group to which you belong as an ordinary user. The procedure to perform this task as root is as follows:

1. Launch a terminal window.

2. In the terminal window, type **su** to acquire root privileges.

 WARNING Some Linux distributions don't allow you to use the su command to acquire root privileges. For example, if you're using the GNOME version of Ubuntu you may instead need to use sudo to launch GNOME Files from the command line.

3. In the terminal window, type **nautilus** to launch GNOME Files (the Files application was called Nautilus in previous versions of GNOME, and the name has stuck around). You can optionally include the path to the directory in which you want Files to start up. If you don't include a path, it will begin by displaying the contents of the /root directory.

 TIP The /root directory is the root account's home directory.

4. Locate the file whose ownership you want to adjust and right-click it.

5. In the resulting menu, select Properties. The result is a Properties dialog.

6. In the Properties dialog, click the Permissions tab. The result resembles Figure 14.1.

7. To change the file's owner, select a new owner in the Owner field. This action is possible only if you run GNOME Files as root.

8. To change the file's group, select a new group in the Group field. If you run GNOME Files as an ordinary user, you will be able to select any group to which you belong, but if you run GNOME Files as root, you will be able to select any group.

9. When you've adjusted the features you want to change, click the X in the title bar to close the window.

If you want to change a file's group but not its owner, and if you're a member of the target group, you can launch GNOME Files as an ordinary user. You can then pick up the preceding procedure at step 4.

FIGURE 14.1   Linux file managers give you access to the file's ownership and permission metadata.

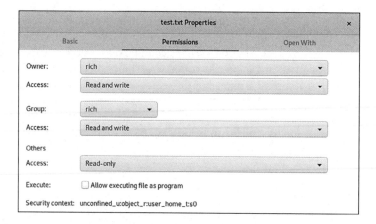

You should be *extremely* cautious about running GNOME Files as root. If you forget you're running this program as root, you can easily create new files as root, which will then require root privileges to make any changes to file ownership or permissions later on. It's also easy to accidentally delete critical system files as root that you could not delete as an ordinary user. For these reasons, I recommend that you use a text-mode shell to adjust file ownership. The change in the prompt makes it easier to notice you're running as root, and if you're used to using a GUI, you're less likely to launch additional programs as root from a text-mode shell than from GNOME Files.

Setting Ownership in a Shell

The command to change the ownership of a file in the preferred text-mode manner is *chown*. In its most basic form, you pass it the name of a file followed by a username:

   The chown command's name stands for *change owner*.

```
# chown rich targetfile.odf
```

This example gives ownership of targetfile.odf to rich. You can change the file's principal owner and its group with a single command by separating the owner and group with a colon (:) or a period (.):

```
# chown bob:users targetfile.odf
```

This example gives ownership of targetfile.odf to bob and associates the file with the users group. To change the group without changing the owner, you can omit the owner, leaving the colon and group name:

```
$ chown :users targetfile.odf
```

Alternatively, you can use the *chgrp* command, which works in the same way but changes *only* the group and does not require the colon before the group name:

```
$ chgrp users targetfile.odf
```

Note that the commands used to change the owner require root privileges, whereas you can change the group as an ordinary user—but only if you own the file and belong to the target group.

The chown and chgrp commands both support a number of options. The most useful of these is -R (or --recursive), which causes a change in ownership of all the files in an entire directory tree. For instance, suppose that the user christine has left a company and an existing employee, rich, must access her files. If christine's home directory was /home/christine, you might type:

```
# chown -R rich /home/christine
```

This command gives rich ownership of the /home/christine directory; all the files in the /home/christine directory, including all its subdirectories; the files in the subdirectories; and so on. To make the transition a bit easier for rich, you might also want to move christine's former home directory into rich's home directory.

 Real World Scenario

Cross-Installation UIDs and GIDs

You may use multiple Linux installations, either dual-booting on one computer or installed on multiple computers. If so, and if you transfer files from one installation to another, you may find that the ownership of files seems to change as you move them around. The same thing can happen with non-Linux Unix-like OSs, such as macOS. The reason is that the filesystems for these OSs store ownership and group information using UID and GID numbers, and a single user or group can have different UID or GID numbers on different computers, even if the name associated with the account or group is identical.

This problem is most likely to occur when using native Linux or Unix filesystems to transfer data, including both disk-based filesystems (such as ext4fs in Linux or HFS+ in macOS) or the Network File System (NFS) for remote file access. This problem is less likely to occur if you use a non-Linux/Unix filesystem, such as the File Allocation Table (FAT) or the New Technology File System (NTFS) for disks, or the Server Message Block/Common Internet File System (SMB/CIFS; handled by Samba in Linux) for network access.

If you run into this problem, several solutions exist, but many of them are beyond the scope of this book. One you can use, though, is to change the UID or GID mappings on one or more installations so that they all match. Chapter 13 describes how to change a user's UID number with usermod and how to change a group's GID number with groupmod. When you are transferring data via removable disks, using FAT or NTFS can be a simple solution, provided you don't need to preserve Unix-style permissions on the files.

Setting Permissions

File ownership is meaningless without some way to specify what particular users can do with their own or other users' files. That's where permissions enter the picture. Linux's permission structure is modeled after that of Unix, and it requires a bit of explanation before you tackle the issue. After you understand the basics, you can begin modifying permissions, using either a GUI file manager or a text-mode shell. You can also set default permissions for new files you create.

Understanding Permissions

Certification
Objective

To understand Unix (and hence Linux) permissions, you may want to begin with the display created by the ls command, which lists the files in a directory, in conjunction with its -l option, which creates a long directory listing that includes files' permissions. For instance, to see a long listing of the file test, you might type

Chapter 5, "Getting to Know the Command Line," introduced the ls command, and describes additional ls options.

```
$ ls -l test
-rwxr-xr-x  1 rich users      111 Oct 13 13:48  test
```

This line consists of several sections, which provide assorted pieces of information on the file:

Permissions The first column (-rwxr-xr-x in this example) is the file's permissions.

Number of Links The next column (1 in this example) shows the number of hard links to the file—that is, the number of unique filenames that may be used to access the file.

Chapter 7, "Managing Files," describes links in more detail.

Username The next column (rich in this example) identifies the file's owner by username.

Group Name The file's group (users in this example) appears next.

File Size This example file's size is quite small—111 bytes.

Time Stamp The time stamp (Oct 13 13:48 in this example) identifies the time the file was last modified.

Filename Finally, ls -l shows the file's name—test in this example.

The string that begins this output (-rwxr-xr-x in this example) is a symbolic representation of the permissions string. Figure 14.2 shows how this string is broken into four parts:

FIGURE 14.2   A symbolic representation of file permissions is broken into four parts.

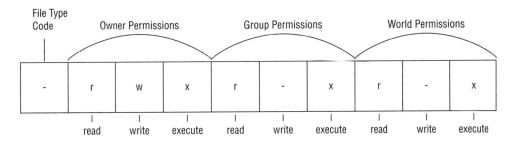

The File Type Code   The first character is the file type code, which represents the file's type, as summarized in Table 14.1. This type character is sometimes omitted from descriptions when the file type is not relevant or when it's identified in some other way.

TABLE 14.1   Linux file type codes

Code	Name	Meaning
-	Normal data file	May be text, an executable program, graphics, compressed data, or just about any other type of data.
d	Directory	Disk directories are files, but they contain filenames and pointers to those named files' data structures.
l	Symbolic link	The symbolic link file contains the name of another file or directory. When Linux accesses the symbolic link, it tries to read the linked-to file.
p	Named pipe	A pipe enables two running Linux programs to communicate with each other in a one-way fashion.
s	Socket	A socket is similar to a named pipe, but it permits network and bidirectional links.
b	Block device	A block device file that corresponds to a hardware device to and from which data is transferred in blocks of more than one byte. Disk devices (hard disks, floppies, CD-ROMs, and so on) are common block devices.
c	Character device	A character device file that corresponds to a hardware device to and from which data is transferred in units of one byte. Examples include parallel and RS-232 serial port devices.

Most of the files you'll manipulate are normal files, directories, and symbolic links.

Owner Permissions   These permissions determine what the file's owner can do with the file.

Group Permissions   These permissions determine what members of the file's group (who aren't its owner) can do with the file.

World (or "Other") Permissions   These permissions determine what users who aren't the file's owner or members of its group can do with the file

In each of the three sets of permissions, the string identifies the presence or absence of each of three types of access: read, write, and execute. Read and write permissions are fairly self-explanatory. If the execute permission is present, it means that the file may be run as a program. The absence of the permission is denoted by a dash (-) in the permission string. The presence of the permission is indicated by the letter r for read, w for write, or x for execute.

Setting the execute bit on a non-program file doesn't turn it into a program, of course; it just indicates that a user may run a file that is a program.

Thus, the example permission string -rwxr-xr-x means that the file is a normal data file and that its owner, members of the file's group, and all other users can read and execute the file. Only the file's owner has write permission to the file.

Another representation of permissions is possible. It's compact but a bit confusing; it takes each of the three permissions groupings of the permission string (omitting the file type code) and converts it into a number from 0 to 7 (that is, a *base 8* or *octal* number). The result is a three-digit octal number. Each number is constructed by starting with a value of 0 and then:

- Adding 4 if read permissions are present
- Adding 2 if write permissions are present
- Adding 1 if execute permissions are present

The resulting three-digit code represents permissions for the owner, the group, and the world. Table 14.2 shows some examples of common permissions and their meanings.

These procedures involve binary numbers and logical, not arithmetic, operations. The arithmetic description is easier to understand, though.

TABLE 14.2   Example permissions and their interpretations

Permission string	Octal code	Meaning
rwxrwxrwx	777	Read, write, and execute permissions for all users
rwxr-xr-x	755	Read and execute permission for all users. The file's owner also has write permission.
rwxr-x---	750	Read and execute permission for the owner and group. The file's owner also has write permission. Other users have no access to the file.
rwx------	700	Read, write, and execute permissions for the file's owner only; all others have no access.
rw-rw-rw-	666	Read and write permissions for all users. No execute permissions for anybody.
rw-rw-r--	664	Read and write permissions for the owner and group. Read-only permission for all others.
rw-rw----	660	Read and write permissions for the owner and group. No world permissions.
rw-r--r--	644	Read and write permissions for the owner. Read-only permission for all others.
rw-r-----	640	Read and write permissions for the owner, and read-only permission for the group. No permission for others.
rw-------	600	Read and write permissions for the owner. No permission for anybody else.
r--------	400	Read permission for the owner. No permission for anybody else.

There are 512 possible combinations of permissions, so Table 14.2 is incomplete. It shows the most common and useful combinations.

Several special cases apply to permissions:

Directory Execute Bits   Directories use the execute bit to grant permission to enter the directory and access files. Even if you have permission to read a file, you must have execute permission on the directory to access the file. This is a highly desirable characteristic for directories, so you'll almost always find the execute bit set when the read bit is set.

Directory Write Permissions   Directories are files that are interpreted in a special way. As such, if a user can write to a directory, that user can create, delete, or rename files in the directory, even if the user isn't the owner of those files and does not have permission to write to those files.

 The usual rules for writing to directories can be modified with the *sticky bit*, which is described later in "Using Sticky Bits."

Symbolic Links   Permissions on symbolic links are always 777 (`rwxrwxrwx`, or `lrwxrwxrwx`, to include the file type code). This access applies only to the link file itself, not to the linked-to file. In other words, all users can read the contents of the link to discover the name of the file to which it points, but the permissions on the linked-to file determine its file access. Changing the permissions on a symbolic link affects the linked-to file.

root   Many of the permission rules don't apply to root. The superuser can read or write any file on the computer—even files that grant access to nobody (that is, those that have 000 permissions). The superuser still needs an execute bit set to run a program file.

Setting Permissions in a File Manager

The procedure for setting permissions in a file manager is similar to that for setting the ownership of a file:

- You normally adjust these settings using the same dialog used to adjust ownership, such as the GNOME Files dialog shown earlier in Figure 14.1.

- You don't need to be root to adjust the permissions of files you own.

- You should use root access for this job only on files you don't own.

   As seen earlier in Figure 14.1, there are three Access items, associated with the Owner, the Group, and Others:

- The Owner item provides two options: Read-Only and Read and Write.

- The Group and Others items both provide Read-Only and Read and Write plus the None option. You can use these options to set the read and write permission bits on your file.

GNOME Files requires setting the execute bit separately by checking the Allow Executing File As Program box. This check box sets all three execute permission bits; you can't control execute permission more precisely with GNOME Files. You also can't adjust the execute permissions on directories with GNOME Files.

 Details on setting permissions vary in other file managers, but the principles are the same as those described here for GNOME Files.

Setting Permissions in a Shell

In a text-mode shell, you can use *chmod* to change permissions. This command is rather complex, mostly because of the complex ways that permissions may be changed. You can specify the permissions in two forms: as an octal number or in a symbolic form, which is a set of codes related to the string representation of the permissions.

 The chmod command's name stands for *change mode, mode* being another name for permissions.

The octal representation of the mode is the same as that described earlier and summarized in Table 14.2. For instance, to change permissions on report.txt to rw-r--r--, you can issue the following command:

```
$ chmod 644 report.txt
```

A symbolic mode, by contrast, consists of three components:

- A code indicating the permission set you want to modify—u for the user (that is, the owner), g for the group, o for other users, and a for all permissions
- A symbol indicating whether you want to add (+), delete (-), or set the mode equal to (=) the stated value
- A code specifying what the permission should be, such as the common r, w, or x symbol, or various others for more advanced operations

Using symbolic modes with chmod can be confusing, so we don't describe them fully here; however, you should be familiar with a few common types of use, as summarized in Table 14.3. Symbolic modes are more flexible than octal modes because you can specify symbolic modes that modify existing permissions, such as adding or removing execute permissions without affecting other permissions. You can also set only the user, group, or world permissions without affecting the others. With octal modes, you must set all three permission bits equal to a value that you specify.

Certification Objective

As with the chown and chgrp commands, you can use the -R (or --recursive) option to chmod to have it operate on an entire directory tree.

TABLE 14.3   Examples of symbolic permissions with chmod

Command	Initial permissions	End permissions
chmod a+x bigprogram	rw-r--r--	rwxr-xr-x
chmod ug=rw report.txt	r--------	rw-rw----
chmod o-rwx bigprogram	rwxrwxr-x	rwxrwx---
chmod g-w,o-rw report.txt	rw-rw-rw-	rw-r-----

Setting the umask

The *user mask*, or *umask*, determines the default permissions for new files and directories. The umask is the value that is *removed* from 666 (rw-rw-rw-) permissions when creating new files or from 777 (rwxrwxrwx) when creating new directories. For instance, if the umask is 022, then files will be created with 644 permissions by default and new directories will have 755 permissions. Note that the removal operation is not a simple subtraction but a bitwise removal. That is, a 7 value in a umask removes the corresponding rwx permissions, but for files, for which the starting point is rw-, the result is --- (0), not –1 (which is meaningless).

You can adjust the umask with the umask command, which takes the umask value, as in **umask 022**. Typically, this command appears in a system configuration file, such as /etc/profile, or in a user configuration file, such as ~/.bashrc.

Using Special Permission Bits and File Features

When you investigate the Linux directory tree, you will encounter certain file types that require special attention. Sometimes you may just want to be aware of how these files are handled, since they deviate from what you might expect based on the information presented in Chapter 8. In other cases, you may need to adjust how you use ls or other commands to deal with these files and directories. These special cases include the "sticky bit," hiding files from view, obtaining long listings of directories, and using special execute permissions.

Using Sticky Bits

Certification
Objective

Before diving into what sticky bits are, it's easier to start out with explaining why we need them. Consider the following commands, typed on a system with a few files and subdirectories laid out in a particular way:

```
$ whoami
rich
$ ls -l
total 0
drwxrwxrwx 2 root root 80 Oct 14 17:58 subdir
$ ls -l subdir/
total 2350
-rw-r----- 1 root root 2404268 Oct 14 17:59 report.txt
```

These commands establish the current configuration; the effective user ID is rich and the current directory has one subdirectory, called subdir, which root owns but to which rich, like all the system's users, has full read/write access. This subdirectory has one file, report.txt, which is owned by root and to which rich has no access. You can verify that rich can't write to the file by attempting to do so with the touch command:

```
$ touch subdir/report.txt
touch: cannot touch `subdir/report.txt': Permission denied
```

This error message verifies that rich could not write to subdir/report.txt. The file, you might think, is safe from tampering. Not so fast! Try this:

```
$ rm subdir/report.txt
$ ls -l subdir/
total 0
```

The rm command returned no error message, and a subsequent check of subdir verifies that it's now empty—in other words, rich could delete the file even without write permission to it! This may seem like a bug—after all, if you can't write to a file, you might think you shouldn't be able to delete it. Recall, however, that directories are just a special type of file, one that holds other files' names and pointers to their lower-level data structures. Thus, modifying a file requires write access to the file, but creating or deleting a file requires write access to the *directory in which it resides*. In this example, rich has write access to the subdir directory but not to the report.txt file within that directory. Thus, rich can delete the file but not modify it. This result is not a bug; it's just a counterintuitive feature.

Although Linux filesystems were designed to work this way, such behavior is not always desirable. The way to create a more intuitive result is to use a *sticky bit*, which is a special permission that alters this behavior. With the sticky bit set on a directory, Linux will permit you to delete a file only if you own it or the containing directory; write permission to the containing directory is not enough. You can set the sticky bit with chown, in either of two ways:

Using an Octal Code By prefixing the three-digit octal code described earlier in this chapter with another digit, you can set any of three special permission bits, one of which is the sticky bit. The code for the sticky bit is 1, so you would use an octal code that begins with 1, such as 1755, to set the sticky bit. Specifying a value of 0, as in 0755, removes the sticky bit.

> Other odd numbers will set the sticky bit, too, but will also set additional special permission bits, which are described shortly, in "Using Special Execute Permissions."

Using a Symbolic Code Pass the symbolic code t for the world permissions, as in **chmod o+t subdir**, to set the sticky bit on subdir. You can remove the sticky bit in a similar way by using a minus sign, as in **chmod o-t subdir**.

Restoring the file and setting the sticky bit enables you to see the effect:

```
$ ls -l
total 0
drwxrwxrwt 2 root root 80 Oct 14 18:25 subdir
$ ls -l subdir/
total 304
-rw-r--r-- 1 root root 2404268 Oct 14 18:25 report.txt
$ rm subdir/report.txt
rm: cannot remove `subdir/report.txt': Operation not permitted
```

In this example, although rich still has full read/write access to subdir, rich cannot delete another user's files in that directory.

You can identify a directory with the sticky bit set by a small change in the symbolic mode shown by ls -l. The world execute bit is shown as a t rather than an x. In this example, the result is that subdir's permission appears as drwxrwxrwt rather than drwxrwxrwx.

The sticky bit is particularly important for directories that are shared by many users. It's a standard feature on /tmp and /var/tmp, for instance, since many users store temporary files in these directories, and you wouldn't want one user to be able to delete another's temporary files. If you want users who collaborate on a project to be able to write files into each other's home directories, consider setting the sticky bit on those home directories or on the subdirectories in which users are sharing files.

> If you delete /tmp or /var/tmp and need to re-create it, be sure to set the sticky bit on your new replacement directory!

Using Special Execute Permissions

As described earlier in this chapter, the execute permission bit enables you to identify program files as such. Linux then enables you to run these programs. Such files run using your own credentials, which is generally a good thing—associating running processes with specific users is a key part of Linux's security model. Occasionally, though, programs need to run with elevated privileges. For instance, the passwd program, which sets users' passwords, must run as root to write, and in some cases to read, the configuration files it handles. Thus, if users are to change their own passwords, passwd must have root privileges even when ordinary users run it.

To accomplish this task, two special permission bits exist, similar to the sticky bit described earlier:

Certification
Objective

Set User ID (SUID)   The *set user ID (SUID)* option tells Linux to run the program with the permissions of whoever owns the file rather than with the permissions of the user who runs the program. For instance, if a file is owned by root and has its SUID bit set, the program runs with root privileges and can therefore read any file on the computer. Some servers and other system programs run this way, which is often called SUID root. SUID programs are indicated by an s in the owner's execute bit position in the permission string, as in rwsr-xr-x.

Set Group ID (SGID)   The *set group ID (SGID)* option is similar to the SUID option, but it sets the group of the running program to the group of the file. It's indicated by an s in the group execute bit position in the permission string, as in rwxr-sr-x. When set on a directory, the SGID option ensures that all files created in the directory are set to the group of the directory instead of the person who created the file.

You can set these bits using chmod:

Using an Octal Code   In the leading digit of a four-digit octal code, set the leading value to 4 to set the SUID bit, to 2 to set the SGID bit, or to 6 to set both bits. For instance, 4755 sets the SUID bit, but not the SGID bit, on an executable file.

Using a Symbolic Code   Use the s symbolic code, in conjunction with u to specify the SGID bit, g to specify the SGID bit, or both to set both bits. For instance, typing **chmod u+s myprog** sets the SUID bit on myprog, whereas **chmod ug-s myprog** removes both the SUID bit and the SGID bit.

Ordinarily, you don't need to set or remove these bits; when necessary, the package management program sets these bits correctly when you install or upgrade a program. You might need to alter these bits if they've been mistakenly set or removed on files. In some cases you might want or need to adjust these values on program files that you compile from source code or if you need to modify the way a program works. Be very cautious when doing so, though. If you set the SUID or SGID bit on a garden-variety program, it will run with increased privileges. If the program contains bugs, those bugs will then be able to do more damage. If you accidentally remove these permissions, the results can be just as bad— programs like passwd, sudo, and su all rely on their SUID bits being set, so removing this feature can cause them to stop working.

Hiding Files from View

Certification
Objective

If you're used to Windows, you may be familiar with the concept of a *hidden bit*, which hides files from view in file managers, by the Windows DIR command, and in most programs. If you're looking for something analogous in Linux, you won't find it, at least not in the form of a dedicated filesystem feature. Instead, Linux uses a file-naming convention to hide files from view; most tools, such as ls, hide files and directories from view if their names begin with a dot (.). Thus, ls shows the file afile.txt but not .afile.txt. Most file managers and dialogs that deal with files also hide such *dot files*, as they're commonly called; however, this practice is not universal.

Many user programs take advantage of this feature to keep their configuration files from cluttering your display. For instance, ~/.bashrc is a Bash user configuration file, Evolution's configuration files go in the ~/.evolution directory, and ~/.fonts.conf holds user-specific font configuration information.

You can view dot files in various ways depending on the program in question. Some GUI tools have a check box you can set in their configuration options to force the program to display such files. At the command line, you can use the -a option to ls:

```
$ ls -l
total 0
drwxrwxrwt 2 root root 80 Dec 14 18:25 subdir
$ ls -la
total 305
drwxr-xr-x 3 kirk users    104 Dec 14 18:44 .
drwxr-xr-x 3 kirk users    528 Dec 14 18:21 ..
-rw-r--r-- 1 kirk users 309580 Dec 14 18:44 .report.txt
drwxrwxrwt 2 root root     80 Dec 14 18:25 subdir
```

Certification
Objective

This example shows the hidden file, .report.txt, in the current directory. It also shows two hidden directory files. The first, ., refers to the current directory. The second, .., refers to the parent directory.

Recall from Chapter 6, "Managing Hardware," that .. is a relative directory reference. This hidden entry is why it works.

Note that renaming a file so that it begins with a dot will hide it, but this action will also make the file inaccessible to any program that uses the original filename. That is, if you rename report.txt to .report.txt, and if another program or file refers to the file as report.txt, that reference will no longer work. You *must* include the leading dot in any reference to the hidden file.

Viewing Directories

Chapter 6 introduced the ls command, including many of its options. One of these deserves elaboration at this point: -d. If you're working in a directory that holds many subdirectories, and if you use a wildcard with ls that matches one or more subdirectories, you may get an unexpected result; the output will show the files in the matched subdirectories, rather than the information on the subdirectories themselves—for instance, starting in a directory with two subdirectories, subdir1 and subdir2:

Certification
Objective

```
$ ls -l subdir*
subdir1:
total 304
-rw-r--r-- 1 kirk users 309580 Dec 14 18:54 report.txt

subdir2:
total 84
-rw-r--r-- 1 kirk users 86016 Dec 14 18:54 mypaper.doc
```

If instead you want information on the subdirectories, rather than the contents of those subdirectories, you can include the -d option:

```
$ ls -ld subdir*
drwxr-xr-x 2 kirk users 80 Dec 14 18:54 subdir1
drwxr-xr-x 2 kirk users 80 Dec 14 18:54 subdir2
```

Summary

File security is important on a multiuser OS such as Linux, and one of the pieces of the puzzle of security is ownership. In Linux, every file has one owner and one associated group. The superuser can set the owner with chown, and either the superuser or the file's owner can set the file's group with chown or chgrp. By itself, ownership is useless, so Linux supports the concept of file permissions, which control which other users can access a file, and in what ways. You can set permissions with the chmod utility. You can view ownership, permissions, and some additional file features using the -l option to the ls command.

Exam Essentials

Describe how Linux tracks file and directory ownership. Each file and directory in the Linux filesystem is assigned one owner and one primary group. You can view the owner and group of a file or directory by using the ls command with the -l option. You can change the owner and primary group assigned to a file or directory using the chown command or just the group by using the chgrp command.

Explain how Linux tracks file and directory permissions.   Linux assigns permissions to files and directories based on a three-level hierarchy—the owner, the primary group assigned to the file or directory, and everyone else on the system. To view the permissions for a file or directory, use the ls command with the -l option. The permissions appear as a set of nine characters, three sets of r (for read), w (for write), and x (for execute), ordered rwx. If a permission is not set, it appears as a dash (-). The first set is the owner's permissions, the second set is the group permissions, and the third set is the permissions assigned to all other users who aren't the owner or in the primary group of the file or directory. You change the permissions assigned to a file or directory by using the chmod command. You can either use the symbolic r, w, and x characters, or you can use an octal mode, where each permission is assigned an octal value.

Explain how Linux makes files or directories hidden.   Linux flags a file or directory as hidden if the file or directory name begins with a period (.). Hidden files and directories don't appear in a standard ls listing unless you include the -a option.

Describe the special bits used for files.   The sticky bit, when assigned to a directory, tells Linux to allow only the owners of files contained in the directory to delete them, even if another user account has write access to the file. The set user ID bit tells Linux to run the file with the permissions of the file owner instead of the actual user account that runs the file. The set group ID bit tells Linux to run the file with the permissions of the file's primary group instead of the primary group of the user account that runs the file.

Review Questions

You can find the answers in Appendix A.

1. What command would you type (as root) to change the ownership of somefile.txt from ralph to tony?

   A. chown ralph:tony somefile.txt

   B. chmod somefile.txt tony

   C. chown somefile.txt tony

   D. chown tony somefile.txt

   E. chmod tony somefile.txt

2. Typing **ls -ld wonderjaye** reveals a symbolic file mode of drwxr-xr-x. Which of the following are true? (Choose all that apply.)

   A. wonderjaye is a symbolic link.

   B. wonderjaye is an executable program.

   C. wonderjaye is a directory.

   D. wonderjaye may be read by all users of the system.

   E. wonderjaye may be written by any member of the file's group.

3. Which of the following commands can you use to change a file's group?

   A. groupadd

   B. groupmod

   C. chmod

   D. ls

   E. chown

4. True or false: A file with permissions of 755 can be read by any user on the computer, assuming all users can read the directory in which it resides.

5. True or false: Only root can use the chmod command.

6. True or false: Only root can change a file's ownership with chown.

7. The __ option causes chown to change ownership on an entire directory tree.

   A. -L

   B. -R

   C. -H

   D. -P

   E. -f

8. The three-character symbolic string _____ represents read and execute permission but no write permission.

    A. -wx

    B. --x

    C. r-x

    D. rw-

    E. rwx

9. The chmod symbolic representation _____ allows all users execute access to a file without affecting other permissions.

    A. u+x

    B. u-x

    C. g+x

    D. a-x

    E. a+x

10. You want to set the sticky bit on an existing directory, subdir, without otherwise altering its permissions. To do so, you would type **chmod_____ subdir**.

    A. o+t

    B. o+w

    C. a+t

    D. g+t

    E. a+w

Chapter

15

Managing Network Connections

OBJECTIVE:

✓ 4.4   **Your Computer on the Network**

These days it's almost a necessity to have your Linux system connected to some type of network. Whether it's the need to share files and printers on a local network, or the need to connect to the Internet to download updates and security patches, most Linux systems have some type of network connection.

This chapter looks at how to configure your Linux system to connect to a network, as well as how to troubleshoot network connections if things go wrong. There are a few different methods for configuring network setting in Linux, and you'll need to know them all for the Linux Essentials exam. First, we'll cover the basic settings required for network connectivity. Next, we'll examine the different tools you have at your disposal that help make configuring the network settings easier. After that, this chapter explores simple network troubleshooting techniques you can use to help find the problem if anything goes wrong.

Configuring Network Features

Certification
Objective You need to configure five main pieces of information in your Linux system to interact on a network:

- The host address
- The network subnet address
- The default router (sometimes called gateway)
- The system host name
- A Domain Name System (DNS) server address for resolving host names

You have three ways to configure this information in Linux systems:

- Manually editing network configuration files
- Using a graphical tool included with your Linux distribution
- Using command-line tools

Trying to manually edit the network configuration files is best left for advanced system administrators and is beyond the scope of this book. For most typical Linux users, you'll never have to mess with the configuration files; the graphical and command-line tools can do all that work for you. The following sections walk through both the graphical and command-line tools.

It's worth noting that there are two types of IP network address schemes in use today. The legacy address scheme is technically referred to as IPv4 but is commonly just called IP. It uses 32 bits to represent a host address. These 32 bits are normally split into four 8-bit values, represented by decimal values, separated by dots (such as 192.168.1.5). Because the world is running out of unique 32-bit addresses to assign to hosts on the Internet, IPv6 was created. It uses 128 bits for addresses. These values are commonly represented as eight groups of four hexadecimal digits, separated by colons (such as 2500:1602:1ce0:eeb0:e900:aa10:fa10:cf33).

Graphical Tools

The *Network Manager* tool is a popular program used by many Linux distributions to provide a graphical interface for defining network connections. Network Manager starts automatically at boot time and appears in the system tray area of the desktop as an icon.

If your system detects a wired network connection, the icon appears as a mini-network with blocks connected together. If your system detects a wireless network connection, the icon appears as an empty radio signal. When you click the icon, you'll see a list of the available wireless networks detected by the network card (as shown in Figure 15.1).

FIGURE 15.1   Network Manager showing a wireless network connection

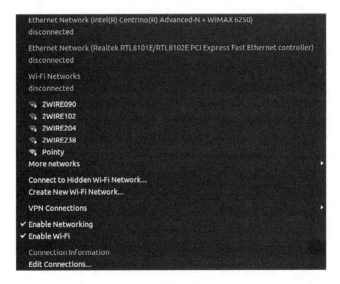

Click your access point to select it from the list. If your access point is encrypted, you'll be prompted to enter the password to gain access to the network.

After your system is connected to a wireless access point, the icon appears as a radio signal. Click the icon and then select Edit Connections to edit the network connection settings for the system, shown in Figure 15.2.

FIGURE 15.2 The Network Connections dialog

Select the network connection you want to configure (either wireless or wired), and then click the Edit button to change the current configuration.

Network Manager allows you to specify the host address, network subnet address, default router, and DNS server names by using the manual configuration option, or you can set the configuration to use Dynamic Host Configuration Protocol (DHCP) to determine the settings. Network Manager automatically updates the appropriate network configuration files with the updated settings.

Certification Objective

🌐 Real World Scenario

Manual DNS Configurations

One topic that the Linux Essentials exam does expect you to know about network configuration files is DNS. You can manually define a DNS server so that the system can use DNS host names. Fortunately, this is a standard that all Linux systems follow, which is handled in the /etc/resolv.conf configuration file:

```
domain mydomain.com
search mytest.com
nameserver 192.168.1.1
```

The domain entry defines the domain name assigned to the network. By default, the system appends this domain name to any host names you specify. The search entry defines any additional domains used to search for host names. The nameserver entry is where you specify the DNS server assigned to your network. Some networks can have more than one DNS server; just add multiple nameserver entries in the file. Be careful, though, as this file may reset the next time you boot your Linux system, depending on how your Linux distribution is configured. To help speed up connections to commonly used hosts, manually enter their host names and IP addresses in the /etc/hosts file on your Linux system. The /etc/nsswitch.conf file defines whether the Linux system checks this file before or after using DNS to look up the host name.

Command-Line Tools

If you're not working with a graphical desktop client environment, you'll need to use the Linux command-line tools to set the network configuration information. Quite a few different command-line tools are at your disposal. This section covers the ones you're most likely to run into (and the ones you'll most likely see on the Linux Essentials exam).

Network Manager Command-Line Tools

Network Manager offers two command-line tools:

- nmtui—Provides a simple text-based menu tool
- nmcli—Provides a text-only command-line tool

Both of these tools help guide you through the process of setting the required network information for your Linux system. The *nmtui* tool displays a stripped-down version of the graphical tool where you can select a network interface and assign network properties to it, as shown in Figure 15.3.

FIGURE 15.3 The Network Manager nmtui command-line tool

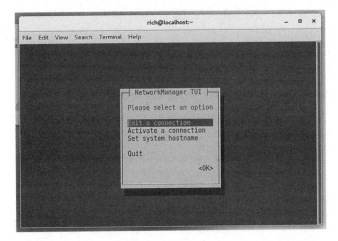

The *nmcli* tool doesn't attempt to use any type of graphics capabilities—it just provides a command-line interface where you can view and change the network settings. By default, the command displays the current network devices and their settings, as shown in Listing 15.1.

Listing 15.1: The default output of the nmcli command

```
$ nmcli
enp0s3: connected to enp0s3
        "Intel 82540EM Gigabit Ethernet Controller (PRO/1000 MT Desktop
  Adapter)
        ethernet (e1000), 08:00:27:73:1C:6D, hw, mtu 1500
        ip4 default
        inet4 10.0.2.15/24
        route4 0.0.0.0/0
        route4 10.0.2.0/24
        inet6 fe80::5432:eddb:51ea:fb44/64
        route6 ff00::/8
        route6 fe80::/64
        route6 fe80::/64
```

The nmcli command uses command-line options to allow you to set the network settings:

```
# nmcli con add type ethernet con-name eth1 ifname enp0s3 ip4
192.168.1.15/24 gw4 192.168.1.254
```

In this example, we set the IP address to 192.168.1.15, the subnet mask to /24, and the default router to 192.168.1.254.

Traditional Command-Line Tools

Certification
Objective

If your Linux distribution doesn't support one of the Network Manager tools, you can use one of four traditional command-line tools:

- ethtool—Displays Ethernet settings for a network interface
- ifconfig—Displays or sets the IP address and netmask values for a network interface
- ip—Displays or sets the IP address, netmask, and router values for a network interface
- iwconfig—Displays or sets the SSID and encryption key for a wireless interface
- route—Displays or sets the default router address

The *ethtool command* allows you to peek inside the network interface card Ethernet settings and change any properties that you may need to communicate with a network device, such as a switch.

By default, the ethtool command displays the current configuration settings for the network interface, as shown in Listing 15.2.

Listing 15.2: Output from the ethtool command

```
$ ethtool enp0s3
Settings for enp0s3:
        Supported ports: [ TP ]
        Supported link modes:   10baseT/Half 10baseT/Full
                                100baseT/Half 100baseT/Full
                                1000baseT/Full
        Supported pause frame use: No
        Supports auto-negotiation: Yes
        Supported FEC modes: Not reported
        Advertised link modes:  10baseT/Half 10baseT/Full
                                100baseT/Half 100baseT/Full
                                1000baseT/Full
        Advertised pause frame use: No
        Advertised auto-negotiation: Yes
        Advertised FEC modes: Not reported
        Speed: 1000Mb/s
        Duplex: Full
        Port: Twisted Pair
        PHYAD: 0
        Transceiver: internal
        Auto-negotiation: on
        MDI-X: off (auto)
Cannot get wake-on-lan settings: Operation not permitted
        Current message level: 0x00000007 (7)
                               drv probe link
        Link detected: yes
$
```

You can change features such as speed, duplex, and whether or not the network interface attempts to automatically negotiate features with the switch.

The *ifconfig command* is a legacy command for configuring network device settings. It allows you to set the network address and subnet mask for a network interface:

Certification
Objective

```
$ sudo ifconfig enp0s3 down 10.0.2.10 netmask 255.255.255.0
```

The *ip command* is more robust in what it can do, and it is becoming the most popular method to use for defining network settings from the command line. The ip utility uses several command options to display the current network settings or define new network settings. Table 15.1 show these commands.

Certification
Objective

TABLE 15.1 The ip utility command options

Parameter	Description
address	Display or set the IPv4 or IPv6 address on the device.
addrlabel	Define configuration labels.
l2tp	Tunnel Ethernet over IP.
link	Define a network device.
maddress	Define a multicast address for the system to listen to.
monitor	Watch for netlink messages.
mroute	Define an entry in the multicast routing cache.
mrule	Define a rule in the multicast routing policy database.
neighbor	Manage Address Resolution Protocol (ARP) or Neighbor Discovery (NDISC) cache entries.
netns	Manage network namespaces.
ntable	Manage the neighbor cache operation.
route	Manage the routing table.
rule	Manage entries in the routing policy database.
tcpmetrics	Mange TCP metrics on the interface.
token	Manage tokenized interface identifiers.
tunnel	Tunnel over IP.
tuntap	Manage Network Tunnel (TUN) or Network Bridge (TAP) devices.
xfrm	Manage IPSec policies for secure connections.

Each command option uses parameters to define what to do, such as display network settings, or to modify existing network settings. Listing 15.3 demonstrates how to display the current network settings using the show parameter.

Listing 15.3: The `ip address show` output

```
$ ip address show
1: lo: <LOOPBACK,UP,LOWER_UP> mtu 65536 qdisc noqueue state UNKNOWN group
default qlen 1000
    link/loopback 00:00:00:00:00:00 brd 00:00:00:00:00:00
    inet 127.0.0.1/8 scope host lo
       valid_lft forever preferred_lft forever
    inet6 ::1/128 scope host
       valid_lft forever preferred_lft forever
2: enp0s3: <BROADCAST,MULTICAST,UP,LOWER_UP> mtu 1500 qdisc pfifo_fast
state UP group default qlen 1000
    link/ether 08:00:27:73:1c:6d brd ff:ff:ff:ff:ff:ff
    inet 10.0.2.15/24 brd 10.0.2.255 scope global noprefixroute dynamic
enp0s3
       valid_lft 84411sec preferred_lft 84411sec
    inet6 fe80::5432:eddb:51ea:fb44/64 scope link noprefixroute
       valid_lft forever preferred_lft forever
$
```

Listing 15.3 shows two network interfaces on the Linux system:

- `lo`—The local loopback interface
- `enp0s3`—A wired network interface

The *local loopback interface* is a special virtual network interface. Any local program can use it to communicate with other programs just as if they were across a network. That can simplify transferring data between programs.

The `enp0s3` network interface is the wired network connection for the Linux system. The `ip` command shows the IP address assigned to the interface (there's both an IP and an IPv6 link local address assigned), the netmask value, and some basic statistics about the packets on the interface.

If the output doesn't show a network address assigned to the interface, you can use the ip command to specify the host address and netmask values for the interface:

```
# ip address add 10.0.2.15/24 dev enp0s3
```

You can then use the `ip` command to set the default router for the network interface:

Certification
Objective

```
# ip route add default via 192.168.1.254 dev enp0s3
```

Then finally, make the network interface active by using the `link` option:

```
# ip link set enp0s3 up
```

Although the `ip` command is a one-stop method for changing network settings, an alternative way to specify network routing settings for your network is the `route` command:

```
# route add default gw 192.168.1.254
```

You can also use the `route` command by itself to view the current default router configured for the system:

```
$ route
Kernel IP routing table
Destination     Gateway          Genmask         Flags Metric Ref Use Iface
default         192.168.1.254    0.0.0.0         UG    0      0   0   enp0s3
192.168.1.0     *                255.255.255.0   U     1      0   0   enp0s3
$
```

The default router defined for the Linux system is 192.168.1.254 and is available from the enp0s3 network interface. The output also shows that to get to the 192.168.1.0 network you don't need a gateway, because that's the local network the Linux system is connected to.

If your network is connected to multiple networks via multiple routers, you can manually create the routing table in the system by using the add or del command-line options for the `route` command. The format is:

```
route [add] [del] target gw gateway
```

where *target* is the target host or network and *gateway* is the router address.

If your network uses DHCP, ensure that a proper DHCP client program is running on your Linux system. The DHCP client program communicates with the network DHCP server in the background and assigns the necessary IP address settings as directed by the DHCP server. Three common DHCP client programs available for Linux systems are:

- dhcpcd
- dhclient
- pump

The dhcpcd program is becoming the most popular of the three, but you'll still see the other two used in some Linux distributions.

When you use your Linux system's software package manager utility to install the DHCP client program, it sets the program to automatically launch at boot time and handles the IP address configuration needed to interact on the network.

Before you can use the `ip` command to assign an address to a wireless interface, you must assign the wireless SSID and encryption key values using the `iwconfig` command:

```
# iwconfig wlan0 essid "MyNetwork" key s:mypassword
```

The essid parameter specifies the access point SSID name, and the key parameter specifies the encryption key required to connect to it. Notice that the encryption key is preceded by an s:. That allows you to specify the encryption key in ASCII text characters—otherwise, you'll need to specify the key using hexadecimal values.

If you don't know the name of a local wireless connection, you can use the iwlist command to display all the wireless signals your wireless card detects. Just specify the name of the wireless device and use the scan option:

```
$ iwlist wlan0 scan
```

 Real World Scenario

Obtaining Wi-Fi Drivers

Unfortunately, Linux driver support for Wi-Fi hardware is fairly weak. If you don't see your Wi-Fi hardware when you try to configure it, you may need to track down suitable drivers. You can begin this task with a tool called lspci, which is described in Chapter 6, "Managing Hardware." Type this command with no options to see a list of available hardware and search that list for a wireless network adapter. For instance, my laptop's lspci output includes the following line:

```
03:00.0 Network controller: Realtek Semiconductor Co., Ltd.m
 RTL8191SEvB Wireless LAN Controller (rev 10)
```

This line identifies the Wi-Fi adapter as a Realtek RTL8191SEvB. A search on Realtek's website turns up a driver; however, this driver has to be compiled locally, which is a topic that's beyond the scope of this book. You also might not be lucky enough to find a driver in this way.

An alternative to using a native Linux driver is to use a Windows driver. This unusual option is possible using a package called ndiswrapper (http://ndiswrapper.sourceforge.net), which enables you to install Windows Wi-Fi drivers in Linux. Not all distributions provide ndiswrapper in their standard package sets, but you can usually find a binary package in an add-on repository.

If all other options fail, you may need to buy new networking hardware. Many USB Wi-Fi adapters are available, but you should research them to find one that has good Linux support. You can also replace the built-in adapters on some laptops.

Basic Network Troubleshooting

After you have a Linux kernel installed, you can take a few steps to check that things are operating properly. This section walks through the commands you should know to monitor the network activity, including watching what processes are listening on the network and what connections are active from your system.

Sending Test Packets

One way to test network connectivity is to send test packets to known hosts. Linux provides the ping and ping6 commands to do that. The ping and ping6 commands send *Internet Control Message Protocol (ICMP)* packets to remote hosts using either the IP (*ping*) or IPv6 (*ping6*) protocols. ICMP packets work behind the scenes to track connectivity and provide control messages between systems. If the remote host supports ICMP, it will send a reply packet back when it receives a ping packet.

Certification
Objective

The basic format for the ping command is to specify the IP address of the remote host:

```
$ ping 10.0.2.2
PING 10.0.2.2 (10.0.2.2) 56(84) bytes of data.
64 bytes from 10.0.2.2: icmp_seq=1 ttl=63 time=14.6 ms
64 bytes from 10.0.2.2: icmp_seq=2 ttl=63 time=3.82 ms
64 bytes from 10.0.2.2: icmp_seq=3 ttl=63 time=2.05 ms
64 bytes from 10.0.2.2: icmp_seq=4 ttl=63 time=0.088 ms
64 bytes from 10.0.2.2: icmp_seq=5 ttl=63 time=3.54 ms
64 bytes from 10.0.2.2: icmp_seq=6 ttl=63 time=3.97 ms
64 bytes from 10.0.2.2: icmp_seq=7 ttl=63 time=0.040 ms
^C
--- 10.0.2.2 ping statistics ---
7 packets transmitted, 7 received, 0% packet loss, time 6020ms
rtt min/avg/max/mdev = 0.040/4.030/14.696/4.620 ms
$
```

The ping command continues sending packets until you press Ctrl+C. You can also use the -c command-line option to specify a set number of packets to send and then stop.

With the ping6 command, things get a little more complicated. If you're using an IPv6 link local address, you also need to tell the command which interface to send the packets out on:

```
$ ping6 -c 4 fe80::c418:2ed0:aead:cbce%enp0s3
PING fe80::c418:2ed0:aead:cbce%enp0s3(fe80::c418:2ed0:aead:cbce) 56 data
bytes
64 bytes from fe80::c418:2ed0:aead:cbce: icmp_seq=1 ttl=128 time=1.47 ms
64 bytes from fe80::c418:2ed0:aead:cbce: icmp_seq=2 ttl=128 time=0.478 ms
64 bytes from fe80::c418:2ed0:aead:cbce: icmp_seq=3 ttl=128 time=0.777 ms
64 bytes from fe80::c418:2ed0:aead:cbce: icmp_seq=4 ttl=128 time=0.659 ms

--- fe80::c418:2ed0:aead:cbce%enp0s3 ping statistics ---
4 packets transmitted, 4 received, 0% packet loss, time 3003ms
rtt min/avg/max/mdev = 0.478/0.847/1.475/0.378 ms
$
```

%enp0s3 tells the system to send the ping packets out the enp0s3 network interface for the link local address.

 These days, many hosts don't support ICMP packets because they can be used to create a denial-of-service (DOS) attack against the host. Don't be surprised if you try to ping a remote host and receive no responses.

Finding Host Information

Sometimes the problem isn't with network connectivity but with the DNS host name system. You can test a host name using the *host* command:

Certification
Objective

```
$ host www.linux.org
www.linux.org is an alias for linux.org.
linux.org has address 107.170.40.56
linux.org mail is handled by 20 mx.iqemail.net.
$
```

The host command queries the DNS server to determine the IP addresses assigned to the specified host name. By default, it returns all IP addresses associated with the host name. Some hosts are supported by multiple servers in a load-balancing configuration. The host command will display all the IP addresses associated with those servers:

```
$ host www.google.com
www.google.com has address 74.125.138.104
www.google.com has address 74.125.138.105
www.google.com has address 74.125.138.147
www.google.com has address 74.125.138.99
www.google.com has address 74.125.138.103
www.google.com has address 74.125.138.106
www.google.com has IPv6 address 2607:f8b0:4002:c0c::67
$
```

You can also specify an IP address for the host command and it will attempt to find the host name associated with it:

```
$ host 107.170.40.56
56.40.170.107.in-addr.arpa domain name pointer iqdig11.iqnection.com.
$
```

Notice, though, that often an IP address will resolve to a generic server host name that hosts the website and not the website alias, as is the case here with the www.linux.org IP address.

Another great tool is the *dig* command. The dig command displays all of the DNS data records associated with a specific host or network. For example, you can look up the information for a specific host name:

```
$ dig www.linux.org

; <<>> DiG 9.9.4-RedHat-9.9.4-18.el7_1.5 <<>> www.linux.org
;; global options: +cmd
;; Got answer:
;; ->>HEADER<<- opcode: QUERY, status: NOERROR, id: 45314
;; flags: qr rd ra; QUERY: 1, ANSWER: 2, AUTHORITY: 0, ADDITIONAL: 1

;; OPT PSEUDOSECTION:
; EDNS: version: 0, flags:; udp: 4096
;; QUESTION SECTION:
;www.linux.org.      IN    A

;; ANSWER SECTION:
www.linux.org.        14400    IN    CNAME    linux.org.
linux.org.         3600    IN    A    107.170.40.56

;; Query time: 75 msec
;; SERVER: 192.168.1.254#53(192.168.1.254)
;; WHEN: Sat Feb 06 17:44:29 EST 2016
;; MSG SIZE  rcvd: 72

$
```

Or you can look up DNS data records associated with a specific network service, such as a mail server:

```
$ dig linux.org MX

; <<>> DiG 9.9.5-3ubuntu0.5-Ubuntu <<>> linux.org MX
;; global options: +cmd
;; Got answer:
;; ->>HEADER<<- opcode: QUERY, status: NOERROR, id: 16202
;; flags: qr rd ra; QUERY: 1, ANSWER: 1, AUTHORITY: 0, ADDITIONAL: 1

;; OPT PSEUDOSECTION:
; EDNS: version: 0, flags:; udp: 4096
;; QUESTION SECTION:
;linux.org.              IN    MX

;; ANSWER SECTION:
```

```
linux.org.        3600    IN    MX    20 mx.iqemail.net.

;; Query time: 75 msec
;; SERVER: 127.0.1.1#53(127.0.1.1)
;; WHEN: Tue Feb 09 12:35:43 EST 2016
;; MSG SIZE  rcvd: 68

$
```

If you need to look up DNS information for multiple servers or domains, the *nslookup* command provides an interactive interface where you can enter commands:

```
$ nslookup
> www.google.com
Server:        192.168.1.254
Address:    192.168.1.254#53

Non-authoritative answer:
Name: www.google.com
Address: 172.217.2.228
> www.wikipedia.org
Server:        192.168.1.254
Address:    192.168.1.254#53

Non-authoritative answer:
Name: www.wikipedia.org
Address: 208.80.153.224
> exit

$
```

You can also dynamically specify the address of another DNS server to use for the name lookups, which is a handy way to determine whether your default DNS server is at fault if a name resolution fails.

Advanced Network Troubleshooting

Besides the simple network tests shown in the previous section, Linux has some more advanced programs that can provide complex information about the network environment. Sometimes it helps to be able to see just what network connections are active on a Linux system. There are two ways to troubleshoot that issue: the netstat command and the ss command.

The *netstat* Command

Certification
Objective

The *netstat* command can provide a wealth of network information for you. By default, it lists all the open network connections on the system:

```
# netstat
Active Internet connections (w/o servers)
Proto Recv-Q Send-Q Local Address      Foreign Address      State
Active UNIX domain sockets (w/o servers)
Proto RefCnt Flags      Type      State      I-Node  Path
unix  2      [ ]        DGRAM                10825   @/org/freedesktop/systemd1/notify
unix  2      [ ]        DGRAM                10933   /run/systemd/shutdownd
unix  6      [ ]        DGRAM                6609    /run/systemd/journal/socket
unix  25     [ ]        DGRAM                6611    /dev/log
unix  3      [ ]        STREAM    CONNECTED  25693
unix  3      [ ]        STREAM    CONNECTED  20770   /var/run/dbus/system_bus_socket
unix  3      [ ]        STREAM    CONNECTED  19556
unix  3      [ ]        STREAM    CONNECTED  19511
unix  2      [ ]        DGRAM                24125
unix  3      [ ]        STREAM    CONNECTED  19535
unix  3      [ ]        STREAM    CONNECTED  18067   /var/run/dbus/system_bus_socket
unix  3      [ ]        STREAM    CONNECTED  32358
unix  3      [ ]        STREAM    CONNECTED  24818   /var/run/dbus/system_bus_socket
...
```

The netstat command produces lots of output, because there are normally several programs that use network services on Linux systems. You can limit the output to just TCP or UDP connections by using the -t command-line option for TCP connections or -u for UDP connections:

```
$ netstat -t
Active Internet connections (w/o servers)
Proto Recv-Q Send-Q Local Address      Foreign Address      State
tcp   1      0 10.0.2.15:58630         productsearch.ubu:https CLOSE_WAIT
tcp6  1      0 ip6-localhost:57782     ip6-localhost:ipp    CLOSE_WAIT
$
```

You can get a list of what applications are listening on which network ports by using the -l option:

```
$ netstat -l
Active Internet connections (only servers)
Proto Recv-Q Send-Q Local Address      Foreign Address      State
tcp          0      0 ubuntu02:domain   *:*                  LISTEN
```

```
tcp      0      0 localhost:ipp           *:*                    LISTEN
tcp6     0      0 ip6-localhost:ipp       [::]:*                 LISTEN
udp      0      0 *:ipp                   *:*
udp      0      0 *:mdns                  *:*
udp      0      0 *:36355                 *:*
udp      0      0 ubuntu02:domain         *:*
udp      0      0 *:bootpc                *:*
udp      0      0 *:12461                 *:*
udp6     0      0 [::]:64294              [::]:*
udp6     0      0 [::]:60259              [::]:*
udp6     0      0 [::]:mdns               [::]:*
...
```

As you can see, just a standard Linux workstation still has lots of things happening in the background, waiting for connections.

Yet another great feature of the netstat command is that the –s option displays statistics for the different types of packets the system has used on the network:

```
# netstat -s
Ip:
    240762 total packets received
    0 forwarded
    0 incoming packets discarded
    240747 incoming packets delivered
    206940 requests sent out
    32 dropped because of missing route
Icmp:
    57 ICMP messages received
    0 input ICMP message failed.
    ICMP input histogram:
        destination unreachable: 12
        timeout in transit: 38
        echo replies: 7
    7 ICMP messages sent
    0 ICMP messages failed
    ICMP output histogram:
        echo request: 7
IcmpMsg:
        InType0: 7
        InType3: 12
        InType11: 38
        OutType8: 7
```

```
Tcp:
    286 active connections openings
    0 passive connection openings
    0 failed connection attempts
    0 connection resets received
    0 connections established
    239933 segments received
    206091 segments send out
    0 segments retransmited
    0 bad segments received.
    0 resets sent
Udp:
    757 packets received
    0 packets to unknown port received.
    0 packet receive errors
    840 packets sent
    0 receive buffer errors
    0 send buffer errors
UdpLite:
TcpExt:
    219 TCP sockets finished time wait in fast timer
    15 delayed acks sent
    26 delayed acks further delayed because of locked socket
    Quick ack mode was activated 1 times
    229343 packet headers predicted
    289 acknowledgments not containing data payload received
    301 predicted acknowledgments
    TCPRcvCoalesce: 72755
IpExt:
    InNoRoutes: 2
    InMcastPkts: 13
    OutMcastPkts: 15
    InOctets: 410722578
    OutOctets: 8363083
    InMcastOctets: 2746
    OutMcastOctets: 2826
#
```

The netstat statistics output can give you a rough idea of how busy your Linux system is on the network, or if there's an issue with one of the protocols installed.

Examining Sockets

The netstat tool provides a wealth of network information, but it can often be hard to determine just which program is listening on which open port. The *ss* command can come to your rescue for that.

Certification
Objective

A program connection to a port is called a *socket*. The ss command can link which system processes are using which network sockets that are active:

```
$ ss -anpt
State      Recv-Q Send-Q Local Address:Port          Peer Address:Port
LISTEN     0      100    127.0.0.1:25                     *:*
LISTEN     0      128        *:111                    *:*
LISTEN     0      5      192.168.122.1:53                        *:*
LISTEN     0      128        *:22                     *:*
LISTEN     0      128    127.0.0.1:631                    *:*
LISTEN     0      100      ::1:25                     :::*
LISTEN     0      128      :::111                     :::*
LISTEN     0      128      :::22                      :::*
LISTEN     0      128      ::1:631                    :::*
ESTAB      0      0        ::1:22                     ::1:40490
ESTAB      0      0        ::1:40490                  ::1:22
users:(("ssh",pid=15176,fd=3))
$
```

The -anpt option displays both listening and established TCP connections, as well as the process they're associated with. This output shows that the ssh port (port 22) has an established connection and is controlled by process ID 15176, the ssh program.

Summary

Connecting Linux systems to networks can be painless if you have the correct tools. To connect the Linux system you'll need an IP address, a netmask address, a default router, a host name, and a DNS server. If you don't care what IP address is assigned to your Linux system, you can obtain those values automatically using DHCP.

Network Manager is the most popular graphical tool used by Linux distributions for configuring network settings. It allows you to configure both wired and wireless network settings from a graphical window. If you must configure your network settings from the command line, there are a few different tools you'll need to use. For wireless connections, use the iwconfig command to set the wireless access point and SSID key. For both wireless and wired connections, use the ifconfig or ip command to set the IP address and netmask values for the interface. You may also use the route command to define the default router for the local network. When your network configuration is complete, you may have to do some additional troubleshooting for network problems. The ping and ping6 commands allow you to send ICMP packets to remote hosts to test basic connectivity. If you suspect issues with host names, use the host and dig commands to query the DNS server for host names. For more advanced network troubleshooting, you can use the netstat and ss commands to display what applications are using which network ports on the system.

Exam Essentials

Describe the command-line utilities required to configure and manipulate Ethernet network interfaces.   To set the IP and netmask addresses on an Ethernet interface, you use the ifconfig or ip command. To set the default router (or gateway) for a network, you use the router command. Some Linux distributions that have Network Manager installed can use the nmtui or nmcli commands, which can configure all three values.

Explain how to configure basic access to a wireless network.   Linux uses the iwlist command to list all wireless access points detected by the wireless network card. You can configure the settings required to connect to a specific wireless network by using the iwconfig command. At a minimum, you'll need to configure the access point SSID value and most likely specify the encryption key value to connect to the access point.

Describe how to manipulate the routing table on a Linux system.   The route command is used to display the existing router table used by the Linux system. You can add a new route by using the add option or remove an existing route by using the del option. Specify the default router (gateway) used by the network by adding the default keyword to the command.

Summarize the tools you would need to analyze the status of network devices.   The ifconfig and ip commands display the current status of all network interfaces on the system. You can also use the netstat or ss command to display statistics for all listening network ports.

Explain how to test network connectivity.   The ping and ping6 commands allow you to send ICMP messages to remote hosts and display the response received.

Describe how Network Manager is used to configure network settings in Linux.   Network Manager provides a graphical interface for changing settings on the network interfaces. Network Manager appears as an icon in the desktop panel area. If your Linux system uses a wireless network card, the icon appears as a radio signal, whereas for wired network connections it appears as a mini-network. When you click the icon, it shows the current network status and, for wireless interfaces, a list of the access points detected. When you open the Network Manager interface, it allows you to set either static IP address information or configure the network to use a DHCP server to dynamically set the network configuration.

Review Questions

You can find the answers in Appendix A.

1. Which two commands set the IP address, subnet mask, and default router information on an interface using the command line? (Choose two.)

   A. netstat

   B. ping

   C. nmtui

   D. ip

   E. route

2. Which command displays the duplex settings for an Ethernet card?

   A. ethtool

   B. netstat

   C. iwconfig

   D. iwlist

   E. route

3. Which command displays what processes are using which ports on a Linux systems?

   A. iwconfig

   B. ip

   C. ping

   D. nmtui

   E. ss

4. What network setting defines the network device that routes packets intended for hosts on remote networks?

   A. Default router

   B. Netmask

   C. Host name

   D. IP address

   E. DNS server

5. What device setting defines a host that maps a host name to an IP address?

   A. Default router

   B. Netmask

   C. Host name

   D. IP address

   E. DNS server

6. What is used to automatically assign an IP address to a client?

    A. Default router

    B. DHCP

    C. ARP table

    D. Netmask

    E. ifconfig

7. Which command would you use to find the mail server for a domain?

    A. dig

    B. netstat

    C. ping6

    D. host

    E. ss

8. Which ifconfig format correctly assigns an IP address and netmask to the eth0 interface?

    A. ifconfig eth0 up 192.168.1.50 netmask 255.255.255.0

    B. ifconfig eth0 255.255.255.0 192.168.1.50

    C. ifconfig up 192.168.1.50 netmask 255.255.255.0

    D. ifconfig up

    E. ifconfig down

9. What command displays all the available wireless networks in your area?

    A. iwlist

    B. iwconfig

    C. ifconfig

    D. ip

    E. arp

10. What command can you use to both display and set the IP address, netmask, and default router values?

    A. ifconfig

    B. iwconfig

    C. router

    D. ifup

    E. ip

Appendix
A

Answers to Review Questions

Chapter 1: Selecting an Operating System

1. A, B, D, and E. The kernel manages the memory, CPU, and devices for programs running on a computer system, so options A, B, D, and E are correct. The kernel does not manage features of the GUI desktop environment, so option C is incorrect.

2. A. The Android OS is used on phones as an embedded Linux system, so option A is correct. The CentOS, Fedora, Mint, and Red Hat Linux distributions are full Linux distributions intended for desktop and server environments, and they are not used in embedded systems, making options B, C, D, and E incorrect.

3. B. Linux's GUI is based on the X Window System. Although macOS provides an X implementation, its primary GUI is Apple's proprietary product. Thus, option B is correct. Option A is incorrect because both Linux and macOS can run most GNU programs. Option C is incorrect because Linux can run on both Apple Macintosh and Microsoft-compatible hardware. Option D is incorrect because macOS includes many BSD utilities. Although most Linux distributions use GNU utilities, you can use BSD utilities in Linux if you prefer. Option E is incorrect because both Linux and macOS support text-mode commands, although in macOS you must use the GUI Terminal application.

4. E. The Linux OS was created by Linus Torvalds while he was a student. Although based on current Linux OSs, it wasn't derived from any of them, so option E is correct, and options C and D are incorrect. The Linux OS is not derived from either macOS or Windows, so options A and B are also incorrect.

5. False. Programs known as terminals enable entry of text-mode commands after you've logged into Linux in GUI mode. You can also switch between multiple virtual terminals by using keystrokes such as Ctrl+Alt+F2.

6. True. The CentOS distribution release cycle is approximately every two years, which is long by the standards of other Linux distributions, some of which have release cycles of just six months.

7. A. The text-mode login prompt is a single text word that prompts you for your user account ID to access the Linux system. The login term is used to prompt for the user to enter his or her userid, so Option A is correct. Options B, C, D, and E are not used as login prompts for the Linux.

8. D. Most attackers who write viruses focus their energy on the Windows platform where they can find the most victims, so there are very few viruses targeted toward Linux systems. Thus, Option D is correct. Commercial software purchased from reputable vendors is not normally considered a security risk, so Option A is incorrect. Linux systems installed on networks should still utilize network routers and firewalls to protect them from outside attacks, so Options B and C are incorrect. Software management packages such as the Microsoft Store are considered a security feature and not a problem, so Option E is correct.

9. C. An alpha software release is the first test version of an application or distribution, which hasn't been fully tested in all environments and most likely contains bugs. The beta software release has been tested in some environments but not all, and it may contain bugs for your particular environments. Thus, Option C is correct. The terms suggested in Options A, B, D, and E are not used to represent standard first and second releases of software packages.

10. A. A rolling release is provided as needed for a Linux distribution, with no specific release dates or version numbers. Thus, Option A is correct. The terms used in Options B, C, D, and E are not commonly used to indicate version types.

Chapter 2: Understanding Software Licensing

1. C. Option C does not describe an open source requirement, and so it is the correct answer. The open source definition specifies that users be able to distribute changes, but it doesn't specify that the license require distribution under the terms of the same license. Options A, B, D, and E all paraphrase actual open source license term requirements.

2. B. Some distributions (particularly "Enterprise" versions that are sold for money) include software that is neither open source nor even freely redistributable, so option B is correct. Distributions as a whole use many licenses, not just one, so option A is incorrect. The MIT license is one of several open source licenses; such software is not an impediment to copying a distribution, so option C is incorrect. Although some distributions, such as Debian, aim to make their main systems fully open source compliant, not all do this, so option D is incorrect. Likewise, not all distributions are composed completely of free software as the FSF uses the term.

3. E. Option E paraphrases one of the four key points in the FSF's philosophy and so is correct. Contrary to option A, the FSF's philosophy does not mandate use of the GPL, much less its most recent version, although the GPL is the FSF's preferred license. Option B is contrary to the FSF's position, which is that free software should remain free; however, this option is compatible with the OSI's philosophy. Although the FSF advocates free software and free OSs, option C is not an explicit part of their philosophy and so is incorrect. Although the FSF wants to see a world dominated by free software, it does not advocate software piracy, so option D is incorrect.

4. True. Courts and laws explicitly recognize computer software as being creative works that are governed by copyright law. In some countries, patent laws also apply to software, although this is not globally true.

5. True. This principle is at the heart of both the free software and the open source software definitions.

6. False. Hardware vendors often do release open source drivers for their products. One caveat is that the release of open source drivers necessarily renders some programming interfaces for the hardware open, which some hardware vendors are reluctant to do.

7. D. The Lesser GPL (LGPL) is a variant of the Free Software Foundation's GPL. Developers often use the LGPL with libraries (collections of code that can be used by other programs).

8. A. The Creative Commons helps to promote the types of freedoms that also concern the FSF and the OSI, but in a broader sense. Its licenses are typically aimed at audio recordings, video recordings, textual works, as well as computer programs.

9. C. The term copyleft came about via a play on the word copyright, reflecting the fact that copyright provisions are used to ensure freedoms that are, in some respects, the exact opposite of what copyright was created to do—that is, to guarantee the freedom of users to copy software, rather than to restrict that right. Copyleft is typically used to reflect the FSF philosophy and the licenses it inspires.

10. E. A bounty is a crowdfunding method that can help bring together users, each of whom individually might not be able to offer enough money to motivate development, to entice programmers to write the desired code. With bounties, the programmer who completes the project first is allowed to collect the project's accumulated funds.

Chapter 3: Investigating Linux's Principles and Philosophy

1. A. Linux's multitasking is preemptive, meaning that the kernel can give CPU time to any process as it sees fit, potentially interrupting (or preempting) other processes. Thus, option A is correct. Linux is a multiuser OS, but multiuser is not a type of multitasking, so option B is incorrect. In a cooperative multitasking OS, applications must voluntarily give up CPU time to each other. Although Linux programs can signal the OS that they don't need CPU time, Linux doesn't rely exclusively on this method, making option C incorrect. A single-tasking OS can run just one process at a time, so option D is incorrect. A single-user OS can support just one user at a time. Such OSs can be either single tasking or multitasking, and in the latter case, can use either cooperative or preemptive multitasking. Thus, option E is incorrect.

2. C. The open source definition includes 10 points, one of which is that users may modify the original code and redistribute the altered version. Thus, option C is correct. Although all open software is available at no charge, nothing in the open source definition forbids selling it, and in practice, many organizations do sell open source software, so option A is incorrect. The open source definition requires distribution of source code but does not require distribution of binaries, so option B is incorrect. Although many open source projects began life in an academic environment, that's not a requirement for open source software, so option D is incorrect. The open source definition does not specify that either an interpreted or a compile language be used, making option E incorrect.

3. D. Evolution is an email reader program. Such programs are commonly used in desktop environments, so option D is correct. Apache is a web server, Postfix is an email server, and BIND is a Domain Name System (DNS) server, which are all unlikely to be run in a desktop computer environment, making options A, B, and E incorrect. Android is the name of a Linux distribution for smartphones and tablets, not a program, so option C is incorrect.

4. False. VMS was an OS for minicomputers and mainframes when Linux was created. On x86 computers, DOS was the dominant OS in 1991.

5. True. Digital video recorders (DVRs) are specialized computers for recording TV shows. Some commercial DVRs such as TiVos, run Linux natively. DVR software for standard PCs, such as MythTV, which runs under Linux, also exists.

6. True. Most server programs do not require the X Window System (X) GUI, so server computer administrators often disable X or even remove it entirely to save disk space and memory and to minimize the risk of security problems.

7. B. The monolithic kernel design incorporates all of the kernel functions into a single program, whereas the microkernel design splits the kernel functions into separate smaller programs. Thus, Option B is correct. An exokernel design provide minimal hardware support in the kernel, relying on external programs for everything else, thus Option A is incorrect. A hybrid kernel are similar to microkernels, but rely on some external programs to operate, thus Option C is incorrect. The terms distributed and unified are not used to describe kernel types, thus Options D and E are both incorrect.

8. D. Shareware allows a program author to release the binary executable program to the public without payment but ask for payment if the program is used. Thus, Option D is correct. Open source software does not require a payment, thus Option A is incorrect. Commercial software requires an up-front payment, making Option B incorrect. Freeware doesn't require any payments at all, making option C incorrect. Viruses are not typically distributed as software packages, making Option E incorrect.

9. B. A desktop Linux system usually utilizes a graphical desktop interface environment for running graphical programs such as word processors and web browsers, thus Option B is correct. Server computers typically don't utilize graphical desktops, making Option A incorrect. Distributed computers are typically servers, which don't utilize graphical desktops, so Option C is incorrect. A client computer may use a graphical desktop, but it's not required, so Option C is incorrect. A laptop computer may also utilize a graphical desktop, but could also be used as a text-only server, so Option E is incorrect.

10. Apache. The Apache software package is a web server program written specifically for the Linux server environment, taking advantage of how Linux handles processes and memory for multiple applications. Thus, Option E is correct. The MySQL program is a database server commonly used in Linux, not a web server, so Option A is incorrect. The LibreOffice package is a word processing program, not a web server program, so Option B is incorrect. The Firefox package is a web browser program, not a web server program, so Option C is incorrect. The GIMP package is a graphics processing program, not a web server program, so Option D is incorrect.

Chapter 4: Using Common Linux Programs

1. B, C, E. GNOME, KDE Plasma, and Xfce are all Linux desktop environments, so options B, C, and E are all correct. (LXDE is also a desktop environment.) The GIMP Toolkit (GTK+) is a GUI programming library. Although GNOME and Xfce are both built atop GTK+, it's not a desktop environment, so option A is incorrect. Evolution is a Linux email client, not a desktop environment, so option D is incorrect.

2. B. The Network File System (NFS) was designed for exactly the task described in the question, so option B is correct. The Simple Mail Transfer Protocol (SMTP) enables one computer to send email messages to another computer, so it's a poor choice for achieving the stated goal, making option A incorrect. The PHP: Hypertext Processor (PHP) language is used to generate dynamic content for web pages, so option C is incorrect. The Domain Name System (DNS) is a protocol for delivering the mappings between hostnames and IP addresses to computers, so it won't achieve the stated goals, making option D incorrect. The Dynamic Host Configuration Protocol (DHCP) enables one computer to provide network configuration information to another one over a network link, so option E is incorrect.

3. C. The main language for the Linux kernel is C, so option C is correct. Although Bash shell scripts control much of the Linux startup process, these scripts are not part of the kernel, so option A is incorrect. Java is often used for web-based applications, but it's not used in the Linux kernel, so option B is incorrect. C++ is a derivative of C that adds object-oriented features to the language, but the Linux kernel uses regular C, not C++, so option D is incorrect. Perl is a popular interpreted language, particularly for tasks that involve processing text, but it's not the language of the Linux kernel, so option E is incorrect.

4. False. LibreOffice forked from the pre-Apache version of OpenOffice.org. Calligra split from the KOffice office suite, which is no longer maintained.

5. True. A denial-of-service (DoS) attack can disrupt a server's operation by directing an overwhelming quantity of bogus data at the server program, or even just the computer on which it runs. This is true even if the server is impeccably managed.

6. True. Python, like JavaScript, Perl, PHP, and shell languages, is interpreted. This contrasts with C and C++, which are two common compiled languages, and with Java, which is somewhere in-between.

7. C. Email client programs enable you to read and write email messages, and can either access a mailbox on your own computer or, using email network protocols, send and receive email over a network. Thunderbird is one common Linux email client. Others include Evolution, KMail, and Mutt.

8. E. Microsoft uses the SMB/CIFS protocol for file and printer sharing. On Linux, the Samba software implements this protocol.

9. B. Programmers must convert a program written in a compiled language from its original source code form into the machine code form. The machine code is run later. Programs written in interpreted languages (such as Python, Javascript, and Perl) are converted on a line-by-line basis to machine code at the time they're run, by a program interpreter.

10. D. Software programs are bundled into a prebuilt package on Linux, which simplifies their installation and management. Packages are then managed on Linux using a package management system (PMS).

Chapter 5: Getting to Know the Command Line

1. A. Pressing Ctrl+A moves the cursor to the start of the line when you are editing a command in Bash, so option A is correct. The left arrow key moves a single character to the left, Ctrl+T transposes two characters, the up arrow moves up one item in the history, and Ctrl+E moves to the end of the line.

2. C, D. Options C and D both describe ways to run a program in the background from a shell, so options C and D are both correct. Neither start nor bg is a command that launches a program in the background. The fg command returns a program to the foreground, meaning that the shell will go back to sleep, which isn't what the question specified.

3. D. The less program, like more, displays a text file a page at a time. The less utility also includes the ability to page backward in the text file, search its contents, and do other things that more can't do. Thus, option D is correct. The grep command searches a file for a specified string, so it doesn't do a task that's similar to more, making option A incorrect. The Hypertext Markup Language (HTML) is a file format, often indicated with the filename extension .html, that's commonly used on the web. As such, it's not a better version of more, so option B is incorrect. The cat command can concatenate two or more files, or display a single file on the screen. In the former capacity, cat doesn't do the task of more, and in the latter capacity, cat is less capable than more. Thus, option C is incorrect. The man command displays Linux manual pages. Although man uses less by default, man is not itself an improved version of more, so option E is incorrect.

4. False. When in the GUI, Ctrl must be added to the VT-switching keystroke, so the correct keystroke in this case is Ctrl+Alt+F3.

5. True. When you want to override man's search order, you specify the desired manual section between man and the command name, filename, or other name on which you're searching.

6. False. Although info pages, like web pages, use hyperlinks to tie related documents together, the two systems use different formats and protocols. Info pages also reside on the computer's hard disk; they require no Internet access to read. For these reasons, info pages are *not* web-based.

7. False. Individual program authors decide on documentation file format based on their own specific needs and preferences. Although some documents are in OpenDocument text format, many documents are not.

8. D. Both the `logout` and the `exit` commands will end a text-mode terminal session.

9. C. Each info page document is known as a node, and the info page system as a whole is an interrelated set of nodes. The nodes are organized on levels.

10. E. The `locate` command searches a database of filenames that is typically updated every 24 hours. Thus, `locate` is much quicker than the `find` command in producing results of files whose names match a specified term.

Chapter 6: Managing Hardware

1. D. The `lspci` command displays information about PCI devices. Since many motherboard features appear to Linux as PCI devices, option D provides a great deal of information about your motherboard, making option D correct. The lscpu command provides information about the CPU but nothing else on the motherboard, so option A is wrong. The Xorg program provides information about the display environment but not the motherboard, so option B is incorrect. The `fdisk` command displays information about a hard drive on the system but not the motherboard, so option C is incorrect. Connecting to web address localhost:631 connects to the CUPS admin web page, which helps you manage printers on your Linux system, but it doesnt tell you anything about the motherboard, making option E incorrect.

2. A, D. Disk partitioning allows you to separate data of different types into different parts of a disk. Examples of reasons to do this include installing multiple OSs and separating filesystem data from swap space. Thus, options A and D are both correct. The ext4fs and ReiserFS values in option B are both filesystem types, and they don't have anything to do with partitioning, so option B is incorrect. The disk attachment types PATA and SATA are types of hard drive interfaces and not partition types; you can't convert one to the other by changing the partition, so option C is incorrect. Partitioning a hard disk doesn't separate the hard disk cache; that's an internal feature of the hard drive, so option E is incorrect.

3. A. Video monitors normally connect to a video card using a standard video interface such as VGA or HDMI, not using the serial USB interface, so option A is the correct selection. Keyboards, external hard disks, printers, and scanners can all connect to the motherboard using a USB interface, so options B, C, D, and E are all incorrect.

4. True. Most CPU families have multiple names. EM64T is one name that Intel has used for its implementation of the x86-64 architecture, and AMD64 is one of AMD's names for the same architecture. Thus, the two names identify the same architecture, and an AMD64 Linux distribution will run on an EM64T CPU.

5. False. The Universal Disk Format (UDF) is a filesystem that's used primarily on optical discs, not hard disks. Using it for a Linux installation on a hard disk would be awkward if not impossible. Linux-specific filesystems such as ext4s, ReiserFS, or btrfs are the only practical choices for Linux installations on a hard disk.

6. True. In Linux, most drivers, including those specified, are provided as part of the kernel. Some other drivers, such as those for specialty video cards, printers, and scanners, exist outside the kernel, although they may also rely on kernel drivers to do their work.

7. B. The x86 hardware architecture refers to 32-bit microprocessor register, making Option B correct. The 8-bit microprocessor was used in the early 8080 microprocessor chip, which doesn't support Linux, so Option A is incorrect. The 64-bit microprocessor is commonly referred to as amd64 in Linux, since AMD was the first to come out with one, thus, Option C is incorrect. Currently Linux doesn't support 128 or 256-bit microprocessors, making Options D and E incorrect.

8. A. Computer hardware requires direct current power electricity to operate, making Option A correct. Three-phase electricity is commonly used for large motors, not computer hardware, making Option B incorrect. Magnetic electricity is generated by rotating magnets, which aren't used in computer power supplies, making Option C incorrect. Static current is created by rubbing two or more objects together creating friction, and is not used in computer power supplies, making Option D incorrect. Solar power is used by converting the energy produced by the sun into electricity, and is not commonly used to power computers, making Option E incorrect.

9. D. The HDMI standard is a modern standard for sending digital video signals to monitors, thus Option D is correct. The VGA, SVGA, and SDI standards are old standards for sending analog signals to monitors, thus Options A, C, and E are all incorrect. The LED standard defines how images are displayed on a monitor, not the video interface, so Option B is incorrect.

10. B and C. The X.org and Wayland X software package are currently used in Linux distributions, making Options B and C both correct. The xFree86 package was the original X software package for Linux, but is no longer in use, making Option A incorrect. The GNOME and KDE Plasma packages are graphical desktop management packages and not X software packages, making Options D and E both incorrect.

Chapter 7: Managing Files

1. A. The mv command moves or renames a file, so option A is correct. The cp command copies a file so that the original is still in place, so option B is incorrect. The ln command creates a link between two files, so option C is incorrect. The rn command in option D is fictitious, so that option is incorrect. The touch command creates a new empty file or adjusts the time stamps on an existing file, so option E is incorrect.

2. C. Because two files (outline.pdf and Outline.pdf) have names that differ only in case, and because FAT is a case-insensitive filesystem, one of those files will be missing on the copy. (Both files will be copied, but the second one copied will overwrite the first.) Thus, option C is correct. The specified cp command does not create links, so option A is incorrect. Because the specified cp command included the -a option, which performs a recursive copy, all of the files in MyFiles will be copied, along with the directory itself, so option B is incorrect. In order to copy all of the files, you will have to change one file's name manually; however, cp won't do this automatically, so option D is incorrect. Because option C is correct, option E is not correct.

3. A, B. If you try to create a directory inside a directory that doesn't exist, mkdir responds with a No such file or directory error. The --parents parameter tells mkdir to create all necessary parent directories automatically in such situations, so option A is correct. You can also manually do this by creating each parent directory separately, so option B is also correct. Option C will have no useful effect; at most, it will change the time stamps on the mkdir program file, but if you type it as a normal user, it probably won't even do that. Options D and E are both based on the premise that you must remove directories that already exist with the names that you want to use, but this isn't true, so these options are both incorrect.

4. True. Symbolic links work by storing the name of the linked-to file in the symbolic link file. Linux reads this filename and transparently substitutes the linked-to file. This process works both on a single filesystem and across filesystems, so the statement is true. Hard links, by contrast, work by providing multiple directory entries that point to a single file. This method of creating a link does not work across low-level filesystems.

5. False. Linux's security features prevent accidental damage when you work as an ordinary user. You must be more careful when you acquire root privileges to perform system maintenance, though.

6. True. The touch command updates a file's time stamps, and for this purpose, a directory counts as a file, so this statement is true.

7. D. The -u and --update options of the cp command tell Linux to update the existing file with the specified file, thus Option D is correct. The -f option forces a copy if the destination file cannot be opened, but doesn't check the file dates, so Option A is incorrect. The -r option copies directories recursively, it doesn't check file dates, so Option B is incorrect. The -s option creates a symbolic link instead of copying files, so Option C is incorrect. The -v option displays more verbose output, it doesn't check the file dates, so Option E is incorrect.

8. D. The -r, -R, and --recursive command-line options of the rm command will recursively remove files from directories, thus Option D is correct. The rmdir command can only remove directories, it can't remove files inside the directories, so Options A, B, and C are all incorrect. The -f option of the rm command only ignores nonexistent files and doesn't prompt before removing the files, it doesn't recursively remove files from directories, so Option E is incorrect.

9. A. The question mark (?) wildcard character matches none, one, or a set of characters in a filename, so Option A is correct. The asterisk (*) matches zero, one, or multiple characters,

not just a single character, so Option C is incorrect. The underscore, period, and dash aren't used as wildcard characters in matching filenames, so Options B, D, and E are all incorrect.

10. B. Most Linux applications store their configuration files in the /etc directory structure. Usually these files are only accessible by root or by the user account the application is started with.

Chapter 8: Searching, Extracting, and Archiving Data

1. A. The grep utility finds matching text within a file and prints those lines. It accepts regular expressions, which means that you can place in brackets the two characters that differ in the words for which you're looking. Option A shows the correct syntax for doing this. The tar utility creates or manipulates archive files, and option B's syntax is incorrect for any use of tar, so that option is incorrect. The find utility locates files based on filenames, file sizes, and other surface features. Furthermore, options C and E both present incorrect syntax for find, and so are incorrect. Option D's cat utility displays or concatenates files, so it won't have the desired effect, making this option wrong.

2. E. The >> operator appends standard output to a file, so option E is correct. The vertical bar (|) is the pipe character; it ties one program's standard output to another's standard input, so option A is incorrect. The 2> operator redirects standard error, not standard output, and it overwrites the target file. Thus, option B is incorrect. The &> operator redirects both standard output and standard error, and it overwrites the target file, making option C incorrect. The > operator redirects standard output, but it overwrites the target file, so option D is incorrect.

3. D. With the tar utility, the --list (t) command is used to read the archive and display its contents. The --verbose (v) option creates a verbose file listing, and --file (f) specifies the filename—data79.tar in this case. Option D uses all of these features, and therefore does as the question specifies. Options A, B, C, and E all substitute other commands for --list, which is required by the question, so all of these options are incorrect.

4. True. The special characters [^x] match any single character except x, and .* matches any sequence of any characters. The string Linus Torvalds is just one of many strings to match the specified regular expression.

5. True. You can use the -size n option in the find command to locate files based on their sizes.

6. False. The zip utility creates or manipulates zip archive files. This file type supports compression directly, as does the zip program. Thus, there's no need to involve another compression program to compress files archived with zip.

7. A. When not used inside brackets within a regular expression, the caret (^) represents the start of a text line. For example, ^172 matches 172 only if it is first in a line of characters.

8. **B.** The cut command can help; in this case it extracts text from specified fields in a file record and displays them. However, no modifications are made to the file.

9. **C.** The &> symbol combination redirects both standard output and standard error from the command or program, and into a designated file (or location).

10. **E.** Lossless compression is just like it sounds—no data is lost, and the compressed data will exactly match the original uncompressed data, after a decompression process.

Chapter 9: Exploring Processes and Process Data

1. **E.** The apt-get command is used to install software packages on Debian-based Linux systems, so option E is correct. The yum and rpm commands are package management commands but are used on Red Hat–based Linux systems, so options A and D are both incorrect. The zypper command is a package management application but is used on openSUSE Linux systems and not Debian-based systems, so option B is incorrect. The dmesg command is used to view the contents of the kernel ring buffer, not to install software, so option C is incorrect.

2. **A, C.** The name of the first process that the Linux kernel runs is set in the boot loader configuration file. That program is normally systemd or init, so options A and C are correct. The bash program creates an interactive shell, so option B is incorrect. The login program creates a login prompt on a terminal, allowing users to log into the system, so option D is incorrect. The grub boot loader program is started by the computer BIOS or UEFI system, so option E is incorrect.

3. **A.** Most Linux distributions that follow the filesystem hierarchy standard (FHS) store log files in the /var/log directory structure, so option A is correct. Using the FHS, the /etc directory is for storing application configuration files, not log files, so option B is incorrect. The /usr directory is for storing noncritical applications, so option C is incorrect. The /home directory is for storing user data, so option D is incorrect. The FHS does not specify a /log directory, so most Linux systems don't create one, making option E incorrect.

4. **True.** Network-enabled package management programs provide a method for ensuring any dependencies required by an application are already installed on the system before installing the application. If not, the package management system either installs them automatically or prompts you to install them first.

5. **True.** The top program allows you to sort the process data based on any data field, but by default it displays the data sorted by CPU usage.

6. **True.** The dmesg command displays the contents of the kernel ring buffer. The kernel ring buffer stores kernel log messages in a limited space. When that space fills up, older log messages are removed to make room for newer messages. Thus, the contents of the kernel ring buffer (and therefore the dmesg output) change as new events occur in the Linux kernel.

7. B. The package database maintains a listing of all software packages installed by the package manager program, making Option B correct. The kernel interfaces with the system hardware, it doesn't manage installed software packages, so Option A is incorrect. The graphical desktop creates a graphical environment to interact with the Linux system, but doesn't maintain the software packages, so Option C is incorrect. The /usr/lib directory contains library files used by programs, but doesn't manage software packages, so Option D is incorrect. The Software updater program is part of the software management system, but doesn't maintain information on installed packages, making Option E incorrect.

8. A. When you launch an application from the Bash shell it becomes a child process of the shell, so Option A is correct. The parent process is the process that launches the new program, not the new program itself, so Option B is incorrect. The terms client and server are used in an environment where one program retrieves information from another, not in the process environment, so Options C and D are incorrect. Parallel processes are programs that are launched from the same parent process. Since emacs is launched from the Bash shell, it is not a parallel process, so Option E is incorrect.

9. C. The /var/log/secure file is a common location for some Linux distributions to place general system messages, so Option C is correct. The secure file is commonly used to track user login information, not general system messages, so Option A is incorrect. The dmesg program displays messages logged into the kernel ring buffer by the kernel; it's not a file that contains general system messages, so Option B is incorrect. The mail file commonly contains messages from the email program on the system, not general system messages, so Option D is incorrect. The wtmp file contains login and logout messages from the system, not general system messages, so Option E is incorrect.

10. E. The dmesg command displays messages stored in the kernel ring buffer, so Option E is correct. The ls command displays directory listings, not kernel messages, so Option A is incorrect. The pwd command displays the current working directory, not kernel messages, so Option B is incorrect. The chmod command changes file and directory permissions, it doesn't display kernel messages, so Option C is incorrect. The cat command displays text files, but since the kernel ring buffer is not a text file you cannot use cat to display it, so Option D is incorrect.

Chapter 10: Editing Files

1. D. LibreOffice, like most word processors, uses a binary format that can't be properly parsed using an ASCII or Unicode text editor. Thus, nano won't be useful in examining such a document, making option D correct. The nano text editor can handle ASCII or Unicode format, so the text files described in options A and C are incorrect. The other document types described in options B and E are all likely or certain to be stored in ASCII or Unicode format, making them incorrect choices.

2. B, E. The F6 and Ctrl+W keystrokes both invoke the search function, so options B and E are correct. The F3 key writes the current buffer to disk, so option A is incorrect. The Esc+S keystroke is an obscure one; it enables or disables smooth scrolling, so option C is incorrect. Ctrl+F moves forward one character, so option D is incorrect.

3. A. In the vi editor, dd is the command-mode command that deletes lines. Preceding this command by a number deletes that number of lines. Thus, option A is correct. Although yy works similarly, it copies (yanks) text rather than deleting it, so option B is incorrect. Option C works in many text editors but not in vi. Option D works in emacs and similar text editors (including nano) but not in vi. Option E, or something similar, works in many GUI text editors but not in vi, so it is incorrect.

4. False. Unicode provides support for most alphabets around the world.

5. False. Support for underlining, italics, multiple fonts, and similar advanced formatting features is present in word processors, not plain-text editors—even GUI text editors lack such support.

6. True. Due to its ease of use, nano is typically the best editor to learn first.

7. B. ASCII is a 7-bit code, meaning that it supports a maximum of 128 characters. Though, in practice, ASCII uses 8 bits, so an extra 128 characters are available, which can encode various control characters.

8. A, C, E. Of the choices shown, the ESC+R and Ctrl+\ key combinations as well as pressing the F4 key will start a search-and-replace activity in the nano text editor.

9. D. Typing u in the vi editor's command mode will undo the last change you made to the text, which is handy.

10. C. While you are in command mode, the ZZ key combination will save any file modifications and then leave the vi editor.

Chapter 11: Creating Scripts

1. A. Before you can run a shell script directly from the command line, you need to allow execute permissions for at least yourself, so option A is correct. You don't need to have the shell script file located in any specific directory as long as you have access to the directory, so option B is incorrect. Typing the bash scriptname will run the script, not compile it, so option C is incorrect. Viruses are extremely rare in Linux, and because you just created the script, the only way in which it could contain a virus would be if your system was already infected or if you wrote it as a virus, so option D is incorrect. Most spell checkers are intended for English or other human languages, so they lack the ability to check for valid Bash commands, such as esac. Furthermore, even if every keyword is spelled correctly, the script could still contain logic bugs. Thus, option E is incorrect.

2. C. The cp command is the only one called in the script, and that command copies files. Because the script passes the arguments ($1 and $2) to the cp command in reverse order, their effect is reversed; whereas cp copies its first argument to the second name, the cp1 script copies the second argument to the first name. Option C correctly describes this effect. Option A ignores the reversed order of the arguments, so this option is incorrect. The cp command has nothing to do with compiling C or C++ programs, making options B and D incorrect. The first line in the script is a valid shebang line, indicating the shell to use to run the script, so option E is incorrect.

3. C. Conditional expressions return a true or false response, enabling the script to execute one set of instructions or another or to continue or terminate a loop; thus, option C is correct. Conditional expressions have nothing to do with licensing conditions, so option A is incorrect, nor do they have anything to do with displaying environment information, making option B incorrect as well. Conditional expressions also don't implement Pavlovian conditioning by themselves (you can create a script to implement that, but the conditional expressions by themselves don't), so option D is incorrect. The conditional expressions also don't cause the script to run only at a specified time of day—you need to use the at or cron facility on the Linux system to do that—so option E is incorrect.

4. False. The $0 variable contains the name of the script, which would be myscript in this example. The first parameter (laser.txt) would be held in the $1 positional variable.

5. True. You can use the for statement to execute a loop a fixed number of times, whereas while and until execute until a test condition is no longer met or is met, respectively.

6. False. The terminal commands don't have the ampersand (&) sign after them to indicate that they should run in background mode, so they will run serially, only one at a time. QuestionID:

7. A. A shell script should contain the shebang line to indicate the shell required to run the script. The shebang line contains the #! characters, followed by the shell path. Thus, option A is correct. Options B and D are both incorrect because they just specify the shell, not the shebang characters. Option C is incorrect because it uses only the pound symbol, which makes the line a comment. Option E is incorrect because it doesn't specify the full path to the shell.

8. D. The echo command is used to display text to the shell user, so option D is correct. The case command compares a value to multiple answers, not display text, so option A is incorrect. The while command performs a loop on a block of code, and doesn't display text, so option B is incorrect. The if command tests a condition and if true, executes a block of code, it doesn't display text, so option C is incorrect. The exit command stops the running script and returns to the shell, passing a numeric exit value, not a text value to display, so option E is incorrect.

9. A. The case command can compare a variable against multiple values and execute different blocks of code based on the matching value, so option A is correct. The while command performs loops, it doesn't compare a variable against multiple values, so option B is incorrect. The if command tests a variable against a single condition, not multiple values, so option C is incorrect. The echo command displays text to the script user; it doesn't compare multiple values, so option D is incorrect. The exit command stops the script and returns to the shell, it doesn't compare a variable against multiple values, so option E is incorrect.

10. E. The exit command stops the script and returns a specified value back to the shell, so option E is correct. The case command compares a variable against multiple values, it doesn't control the script return value, so option A is incorrect. The while command performs a loop on a code block, but doesn't control the script return value, so option B is incorrect. The if statement allows you to test a variable against a value, but not control the script return value, so option C is incorrect. The echo statement displays text for the script user, but doesn't control the script return value, so option D is incorrect.

Chapter 12: Understanding Basic Security

1. **A.** UID 0 is reserved for the system administrator's account, also known as root, so option A is correct. The first ordinary user account is not a system account, and its UID is normally 500 or 1000, depending on the distribution, so option B is incorrect. Because A is correct, C cannot be correct. The association of UID 0 for administrative tasks is very basic in Linux, so you won't find variation on this score, making option D incorrect. Since the root account is not low-privilege, option E is also incorrect.

2. **A, C, E.** The /etc/passwd file's fields specify the username, an encrypted password (or x to denote use of shadow passwords, which is more common), a UID number (option A), a single default GID number, a comment field that normally holds the user's full name, the path to the account's home directory (option C), and the path to the account's default text-mode shell (option E). Option B is incorrect because, although /etc/passwd includes the user's default group, the user may belong to additional groups that are defined elsewhere. Option D is incorrect because the user's default desktop environment is not defined in /etc/password.

3. **A.** The sudo command is the usual way to execute a single command as root, and option A gives the correct syntax to use it as the question specifies. There is no standard root command, so option B is incorrect. The passwd command changes passwords, so option C is incorrect. Although you can use su to execute a single command as root, you must use it with the -c option to do this, as in su -c "cat /etc/shadow", so option D is incorrect. Option E's admin is a fictitious command, so this option is incorrect.

4. **False.** The whoami command displays your username only. The id command displays your username, your UID number, your primary group name, your primary GID number, and the group names and GID numbers of all your groups.

5. **False.** The name for the group data file in Linux is /etc/group, not /etc/groups.

6. **True.** It's possible to do more damage to a computer as root than as an ordinary user. Thus, you should be extra cautious when using root—run only trusted programs, double-check your commands for errors, and so on.

7. **D.** The /etc/passwd file contains not only user account information such as the username, primary group ID, and default shell, but it also contains the UID associated with each username.

8. **B.** While the who and the who -q commands will display who is currently logged into the computer, only the w command will also display what programs they are currently running.

9. **E.** System accounts have UIDs above 0, but below 500 or even 1,000, depending on the distribution's configuration. The root account typically has a UID of 0.

10. **C.** A company policy that demands the sudo command is used to acquire root privileges sets a desirable nonrepudiation environment in which actions cannot be legally denied.

Chapter 13: Creating Users and Groups

1. C. The userdel command deletes an account, and the -r switch to userdel causes it to delete the user's home directory and mail spool, thus satisfying the terms of the question. Option A deletes the account but leaves the user's home directory intact. Option B does the same; the -f option forces account deletion and file removal under some circumstances, but it's only meaningful when -r is also used. Option D's command will probably have no effect, since rm works on directories only in conjunction with -r, and /home/nemo is probably the user's home directory. Option E's rm command deletes the user's home directory (assuming it's located in the conventional place, given the username) but doesn't delete the user's account.

2. B. The password in option B uses a combination of upper- and lowercase letters, numbers, and symbols, and it doesn't contain any obvious word. Furthermore, it's a long password. All of these characteristics make it unlikely to appear in an intruder's password dictionary and make it hard to guess. Thus, option B represents a good password, and the best of those shown. Option A is the name of a well-known celebrity (at least in the Linux world!); such a name is likely to appear in password-cracking dictionaries, and so makes a poor password choice. Option C is an extremely common password, which makes it a bad choice. Furthermore, it's short and it consists of just one symbol type (digits). Option D is another popular (and therefore very poor) password. It's a single common word in all lowercase and it contains no numbers or other nonalphabetic symbols. Although option E is fairly long, it consists entirely of lowercase letters, and its three related words, making it a poor password too.

3. A. The groupadd command creates a new group, as described in option A, so that option is correct. To add a user to a group, as suggested by option B, you would use the usermod utility. No standard command imports group information from a file, as option C suggests, so this option is incorrect. (Some network user management tools do provide such functionality, though.) To change a user's default group or list of supplemental groups, you would use usermod, so options D and E are both incorrect.

4. True. System accounts have UID values between 0 and some number (normally 499 or 999), whereas user accounts have UID values above that number (starting at 500 or 1,000, typically).

5. False. The usual command-line command for changing passwords is passwd.

6. True. Although the userdel command's -r option deletes the user's home directory and mail files, this command doesn't track down the user's files stored in more exotic locations. You can use find to locate such files if you want to delete them or transfer ownership to another user.

7. D. The useradd command with -u 2019 thor will create a new user account, with the username thor and give it a UID of 2019.

8. B. In order to modify a user account with the username of carol to a username of marvel, you must issue the usermod -l marvel carol command using super user privileges.

9. E. The -r option used with the groupadd command will allow you to create a system group (as long as you have super user privileges).

10. C. The /etc/group file contains group data such as the group's name, associated GID, and a list of group members.

Chapter 14: Setting Ownership and Permissions

1. D. The chown command changes the owner assigned to a file. You list the new file owner first, then the filename, making option D correct. You can't change file ownership using the chmod command, making options B and E incorrect. The new file owner must be listed first by itself, making options A and C incorrect.

2. C, D. The d at the start of the symbolic file mode indicates that wonderjaye is a directory. The first set of permissions (rwx) indicate the directory owner has read, write, and execute permissions on the directory. The second and third sets of permissions (r-x and r-x) indicate that the directory's primary group and all others have read and execute permissions on the directory. Thus, options C and D are correct. A leading l character would indicate the file is a symbolic link, so option A is incorrect. A leading dash would indicate the object is a file, but since the leading character is a d option B is incorrect. For members of the group to have write permissions to the directory, the second set of permissions must include the w character, which it doesn't, so option E is incorrect.

3. E. The chown command allows you to change both the file's owner and group, so option E is correct. The groupadd command allows you to add a new group to the system, not change the group assigned to a file, so option A is incorrect. The groupmod command allows you to modify details of a group definition, not change the group assigned to a file, so option B is incorrect. The chmod command allows you to change the permissions assigned to a file, not the file's primary group, so option C is incorrect. The ls command allows you to display the file owner, group, and permissions using the -l option, but it doesn't allow you to change the file's group, so option D is incorrect.

4. True. The octal mode permission 755 represents the symbolic mode -rwxr-xr-x. The third set of permission characters indicates the permissions for all users on the system, so all users have read permission on the file.

5. False. The chmod command allows users to change the permissions assigned to a file or directory. Any user can change the permissions of files and directories that the user owns; therefore, any user can use the chmod command.

6. True. An ordinary user can use chown to change a file's group to another group the user belongs to, but ordinary users can't change the ownership of a file—only the root user can do that.

7. B. The -R (or --recursive) option allows Linux to recursively change the ownership of a directory and all files and directories under it, so option B is correct. The -L option tells Linux to follow any symbolic links encountered in the directory, not recursively change the entire directory tree, so option A is incorrect. The -H option tells Linux to follow the symbolic link if it's listed as the command-line argument, not recursively change ownership in the entire directory; so option C is incorrect. The -P option tells Linux to not follow any symbolic links in the directory, not recursively change ownership in the directory tree, so option D is incorrect. The -f option tells Linux to suppress any error messages, not recursively change ownership on an entire directory tree, so option E is incorrect.

8. C. Symbolic permissions are indicated by the three-character string rwx. If a permission is not present, the character is replaced by a dash, so to remove write permissions you would use the character set r-x, making option C correct. The -wx symbol indicates write and execute permissions, so option A is incorrect. The --x symbol indicates no read and write permissions, only execute permissions, so option B is incorrect. The rw- symbol indicates read and write permissions but no execute permission, making option D incorrect. The rwx symbol indicates read, write, and execute permissions, so option E is incorrect.

9. E. The chmod command uses the character a to represent permissions assigned to all users. To add a permission, you use the plus sign (+), and to represent execute permissions you use the x character. Thus, option E is correct. The u+x symbol assigns execute permissions to only the user, not all users, so option A is incorrect. The u-x symbol removes execute permissions from the user and doesn't change the permissions for everyone else, so option B is incorrect. The g+x symbol adds execute permissions to the group but not for all users, so option C is incorrect. The a-x symbol removes execute permission for all users—it does not add it—so option D is incorrect.

10. A. To add a sticky bit to a directory you use the t character and add it to the owner permission set (o), so option A is correct. You add the sticky bit permissions to the owner, not the group, or all users, so options C and D are incorrect. The w character is used to assign write permissions, not the sticky bit, so options B and E are incorrect.

Chapter 15: Managing Network Connections

1. C, D. The nmtui command provides an interactive text menu for selecting a network interface and setting the network parameters, and the ip command provides a command-line tool for setting network parameters, so both options C and D are correct. The netstat command displays information about network connections but doesn't set the network parameters, so option A is incorrect. The ping command can send ICMP packets to a remote host but doesn't set the local network parameters, so option B is incorrect. The route command sets the routing network parameters but not the IP address or subnet mask, so option E is incorrect.

2. A. The `ethtool` command displays features and parameters for network cards, so option A is the correct answer. The `netstat` command displays network statistics and connections, so option B is incorrect. The `iwconfig` and `iwlist` commands are used to set wireless network parameters not Ethernet card settings, so options C and D are incorrect. The `route` command sets or displays routing information and not Ethernet card settings, so option E is incorrect.

3. E. The `ss` command displays a list of the open ports on a Linux system, along with the processes associated with each port, so option E is correct. The `iwconfig` command sets wireless network information, not open ports, so option A is incorrect. The `ip` command displays or sets network information on a network interface but doesn't display open ports, so option B is incorrect. The `ping` command sends ICMP messages to a remote host but doesn't display any open ports, so option C is incorrect. The `nmtui` command allows you to configure network parameters for a network interface but doesn't display the open ports on the system, so option D is incorrect.

4. A. The default router is used to send packets from the local network to remote networks, so to communicate with a remote host you need to define the default router address, making option A correct. The netmask only defines the local network—it doesn't define what to do with packets for remote hosts—so option B is incorrect. The host name and IP address only define features of the local host, so options C and D are incorrect, whereas the DNS server defines how to retrieve the IP address of a host based on its domain name, so option E is incorrect.

5. E. The DNS server maps the host name to an IP address, so you must have a DNS server defined in your network configuration to be able to use host names in your applications. Thus, option E is correct. The default router only defines how to send packets to remote hosts—it doesn't map the host name to the IP address—so option A is incorrect. The netmask value defines the local network, not how to map host names to IP addresses, so option B is incorrect. The host name and IP address define features of the local host, so options C and D are incorrect.

6. B. The Dynamic Host Configuration Protocol (DHCP) is used to assign dynamic IP addresses to client workstations on a network, so option B is correct. The default router can't assign addresses to devices, so option B is incorrect. The ARP table maps the hardware address of the network card to IP addresses but doesn't assign the IP addresses, so option C is incorrect. The netmask value determines the network address but not the IP address of the host, so option D is incorrect. The ifconfig command can set the static IP address of the host but doesn't automatically assign the IP address, so option E is incorrect.

7. A. The `dig` command can display individual host records for a domain, which you can use to find the MX mail host for the domain, so option A is correct. The `host` command only displays host IP address information—it can't determine the server type from the DNS records—so option D is incorrect. The `netstat` and `ss` commands display active network connections but not the remote host types, so options B and E are both incorrect. The `ping6` command sends IPv6 ICMP packets to test remote hosts but can't tell if the remote host is a mail server, so option C is incorrect.

8. A. The `ifconfig` command must specify the network interface, the IP address, then the netmask option before the netmask address. You can use the up or down option to place the network card in an active or inactive state by default, but it's not required. Option A is the only option that uses the correct values in the correct order. Option C is close but fails to specify the network interface. Option B is not in the correct format, and options D and E fail to list the necessary configuration settings.

9. A. The `iwlist` command displays the available wireless network access points detected by the wireless network card, so option A is correct. The iwconfig command configures the network card to connect to a specific access point but doesn't list all of the detected access points, making option B incorrect. Option C specifies the `ifconfig` command, which is used to assign an IP address to a wireless network card, but doesn't list the access points. The `ip` command specified in option D likewise can be used to set the IP address of the card but doesn't list the access points. Option E, the `arp` command, maps hardware addresses to IP addresses so that you can find duplicate IP addresses on your network, but it doesn't list the wireless access points.

10. E. The `ip` command allows you to both display and set the IP address, netmask, and default router values for a network interface, so option E is correct. The `ifconfig` command can set the IP address and netmask values, but not the default router. The iwconfig command is used to set the wireless access point settings, and the router command is used to set the default router but not the IP address or netmask values. The `ifup` command only activates the network interface—it can't set the address values.

Appendix B

Setting Up a Linux Environment

If you don't have access to a system running Linux to study for the Linux Essentials certification exam, consider setting up your own learning space on a laptop or desktop. Your learning space needs to be an environment where you can freely explore Linux and its various distributions (called *distros* for short).

Creating a virtualized environment for your Linux learning space is ideal. This setting will allow you to boot multiple Linux distributions at the same time (provided you have enough computer resources), enabling you to move quickly between them, and to provide compare-and-contrast experiences. In addition, you can explore networking utilities more thoroughly in such an environment.

For a virtualized environment, you need to create a virtual machine. A virtual machine is a simulated computer system that appears and acts just like a physical machine. It can be created using a software application on a laptop or desktop. We like Oracle VirtualBox (virtualbox.org), because it's free and provides an accurate Linux experience. You can obtain and install VirtualBox on a Windows or macOS system. The VirtualBox website is loaded with helpful documentation, and it has community forums to help you create your Linux learning space. Also, there are several youtube.com videos to help with installing the VirtualBox software on your computer.

For this book, the primary Linux distributions used were Linux Mint 18.3 LTS with the Cinnamon Desktop (linuxmint.com), and Fedora 30 Workstation (getfedora.org). You can obtain the distributions on these websites and find helpful documentation.

As time goes on, new Linux Mint and Fedora distribution versions will be available. Although it is always tempting to get the latest and greatest version, it is not beneficial to use it in your learning space. Remember that the LPI Linux Essentials certification exam objectives are static—until the next time the certification exam is updated. Therefore, it is wise to use the distribution versions that were available at the time of the certification exam's creation.

You'll want to download at least one of the distributions' installation files (called an *ISO file*, because its file extension is .iso) from their website. Be aware that these distros update their software every six months to a year. Thus, if you cannot find the ISO file on the distribution's primary download page, try these locations:

- Fedora 30 Workstation: dl.fedoraproject.org/pub/fedora/linux/releases/30/ Workstation/

- Linux Mint 18.3 LTS: linuxmint.com/download_all.php

When you have the ISO file, install it to VirtualBox. If you need some additional assistance in accomplishing this last task, then on a computer system with access to the Internet open your favorite web browser, and in the search engine, type **How to install Linux using VirtualBox**. You should find several websites with helpful information to get your study environment built.

Index